PATRICK WHITE was born in London in 1912, the son of an Australian pastoralist. He received his schooling in Australia and Britain, and read French and German at King's College, Cambridge. In his early years between study he was a jackeroo in northern New South Wales, travelled through most of Western Europe and the United States, and served as an intelligence officer in the Royal Air Force during World War II in the Middle East and Greece. After the war he returned to Australia and settled on a property at Castle Hill, outside Sydney. He was awarded the Australian Literary Society Gold Medal for his novels *Happy Valley* and *The Tree of Man*; and the Miles Franklin Award twice: in 1958 for *Voss* and in 1962 for *Riders in the Chariot*. He was awarded the Nobel Prize for Literature in 1973.

His novels include: *The Aunt's Story* (1948), *The Tree of Man* (1956), *Voss* (1957), *Riders in the Chariot* (1964), *The Solid Mandala* (1966), *The Vivisector* (1970), *The Eye of the Storm* (1973) and *A Fringe of Leaves* (1977). In 1981 he published a self-portrait, *Flaws in the Glass*. His first group of plays are: *The Ham Funeral* (1961), *The Season at Sarsaparilla* (1962), *A Cheery Soul* (1963) and *Night on Bald Mountain* (1964).

Following the revival of *The Season at Sarsaparilla* in 1976 at the Sydney Opera House, Patrick White returned to the stage with *Big Toys* (1977) which he wrote for the director Jim Sharman and three actors, two of them being members of the cast of *The Season at Sarsaparilla*. The same year he wrote the screenplay *The Night the Prowler*, based on his own short story, which was also directed by Sharman and received its premiere in 1978. Following Sharman's appointment as director of the State Theatre Company of South Australia for 1982–83, White wrote two plays for the company, *Signal Driver* (1982) and *Netherwood* (1983).

Patrick White died in Sydney in 1990.

Also by Patrick White

Plays

> *Big Toys*
> *Signal Driver*
> *Netherwood*

Novels

> *Happy Valley*
> *The Living and the Dead*
> *The Aunt's Story*
> *The Tree of Man*
> *Voss*
> *Riders in the Chariot*
> *The Solid Mandala*
> *The Vivisector*
> *The Eye of the Storm*
> *A Fringe of Leaves*
> *The Twyborn Affair*

Short Stories

> *The Burnt Ones*
> *The Cockatoos*

Self-portrait

> *Flaws in the Glass*

PATRICK WHITE

COLLECTED PLAYS

Volume I

CURRENCY PRESS · SYDNEY

AUSTRALIAN DRAMATISTS SERIES
General Editor: Katharine Brisbane

First published in 1965 as *Four Plays by Patrick White*, by
Eyre and Spottiswoode, London.
This edition published in 1985 by
Currency Press
PO Box 2287
Strawberry Hills NSW 2012
www.currency.com.au, enquiries@currency.com.au

Reprinted 1993, 2002

NATIONAL LIBRARY OF AUSTRALIA CARD NUMBER
and ISBN 0 86819 124 8

Printed in China through Colorcraft Ltd., Hong Kong
Cover design by Kevin Chan

Publication of this title was assisted by the Commonwealth
Government through the Australia Council, its arts funding
and advisory body.

FOREWORD

KATHARINE BRISBANE

The late 1950s was a remarkable moment in the development of the indigenous Australian theatre. Out of a swell of sudden optimism came a handful of plays: *Summer of the Seventeenth Doll*, *The Slaughter of St Teresa's Day*, *The Shifting Heart*, *The One Day of the Year*, which sought to convey the Australian way of life on to the mainstages of Australia.

At the best of times the Australian theatre had never had much room for the indigenous playwright. By the time of the Great Depression, when the last of the actor-managers were no more than a memory, the Australian stage offered nothing but imports from Broadway and Shaftesbury Avenue. In 1955 the *Doll* was hailed as the harbinger of a great new theatre.

The task those playwrights set themselves was to create for Australian audiences their own familiar world by the rules of the dominant, wholly British, stage conventions or those of the Hollywood movie. Unlike Australian writers of a decade later who created their own theatrical environments, the 50s playwrights took their cue from an overseas commercial theatre. A measure of their success has inevitably been the degree to which the life of the play has burst these bounds and engaged the Australian audience directly.

While the *Doll* was making its name around the world and *The One Day of the Year* was fighting its battles with the first Adelaide Festival and the Returned Services League, the first of

Patrick White's major plays, *The Ham Funeral*, was gestating. Originally written in 1947, it had lain in the dark for thirteen years before being brought into the light by the Adelaide Theatre Guild on 15 November 1961. Encouraged by the response of the young people about him, Patrick White began to give his full attention to the stage and by 1964 had produced the body of work in this volume. It was an inspirational period in his literary output: having published *Voss* in 1957, he followed it with *Riders in the Chariot* in 1964 and *The Solid Mandala* in 1966.

White's contribution to the stage at this point was twofold. First, as a literary figure of international reputation, he came from a world very different from the popular working-class culture represented by authors of the plays listed above and his perspective upon that culture was accordingly very different. Second, his European multi-lingual education had exposed him to a greater variety of style than the simplicities of domestic drama and musical comedy afforded in Australia; and the expressionist forms he drew upon in his novels, particularly of that period, extended naturally into his plays. It is as if the very innocence of the limitations of the Australian theatre at that time had freed him to draw effortlessly upon his poetic imagination.

Today in the mid-80s we at last have a theatre rich in technical resources and alert to new forms; and one which has belatedly caught up with the dramatic forces of Europe in the twentieth century. Strindberg has begun to take his place alongside Chekhov and Ibsen as a master of the modern theatre and audiences of our major companies are being introduced to works in translation of romantic, expressionist and surreal writers like Kleist, Wedekind, Handke and Witciewicz.

The younger writers who have grown up with this developing theatre are, like White, also innocent of its limitations. The new plays range in setting across the world, their structures flash from scene to scene in a manner taken directly from film. Even their seniors, who ten years ago were holding strictly to a handful of actors and one set, now range free and fluent. The visual has become the primary response of the theatre today, to the point that in some circles the word itself has been superseded.

It has taken all these developments for his homeland to begin to come to terms with the plays of Patrick White. After 1964 these four were shelved by the theatre and only glimpsed between covers by those who valued their literary interest. Meanwhile other radicals embraced the 'poor theatre' theory as a way to new indigenous forms. It was 1976 before the theatre director Jim Sharman, a man as preoccupied as White with the task of communicating in physical terms the landscape of the imagination, brought him back to the theatre with a production of *The Season at Sarsaparilla* at the Sydney Opera House. The popular production drew from the author an immediate response: *Big Toys*, a Mozartian indictment of Australia's yellowcake mining activities, was performed the following year. In 1979 Sharman directed another revival, this time *A Cheery Soul*. The production not only demonstrated our new capacity to meet the demands of expressionist drama but in the character of Miss Docker it supplied a challenge which Robyn Nevin met with such brilliance that the performance set a new standard in achievement for the rapidly-changing acting profession.

Sharman's appointment as director of the State Theatre Company of South Australia for 1982–83 resulted in the commissions of *Signal Driver*, a journey through the life of a working couple, and *Netherwood*, a satirical look at the common repressions and ambivalent sexuality which seem to dog the Australian character.

White has been commonly called a symbolic or expressionist playwright, in that his writing is a reaction against naturalism and seeks to represent spiritual before social reality. But while the tone of the European expressionists and their precursors was, on the whole, pessimistic, and often obsessional, White's plays, like his novels, explore the dead heart of Australia and find it not only teeming with life but endowed with a leathery will to survive. The theme of all the plays in this volume is the journey towards a recognition of the basic forces of life. In *The Ham Funeral* the young poet makes his way slowly from the shelter of his dreams, through the ugly assaults of birth, death and lust, to the emotional freedom he longs for. In *The Season* at *Sarsaparilla* puberty, maturation and reconciliation are the recurring cycle. In *A Cheery Soul* the comforts of ignorance give way to the rude recognition that life cannot be easily contained; and in the last play Bald Mountain is the scene of a heroic tussle between the forces of sterility, represented by the intellect, and those of the flesh.

It is characteristic of White's writing that the spirit is as tangible as the flesh and the inanimate as the animate. Such are, of course, theatrical devices and he employs them unself-consciously, from the girl–anima in *The Ham Funeral* and the mysterious powers of Miss Quodling, the goat woman, in *Night on Bald Mountain*; to the music-hall avatars or beings who stand guard over Theo and Ivy Vokes in *Signal Driver* and the surreal childhood evocations in *Netherwood*. And because psychological reality is uppermost in his plays he is able to leap the barrier which to some, in the 60s, seemed insuperable, but in White's imagination was never present: that is, to give to the conventionally inarticulate character the means to express an inner life. And just as the characters reveal vitality where some might expect none, so does their environment. The house in *The Ham Funeral*, the 'sundown' home in *A Cheery Soul*, the mountain in *Night on Bald Mountain* are as animate as the people who inhabit them.

Because of his international stature as a novelist, more has been written about the unique qualities of these remarkable plays than about the work of any other Australian playwright; and we have included a bibliographical note at the end of this book, for which we are indebted to May-Brit Akerholt. Yet, ironically, Patrick White's plays have received less attention on stage than those of any other leader in the Australian field. In an electronic age when the power of the literate imagination is waiting to be rediscovered, the freedom and subtlety of these works offer a special challenge to the modern Australian theatre. Today the theatre owns both the minds and the resources to redress the balance: I hope this new edition will help to bring to public attention again the early work of an extraordinary dramatic imagination.

CONTENTS

Jan Hamilton as Miss Dando, Annie Byron as Mrs Watmuff, Robyn
Nevin as Miss Docker, Pat Bishop as Miss Perry, Peter Carroll as Mrs
Jebb and Paul Johnstone as the ghost of Tom Lillie in the the Sydney
Theatre company production of A Cheery Soul, at the Sydney Opera
House, 1979, directed by Jim Sharman, designed by Brian Thomson. Photo
by Branco Gaica.

THE HAM FUNERAL

Joan Bruce as Mrs Lusty and Hedley Cullen as the Landlord in the Adelaide University Theatre Guild production of The Ham Funeral, *1961.*

The Ham Funeral was first performed by the Adelaide University Theatre Guild at the Union Theatre, Adelaide, on 15 November 1961 with the following cast:

YOUNG MAN	John Adams
LANDLADY	Joan Bruce
LANDLORD	Hedley Cullen
GIRL	Anne Dibden
FIRST LADY	Pat Griffith
SECOND LADY	Kathleen Steele–Scott
FIRST RELATIVE	Dennis Olsen
SECOND RELATIVE	Don Porter
THIRD RELATIVE	Tony Georgeson
FOURTH RELATIVE	Brian Bergin

Directed by John Tasker
Designed by S. Ostoja Kotkowski

CHARACTERS

LANDLORD
LANDLADY
YOUNG MAN
GIRL
TWO LADIES
FOUR RELATIVES

SETTING

A lodging-house and the streets of London, about 1919.

ACT ONE

Before the CURTAIN *rises, the* YOUNG MAN *appears, and speaks the following prologue. He is dressed informally, in a fashion which could be about 1919. He is rather pale. His attitude throughout the play is a mixture of the intent and the absent, aggressiveness and diffidence.*

YOUNG MAN (*yawning, addressing the audience*) I have just woken, it seems. It is about ... well, the time doesn't matter. The same applies to my origins. It could be that I was born in Birmingham ... or Brooklyn ... or Murwillumbah. What *is* important is that, thanks to a succession of meat pies (the gristle-and-gravy, cardboard kind) and many cups of pink tea, I am *alive*! Therefore ... and this is the rather painful point ... I must go in soon and take part in the play, which, as usual, is a piece about eels. As I am also a poet ... though, to be perfectly honest, I have not yet found out for sure ... my dilemma in the play is how to take part in the conflict of eels, and survive at the same time ... becoming a kind of Roman candle ... fizzing for ever in the dark. (*Somewhat stern*) Probably quite a number of you are wondering by now whether this is your kind of play. I'm sorry to have to announce the management won't refund any money. You must simply sit it out, and see whether you can't recognize some of the forms that will squirm before you in this mad, muddy mess of eels. As it heaves and shudders, you may even find ... you have begun to feed ... on memory ... (*more relaxed, as if returning to his private world*) Let me remind you of a great, damp, crumbling house in which people are living. Remember? Perhaps you have only dreamt it. Some of the doors of the house have never been seen open. The people whose protection they are intended to ensure can be heard bumping about behind them. Sometimes these characters fry little meals for their temporary comfort. Sometimes it sounds as though they are breaking glass. As far as we know, nobody has ever committed a murder in this house of ours, but it could be ... (*slowing up, thoughtfully*) Certainly murder has often been *contemplated* . . . (*looking at his wrist-watch*) . . . towards five o'clock . . . when the fingers have turned to bones . . . and the sky is green. There are the voices, too. Not only the voices of the walls. There are the voices of the gas-fires, full of advice that we haven't the courage to take. And the mirrors in the deal dressing-tables . . . well, you can never believe *them*. They are living lies, down to the last vein in their eyeballs. So, we turn our backs. But look again. The land-lady, you're going to see, spends an awful lot of her time looking again. And I . . . but I know already. I know too much. That is the poet's tragedy. To know too much, and never enough. (*Defensive*) You are right in suspecting I can't give you a message. The mes-sage always gets torn up. It lies at the bottom of the basket, under the hair, and everything else. Don't suggest we piece it together. I've found the answer is always different. So . . . the most I can do is give you the play, and plays, of course, are only plays. Even the great play of life. Some of you will argue that *that* is real enough . . . (*very quiet and diffident*) . . . but can we be . . . sure? (*Returning to the surface, dry*) Thank you. We'd better begin now.

EXIT *behind the* CURTAIN.

CURTAIN *rises on Scene I. Basement of the lodging-house – that is, the lower half of the picture; for the present the stair-well,* BACK, *and the hall and two ground-floor bedrooms* ABOVE *remain in darkness.*
BACK CENTRE *a door standing open on the darkened stair-well.* R. *and* L. *are the area windows, through which the light palely filters. Against the wall,* R., *is an enormous iron bedstead with brass knobs. A kitchen table,* C. *At least six kitchen chairs, some at the table, some dispersed. Against the wall,* L., *a gas-stove of an antique variety, and a dresser. The action of the play will also reveal that there is an invisible dressing-table against the 'fourth wall', so that anybody making use of the mirror must expose themselves fully to the audience. An invisible sink against the same 'wall', to the* LEFT, *on the kitchen half of the basement. The whole is lit by an isolated unshaded electric bulb.*
The LANDLORD *is seated on one of the deal chairs beside the kitchen table. He sits with his legs apart, facing the audience. He is a vast man, swollen, dressed from neck to ankle in woollen underclothes, of a greyish*

colour, and in carpet slippers. His face is pallid, flushing to strawberry in the nose, and in a wen on one cheek. He wears a thick, drooping moustache, and is smoking a short, black pipe. The LANDLADY *is also seated at the kitchen table, with a saucepan, peeling potatoes. She is a large woman in the dangerous forties, ripe and bursting. Her hair, still black, is swept up untidily in a vaguely Edwardian coiffure. She is wearing a shabby white satin blouse, dark skirt, and an old pair of pink mules.* LANDLADY *continues to peel potatoes, but with mounting boredom and distaste.*

LANDLADY (*laying down the knife, pushing things away from her*) I'm just about sick of peelin' bloody pertaters! Don't yer understand, Will? (*Disgusted*) You wouldn't!

(LANDLORD *looks at her expressionlessly for a moment, then continues to stare and smoke.*)

I'm sick of it! I'm sick. . . .

LANDLORD Why?

LANDLADY Why? Lord, I dunno *why*! (*Yawns and stretches*) Aooh, nao! (*Then relaxes on her chair, momentarily helpless*) I dunno much. Else I wouldn't be sitting 'ere. Thursday I went to the theayter. It was lovely. A bunch of toffs in satin . . . gassin' about love and nothink. An' when I come out, the rain 'ad stopped, an' the blossom sticky on the chestnut trees. You could smell it, that strong and funny. It nearly bust my 'ead open. . . . (*Angrily, pushing the potato peelings farther away from her*) Then I come 'ome!

(LANDLORD *noisily clears his throat.*)

Yes, that's wot *I* felt! Twenty years listenin' to the damp, an' the furniture, an' your 'usband's breathin'!

(LANDLADY *gets up, goes to the invisible dressing-table in the 'fourth wall', looking into the mirror, touching her hair.*)

(*Sighing*) Twenty years, an' more, since that day at 'Ighgate. . . . (*Seductively, more to the mirror than to her husband*) Remember? I said: 'Praps the grass ain't quite dry. ''Oo cares, says you.' I says: 'Not me.' I was a bit afraid. 'Ow your breath scorched, Will. I seen the pores of yer skin, like they was in one of them mikerscopes. You smelled of soap an' beer. I could feel me own breath, strugglin' to fan your fire. Well, we was burnt. We was burnt up. Now I

listen to you breathe, and it's regular as the silence and the clocks.
(LANDLORD *heaves a snorting sigh, but whether in sympathy or contempt, it is not possible to tell.*)
(*Pulling herself together*) But I got used to it. The way you do get used to things. The way the iron becomes part of the tree, when it's eaten into it. . . .
(*She goes and puts her hand on his shoulder, so that for the moment they make a monumental, if primitive whole.*)
I loved you, Will. Afterwards, I even got to like yer, and wanted you about. We were two bodies in the bed. I could return to you out of my dreams . . . push against your hot side. You didn't wake, ever. But you was solid.
(LANDLORD *grunts and stares.*)
(*Withdrawing her hand, angrily*) You were that, all right!
(*She carries potato-peelings and disposes of them briskly, somewhere near the stove,* L.)
Anyway, 'ere's for a cup of tea. And a slice of somethink. I'm 'ungry.
(*She takes down a teapot from the dresser.*)

LANDLORD You're always 'ungry.

LANDLADY (*laughing, good-natured now, as she goes to the kettle to warm the pot*) Yes. I am. (*Coming forward to the invisible sink, to swill and empty the pot*) I like to eat. I like somethink you can get yer tongue round. A nice piece of fat 'am, for instance. (*Emptying pot into sink*) Or a little bowl of stewed eels. Or a chop with the kidney on it. Or even a bit of bread and drippin', with the brown underneath. (*Filling pot with tea at the dresser*) Yes, there's no end to pleasure, if yer come to think.
(*Fills pot with hot water, and stands it on the table.*)
(*Thoughtfully*) That reminds me, Will . . .
(LANDLORD *stares and smokes.*)
. . . that young man upstairs . . . beats me wot pleasure 'e gets. 'E don't go nowhere. Lies an' sleeps, or stares at the ceilin', as if 'e was sick . . . or barmy.

LANDLORD (*grunting*) 'E's a poet.

LANDLADY 'E's a bloomin' corpse for all the life 'e lives. Lyin' with 'is 'ands under 'is 'ead. An', d'you know, Will, once I caught 'im listenin' at the room opposite. Settled down to it, proper, like. (*Starts to bring cups*) You would'uv said 'is ear was growin' out of the door.

LANDLORD Up to no good.

LANDLADY (*giggling*) Wot! D'you mean Phyllis Pither? Oh, my!

LANDLORD Ain't she t'other side of the door?

LANDLADY Yes.

LANDLORD Well.

LANDLADY Go on! Phyllis Pither! (*Starts to cut slices of bread*) Nao, serious, Will. I feel sorry for that young man. Let's ask 'im down now and again, and act a bit sociable. (*Withdrawing into herself for a moment*) Jack would'uv been 'is age by now. (*Coaxingly*) Eh? Feed 'im up a bit. The skin under 'is eyes 'as turned quite blue. Wot do you say, Will?

(LANDLORD *grunts*).

LANDLADY That's right. Knew you'd come round. You're not a bad stick. (*Wipes her hands on a towel*) Does you good to 'ave company once in a while. (*Goes quickly to dressing-table mirror in 'fourth wall', and touches her hair*) A fresh face, an' you forget yer own. (*Meditatively*) When I walk down the street, I often feel I could take the faces . . . I could eat 'em up. If they only knew! But there they are . . . (*disgusted*) . . . they might be a lot of cherry stones! (*Touches her own face and frowns*) Makes yer sick! (*She turns quickly*) Well, I'll fetch 'im down. . . . (*Pauses as she catches sight of the* LANDLORD'S *figure*) I say, Will, wot about you in them old underwears?

LANDLORD (*staring in front of him, without flinching*) Wot's wrong?

LANDLADY Why, nothink . . . I suppose. . . .

(*She goes out,* BACK. *As she does so, the basement darkens, and the stairway, and hall above,* C., *are illuminated.*)

SCENE TWO · THE STAIRS

LANDLADY (*pausing at the stairs*) This part of the 'ouse 'as never been warmed. I bet not even a first-class weddin' could chafe life into the stairs. Not all the rice an' rudery in the world. (*Starting to mount*) I've always been a bit afraid. . . . A lady could get 'er neck broke . . . not by fallin', neither. (*Mounting*) The mice squeak behind the skirtin'-boards. Look 'ow the damp's spread. You could teach geography off of the wall. (*Pausing as she mounts, tracing an outline with her finger*) 'Ole continents to them that knows. Africa couldn't be darker to me. Once I almost screamed. Then I wondered if anyone would 'ear me. Other people are deaf, you know. (*Getting her breath*) I hate the stairs. There's a great deal I hate. There's a lot that refuses to be loved. (*Reaching the hall above*) I could love, too, if they'd let me. (*Pausing for a moment by the street door*) Once I heard a voice in the street, somebody trying to get in. But when I opened, 'e said it was the wrong door. (*She approaches the door of the* YOUNG MAN'S *bedroom. This occupies the* UPPER LEFT *part of the stage.*)

(*Pausing outside, listening*) Listen! You can 'ear 'im. You can 'ear 'im already. Lyin' on the bed. Doin' nothink. Once 'e wrote a poem. I picked it out of the basket, along with the razor blades, and a piece of lilac 'e must 'ave pinched from somewhere. I couldn't read 'is poem, but the paper was still warm, as if 'e'd clenched it quite a while. Although 'e's been 'ere all these months . . . or is it years? . . . I'm buggered if I can remember 'is name. I call 'im Jack. (*She knocks on the door*) Hey, are you there, young man? 'S me, Jack. Can you 'ear? Or am I speakin' to a dummy?

SCENE THREE · YOUNG MAN'S BEDROOM

In the silence following the LANDLADY'S *words, the room floods with a pale afternoon light. There is a window,* BACK, *a black branch with a few early leaves cutting across the pane. A narrow iron bed with head against the wall,* L. *A crimson plush arm-chair, with comfortable, rounded shoulders,* R. FORWARD. *Against the 'fourth wall' there would be a dressing-table. The* YOUNG MAN'S *coat is hanging from a hook on the door leading to the hall.*

THE YOUNG MAN *himself is stretched on the bed, in shirt and trousers, and wearing his shoes. His hands are behind his head, and he is staring at the ceiling.*

YOUNG MAN (*to the* LANDLADY, *as she waits for admission*) It's your house, and the door isn't locked.

(*He continues to stare at the ceiling.*)

LANDLADY (*opening the door, entering*) That's a nice thing to say to a lady 'oo means well. Not up yet, eh? (*She wanders about the room, touching things*) And 'ere it is . . . evenin'. A nice evenin', too. A bit raw, but 'ealthy like. (*Looking out of the window*) There's the girls goin' on the job. Their 'ips 'aven't loosened yet. They've still got to warm the pavement. (*Turning back into the room*) An' you not up! Well, I suppose you're yer own master.

YOUNG MAN (*wryly, still staring at the ceiling*) I like to think so.

LANDLADY A poet, anyways.

YOUNG MAN Once I wrote a poem. . . .

LANDLADY That was the one I found in the basket.

(YOUNG MAN *immediately raises himself on an elbow. Looks at her.*) Not that I read it, of course. I never could read an educated 'and. (YOUNG MAN *sinks back on the bed, apparently satisfied.*) But I like a good bit of poetry. I love a love poem. (*Sighing*) Yes.

YOUNG MAN (*again rising on his elbow, looking at her*) Tell me, Mrs Lusty, do you expect much of life?

LANDLADY Expect? I don't expect. I take wot turns up.

YOUNG MAN I hope I still expect.

LANDLADY (*yawning*) You're barmy. Or clever.

(*She sits down comfortably in the plush chair.*)

YOUNG MAN (*propped on his elbow, looking inward at his own experience*) I'm certainly not clever. Sometimes my lack of cleverness makes me desperate. It seems that everybody else understands which button to press, which lever to pull, which tablet to take, to achieve the maximum happiness or the required dream. At least, that's what their faces claim. Sometimes I stand in the street and watch them. Then my ignorance begins to choke me. The answer is either tremendously simple, or tremendously involved. But either way, it's something I still fail to grasp.

LANDLADY You poor kid!

YOUNG MAN When I was a boy, I mooned about in a garden. I tried to fit words to the sounds of nature and the shape of lilacs.

LANDLADY Always said you was a screw loose!

YOUNG MAN No one before myself had ever heard or seen. I had to prove it. Then I found I couldn't. (*Slips back to his original position, staring at the ceiling*) Or I haven't yet.

LANDLADY Don't lose 'eart. You'll write lots of lovely poems.

YOUNG MAN (*laughs*) Since they fetched up their breakfast, men are less inclined to listen to the cuckoo. And I'm not reconciled to the stench of vomit.

LANDLADY Eh?

YOUNG MAN Nothing. (*Turning on his side to look at her*) How you long to be kind. You'd like to devour the world, and keep it warm inside you. But as that isn't possible, you touch, and touch, and touch, and offer slices of bread smeared with rancid dripping.

LANDLADY Wot if I *was* goin' ter suggest you come and 'ave a bite with me and my old man! There's no 'arm done. There's nothing like food in yer stummick for putting things right in yer head. (*Advancing on him, taking his hand*) And if I take your hand, it's because it's cold, Jack. It is. Cold as a dead canary's claw.

YOUNG MAN (*withdrawing his hand quickly, looking at it*) My name is not Jack.

LANDLADY It might have been.

YOUNG MAN (*making to ward her off with his elbow*) Are you going to *touch* me again?

LANDLADY Death itself couldn't touch *you*, yer little bastard!

YOUNG MAN Oh, dear Mrs Lusty, I'm all you say. But admitting doesn't help. Now tell me about your poor dead child.

LANDLADY There's nothink to tell. There wasn't time. 'E died. It was Saint Swithin's Day. That's all.

YOUNG MAN Sad. But it might have been sadder. He might have sprouted from your area, all muscles and malignancy, and over-run the world. Or they might have stoned him for a saint. Or he could have turned out so pale, nobody noticed him.

LANDLADY Whichever way, 'e would 'uv needed 'is tea.

YOUNG MAN (*sitting up, dangling his legs over the side of the bed*) How remorseless you are! And I my bread and dripping.

LANDLADY You'll come then, Jack? It'll liven Will up.

YOUNG MAN (*grimacing*) He's landlord enough dead. Can't imagine him alive.

LANDLADY Will's all right.

YOUNG MAN Everything's 'all right'. The pity is it's never 'better'.

LANDLADY (*limping and wincing as she goes towards the door*) To-night my bunion 'urts like 'ell. Wonder wot that means?

YOUNG MAN An accident. Or just a letter . . . the most brutal of all threats. . . . Or perhaps a stranger opening the door . . . her arms full of flowers. . . .

LANDLADY We don't get no strangers 'ere.

YOUNG MAN (*cautiously*) Tell me, Mrs Lusty, before you go, what is in the room across the hall?

LANDLADY Why, it's me other front room.

YOUNG MAN Just another bedroom.

LANDLADY In every way h'identical.

YOUNG MAN And occupied. . . .

LANDLADY Since I don't know when.

YOUNG MAN Sometimes she puts her mouth to the door. I can almost hear the words if I hold my ear. . . .

LANDLADY She wouldn't be so bold!

YOUNG MAN I can hear her skirt rubbing the paper. It has the sound of very thin ice. The air is filled with intolerable lilacs . . .

LANDLADY Potty, that's wot you are! I always said. There's no one but Phyllis Pither in there. A young lady as works for a firm of gas-fitters in Kennington. In every way a steady girl. Gives 'er wages to an auntie 'oo suffers from Bright's Disease . . .

YOUNG MAN . . . filling the air, heavier than eyelids . . .

LANDLADY . . . Phyllis leaves early, an' comes 'ome late. Most nights she goes to bed with an aspirin and a cold.

YOUNG MAN (*jumping off the bed*) I am exorcized! Or am I?

LANDLADY Aoh, come on! Stop yer jaw! (*Moves towards the door*) My tongue's 'angin' out for a cuppa.

(LANDLADY *goes into the hall*)

YOUNG MAN Yes. I'm coming.

LANDLADY A proper windbag!

EXIT LANDLADY *down the dark stairs.*

(*still grumbling*) My feet ache that bad. . . . I could'uv walked all the way from Putney. . . .

(*She goes into the still unlit kitchen.*)

(YOUNG MAN *makes sure she has gone. Leaves his room, crosses the hall to the door of the second bedroom,* L. *Leans against the door, arms outstretched, cheek pressed to the panel.*)

YOUNG MAN All my life the present moment has just failed to materialize. Completeness is something I sense, but never yet experienced. There is always the separating wall.

(*The other side of the door a patch of light forms, in which are visible a hand and an arm in a long white glove. The fingers barely rest on the intervening door, at the point where the* YOUNG MAN'S *head is resting on the other side. The hand remains motionless, but with a kind of still grace and poetry.*)

YOUNG MAN Often I hear your voice. But the words remain indistinct. I could swear to the touch of your fingers, without actual pressure. If I could feel certain, this door might vanish. Or am I just an impostor . . . trying to draw a bouquet out of the air, without having learnt the trick? Or is there? Or is there a bouquet? Where are the stiff flowers, trembling on their wire stems?

LANDLADY (*calling impatiently from the kitchen below*) Hey, Jack, wotcher playin' at? I like ter know 'ow I stand. Are yer comin', or aren't yer? 'Ere's this nice tea, stewin' in the pot. . . .

YOUNG MAN Is this the most we can expect? The figures in the basement? The silent landlord and his bursting wife. . . .

(*Light in the second bedroom fades. The* YOUNG MAN *winces against the separating door.*)

(*Striking the door with palm of his hand*) I've had my answer! I hold my still, cold poem, stiller and colder than the landlady's dead child. . . . (*Tears himself away from the door with an effort*) (*calling to* LANDLADY) Coming, Mrs Lusty! (*Dashes into his room, snatches the coat from the hook behind the door. As the lower stairs light up, he is back in the hall. Bedroom fades.*) (*Running downstairs, bundling into his coat, calling*) Don't say I ever spoilt a party! I'll be there before my own voice!

SCENE FOUR

Basement floods with light and the stairs fade as YOUNG MAN *enters.*
LANDLORD *is sitting in exactly the same position as before.* LAND-
LADY *is back at the kitchen table, cutting slices of bread, and spreading
them with dripping.*

YOUNG MAN (*entering, to* LANDLORD) How're they treatin' yer,
Mr Lusty?
(*He sleeks down his hair. His manner has become cocky, and rather
vulgar.* LANDLORD *does not answer. Sits staring ahead, smoking.*)
(*Rubbing his hands together, heartily*) I'm fine meself. Thanks for
inquiring. (*Panting*) On these fresh spring evenings my breff
goes on ahead like the spirit of health.

LANDLADY (*on her dignity, spreading dripping*) I thought you'd
died. (*A silence*)

YOUNG MAN (*himself again*) I might have. Or someone. To justify
this funeral.

LANDLADY 'Ere, young man! Elders and betters, you know. An'
drippin' thrown in. Let us talk about somethink nice and bright.
There's other flowers besides everlastin's. (*Pushing tea and bread
and dripping towards the* YOUNG MAN) An' you, Will Lusty . . .
(*passing same to her husband*) tell us a story of yer youth, when
you threw the big buck nigger on the grass, and I kissed you on
the mouth 'cause I was proud.

LANDLORD (*spitting out a mouthful, throwing the slice back on the
plate*) This stinks! It stinks!

YOUNG MAN It might, too.

LANDLADY It's you, Will. Your bloody mouth's foul with silence.

YOUNG MAN (*mock heroic*) Then she threw 'im on the grass, 'is
muscles turned to fat!
(LANDLORD *calmly wipes stem of his pipe on his arm, re-lights, and
continues smoking.*)

LANDLADY (*to* YOUNG MAN) No one asked lip from you.

YOUNG MAN That was irony, Mrs Lusty. I'd no more think of
offering you cheek than I'd throw a pat of butter to a steamroller.

LANDLADY (*tearfully*) All you get is words . . . good, bad, or
doubtful. Or else it's silence. (*Shivers*) That's worse.

LANDLORD Yes, you suffer, Alma Lusty!

LANDLADY Wot come over *you*? I wasn't askin' for sympathy.

LANDLORD You ask me for the story of me youth. You'd ask me in the same breath for a basinful of blood.

YOUNG MAN (*rubbing his hands*) Ding dong! Now they're at it!

LANDLADY (*raucously contemptuous*) This is Christmas! Will Lusty found 'is tongue! If a court'ud asked me was you still there, I wouldn't 'uv known wot to answer. Reminds me of a kid I used to be friendly with . . . got me to take a squint at a fart 'e'd caught in a bottle. . . .

LANDLORD Well?

LANDLADY "Oo's to know,' I says, 'if it didn't get away?'

LANDLORD And wot did 'e say to that?

LANDLADY (*tossing her head, out of patience*) Aoh, I for*get*!

LANDLORD Never knowed Alma to forget.

LANDLADY (*emphasizing with one fingertip on the table*) The point is, Will, you've e-vap-er-ated! (*Smiles to herself, smugly pleased*) See? You went an' left us.

LANDLORD If I left yer, something must'uv brought me back. (LANDLADY *hunches her shoulders, grits her teeth.*)

LANDLADY All your life you wasn't there! All your life!

LANDLORD 'Arp! 'Arp! My life's been that simple, it doesn't bear tellin' about. I was a boy. I grew. I met a woman 'oo became my wife. . . .

LANDLADY That was simple! Lord save us!

LANDLORD We bought the little sweetshop out at Croakers' Pond . . .

LANDLADY (*sentimental*) The little sweetshop!

LANDLORD . . . because you thought you fancied it. Well, we sold the little business. You said the bell made yer nervous. I took up wrestlin' . . . for the exercise. Then I found I could do it good.

LANDLADY You did it good. . . .

LANDLORD (*moved and repelled*) I can't add nothink to that. It's done. I threw Joe 'Arris, and Billy Doyle, and Patsy Lonergan. I 'eld 'em to the ground till their ribs and thighs was crackin'. I could feel the whole world give in me hands. The mob would let fly with their caps and their voices. An' there was always one tart louder than the rest. She told me I'd won. She told me I was Gawd. Then, when I could no longer 'old their faces in the dust, an' the stink of sweat 'ad begun to make me sicken, she let me know we'd reached 'ell by a short cut.

LANDLADY It's 'arder for the woman. The woman's the man's shadow.

LANDLORD Listen to the tap drip in the sink. Listen to its words. Soft and pitiful. We promise ourselves we'll change the washer. But we don't.

YOUNG MAN Is this a tragedy? Or is it two fat people in a basement, turning on each other?

LANDLADY But it's life I'm after, Will. (*Vague gesture*) That's why I can't stick all this. That's why the old days are still glossy as a postcard.

LANDLORD (*shifting his thighs, contemptuously*) Life!

LANDLADY I can taste the whelks! I can hear the flares! You can see right inside of a person by the light of acetylene flares.

LANDLORD I sit 'ere. I am content. Life, at last, is wherever a man 'appens to be. This 'ouse is life. I watch it fill with light, an' darken. These are my days and nights. The solid 'ouse spreadin' above my head. Only once in a while I remember the naked bodies . . . knotting together . . . killing theirselves . . . and one another. . . . Bloody deluded!

YOUNG MAN He's a sensitive beast, this landlord, inside his under-clothes. And I disliked him. I loathed him. I was almost afraid. Perhaps this is why.

LANDLADY But it's natural, Will, to fight. And love.

LANDLORD (*laughing in his throat, speaking not particularly to his wife, spreading his hand on the table-top*) This table is love . . . if you can get to know it. . . .

LANDLADY (*Going and leaning on the dresser*, L., *her hands in her thick hair, in an attitude of desperation and boredom, choking*) I'll suffocate!

YOUNG MAN And *my* lungs are bursting, with enthusiasm and excitement . . . now that his flesh has opened, and I look inside. (*Moving his chair closer to the* LANDLORD) Perhaps he can answer questions. I no longer notice the knob on his face.

(LANDLADY *turns suddenly.*)

LANDLADY (*menacing*) You keep off!

YOUNG MAN (*turning to her, in amazement*) I had forgotten the landlady.

(LANDLORD *sits as before, intent on some problem of his own.*)

LANDLADY Everyone forgets the landlady. (*To* YOUNG MAN) But *you* ought to remember.

YOUNG MAN I? I don't understand.

LANDLADY (*laughing*) Oh, they're all alike! 'Cold puddin' is cold puddin',' they say, 'it didn't oughta be warmed up.' (*Half angry, half tender*) But warmth . . . warmth is everything. (*Advancing on the* YOUNG MAN) Pretendin' to forget!

YOUNG MAN (*cocking an eye at the* LANDLORD, *speaking with the same vulgar assurance he assumed on his entrance*) What price the landlord now? You win, Alma! You always did!

LANDLADY (*putting her arms round his neck, at the same time standing back so as to look at him, laughing sensually and relieved*) I knew you'd remember. You can remember each line we wrote to the poste restante. You can remember the leg above the boot. They was a pretty little pair of boots. Glassy kid. I can remember the taste of seaweed on your mouth. Up on the promenade, the band had started on 'The Quaker Girl'. As if you could forget! Why, *Fred*!

YOUNG MAN (*not quite freed from his own identity*) Fred?

(LANDLORD *slams his hand on the table, and quivers.*)

LANDLADY (*looking at* LANDLORD, *shouting vindictively*) Wot if I said it!

(*She pushes aside the* YOUNG MAN, *who has only been instrumental in evoking the scene.*)

LANDLORD You bitch! I told you to never. . . .

LANDLADY As if it wasn't finished! But 'ow can I forget wot I can still feel?

LANDLORD You bitch!

YOUNG MAN (*to himself*) Am I the chorus to this play? No one ever cursed the chorus. Serpents only slither from the sea to strangle those who are big enough.

LANDLORD (*contemptuously, to* LANDLADY) Because *you* can still feel! (*Wipes his face with his hand, speaking with great emotion, although restrained*) Only once I set eyes on *Him* ... before 'e disappeared ... in the rain, an' the gaslight. .... Did I say only once?

YOUNG MAN (*still a chorus to the drama*) You did, Landlord. But the room still quivers.

(*A brief silence.*)

LANDLORD (*producing a recollection from the depths*) Well, I seen 'im again ... in the face of that dead kid. I seen that little blue, queasy, wizened pimp ... lookin' at me out of the coffin ... through the closed eyelids. You'd pulled a piece of geranium, an' stuck it in 'is ... you couldn't 'ardly call it a hand. I never smelt geranium since without I felt choked.

LANDLADY (*holding herself, in agony*) Wot of it? I 'ad a child. For a few days I held 'im in my arms. 'Oose child? 'Oo cares!

YOUNG MAN I could offer pity. But pity is an abstraction of other people's sorrows.

LANDLORD (*to* LANDLADY) You admit all right. ...

LANDLADY I 'ad a child. It died. That's all I admit.

LANDLORD The little, blue-faced, wizened pimp!

LANDLADY (*bowing her head*) I admit that 'urts still.

YOUNG MAN Now, where's the landlord, whose words for a moment brought the furniture to life? He's about to eat his wisdom. He's still only a man!

(LANDLORD *has raised himself heavily but methodically out of his chair. Staggers towards the* LANDLADY.)

LANDLORD (*hitting her over the side of the face*) The little bastard!

(*A silence before* LANDLADY *speaks.*)

LANDLADY I can't cry, Will. I loved 'im. ...

(LANDLORD *returns heavily to his chair, sits in same position as before.*)

YOUNG MAN (*moved*) In the end, there is nothing I can do to cut their tangle. They must fumble, and bungle, and loosen the knot for themselves.

(YOUNG MAN *turns towards the stairs,* BACK.)

LANDLADY (*to* LANDLORD) ... just as I loved *you*, Will. And other men. Or tried to. Only it dies too soon. It dies in your arms. (*Basement darkens.*)

SCENE FIVE · THE STAIRS

The stairs come to life as the YOUNG MAN *mounts with apparent weariness and disillusion.*

YOUNG MAN (*sighing, counting to himself*) One . . . two . . . three. . . . In the evening a mute monotony fills the stairs . . . the resentment of all the feet that ever trod the carpet. Look. The cockroach popped by the landlady's old pink slipper. . . . There's the corner where a friend, or lover, was overcome by Saturday night . . . and the stair where the broken rod was never replaced . . . not even after the plumber took a tumble. . . . Fatal, melancholy, passionate moments crowd upon the stairs . . . but none of them ever broke the monotony for long. . . . So resentment creeps back . . . and back . . . as we mount . . . endlessly. . . .
(*Emerging at the top, he comes* FORWARD, *facing the audience.*)
(*Somewhat breathless after negotiating the stairs*) . . . hoping to burst out . . . show we are independent creatures . . . no connection with the landlord and his wife . . . only waiting to be recognized . . . for our brilliant minds, noble instincts, romantic appearance, generous acts! (*Pause*) Strange we have been overlooked. . . . It can't continue. It won't! (*Pause*) But the silent house doesn't confirm. It only echoes. (*Turning, going towards his room*) The evenings of spring are merciless.
(*Goes into his room, which* LIGHTENS *as stairs* FADE.)
Purpose dwindles . . . if one ever had a purpose. . . . (*Almost in a panic*) What . . . what is intended? (*Desperate*) If one could only . . . find . . . out. . . .
(*Goes back quickly and purposefully into the hall.*)
(*Approaching door of bedroom opposite*) If you would tell me! You!
(*Light drifts through second bedroom, which occupies the upper* RIGHT-HAND *portion of the stage. It is, as the* LANDLADY *said, furnished in exactly the same way as the room occupied by the* YOUNG MAN — *iron bed, plush-chair, etc., disposed as already described.* CENTRE, *facing the closed door which the* YOUNG MAN *is addressing, a* GIRL *is seated — upright, grave, dressed very simply*

and unobtrusively, in white. Her fair hair is worn long. Her expression is remote, but radiant.)

GIRL Yes?

YOUNG MAN (*smiling, incredulously*) Ah, you are there then! Door or no door, I can tell when it happens. (*Goes and stands close to the door, cheek against it, eyes closed, smiling and content*) You are very close now. But I hoped you would tell me how I might come closer.

GIRL (*gently, but firmly*) That is something which can't be taught.

YOUNG MAN I was afraid of that.

GIRL You're afraid of so much.

YOUNG MAN Who isn't?

GIRL I am not.

YOUNG MAN There! You become remote again.

GIRL Shall I show you how close? As a little boy you would gobble angelica and cherries, and afterwards look for somebody to blame.

YOUNG MAN Intuition itself! Tell me some more.

(*The* GIRL *leaves the chair, comes to the separating door standing close to it, so that she is in more or less the same position as the* YOUNG MAN *on the other side.*)

GIRL All right. What would you like to hear?

YOUNG MAN Usually I don't have to tell you.

GIRL (*her voice intimate, but distinct*) The mountain? The mist was cold behind your bare knees. The valleys were rolling with the white mist. The parrots flew screaming . . . the wedge of black cockatoos. . . . You held the sheet of paper in your hand. You had not yet found words. . . .

YOUNG MAN Yes? But now your voice sounds distant.

GIRL Distant as childhood.

YOUNG MAN (*impatient*) Yes, yes! Go on!

GIRL Where the shrubbery ended, there was an oval bed of lilacs, which remained wet even after the sun had risen above the cypresses. The long, bosomy sprays of lilac would press against your soaking shirt . . . the dreamy scents drench you with words and longing. The sun was rising . . . rising . . . bursting on the crests of the trees. You were on the verge! Then, suddenly, you had never felt emptier . . . and went away sneezing . . . and didn't stop all that spring. So they sent you to live in a climate where the landscape had been drained of every possible excitement and interest . . . dry . . . healthy . . . interminable.

YOUNG MAN That was a bit of an anti-climax!

GIRL So was adolescence.

YOUNG MAN Where do we go from there?

(*Pause.*)

GIRL I should really leave you. Unless. . . .

YOUNG MAN (*desperate*) You're going to deny me the little you give?

GIRL (*yawning*) The question is: What do you make of it? The answer: Nothing.

YOUNG MAN (*downcast*) I agree. I haven't yet. But if you remain the other side of the door, we can never complete each other.

GIRL (*sharply, raising her head*) Complete!

YOUNG MAN A comfortable, smug, even ugly word . . . but desirable.

GIRL (*sternly*) For you, death in two syllables.

YOUNG MAN (*beating on the door with his hands*) Then tell me what is the most I can expect? How am I to discover?

GIRL (*stalling*) Discover?

(*She retreats to* CENTRE *of her room, and at same time the* YOUNG MAN *seems propelled like an automaton, back from the door, across the hall, to the* CENTRE *of his.*)

GIRL It is in the air, it is in the wall. . . .

(*She goes* BACK, *feverishly, stands looking out of her window. Simultaneously, the* YOUNG MAN *goes to his.*)

GIRL . . . the bough taps out the answer on the window. It is even in the basement . . . where the landlord's teeth have left their bite in the stale crust, and potato peelings are oracles to those who learn how to read them.

(*She has moved restlessly back to her position at the door, but the* YOUNG MAN, *while beginning to follow suit, firmly resists the impulse on mention of the basement, and remains standing* CENTRE *of his own room.*)

YOUNG MAN You, too, point to the basement! I hadn't bargained for that.

GIRL We're inclined to overlook the landlord.

YOUNG MAN (*as if asleep*) The landlord said. . . . What was it the landlord said?

GIRL (*moving restlessly back to* CENTRE *of her room*) Ah, what was it?

YOUNG MAN (*driven, sleepwalking*) I must ask. . . . (*Moving towards door which connects with hall*) I must ask the landlord.

GIRL Too late. . . .

(GIRL'S *bedroom fades, as a scream is heard from the dark of the basement. It is the* LANDLADY'S *voice.* YOUNG MAN *stands transfixed, listening,* CENTRE *of his room.*)

YOUNG MAN (*whispering*) Too late. . . . (*Goes quickly into hall, to door of the second bedroom, calling*) You, there! (*Shouting*) When I need your advice most, you leave me!

(LANDLADY *is heard crying and lamenting in the dark.*)

LANDLADY'S VOICE Ah, Will, Will, you haven't left me!

YOUNG MAN (*to himself, facing audience*) Which of us is more lost, the landlady or I, it is difficult to say.

LANDLADY'S VOICE (*calling from dark, apparently to* YOUNG MAN) Where are yer? Where are yer? Am I alone in this great damp house?

YOUNG MAN (*righting his collar, calling*) Coming, Mrs Lusty!

(*As he races downstairs they light up. Hall and stairs fade as soon as he enters basement.*)

SCENE SIX · THE BASEMENT

BASEMENT *lights up as* YOUNG MAN *reaches bottom of the stairs. Same as before, except that the* LANDLORD *is now lying on the floor beside his chair, his pipe dropped somewhere near him.* LANDLADY *is kneeling, bending over him, trying to warm, envelop him.*

LANDLADY (*blubbering*) Dear Will! Speak! Just one word, Will. It's me. I know! I know! But speak!

(*As* YOUNG MAN *enters, he hesitates a moment in doorway.*)

(*On her knees, turning to address him*) See, boy. . . . Will . . . died.

YOUNG MAN (*preparing to protest*) But he can't. . . .

LANDLADY (*laying her open hand on* LANDLORD'S *eyes, wiping his face with her apron*) He's gone. I know. The life'd left 'im already before I touched 'im. Will is dead!

YOUNG MAN (*coming forward slowly*) Have it your own way then.

LANDLADY (*looking down*) That's wot Will used to say. Well, 'e's said it for the last time.

YOUNG MAN (*absorbed by sight of dead* LANDLORD) Who would really believe there could ever be a last time?
(*Continues staring closely at* LANDLORD.)

LANDLADY Wot are yer starin' at?

YOUNG MAN I've never seen a dead body. . . .

LANDLADY (*as the truth sweeps over her afresh*) Will . . . a *dead* . . . .
(*She cannot restrain herself.*)

YOUNG MAN (*shaking her*) Mrs Lusty! We must do something for the dead . . . for your *husband*! It isn't correct. . . .

LANDLADY (*pulling herself together*) No. 'T'ain't decent. (*Picking up* LANDLORD'S *pipe, half angrily, half sorrowfully*) 'Is bloody pipe! (*Whimpering, holding pipe to her cheek*) Coolin' fast. . . . 'Ow I used to hate it . . . when I'd 'ear the spit cracklin' in the bowl. It was as if Will was doin' it a'purpose. Will did everythink a'purpose. . . .
(*She gets up.*)

YOUNG MAN (*taking* LANDLORD *by the armpits*) See . . . I'll take like this . . . (*trying to lift*) and you the feet. . . .
(LANDLADY, *blubbering, takes* LANDLORD *by the feet.*)

LANDLADY Ah, Will, Will, who'd ever 've thought you wouldn't die in yer bed!

YOUNG MAN Not too far from it, though. (*Struggling*) Thank the Lord, he . . . didn't die . . . in his bath.

LANDLADY We 'eat the water . . . Saturdays.

YOUNG MAN That does . . . restrict.
(*They struggle to the bed, deposit body of* LANDLORD – *head at the foot, feet on the pillow.*)

LANDLADY Look, boy, wot we've been an' done!

YOUNG MAN I'm not surprised. I've never handled such a dead weight. I mean . . . I. . . .
(*He begins to hiccup uncontrollably.*)

LANDLADY (*as they manoeuvre the body right way round on the bed*) Will was always solid. Even as a young boy . . . in a photo. . . . Will was a . . . big . . . boy. . . .
(*She tails off into a whimper, which is punctuated by a hiccup from the* YOUNG MAN.)

YOUNG MAN I'm sorry. Things are somehow never quite . . . (*hiccup*) . . . as they ought to be.

LANDLADY Don't know about that. (*Bustles to dresser and takes a cup*) This nearly always works. (*Fills cup at the invisible sink*) I 'ad it from a lady called Mrs Moylan, 'oo was often took this way. (*Handing the cup*) 'Ere. 'Old yer breath, stick yer fingers in yer ears, count twenty, and drink from the back-side. Then if you're . . . not better . . . (*suppressing a whimper*) . . . I don't know wot to suggest. . . .

YOUNG MAN (*trying to carry out some of the acrobatics the* LANDLADY *has prescribed, but without giving these exercises his undivided attention*) How did he die, Mrs Lusty?

LANDLADY 'E just died. Without a word. Without even a fit. (*Holding her face*) Oh, God! Oh, dear!

YOUNG MAN (*sitting down, holding the cup, thoughtfully*) When it happens, it's easy as that.

LANDLADY But without even a word! I didn't say goodbye to 'im!

YOUNG MAN The truth stops where words begin. You would have trotted out the tired sentiments of others. It's better to cry when it's all done. . . . (*Setting cup on the table*) Or even hiccup . . . if it takes you that way.

LANDLADY I could'uv said. . . .

YOUNG MAN Not you, Mrs Lusty. Don't become obsessed by words.

LANDLADY You educated people are a jealous lot.

YOUNG MAN Now and then we do know best.

LANDLADY I would'uv said. . . . (*Leaves off in a whimper, slops towards the dressing-table at the 'fourth wall'*) Only Tuesday I said I'd mend 'is jacket. (*Calming*) I went to the theayter instead. (*Staring out at the audience, into the invisible glass*) They was doin' a drama. (*Begins to take down her hair*) You wouldn't believe the things that 'appened. They blew up a real bloomin' train! Every-

body killed. (*Staring at herself, and other things*) But they all got up at the end, and bowed. There wasn't no . . . funeral.
(*Takes up an invisible brush from dressing-table, and begins to brush her hair.*)

YOUNG MAN (*nervously, glancing at the dead* LANDLORD) We must do something, Mrs Lusty.

LANDLADY Wot, *again*? We only just laid 'im on the bed.

YOUNG MAN There's always something to be done . . . before the corpse takes over.

LANDLADY (*brushing hair, frantically*) Oh, leave off, can't yer? Leave me to brush me hair! I wish I was at the theayter. There's nothing so snug as red plush . . . even when you're only lookin' down at it from the gods.

YOUNG MAN But there's got to be a funeral. . . .

LANDLADY Don't I know it! That's why Will Lusty died. 'E 'ad it worked out.

YOUNG MAN But funerals, Mrs Lusty, are nice. Baked meats, and a good, warm cry.

LANDLADY Oh, I shan't let 'im down. (*Brushing calmly now, but with purpose*) It'll be respectable. It'll be somethink ter talk about. It'll be a 'am funeral.

YOUNG MAN Am?

LANDLADY 'Am, silly! Wot you eat. It never was seen in this street. Bill Piper got faggots. And Mrs Ruddock a leg of mutton. But it'll be 'am for Will Lusty, if 'is widow busts!

YOUNG MAN (*recollecting, to himself*) The first time I'd ever looked at a dead face. . . . And it looked back . . . as though . . .

LANDLADY (*brushing, softly*) Besides, I loved Will. As much as you're allowed to love. . . .

YOUNG MAN (*to himself*) . . . as though he'd intended to do a bunk . . . to leave me holding the stage. . . . It depends on me in a way it's never done before. . . .

LANDLADY (*sighing*) If you was allowed to love. But you aren't. And it curdles. It turns sour. . . .

YOUNG MAN (*appalled*) It depends on *me*! (*In revolt*) ME! (*Jumping up, shouting at* LANDLADY) For God's sake, stop brushing your hair!

(LANDLADY *stands arrested in the act of brushing.*)

LANDLADY (*also shouting*) I must do somethink, mustn't I?
(*She breaks into a stormy crying.*)

YOUNG MAN (*holding his head, speaking rapidly*) Yes, yes, I know!
This is the first time anything has happened to me. It's difficult to
think.
(LANDLADY *goes back to the bed where the body of the* LANDLORD
*is lying. She slips down beside the bed, huddling, with her head against
the side.*)

LANDLADY It's been 'appenin' ter me all me life. From the moment
I was born. An' death's the least! (*Taking* LANDLORD'S *hand*)
Ah, Will, Will!

YOUNG MAN (*wincing*) Let us fondle our dead selves! We can't
stroke too much . . . enjoy our sorrow.

LANDLADY (*rubbing her cheek against the* LANDLORD'S *hand*) Why
not, I ask? While it lasts. They box it up quick enough.

YOUNG MAN But other people must have their say. Tell me, Mrs
Lusty, are there any relatives?

LANDLADY (*disgusted*) At least twenty-six.

YOUNG MAN They must be brought, of course.

LANDLADY (*dully*) Why?

YOUNG MAN Why? Because . . . (*as a bright afterthought*) . . . why,
to eat the ham.

LANDLADY Ah, the 'am.

YOUNG MAN And to say the neat, consoling things people do say on
such occasions.

LANDLADY I'll know enough, my lad. I'll know the questions an'
the answers.

YOUNG MAN That's beside the point. It's not what we know. The
voices of relatives must express approval. That'll make an honest
woman of you.

LANDLADY (*ruefully*) I'd 'uv thought, by this, that was beside the
point, too.

YOUNG MAN (*imperiously*) Leave it to me, Mrs Lusty. Where do all
these people live?

LANDLADY Number eleven, Ethel Grove.

YOUNG MAN (*going towards door*, BACK) A grey house . . .

LANDLADY (*raucously*) . . . with the scabs peelin' off . . .

YOUNG MAN . . . and scurf falling . . .

LANDLADY (*infected by a hysterical kind of gaiety*) . . . with the windows sealed down . . .

YOUNG MAN (*from the door, calling back, triumphantly*) . . . because when they're open, the curtains have a habit of waving in the wind!

LANDLADY (*leaning against the bed, laughing in spite of herself*) I always said you was off yer nut!

YOUNG MAN Well, so long, Mrs Lusty. I'll be on my way!
(*Turns and runs up the stairs, two at a time. Stairs and hall light to receive him.*)

LANDLADY (*calling after him*) Cracked!
(*Basement* FADES)

YOUNG MAN (*running upstairs*) I would be . . . if I stayed . . . five minutes longer . . . in this deadly house . . . I must breathe!
(*Pauses for moment in hall, near the street-door.*)
(*Turning and looking back*) Listen to it! The landlord's called in the last cockroach!
(*As he* EXITS *into the street, a drop falls, concealing the rooms of the lodging-house.*)

SCENE SEVEN · A STREET

To be played in front of the drop. Lamp-post, R., *and a length of kerb-stone to accommodate one character as a seat. Another lamp-post,* L., *under it an over-flowing garbage-tin.*

A LADY *is rummaging through the tin.* A SECOND LADY *is seated,* R., *on the kerb.*

FIRST LADY, *rather ancient, is dressed in all kinds of splendour: net, lace, all a rusty-black – sequins, a tiara from which the glitter has gone.*

SECOND LADY, *rather more ancient, similarly dressed, but obviously fonder of feathers. A little supper hat with one sad peacock feather crowns the whole.*

FIRST LADY (*rummaging in the bin*) Some people throw away only what they don't need. That's something I noticed soon as I come into the discard trade.

SECOND LADY But there's always the surprises, dear.

FIRST LADY Of course. There's the surprises. It's the surprises that keeps yer goin'.

(*Out of the bin she fishes a bloater with some of the flesh still on it.*)

There! Yer see? There's as pretty a backbone as a person would ever find.

SECOND LADY To them that cares for fish.

FIRST LADY (*grande dame*) I can't tempt you, then?

SECOND LADY Oh, dear, no. It's kind. But I just 'ad a bite . . . on a corner in Charlotte Street.

(FIRST LADY *proceeds to pick the bloater.*)

FIRST LADY (*nostrils suddenly distended over the fish*) That reminds me of something.

SECOND LADY What, then? You know I try to be well-informed.

FIRST LADY A bath 'eater.

SECOND LADY Why a bath 'eater?

FIRST LADY Why, it blew up, and 'it me in the nose.

SECOND LADY If you must fiddle with a bath 'eater, of course it'll blow up.

FIRST LADY Seriously, though, Mrs Fauburgus, it does the pores good to unstop them once in a while.

SECOND LADY *My* pores would put up with no such monkey business, Mrs Goosgog. Not on yer life.

(FIRST LADY *rummages again in the dust-bin.*)

FIRST LADY Ah, well, it takes all kinds to make a tasty dust-bin.

(*She draws out a string of enormous pearls.*)

(*Displaying the necklace*) Do you believe in that one?

SECOND LADY I've not believed in anythink in life since a copper pinched me maidenhead.

FIRST LADY (*trying a pearl with her teeth*) Celluloid! (*Swallows the pearl*)

SECOND LADY I'm not surprised. There's no tellin' nowadays what won't turn up in celluloid.

FIRST LADY (*consuming pearls, one by one*) But it has its uses . . . and is light . . . and cheap . . . only a bit monotonous.

(*She drops the string with remaining pearls back into the bin.*)

SECOND LADY Are there no letters? There's nothink I like better than a read of a good letter. Look and see, Mrs Goosgog, if you can't find us a letter. I'm inclined to feel melancholy at this hour of night.

FIRST LADY Anything to oblige a friend. But banana skins, Mrs Fauburgus, are fatal to letters.

SECOND LADY Letters are fatal.

FIRST LADY (*fishing one out of the bin*) Here's one. It's all mauve.

SECOND LADY And scenty? It must be scenty.

FIRST LADY It's scenty all right!

SECOND LADY (*impatient*) Go on, then, read it!

FIRST LADY (*reading carefully*) 'Dear Harry ... thank you for yours with ex ... planations ... but I have reached the point where ... suf ... fering is too ex-cruci-atin'. . . . (*To* SECOND LADY) Style, eh? (*Continues*) I used to think it was a luxury. I could have suffered and . . . (*squinting at the letter*) . . . suffered. Well, of course, I have ... wrote you all this before ...' (*squinting again*)

SECOND LADY (*anxiously*) Go on, dear. What are yer waitin' for?

FIRST LADY This letter seems to of got mixed up with the ter-marter sauce.

SECOND LADY Oh, dear! That does 'appen to letters.

FIRST LADY (*deciphering with difficulty*) '. . . wrote you all this before, and shall continue to write . . . because it has become a habit . . . if I do not kill myself. . . .'

SECOND LADY They do, you know. They go out to the post-box. Then they come in and kill theirselves . . . just out of devilment.

FIRST LADY (*meditatively, eating the letter*) What gets inter people? Now, when I was in the circus. . . .

(SECOND LADY *comes across to the bin, to rummage.*)

SECOND LADY What was you doin' in the circus, dear?

FIRST LADY 'Andin' up the swords to my old man.

SECOND LADY What became of yer old man?

FIRST LADY 'E swallowed too 'ard.

(*They look at each other, and scream with laughter.*)

SECOND LADY (*rummaging in the bin*) Oh, dear, this ain't a very rich bin.

FIRST LADY There's no tellin'. The best bits are inclined to work towards the bottom.

(*Enter* YOUNG MAN, R. *He is preoccupied, his coat collar turned up as a protection against night, cold, and thoughts.*)

YOUNG MAN (*hesitating, to himself*) A grey house, where heads will emerge from the windows . . . scenting a corpse. . . .

(*He holds back,* R., *head down, as if wrestling with his doubts and fears.*)

(*To himself*) But they'll carry the load. I shall retire again, into a corner, and dream . . . consider the acts of mercy I never perform, while the box is carried out by the relatives in black.

(YOUNG MAN *faces the audience with his thoughts.*)

It'll be safer then. When I ran out on this charitable errand, leaving the fat, huddled woman, it was because I was afraid. I was afraid of the dead landlord lying on the bed. Once this evening he glimmered for a moment, and I almost saw his soul. But when I looked again, he was dead. *That* was the landlord! Even alive, he was waiting to putrefy . . . a mound of uncommunicative flesh.

(*Shaking off the vision with loathing*) It'll be safer when he's disposed of. So I run to fetch the relatives.

(*Under the lamp-post,* L., *the* TWO LADIES *look towards* YOUNG MAN, *longing to sympathize.*)

FIRST LADY (*sighing*) A fair young man, with a fair moustache just beginning! Touch the fluff, and it flies away. . . .

SECOND LADY A fair moustache once made me cry . . . when I was young. . . .

YOUNG MAN (*still to himself, doubting*) So I'll run to fetch the relatives. . . .

FIRST LADY Daisies and buttercups . . . what wouldn't I give for a field of grass . . .

SECOND LADY . . . where hares bed, in nests of grass. . . .

YOUNG MAN (*to himself*) . . . though who knows, perhaps it's safer to cut and run. . . .

FIRST LADY (*to* YOUNG MAN) Hey . . . Eustace! Got something on yer mind?

YOUNG MAN (*putting his hands in his pockets, standing his ground*) Nothing particular, thanks. Who are you?

FIRST LADY We're two professional ladies.

YOUNG MAN At your age?

SECOND LADY (*cackling*) Nao, nao! We're in the bits-and-pieces business.

YOUNG MAN (*with distaste*) So it seems.

SECOND LADY Lardy da! At least it 'olds a body together, and that's more than thinkin' never did for no one.

YOUNG MAN (*wryly*) Perhaps you've hit the nail on the head.

FIRST LADY (*skipping forward*) I'll let you into a secret. (*Behind her hand*) We're the knockabout girls of the piece.

YOUNG MAN I thought it was all knockabout.

FIRST LADY Yes. But our part won't kill yer.

SECOND LADY No knives in our garters.

FIRST LADY Won't tickle yer ribs with anything sharper than a fevver.

YOUNG MAN I could cry . . . if it was the Anglo-Saxon thing to do.

SECOND LADY Go on, dear. Cry. Everythink's meant to come out, whether it's wind or water.

YOUNG MAN You don't realize. My landlord died.

FIRST LADY Everyone has a dead landlord . . . tucked away . . . somewhere.

SECOND LADY An' rats galore . . . eatin' their 'eads orf . . . after midnight.

FIRST LADY And paper roses . . .

SECOND LADY . . . with desperate breff . . .

FIRST LADY . . . and a mother's love . . .

SECOND LADY . . . to bail you out.

YOUNG MAN (*bowing*) Thank you for your sympathy. Lull me some more. Not with love, though.

SECOND LADY (*running to the bin*) With a bloater?
(*Whisks the fish-skeleton under* YOUNG MAN'S *nose.*)

YOUNG MAN Cripes!

FIRST LADY (*running to the bin*) Or tom-cat perished Saturday night, tryin' to sneak across Holborn? (*About to draw out the cat. Stops. Stares into bin. Pauses. Lets out a long, thin, terrible scream.*)

SECOND LADY (*holding her ears*) Oh, 'ark at 'er! She's remembered somethink she lost.

FIRST LADY Murder! Murder! Murder!

SECOND LADY It's the bloater. There was never nothink like a bloater for makin' a person repeat.

(SECOND LADY *goes and looks into the bin. She too lets out a scream, or series of dry, gasping retches.*)

(*Protesting*) 'Ere, it wasn't me!

FIRST LADY Tell that to the magistrate.

SECOND LADY It's never so much the perlice. . . .

FIRST LADY Perlice is easy as cheese. Nao . . . it's the conscience!

SECOND LADY (*queasily*) Luvva *duck.* . . .

(TWO LADIES *steal away, supporting each other.*)

(YOUNG MAN *has stood transfixed, watching the proceeding. Now he goes slowly but deliberately to look.*)

YOUNG MAN (*staring into bin, pausing, then very gently*) Poor little fellow! (*Suddenly in revolt, shouting*) There was never such brutality. . . . (*On second thought*) Or was it . . . so very brutal? (*Again gently compassionate*) You died too soon . . . or weren't even born. No angel struck you on the mouth, to silence what you already knew. Your love returned into love, without ever feeling the thumb-screw and the rack. Tender, humorous foetus! Such a one the landlady might have carried, and dropped almost without knowing, and tried bitterly to remember. Dreams wear no faces when it is important to identify them.

(*Suddenly coming down,* FORWARD.)

(*Protesting*) So much for visions! Who'll ever tell where the flesh begins . . . or ends? The landlord and the dead child are one. But who am I? (*Calmer*) I'm forgetting, though. It's easy for a poet. While the woman sits in the basement, listening to her memories tick, playing with the ends of her hair, I've failed to produce the relatives . . . (*turning towards the drop,* BACK) . . . though this could be their house.

HOUSE (*in long, stony echo, the voice of a cold, old man*) Could be . . . could be. . . .

SCENE EIGHT · OUTSIDE A HOUSE

House has a closed, grey look. There is a door which opens, and solid steps. Windows of the ground, first, and second floors are visible, and will open.

YOUNG MAN (*contemplating the façade*) Probably never opened since Will Lusty escaped into life. After that it relapsed . . . into mutton-fat and linoleum. (*Brisker*) But here goes. I've started to tell myself I'm a man of action.
(*Mounts steps, and knocks loudly on the door.*)
(*Holding his ear to the door, calling*) Anyone there?
(*A pause.*)

HOUSE (*echoing coldly*) Anyone . . . airrr . . . ?

YOUNG MAN (*listening*) Someone at a great distance getting into his slippers . . . and coming . . . and coming . . .

HOUSE (*echoing*) . . . comm . . . inggg. . . .
(YOUNG MAN *starts back down the steps, holding an arm to his face for protection, as* FOUR RELATIVES *pull up the windows and pop their heads out, one at the ground floor, two at the second, and one at the third. (Alternatively, one could be made to stick his head out of a trap, as if from the area basement.) All* FOUR RELATIVES *exactly alike – soap-coloured, lean, with drooping, straw moustaches.*)

RELATIVES (*in unison*) Is it Will?

YOUNG MAN (*retreating in panic against the lamp-post*) Yes!

FIRST RELATIVE We knew'd it'd be about Will.

SECOND RELATIVE There was every indication.

THIRD RELATIVE A knockin' at the door Friday night.

FOURTH RELATIVE A mouse sang behind the wainscot.

FIRST RELATIVE So what could you expect?

YOUNG MAN I don't know, I'm sure. Frankly, though, I expected you to be more rational.

FIRST RELATIVE What did Will tell yer?

YOUNG MAN Nothing.

SECOND RELATIVE Will never spoke.

YOUNG MAN Only once. And I didn't understand. Then, when I went back to ask, he was already dead.

THIRD RELATIVE We knew'd it'ud happen. It was a bad business.

YOUNG MAN You're not suggesting . . . ?

FIRST RELATIVE (*convinced*) Will Lusty died of his wife.

   (FOURTH RELATIVE *lets out a thin, lascivious laugh.*)

YOUNG MAN Not really. She even loved him at times . . . which is the most we can expect of anybody.

   (RELATIVES *shake their heads.*)

THIRD RELATIVE Never trusted Alma.

FOURTH RELATIVE Alma Jagg. Of Edmonton.

FIRST RELATIVE A red, plump girl. She stood on the doorstep, and her arms mottled in the wind.

SECOND RELATIVE She smelled of milk. And celery.

THIRD RELATIVE And crushed nettles.

   (FOURTH RELATIVE *lets out his thin laugh.*)

FIRST RELATIVE She turned into a shrew that no blouse could contain.

YOUNG MAN That may be. But Will Lusty's dead. And now she's trailing on the floor, like any poor rag. The wind's quite gone out of her.

FIRST RELATIVE No doubt she wants us to assist in choosin' a decent casket.

YOUNG MAN That's more or less the idea.

SECOND RELATIVE And a solid marble stone . . . with hands clasped in eternal agreement.

YOUNG MAN We hadn't ventured as far as that. But she'd like you to come. And to the funeral. It will be a . . .

FIRST RELATIVE (*nodding his head, ponderously*) . . . a ham funeral.

   (YOUNG MAN *starts.*)

YOUNG MAN (*looking at* FIRST RELATIVE) There can't be much that's unexpected.

FIRST RELATIVE (*sharply*) There's one thing, young man.

THIRD RELATIVE Very definitely.

YOUNG MAN Yes?

FOURTH RELATIVE (*laughing thinly*) What we'd like to know is: Where do *you* come in?

YOUNG MAN (*retreating*) I?

FIRST RELATIVE Yes! You!

YOUNG MAN (*rattled*) Really, I . . . I have to find out. You must give me time. Please! There are moments when I can touch fire, but . . . just now . . . if you'll accept me as the Greek messenger, I'll be most grateful.

(*Looks behind him desperately, as if in search of help.*)

FIRST RELATIVE (*darkly*) Your shadow's on the ground behind yer.

FOURTH RELATIVE He still hasn't answered the question.

YOUNG MAN (*considering*) I haven't, because . . . people living together in a house walk with their hands outstretched. Sometimes they touch one another. But only learn their shapes. That puffy object, the landlord, should have been obvious enough. He wasn't. He remained as obscure as the chair on which he sat . . . complete, but telling no secrets. At times I hated him for his ugliness and squalor. I feared his strength. Once, very briefly, I almost loved him. (*Losing his temper*) Damn you, can't you see I'm obsessed by the landlord? (*Recovering control, quietly*) Now, will you come? I'll take you to his dead body.

FIRST RELATIVE Not so badly put, young man.

FOURTH RELATIVE (*still suspicious*) Even varnished oak has splinters.

YOUNG MAN (*at the end of his patience*) I am waiting.

FIRST RELATIVE I wouldn't be surprised if you didn't 'ave ideas about yerself. But . . . (*with a last look of disapproval*) . . . wait till we fetch our 'at and galoshes.

(RELATIVES *withdraw their heads simultaneously.*)

YOUNG MAN (*coming forward, addressing the audience*) While the relatives pick their hats from the antlers where they sprout, and rummage after perished rubber, the dead man has quietly removed himself. So the funeral will be for the living. That is the funny, or the tragic part. But we'll eat the landlady's great ham. (*Looking skyward*) And there'll always be the stars . . . if they don't begin to explode in one's face. . . . (*Door of house opens, and* FIRST RELATIVE *appears, carrying a black bowler hat and loosely-furled umbrella.*)

FIRST RELATIVE (*cheerfully*) There we are!

(*Closes door behind him.*)

YOUNG MAN Where are the others?

FIRST RELATIVE What others?

(RELATIVE *puts on his hat.*)

YOUNG MAN (*helplessly*) Just as you like. Let's get going then.
(*Starts to move off smartly.*)

FIRST RELATIVE (*catching him by the arm, restraining*) Easy does it!
I fell down last year at Ramsgate. (*Chuckling*) And Will Lusty
can't give us the slip!
(*They move* OFF, L.)

ACT TWO

SCENE ONE · THE BASEMENT

Same as before, except that the LANDLORD *is no longer present, the bed is made, and covered with a quilt, and there is a general swept-and-garnished look. On the kitchen table there is a large boiled ham, bottles, and glasses filled with stout. The* FOUR RELATIVES *are dotted about the room, upright on kitchen chairs. On the bed, their four bowler-hats. The* LANDLADY *is seated behind the table, monumental in black. Beside her is an empty chair, and on the table in front of it, a full glass.* AFTER *the* CURTAIN *rises, the actors hold the picture for a brief space.*

FIRST RELATIVE (*sighing*) Ah, well!

LANDLADY (*rousing herself, to* FIRST RELATIVE) Another slice, cousin?

FIRST RELATIVE I don't mind, Alma. I don't mind. . . .

SECOND RELATIVE (*to* THIRD RELATIVE) 'E'll mind in the night. There's many a resurrection after 'am.

(*As other thoughts take possession of her, the* LANDLADY *momentarily closes her eyes, holds her handkerchief to her mouth.* FOURTH RELATIVE *titters.*)

THIRD RELATIVE Ssh! We must respect the feelin's of the widow.

FOURTH RELATIVE Still in the mothball stage too.

(LANDLADY *continues to serve the ham, passing the helping to the* FIRST RELATIVE.)

FIRST RELATIVE Perhaps on second thoughts, Alma, in these sad circumstances it would be more appropriate not to . . . stuff.

LANDLADY (*passionately*) Eat, damn yers! Fill yer bellies! That's wot it's 'ere for!

FIRST RELATIVE I was only suggestin', of course. Out of propriety. (*He starts to eat the ham.*)

LANDLADY There's nothink like food. 'Specially now. If you stuff yer mouths, they can't get inter mischief.

FIRST RELATIVE It was our intention to pay a tribute to our relative 'oo 'as just passed on.

LANDLADY (*unconvinced*) Or to 'ave a dig at the livin'!

FIRST RELATIVE (*rising undeterred, formal, dignified*) It remains our intention, Alma, to do the necessary by Will Lusty. 'E was a silent man, certainly, but not one that you could overlook. (*From a great depth*) '*Deep*' is perhaps the word for Will. Never ever opened a book, but could read the grain in a table simply by passin' 'is 'and across it . . . like as if 'e was blind. In the days when 'e kept the little sweetshop out at Croakers' Pond, 'e never needed to 'ear the bell to know customers were on the step. 'E'd go on out, and there 'e'd be, ready to weigh the aniseed balls and lickerish all-sorts. . . .

LANDLADY (*swaying, eyes closed*) And the 'conversations'. . . . Don't forget the 'conversations' . . . with the motters printed onter them. You wondered whether there was any truth . . .

FIRST RELATIVE (*frowning*) We must ask you, Alma, not to . . .

LANDLADY . . . any truth in wot the printed motters told yer.

FIRST RELATIVE The truth is told in time, Alma, and don't lick off as easy as the printed motter on a 'conversation'.

(LANDLADY *nods her head.*)

LANDLADY The truth was always stickier.

FIRST RELATIVE Now where was we . . . (*clearing his throat*) . . . if the lady's goin' to allow. . . . The children. . . . Yes! (*picking up the thread*) Little children would lower their eyes . . . knowin' that Will would tell what they 'ad not yet thought of. The boys 'oo 'ad not yet learnt to twist the wing off a live bird. Little girls, 'oo 'ad not yet found their way into the cow-parsley and docks, dawdled sweetly . . . sucking sherbet out of paper-bags. Will *knew*. . . . Pardon me! If 'e didn't interfere in anything 'e saw must 'appen, it was because 'e believed a human bein' must purge 'imself of 'is own evil . . . like anythin' . . . well, anythink else. Will was gentle. That was 'is weakness. When I say 'weak', I don't mean 'e wasn't strong. Took up wrestlin' as a 'obby. Got so good, they give 'im a valuable silver belt. (LANDLADY *nods*) But Will was gentle. Anyways, till the end. 'Ere in this very 'ouse . . . which nobody would say 'e was not the pillar of . . . there was never an inmate 'oo did not listen for the landlord's breathin'. Slow and gentle. Risin' out of the depths of the house. Expandin' the walls as if they 'ad been ribs. . . .

(LANDLADY *takes a deep breath.*)

But Will married. That was the other side of the medal. There 'e wrestled and was thrown. Even out at Croakers' Pond, she developed the 'abit of countin' the ivy leaves as she waited. The bell on the shop door was music. 'Ere in the upper rooms, she would sit with the whores on nights when they felt too damn drab to face goin' on the beat. Sat an' played at cat's-cradle. Stitchin' the string into gates an' mattresses. Will knew, of course. Because Will knew. And the goodness in 'im turned to pus. That's wot I reckon 'appened. Will bust at last infected by 'is missus's life. (*Looking at* LANDLADY) Now 'is missus. . . .

LANDLADY Thanks! I'm not all that simple. I know my life inside out.

(*She tosses off what remains of her tumblerful of stout.*)

SECOND RELATIVE (*leaning forward*) Do you, though?

THIRD RELATIVE (*whispering*) I wonder!

(LANDLADY *stands up quickly, facing all insinuations.*)

FIRST RELATIVE (*not really trying to convince, as he subsides windily into his chair*) She's not afraid.

LANDLADY No . . . why should I be afraid . . . ? I'm not afraid . . . of nothink. Wot is there to be afraid of, anyways?

SECOND RELATIVE Not the sound of your own feet . . . on a stone floor . . . in a deserted house . . . at dusk?

THIRD RELATIVE Not the sudden scream of a chair . . . ?

FOURTH RELATIVE Not the space you press against in the empty bed . . . ?

(LANDLADY *tosses her head.*)

LANDLADY Pffh! If I want me flesh to creep, I have a read of the Sunday paper.

FIRST RELATIVE Or really search in your mind, Alma Lusty?

LANDLADY (*rounding on him*) 'Ere wot *is* this? Wot'uv I done?

FIRST RELATIVE Whether you done it or not, it's the thought that counts.

LANDLADY (*knotting her hands*) Will died natural . . . if that's wot yer mean. So 'elp me!

SECOND RELATIVE Will didn't die by the knife . . .

THIRD RELATIVE . . . or by any chemist's bottle . . .

FOURTH RELATIVE . . . but 'e might have done.

FIRST RELATIVE 'E did. Will Lusty died many a time. Time out of mind.

(LANDLADY *tosses her head.*)

LANDLADY (*twisting her apron, laughing hoarsely*) 'Oo 'asn't done a murder . . . once or twice . . . in their imagination?

FOURTH RELATIVE (*coming very close to her*) But nobody's done it so often . . . or so well.

SECOND RELATIVE (*approaching her, softly*) Remember 'ow the blood ran, as you turned the knife in 'is side? Your long black hair was wet. . . .

THIRD RELATIVE (*approaching her, whispering*) Remember 'ow 'is eyes wondered, after 'e put down the glass? 'E 'ad the puzzled, china eyes of a bull . . . as it folds its legs . . . and thumps the earth. . . .

(LANDLADY *goes* FORWARD, *in great agitation, towards the invisible dressing-table with its mirror.*)

LANDLADY Leave me alone, can't yer? Wot 'uv I done?

FOURTH RELATIVE (*laughing his thin laugh*) Ain't we tellin' yer?

FIRST RELATIVE When you saw that man roll from his chair, Alma Lusty, an' die for the last time, I wonder you screamed!

(LANDLADY *stares horrified at her own reflection in the invisible glass.*)

LANDLADY I screamed 'cause I was afraid . . .

FOURTH RELATIVE (*laughing*) She was actually afraid!

LANDLADY (*still staring at the mirror*) . . . to see it 'appen at last. I never thought 'e would lie so still. I never thought my heart would beat that loud. (*In horror, to the mirror*) I was afraid somebody might 'ear it.

SECOND RELATIVE She was afraid!

LANDLADY But I screamed, too . . . (*closing her eyes*) . . . because I loved 'im. . . .

FOURTH RELATIVE Tt-tt-tt!

LANDLADY I was ashamed. Will's face saw more than any mirror. Sometimes 'e looked under the skin.

THIRD RELATIVE So you wanted 'im dead. . . .

LANDLADY Yes. You wouldn't understand. Not any of yers. You was born all-of-a-piece.

FIRST RELATIVE We certainly never done a murder, Alma.

LANDLADY Nor never loved. Exceptin' yerselves . . . yer hollow faces in the glass . . . an' the black cockroach, squintin' down at yez off the shelf.

FIRST RELATIVE All right. We never loved.

SECOND RELATIVE We never loved the butcher . . .

THIRD RELATIVE . . . or the baker . . .

FOURTH RELATIVE . . . or the man that reads the gas meter!

(FOURTH RELATIVE *shrieks with laughter.*)

(LANDLADY *subsides, exhausted, into the chair in which she was sitting before.*)

FIRST RELATIVE (*pointing to empty chair beside* LANDLADY, *and the full glass waiting in front of it*) We never loved Will Lusty that much, that we keep an empty chair and a full glass waitin' for 'im, after 'e's dead!

(LANDLADY *looks aghast and sideways at something non-existent.*)

LANDLADY (*realizing*) That is for a young man wot lodges 'ere. A respectable young feller. Only where 'e's got to now, I don't just know.

FIRST RELATIVE O-ho!

SECOND RELATIVE 'E'll come back.

THIRD RELATIVE 'E'll come back.

FOURTH RELATIVE Nobody escapes.

FIRST RELATIVE (*to* LANDLADY) In the meantime, fill up yer glass. It's empty.

(LANDLADY *does so with eager hand.*)

LANDLADY You've said the word, cousin. Me spirits are as low as the floor. An' that ain't right.

(*She swallows half a tumblerful.*)

SECOND RELATIVE T'ain't.

THIRD RELATIVE This is a funeral.

FOURTH RELATIVE Of poor Will Lusty, 'oo was mild as 'am.

LANDLADY (*feelingly*) Not always, 'e wasn't!
(*Helps herself to another slice of ham.*)

SECOND RELATIVE 'Am '*as* been known to protest.

FIRST RELATIVE (*to* LANDLADY) Will liked a joke, too.
(LANDLADY *sits and stares ahead.*)

FIRST RELATIVE Eh? Didn't 'e, Alma?

LANDLADY (*rousing herself, faintly*) Why . . . yes. Will liked a good laugh.

FIRST RELATIVE Used to laugh, didn't 'e, when people fell down?

LANDLADY (*mechanically*) Yes. 'E did.

FIRST RELATIVE Specially when they fell on their behinds?

LANDLADY Yes. Will laughed loudest.

FIRST RELATIVE (*accusingly*) Why?

LANDLADY I don't know.

FIRST RELATIVE Because it's funny, ain't it?

LANDLADY (*the idea taking root*) Yes. It's . . . funny!
(*She sniggers.*)

FIRST RELATIVE And people are not supposed to lose their balance.

LANDLADY (*beginning to shake*) But they do!

FIRST RELATIVE (*slapping the table*) They do!
(LANDLADY *begins to lose control.*)

LANDLADY (*laughing*) And are never the same again. . . . Lusty used to say . . . Will said: A man only 'as to bounce like a ball to know 'ow much of 'is will is free.

SECOND RELATIVE Our relative was a philosopher . . .

THIRD RELATIVE . . . as well as a wrestler.

FOURTH RELATIVE It's much the same thing. Eh, Alma?

LANDLADY 'Ow do I know? (*drying her eyes*) I don't know nothink.
(*About to lose control again*) 'Ave another slice of 'am?
(*She bursts.*)

LANDLADY (*howling with laughter*) Aoh, go on! Wot 'uv yer done to me? There's nothink ter laugh about . . . nothink funny at . . . all. . . . Me ol' man's just . . . died. . . .
(*At this the* FOUR RELATIVES *roar too.*)
(BASEMENT *darkens.*)

SCENE TWO

Simultaneously the YOUNG MAN'S *bedroom appears. He is discovered standing isolated,* CENTRE.

YOUNG MAN I haven't gone down yet, because I can't face the mourners. Even at a distance you can hear the creaking of their black thighs, and their thin shoulders, green at the seams. How their moustaches twitch and glisten to deliver twisted truths! They are letting the landlady have it, poor cow. She lashes her tail, and tosses her head, and lows. But she can't throw them off. Her conscience sticks to her. Her confused soul lumbers through the labyrinth, laughing when it should cry, and crying when it should laugh. Such confusion is catching. If it weren't for that I might have gone down.

(The other bedroom lightens. The GIRL *is standing in its* CENTRE, *on the same spot and in the same attitude as the* YOUNG MAN.*)*

GIRL Walls are no protection from thoughts. Sorry if I overheard you.

YOUNG MAN *(indifferent at present)* I'd forgotten you were there.

GIRL So much the better.

YOUNG MAN And now that you are, I doubt if I have the strength for one more attitude.

(He goes and sits in the plush armchair, the GIRL *following suit in the twin in her own room.)*

GIRL *(laughing)* Splendid! One day you may discover you're standing on your own feet.

YOUNG MAN I no longer care.

GIRL For the moment you're disgusted by what you begin to suspect may be life.

YOUNG MAN *(protesting)* That poor Judy they're bashing in the basement? Never!

(He jumps up and goes defiantly to CENTRE *of his room.)*

GIRL *(neither agreeing nor disagreeing)* Well. . . .

YOUNG MAN Once I almost took the world in my hands. It was a lovely ball of coloured glass. . . .

GIRL But it would have broken.

YOUNG MAN Once I almost wrote a play, in which the situations were too subtle to express.

GIRL (*ironical*) But the attitudes were your own, and would have given you endless pleasure.

YOUNG MAN (*going quickly through the hall, to door of second bedroom, menacingly*) I didn't ask for any of this!

GIRL (*going similarly to the door on her side*) Nobody asked for their own misgivings. Now won't you go on?

YOUNG MAN No. I've dried up.

GIRL Like the subtle play. And the world has turned to a ball of mud, that stinks and stinks in your hands.

YOUNG MAN (*after a moment, sheepishly*) Yes.

GIRL (*rounding on him, furiously*) And don't you think you're responsible? For some of it, at least?

YOUNG MAN (*also rounding, defensive and aggressive at the same time*) Then what do you expect me to do?

GIRL (*resting her head against door, closing her eyes, as if helpless and exhausted*) My dear simpleton! If it could be *spoken*!

YOUNG MAN (*spreading the palm of his hand on the door*) Yes. Yes. Doesn't matter. Lie still. I can almost touch you. I can . . . feel your . . . cheek . . . forming under my hand!

GIRL (*for a moment allowing herself to succumb*) And if I put my mouth to the door, your lips would fit into the groove. . . .

YOUNG MAN (*resting his cheek against the door*) . . . and we should be complete . . . at last. . . .

(GIRL *opens her eyes suddenly, and starts away from the door. Moves towards* CENTRE *of her room.*)

GIRL It's so easy to delude oneself.

YOUNG MAN (*also drawing away from the door, exasperated*) Let us, for God's sake, delude ourselves in *some* small way!

(*Crosses hall, and moves towards* CENTRE *of his own room.*)

GIRL (*firmly*) You must go now.

YOUNG MAN (*discouraged*) Where?

GIRL You know without my telling.

(*There is a wave of laughter from the basement.* YOUNG MAN *listens with obvious distaste.*)

YOUNG MAN (*to* GIRL) You, too! You're forcing me back to the

dead landlord . . . tying him to me . . . like a great weight. . . .
(*Puts hands to his throat, as if feeling a dead weight that must pull him under.*)

GIRL (*remorseless*) . . . reminding you of his reality. . . .
(*Light returns to basement, disclosing* LANDLADY *and* RELATIVES *in same grouping as before.*)
And these people, performing the great conjuring act, out of their shabby opera hat. . . .

YOUNG MAN These people are less convincing than the landlord himself.

GIRL . . . these people are as real, and as unreal, as your own face in the depths of the glass.
(LANDLADY *and* RELATIVES *come to life in a tremendous gust of laughter.*)

SCENE THREE · THE BASEMENT

During the following brief scene the bedrooms above remain lit, the YOUNG MAN *and* GIRL *holding their positions* CENTRE *of their respective rooms.*

FIRST RELATIVE (*slapping his thigh, telling a story*) . . . and then Will took the crowbar in 'is 'ands . . .

SECOND RELATIVE Will 'ad big 'ands. With rivers of blue veins . . .

THIRD RELATIVE . . . and a tattooed flooer de lees . . .

FOURTH RELATIVE . . . an' Je . . . Jesus Christ in a crown of thorns. . . .

FIRST RELATIVE (*exasperated*) Will Lusty took the crowbar, didn't I say?

LANDLADY (*to* SECOND RELATIVE, *blearily*) 'Ave another slice of 'am, cousin. It's nice.

FIRST RELATIVE (*persevering*) 'E took the *crowbar*! (*Stands to re-enact the scene, and* LANDLADY *and* OTHER RELATIVES *lean forward, and fix him with bemused attention*) 'E took it in 'is 'ands. And before yer could say knife, 'e'd twisted it into 'andlebars!

SECOND RELATIVE (*without begging to differ*) A croaky 'oop!

THIRD RELATIVE A streak of lightnin'!

LANDLADY I'm buggered if it was anythink of the sort. It was a true-lovers' knot!

FIRST RELATIVE (*slapping* LANDLADY *on the thigh*) Alma said it!

FOURTH RELATIVE (*popping his head over* LANDLADY'S *shoulder, giggling*) Alma would!

(ALL *roar*.)

SCENE FOUR

During following scene, basement remains lit. LANDLADY *and* RELATIVES *hold their positions.*

YOUNG MAN They'll bate her till she's raw and bleeding.

GIRL Her dreams have been bloodier.

YOUNG MAN Are you a specialist in tortures?

GIRL Am I your other self?

YOUNG MAN My head's reeling with probabilities.

GIRL Even so . . . it's time you went down to the others.

YOUNG MAN (*an automaton*) Time . . . I . . . went . . . down. . . .

GIRL Aren't you already going?

YOUNG MAN Yes . . . I'm . . . go. . . .

GIRL To play your part in the charade.

(YOUNG MAN *pauses at door of second bedroom*.)

YOUNG MAN (*addressing the door*) And what about you?

GIRL Oh, I shall be there. Don't worry. I shall be sitting on your right hand!

(GIRL *and her bedroom fade*.)

YOUNG MAN (*mechanically*) And so I return to the basement . . . if I've ever really left it.

(*As he moves towards the stairs, the* YOUNG MAN'S *room and hall fade*.)

SCENE FIVE · THE BASEMENT

Stairs light as YOUNG MAN *descends hesitantly. At same time, the group of* MOURNERS *in the basement animates again.*

LANDLADY (*to* FIRST RELATIVE) Another slice, cousin?

FIRST RELATIVE I don't mind, Alma. I don't mind.

LANDLADY (*coyly, stifling a belch*) Reminds me of . . . me weddin' night!

FOURTH RELATIVE Oo-ER, tell us, Alma!

LANDLADY We 'ad a 'am.

SECOND RELATIVE (*singing*) 'They wouldn't believe me!
                          They wouldn't believe me!'

LANDLADY A tre-*mend*-jous 'am! Well, to cut a story short . . . (*coyly*) . . . because weddin' nights *are* short . . .
(*Roars from the* RELATIVES.)

THIRD RELATIVE (*slapping his thigh*) I bet Alma's was the shortest!

LANDLADY I wakes, see? There's a slice of light beneath the blind. Mornin', see? I turns to my Will. Me, the blushin' bride! "Oly smoke!' I cries. I pulls back me 'and. No Will beside me in the bed. Know wot there was?

RELATIVES (*leaning forward*) What?

LANDLADY Will, a course . . . I finds out later . . . is makin' a cuppa. But beside me in the bed . . . you'll never guess . . . the bleedin' 'am!

FIRST RELATIVE What did I tell yer? Will was always a jokey one!
(ALL *roar.*)
(THE YOUNG MAN *has reached the door of the basement,* BACK. *Stairs fade out. He looks in at the convulsed* LANDLADY *and* RELATIVES. ALL *turn and stare back at him.*)
(*There is a silence.*)

FIRST RELATIVE (*at last*) Bless me if it ain't the young lord!

LANDLADY (*encouraging, to* YOUNG MAN) Why, Fred! Come an' sit alongside of me. (*Patting the chair*) Ain't I been dustin' yer chair down . . . all this time?
(*On table, in front of chair, the full glass is still waiting.*)

FOURTH RELATIVE Oho! Fred, eh?

LANDLADY (*patting the chair, tittering at* RELATIVES) Yes. Didn't yer know?

FIRST RELATIVE No!

(YOUNG MAN *advances shyly, sits on the edge of the chair.*)

LANDLADY (*encouraging*) Don't be afraid, dear. These is friends.

SECOND RELATIVE A comparatively *young* man!

THIRD RELATIVE Quite a boy!

FOURTH RELATIVE But well-developed!

(*Silence.*)

LANDLADY (*to* YOUNG MAN) There! Drink, dear.

(YOUNG MAN *sips stout, but without pleasure.*)

LANDLADY (*to* RELATIVES) Fred's shy . . . (*bridling*) when there's company.

YOUNG MAN (*diffidently*) I wanted to pay my respects to the widow of the. . . .

LANDLADY (*fuddled*) That's all right, dear. That's over. Now we've begun again.

SECOND RELATIVE She's right.

THIRD RELATIVE By 'rithmatick!

FIRST RELATIVE (*intoning*) If you give it time, even marble recovers its circulation . . .

FOURTH RELATIVE . . . the nettle is silent that screeched in the gritty wind . . .

SECOND RELATIVE . . . the eye is dry . . .

THIRD RELATIVE . . . dry.

LANDLADY (*sniggers*) Dry! No doubt . . . (*drinks*) . . . about that. Couldn't get me words out without a little bit of assistance. Death's a dry business. (*Remembering something*) Nothing drier . . . (*tortured*) . . . 'xceptin' love. . . .

YOUNG MAN Look here, do you have to tell them any more?

LANDLADY I don't have to tell . . . only what I . . . believe. But what do I believe . . . (*touching her bust, looking at her hands*) . . . since they took it away from me?

FIRST RELATIVE (*taking the cue*) Personally I never believed there was a pair of 'ands inside those gloves . . . wringin' theirselves as the earth fell on the coffin.

FOURTH RELATIVE An' what about all that plaster stuff they put under glass for funerals? Was you taken in by that? It could have been . . . sugar. Same as at a weddin'.

LANDLADY (*patting the* YOUNG MAN) They're right, dear. Everythink begins . . . over and over again.

(YOUNG MAN *has pushed away his glass, continues to stare from one to another of the* MOURNERS.)

LANDLADY Drink up, duckie. You an' me's alive!

YOUNG MAN (*rising, backing away*) But you smell of moth . . .

FIRST RELATIVE That's a compliment to pay a widow and 'er relatives!

(ALL *laugh, except* LANDLADY, *who is becoming maudlin, and* YOUNG MAN, *who is frozen with disgust.*)

LANDLADY (*tearfully*) Why do I deserve this? Everythink slips through me fingers. I got a chill, too, standin' by Will Lusty's grave.

YOUNG MAN (*to* RELATIVES) How long do you people usually indulge in the sentiments?

FIRST RELATIVE (*taking it as a hint, rising, very dignified*) No longer than we're wanted.

(*Other* RELATIVES *follow suit.*)

SECOND RELATIVE I assure you!

THIRD RELATIVE Sentiments, indeed!

FOURTH RELATIVE Facts as plain as the parson's nose!

LANDLADY (*peering round, to* YOUNG MAN) 'Ave you put yer foot in it, love?

YOUNG MAN (*to* RELATIVES) You've had a good laugh. You've buried the dead. Your heads whirl with recollections and lascivious hopes. (*Pointing*) Now, gentlemen, your hats are on the bed.

(RELATIVES *get up to take their hats.*)

SECOND RELATIVE (*taking hat*) The master mind takes over.

THIRD RELATIVE (*hat in hand*) 'E's welcome.

FOURTH RELATIVE (*ditto*) We leave you the empty house, young man.

(SECOND, THIRD *and* FOURTH RELATIVES *move* BACK *towards door.*)

YOUNG MAN (*not so sure of himself, almost putting out his hand to stop them*) That's a pretty liberal bequest. After all . . .

FIRST RELATIVE (*taking up hat from bed*) Did 'e say a empty house? (*Going towards door*) Not quite! It's got the landlady in it! (RELATIVES *roar. Group for a moment at the door.*)

LANDLADY (*rousing herself*) Wot's all this? Wot about me?

YOUNG MAN Nothing. The people are going.

RELATIVES (*singing, to any drunken tune, all together*)

> 'Oo can tell
> If the light'ouse bell
> 'S ringin' for the wreck
> Of the Hesperus?
>
> We only know
> That the undertow
> 'S strong as hell
> Round the rocks. . . .

(*Cheers and jeers from* RELATIVES *as they go out to stairs.*)

LANDLADY (*holding her temples*) Wasn't it somethink about the moon? Didn't they put the moon out, Jack?

YOUNG MAN If they didn't, they'll have a good try. But I shouldn't worry.

LANDLADY You sound kind, young man.

(*She looks at him, surprised.* RELATIVES *mounting stairs.*)

RELATIVES (*singing drunkenly*) We only know
That the undertow. . . .

LANDLADY (*still staring at* YOUNG MAN) Kind!

YOUNG MAN (*sitting down, sighing*) Not really, Mrs Lusty. I've just done something which happened to be expedient. That's the way great virtues get thrust on people who don't deserve them.

FOURTH RELATIVE (*on stairs, singing*)

> Aaooh . . . me old oak bucket
> Got a 'ole in it,
> Me poor little bucket
> Went down. . . .

SECOND RELATIVE (*on stairs*) I'll bloomin' bust if I don't. . . .

OTHER RELATIVES Sssh!

LANDLADY (*to* YOUNG MAN) Whatever you tell me, then. I don't know much.

(RELATIVES *reach hall, and prepare to negotiate front door.*)

THIRD RELATIVE (*to others*) Hey, wait a mo!

FOURTH RELATIVE (*leaning over banisters*) Listen to 'em down there! They're at it!

YOUNG MAN (*to* LANDLADY) You know enough. What you're intended to, anyway. More than that might seem less generous.

FIRST RELATIVE (*aping* LANDLADY, *his hand cupped to his mouth, calling down into stairwell*) Another slice of 'am, young man? Another slice of 'am?

(RELATIVES *cannot contain their laughter as they* EXIT *into street. Door bangs, stairs and hall darken.*)

SCENE SIX · THE BASEMENT

LANDLADY (*accepting the* YOUNG MAN'S *statement*) P'raps you understand. You got edgercation. I only know wot I'm told. An' wot I can 'old in my two hands.

(*She glances at an area window, from which the last malignant light has faded. In herself a faint glimmer of the devil.*)

But I can always pull the curtains an' make it snug. (*Doing so*) There now? See?

(YOUNG MAN *sits staring in front of him, elbows on table.*)

(*Returning to table*) You think I'm drunk. I'm not. Only tipsy. An' tipsy's warm!

(YOUNG MAN *continues disinclined to speak.*)

You're down. (*Touching him*) Wot are yer down about?

YOUNG MAN I was wondering what I could say to you.

LANDLADY Will didn't wonder. 'E just sat.

(YOUNG MAN *shudders, so that* LANDLADY *removes her hand.*)

YOUNG MAN That's what I'm afraid of. Will sat. (*Speaking as stolidly as* LANDLORD, *but without burlesquing his voice*) He was content. This house is life. I watch my house fill with light, and darken. These are my days and nights. The house spreads solid over my head.

LANDLADY (*agitated*) Gawd, yes, that was Will! Pull yer neck out, boy, before you fall!

YOUNG MAN But Will was wise. This table is love, if you can get to know it . . .

(YOUNG MAN *stares in front of him.*)

LANDLADY (*bitterly*) A fat lot Will knew! 'E sat an' stared, an' belched . . . when the wind got too sour for his stummick.

YOUNG MAN (*to himself*) . . . if you can get to know it.

LANDLADY (*desperate*) Speak to me, can't yer? Before I lose you, too. . . .

(*Goes impulsively and seizes* YOUNG MAN *by the arm, but he gets up and extricates himself.*)

YOUNG MAN Words are bridges that won't bridge. They break.

LANDLADY (*passionately*) Let 'em!

(*A silence in which they stand facing each other.*)

(*Putting a hand to her face*) Wot's wrong?

(*As* YOUNG MAN *continues to look through her, she goes* FORWARD *to the invisible mirror, stares into it, touches her face.*)

Wot's wrong with me?

YOUNG MAN I saw your face.

LANDLADY It's the same one, ain't it?

(*Turns on him angrily.*)

YOUNG MAN I saw your face!

LANDLADY (*glancing again at mirror*) T'ain't worn all that well . . . but t'ain't all that bad. Gentlemen still turn round on cold days. I 'ad a colour once.

YOUNG MAN I saw your face. It was *horrible*!

LANDLADY (*trembling with rage*) Then why the hell 'uv you only just made up yer mind? You've seen it often enough. Get out, you dirty bastard! Get out! I'm tired. . . .

(YOUNG MAN *turns to go.*)

Pack yer traps, an' let me 'ear the door bang. So's I'll know.

(YOUNG MAN *goes towards door*, BACK.)

(*Putting out her hand*) No, boy. Don't! I'll be alone then. Don't go! I got a face like a stewed rag. I know. But don't go!

(YOUNG MAN *turns at door, though it is not yet clear whether he means to stay or leave.*)

(*Eagerly, placing a kitchen chair*) There, boy! Sit!

YOUNG MAN (*ironically, but sadly*) And you will be less alone . . . ?

(*Comes back and sits on the chair, mechanically, the* LANDLADY *standing beside him, like a ventriloquist beside a doll.*)

LANDLADY (*in a washed-out voice*) There! Comfy?

YOUNG MAN (*sighing, but dutifully*) Yes.

LANDLADY Let me take your 'and.

YOUNG MAN (*without really protesting*) Am I a child?

LANDLADY Less. You'd find out, Jack, if I was to 'old yer 'ead against my breast.

YOUNG MAN I'm weaned, you know.

LANDLADY No man ever really leaves the breast. That's our weapon. The softest weapon in the world.

(YOUNG MAN *detaches his hand.*)

YOUNG MAN So well armed. Then why are you afraid of losing?

LANDLADY Nothing is all that certain. (*Inspired*) I'd wrap you up with me best kid gloves, an' put you in a box, an' lock it tight.

YOUNG MAN No go! Thieves can break in while you're out at the grocer's.

LANDLADY This is all talk, Jack. I'll *show* you!

YOUNG MAN (*edgy*) How?

(*Gets up, moves away. The following scene is played like a kind of ritual dance.*)

LANDLADY Well . . . (*twitching the corner of her apron, speaking in a light, bantering tone, that is also determined and tentative*) . . . I'll give you presents.

(*Follows* YOUNG MAN.)

YOUNG MAN (*moving away*) What?

LANDLADY Box of pencils.

YOUNG MAN No-no.

LANDLADY A toffee apple.

(YOUNG MAN *laughs, shakes his head. Continues moving away, with* LANDLADY *following.*)

I'll give you a kiss to remind yer of yer mother.

YOUNG MAN I'd always hoped I was an orphan.

(*Moves away.*)

LANDLADY A nice, soft doorstep, then!

(*She snatches at him. He avoids. Retreats behind a chair.*)

YOUNG MAN Not if I know it!

LANDLADY (*quickening her pace*) Oh, dear, you can never lessen the distance! You can never explain to a person!

YOUNG MAN Why try? When the meaning's panting down his neck. . . .

LANDLADY It ought to be made . . . easier.

YOUNG MAN This isn't . . . exactly . . . *algebra*.

LANDLADY Algy . . . ? Algy 'oo?

YOUNG MAN A dry . . . standoffish kind of . . . fellow. . . .

LANDLADY That seems to be the sort . . . it's my luck . . . to get in with.

(*Silence broken by action and panting, grabbing, stifled laughter and escape.*)

(*In pursuit, heated*) You lead a woman a fine dance!

YOUNG MAN Of which she knows every step.

LANDLADY (*laughing*) Round and round, eh?

(*He upsets a chair in her path.*)

YOUNG MAN And nothing barred.

LANDLADY (*laughing, breathless, but pursuing*) It's all in the game . . .

YOUNG MAN . . . of deadly earnest . . .

(LANDLADY *continues to pursue, still laughing, but silent now, from chair to chair.*)

. . . until you have him exhausted.

(*He flops down on a chair*, R.)

LANDLADY Then it's lovely. (*Advancing on him*) That is closest. All tired lads are ready to be touched. (*Holding the back of her hand to his cheek*) Feel?

YOUNG MAN (*fascinated, but repelled*) You're all feelers. Your thoughts, even, put out tentacles. Memory becomes an octopus.

LANDLADY I don't know about that. (*Almost in recitative*) But I was never a slow one. Nor cold. A cold colour, but not cold. Alma Jagg breathed life into the hedges. The frost melted when I lay beneath 'awthorns. I touched the warm, moist earth with my 'and. Afterwards, when flowers come, I lay back . . . an' crushed 'em. (*Closing her eyes*) 'Ow they smelt, Fred! Remember?

YOUNG MAN (*stirs uneasily, also in recitative*) The green smell of young sap. . . . Yellow pollen on your nose. . . . The criss-cross pattern on your cheek, which had suffocated flowers. . . .

E

(*He turns and looks up at her, as if dependent on her for the vision he cannot quite accept.*)

LANDLADY (*triumphantly, looking down into his eyes*) Well? An' didn't the clouds sail then? When we looked up at them through the trees?

YOUNG MAN I looked at clouds . . .

(*Withdrawing from* LANDLADY, *he moves away into a remoter corner of the kitchen.*)

(*shamefaced*) . . . only I didn't realize you were looking too.

LANDLADY (*alone and absent*) Clouds don't sail that way . . . not now . . . not that I've seen for some time.

YOUNG MAN (*recovering self-possession, laughing bitterly*) You're a spellbinder, you are! You know how to ring the changes.

LANDLADY Wot else 'as a person got? That, an' the theayter.

YOUNG MAN You played *me*, all right!

LANDLADY Aoh, Fred, 'ow you create!

YOUNG MAN Cut out the Fred. It doesn't fit.

LANDLADY T'ain't a question of names. (*Goes to him again*) An' you know it isn't, Fred! (*Taking him by the arms, above the elbows*) That's why I can feel yer tremble!

YOUNG MAN (*to himself*) . . . for my own thoughts.

LANDLADY Do yer know so much?

YOUNG MAN Or is it for your neck?

(*Puts his hands on her throat.*)

LANDLADY (*scornfully*) Why, you 'ave grown into a man! A man's always ready to kill a woman for 'is own thoughts.

YOUNG MAN Then, you *are* afraid?

LANDLADY Not afraid. (*Backing*) No one knows wot they're capable of. That's all.

YOUNG MAN (*flatly, following*) You're afraid. The truth is terrible before you know it. Then . . . when you do . . . it becomes most terrible.

LANDLADY (*backing against side of bed*) There are times when you got to try yer luck.

(YOUNG MAN *follows. Stretches out his hand like an automaton.*)

LANDLADY (*putting his hand in her breast*) See? I can't 'elp it if I tremble too. Aoh, Fred, I'm in a proper uproar! (*Takes him in her arms*) Let me 'old yer! Put yer 'ead 'ere . . . close to me neck . . . where it fits . . . warm!

YOUNG MAN And let the senses finish me off!

LANDLADY You'll soon learn where yer hinges are!

YOUNG MAN (*half triumph, half disgust*) I'm learning!

(*Difficult to tell whether he is drawn down by the* LANDLADY, *or whether he topples her backwards on the bed in their all-absorbing embrace.*)

LANDLADY This way the clock stops. . . .

YOUNG MAN This way the sea sucks . . . but under . . . under. . . .

LANDLADY (*as her mouth takes possession of his*) Wot price yer bloomin' poetry now?

(YOUNG MAN *begins to struggle against her.*)

YOUNG MAN (*struggling*) I'm damned if I'll wear the landlord's old glove!

LANDLADY I could die . . .

YOUNG MAN (*trying to wrench himself free*) I'm . . . damned. . . .

LANDLADY . . . willin'ly. . . .

(*Brief silence; panting and struggle.*)

YOUNG MAN (*brutally, quickly, between his teeth*) You'll never sink me deeper than I've sunk!

LANDLADY That's not . . . I never lived . . . only now. . . .

YOUNG MAN So they say!

LANDLADY True enough. But no one never ever believes.

(YOUNG MAN *at last succeeds in wrenching himself free. Puts his knee on her stomach, hands on her throat. Presses.*)

YOUNG MAN (*viciously*) Then, die . . . then. *Die. . .* !

LANDLADY (*strangled scream*) Ahhhhhhhh!

(LANDLADY *tears herself away, staggers, falls forward on floor,* CENTRE, *crying.*)

YOUNG MAN Lie there in your own sweat! I'd call you 'whore' if I hadn't made you one.

LANDLADY (*gasping and crying*) You didn't kill me, Jack, but couldn't 'uv done a better job if you 'ad.

YOUNG MAN You'll recover . . . and enjoy your bruises. You've as good as shown us that already.

LANDLADY I'm a woman, I suppose.

67

YOUNG MAN But flesh, unfortunately, isn't the final answer.

LANDLADY Get out, then . . . now that you've seen me.

YOUNG MAN My legs have never been more willing.

(*Goes out,* BACK. *Stairs light.*)

LANDLADY (*in a renewed burst of sobbing*) Oh, God! Will! Will! I don't know wot I done . . . to be shut up in this body . . . an' nobody to open it an' let me out. . . .

(*Basement fades.*)

SCENE SEVEN · THE STAIRS

YOUNG MAN (*running up stairs, jubilantly*) I could clear this old frayed carpet at one leap . . . catapult into the night . . . let the cold clean me. . . . (*Pausing near top*) Down below, a fat woman lies crying on the flags, a last slobber of passion on her mouth. . . . Ugh! (*Continues to mount, slower*) Anyhow, she's disposed of. I am free. I couldn't have made a better escape if she'd been packed into a box along with the landlord. (*Pauses on reaching hall*) I . . . am free . . . aren't I? Or has the prig simply taken over? I am a poet, I said. I shall possess the infinite. Or am I just an ineffectual prig, looking at the world through a telescope . . . (*hesitating outside his own door*) . . . through the wrong end?

(*His room lights up, but he does not enter. Stairs fade.*)

SCENE EIGHT

The Hall, and, subsequently, both Bedrooms. YOUNG MAN *walks quickly across hall to door of second bedroom.*

YOUNG MAN I *must* know. *You!* Tell me! (*Bangs on the closed door*) Are you there?

(*The adjoining room remains in darkness.*)

(*Thumping wildly*) What's happened? Has the door thickened? Have you left me? Hello! Can't you see I'm desperate?

(*Adjoining room slowly lightens. The* GIRL *is seated on an upright chair on the farther side, her back to the door. Her expression is severe.*)

GIRL (*coldly*) Everyone is desperate.

YOUNG MAN Yes ... of course ... but in a crisis, it's only human to ask for a sign. And I do ask for *some* sign.

GIRL (*sadly*) You must look in your own heart.

YOUNG MAN But I am I.

GIRL And what am I ... but you?

YOUNG MAN It's true, then. ...

GIRL (*gently*) I was ashamed just now.

YOUNG MAN When?

GIRL Down there in the basement.

YOUNG MAN There was no other way out.

GIRL (*sighing*) No. (*Gets up from her chair*) Not yet. You weren't up to it. (*Advances towards separating door*) The landlady has won the round.

YOUNG MAN Won?

GIRL No doubt about it. (*During following, she moves restlessly about the room*) She lies in a heap on the kitchen floor. Her only medals are her bruises. Smudgy, sludgy Mrs Lusty! Bust! But she still has her simplicity. That's one bridge the devils fail to destroy in leaving. She doesn't know it yet ... listening, snivelly, to the clocks. Her innocence has even dredged a kind of beauty out of the ruins of her face. If you had stayed, you might have recognized, and forgiven.

YOUNG MAN (*dismissing the possibility, with disgust*) I held her sweaty body ...

GIRL ... in which the life beat and struggled.

YOUNG MAN Her face was hideous ...

GIRL ... hoping she might express herself ... just that once more.

YOUNG MAN (*contemptuously*) Express!

GIRL Those who live also create.

YOUNG MAN In that case ... I have nothing more to say.

(GIRL *comes close to the door.*)

GIRL (*now tender and persuasive*) No. You are beginning. There is no end where there is beginning. Beginning must follow end. Endlessly. (*Making of it an incantation*) On many future occasions you'll wrestle with the figures in the basement ... passion and compassion locked together. Sleepers are stirring in other rooms to hear their dream interpreted in words. The hands are curled . . . waiting to open.

(YOUNG MAN *leans his head against the door, lulled by possibilities. His face is full of wonder.*)

GIRL Your eyes see already.

YOUNG MAN Only yours will convince me. (*Hardening*) I'll smash the door if necessary!

GIRL (*again severe*) Never!

YOUNG MAN We'll see!

GIRL (*a long, cold cry*) Never!

(YOUNG MAN *starts to rattle the door-handle, then to batter the door itself with his fist, then his shoulder.*)

YOUNG MAN *You realize . . . ?* You've lost control of your puppet. . . .

(*As he continues to batter the door, the figure of the* GIRL *is seen moving desperately about the room, almost like a bird in a cage, in search of a possible avenue of escape.*)

GIRL (*panic-stricken*) Break, then!

YOUNG MAN (*throwing his weight against the door*) I'll . . . run the . . . risk . . .

GIRL (*poised, waiting for the decisive moment*) . . . and find NOTHING!

(*As the* YOUNG MAN *bursts through the door, staggering, and still off balance, the* GIRL *disappears into thin air, i.e. she slips behind the gauze-wall at back as lights fade from it. Before her exit, she must let fall a spray of white lilac from the folds of her skirt.*)

(*On entering,* YOUNG MAN *looks quickly round deserted room, touches the air.*)

YOUNG MAN (*dazed*) She was right. We never meet . . . (*putting his hands to his eyes*) . . . for more than a moment. Foolish of me to have expected more. . . . (*Stands swaying, looking down, at a loss*) What's this? (*Stoops, and picks something up*) A spray of lilac. White lilac! How we wrote . . . the pale, exquisite verses of adolescence . . . to find they have turned . . . (*crushing the lilac, throwing it away*) . . . brittle! (*Leans against frame of communicating door*) At least the landlady's poem speaks . . . after the fashion of imperfect flesh. (*Crosses the hall, wearily enters his own room*) Lunging and plunging, she raped life, and won . . .

(*He throws himself on his bed.*)

... whereas *my* attempts have amounted to little more than acts of self-abuse in an empty room.

(*He lies on his back, looking up at the ceiling.*)

Well, here we are ... back where we began ... amongst the everlasting furniture. This bed on which the nights creak.... (*Rolling over onto an elbow, indicating*) The washstand's not ambiguous. Or dressing-table ... except perhaps the reflection in the glass. (*Touching his actual face*) But the bones are there. (*Gets up, goes and looks into the mirror*) The eyes can see. And all the time, life of a kind has been seeping through the cracks in this house ... (*going to window*) ... flowing through the streets in waves of faces. (*Lays his cheek against the pane*) If I go down myself, I am swallowed up. Or else ... (*slowly, thoughtfully leaving the window*) ... or else. ...

(*He goes out into the hall.*)

(*As the* YOUNG MAN *finishes his soliloquy, an actual* GIRL *lets herself in at the front door. The wordless part should be played by same actress who has appeared as the insubstantial anima. The actual* GIRL *is pale, dreary, rather catarrhal, wearing gold-rimmed spectacles, dowdy hat, street coat – clothes all of an indeterminate colour. She goes immediately into the bedroom in which the* GIRL-*anima materialized, closes door, and is occupied with a certain amount of humdrum business before she is faded out – i.e.° she can remove her hat and coat, blow her catarrhal nose, chafe hands, run a hand over the dressing-table for dust, swallow a couple of aspirin with help of a glass of water, and so on, provided everything very prosaic.*)

YOUNG MAN (*glancing back at* GIRL, *laughing softly, compassionate rather than contemptuous*) Phyllis Pither!

(*He approaches the stairs.*)

(*Calling*) Mrs Lusty!

(*Starts to go down.*)

(*Calling*) Are you fit to be seen?

(*Continues to descend.*)

(*After a pause*) Or are you still a dreadful sight?

(*Reaches basement door. Hesitates.* GIRL *in the room above is faded out.*)

SCENE NINE · THE BASEMENT

YOUNG MAN (*still outside the door*) Are you there, Mrs Lusty? I've come to say goodbye. I'm going away.

(*The basement lightens. Stairs and hall die.*)

(YOUNG MAN *goes into the kitchen, where* LANDLADY *is lying in same position as before.*)

YOUNG MAN What, still there!

(*He goes towards her, purposefully now.* LANDLADY *stirs, and sits up, grimacing at her own stiffness, supporting herself on one arm.*)

LANDLADY Did I dream a man called Will Lusty died? And you. . . .

(*She looks at the* YOUNG MAN, *and quickly decides to say no more.*)

YOUNG MAN Who's to say where the dream begins . . . ever . . . whether it's a dead landlord, or a declaration of love.

LANDLADY I expect it 'appened, boy. All of it. It does! Besides, I still got the bloomin' 'am between me teeth. An' me mouth's all dry from stout and argy-bargy.

YOUNG MAN (*holding out his hand*) Come on!

LANDLADY (*smiling*) It was a lovely funeral, though.

YOUNG MAN Better get up, or your machinery'll stay cockeyed.

(*He helps her, and she gets to her feet painfully.*)

LANDLADY (*wincing*) Aoh! Me bloody bones 'ave turned to stone!

(*She rubs her cold arms.*)

YOUNG MAN That sounds better!

LANDLADY If it's language yer mean, I know ladies 'oo get 'igher marks.

(*Goes to table, and sits down at it.*)

Wot's all this about yer goin' away?

YOUNG MAN Yes. Tonight. At once.

LANDLADY Wot's got into yer?

YOUNG MAN I . . . don't know.

LANDLADY An' where are yer goin'?

YOUNG MAN I don't know that either.

LANDLADY Wot a lather of nothink! An' yer socks not darned! Did you pack yer things?

YOUNG MAN You know I haven't any. Except the spare shirt. And
I lost that.

LANDLADY Well, things do happen. And 'ere's me . . . a relic!
(*Nodding*) A relic all right when you're gone! (*Loudly*) You know,
I quite like you, yer little bugger!

YOUNG MAN That's why I came to say goodbye. (*Pauses*) Well. . . .
(LANDLADY *gets up. Goes slowly towards him.*)

LANDLADY Then it's goodbye, Jack.
(*She takes his hand in both hers, holding it to her.*)

YOUNG MAN Goodbye, Mrs Lusty.
(*He allows her to hold his hand for a moment, then takes her face in
his hands, and kisses her on the forehead.*)

LANDLADY You aven't been that close, Jack . . . not since I carried
yer.

YOUNG MAN (*quickly*) We'll waste a lot of words if I don't get
going.
(*Turns towards door. Stairs and hall light up.* YOUNG MAN *runs up
the stairs.*)

LANDLADY (*following to basement door, watching, calling after him*)
So long, boy! Send us a pitcher post-card now and agen! Let's
know you're alive and kickin'! But write plain.
(YOUNG MAN *turns at top of stairs.*)

YOUNG MAN (*calling back*) So long, Mrs Lusty! I'll be on my way!

LANDLADY (*at breaking point*) Then go, boy! *Go!* GO!
(*Basement and stairs fade. Only the hall remains lit.*)

SCENE TEN · THE HALL

(YOUNG MAN *pauses a moment in the hall.*)

YOUNG MAN (*thoughtfully*) How warm her face was . . .
(*He goes towards front door.*)
. . . and touching . . .
(*He opens the door on a night placid with moonlight.*)
. . . lovely in its way . . . the way of those who've lived, and con-
fessed, and survived their own confession. Well, here's the street.
(*Looking out through doorway*) The night was never stiller, or

73

closer, I could put out my hand and touch it . . . like a face. . . .
(*He leaves the house, goes into the street. As the door closes the whole
of the back wall dissolves, so that the* YOUNG MAN *is seen walking
into the distance through a luminous night.*)

CURTAIN

THE SEASON AT SARSAPARILLA

A Charade of Suburbia

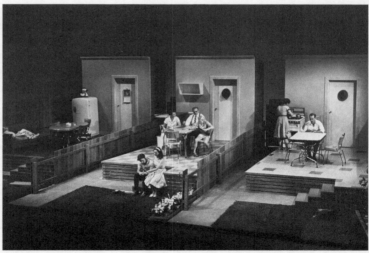

The State Theatre Company of South Australia production of The Season at Sarsaparilla *at the Playhouse, Adelaide, 1984, directed by Neil Armfield, designed by Stephen Curtis. Above: the Pogson family: John Clayton as Clive, Maggie Dence as Girlie, Odile Le Clezio as Judy and Rebe Taylor as Pippy. Below: the three boxes. Photos by Grant Hancock.*

The Season at Sarsaparilla was first performed by the Adelaide University Theatre Guild at the Union Theatre, Adelaide, on 14 September 1962 with the following cast:

JOYLEEN POGSON (PIPPY)	Elizabeth Steel
GIRLIE POGSON	Carmel Millhouse
DEEDREE	Bronwen Courtney
HARRY KNOTT	Wayne Anthoney
NOLA BOYLE	Zoe Caldwell
CLIVE POGSON	John Haynes
MAVIS KNOTT	Morna Jones
JUDY POGSON	Barbara West
ROY CHILD	Terence Stapleton
RON SUDDARDS	Don Barker
JULIA SHEEN	Barbara Dennis
ERNIE BOYLE	Cliff Neate
MR ERBAGE	Hedley Cullen
ROWLEY MASSON (DIGGER)	Leslie Dayman
FIRST AMBULANCE MAN	Ron Dix
SECOND AMBULANCE MAN	Albert Havard

Directed by John Tasker
Designed by Desmond Digby

CHARACTERS

HARRY KNOTT, in men's wear
MAVIS KNOTT, his wife
ROY CHILD, her brother, a teacher
CLIVE POGSON, a business executive
GIRLIE POGSON, his wife
JUDY POGSON, his daughter, studying the violin
JOYLEEN (PIPPY), their little girl
DEEDREE, her little friend
ERNIE BOYLE, a sanitary man
NOLA BOYLE, his wife
ROWLEY MASSON (DIGGER), a mate
RON SUDDARDS, a post–office clerk
JULIA SHEEN, a model
MR ERBAGE, an important person
TWO AMBULANCE MEN

SETTING

Mildred Street, Sarsaparilla, a fictitious outer suburb of Sydney, summer, 1961.

ACT ONE

When the lights go up on the three homes in Mildred Street, there is an outburst of BARKING *as from a pack of dogs somewhere in the distance.* PIPPY POGSON *appears in the kitchen from one of the invisible rooms of the* POGSON *home,* C. *A forthright and astute small girl. Runs through the kitchen, very determined, opens the invisible back door, pauses for a moment, looking and listening. Runs down the steps into the yard. Comes* FORWARD, *pulls open an invisible back gate. She is perhaps out to investigate the barking dogs. She stands at the gate (i.e. at the footlights) listening, shading her eyes, looking up and down the lane.*

GIRLIE POGSON, *her mother, is heard calling from front part of her house.*

GIRLIE (*calling, off stage*) Pip-py? . . . Pip-py?
   (PIPPY *scowls. Explodes under her breath. Runs and hides under the house.*)
   (BARKING *continues spasmodically, gradually dying.*)
   (GIRLIE POGSON ENTERS *her kitchen. A small spruce woman in her forties. Not a hair out of place, and never will be. Everything must be nice, even if you pay the price.* MRS POGSON *wears all the marks of anxiety and a respectable social level.*)
GIRLIE (*calling, quite viciously by now, as she looks out of back door*)
   Joy-leen!
(*Returns in despair into the kitchen.*)
It's the holidays. It's the holidays. Always like this in the holidays.
And now those dogs! It shouldn't be allowed.
   (*Glances at herself in a wall-mirror in passing. Corrects a hair, touches her frown, sighs. Goes out,* BACK, *into front part of her house.*)
   (*At the same time* DEEDREE ENTERS *from the front garden. Slightly younger than her friend* PIPPY, *more innocent, easily put*

upon. DEEDREE *is the eternal stooge. She is carrying two milk bottles, a loaf, and the newspaper.*)

DEEDREE (*tentatively, calling*) Pip-py? Pip-py? Where are yer?

(PIPPY *sticks her head out from under the house.*)

PIPPY (*scowling*) I'm here. Gee, you're early, Deedree. Didn't you have your breakfast? Mum won't give you any if you haven't.

DEEDREE Course I had me breakfast. Didn't you?

PIPPY (*angry*) No. Yes!

(*She comes out from under the house.*)

I wasn't hungry. But I had some to keep *her* quiet.

DEEDREE Is she going crook?

PIPPY Always.

DEEDREE What about?

PIPPY Oh, everything.

(DEEDREE *just stands.*)

Says I know too much.

DEEDREE (*devotedly*) You do know an awful lot, Pippy.

PIPPY Well, I can't help that. It just comes to me.

(*During the foregoing,* GIRLIE POGSON *re-enters her kitchen, starts (in mime) to get the next round of breakfast.*)

DEEDREE Monica Jeffreys is gunna read through the dictionary.

PIPPY (*contemptuous*) Monica Jeffreys! Sooky thing!

DEEDREE She's got as far as B.

PIPPY I don't have to read the dictionary.

DEEDREE (*indicating loaf, milk and paper which she is carrying*) What am I gunna do with these, Pippy?

PIPPY (*jerking her head at the kitchen*) Give them to *her*. It'll sweeten her up.

DEEDREE (*doubtful*) Ah!

GIRLIE (*calling back into the house*) If you're not careful, Clive, you'll miss the bus . . . and who's to blame. . . .

(DEEDREE *has mounted the back steps.*)

DEEDREE (*at kitchen door*) Mrs Pogson! It's me, Mrs Pogson. (*Simpering*) Always bright and early!

GIRLIE That is something you need never tell me, dear. (*Comes and takes* DEEDREE's *offering*) But thank you, Deedree, all the same.

(GIRLIE *glances out of the door, catches sight of* PIPPY.)

That is where you are, Pippy. Did you hear me call?

PIPPY (*kicking the ground*) Yes.

GIRLIE And why didn't you come?

PIPPY I didn't feel like it.

GIRLIE Ooh, you bold little girl! I'll tell your father, Joyleen. One day you'll catch it.

PIPPY (*chanting*)   One day, one day
                       I shall learn to fly.
                       I'll pin little wings on me shoulders,
                       And fly....

GIRLIE Ooh, you are the rudest little girl! And *my*, not me, Joyleen.

(DEEDREE *has a fit of the giggles.*)

What's the matter with you, Deedree Inkpen?

DEEDREE Oh, nothing, Mrs Pogson.

GIRLIE Well, if it's nothing, there's every reason for controlling yourself. (*Looking out*) Now, you children, I don't want you running in and out, marking the lino. The holidays are always death to anybody's lino.

DEEDREE Yes, Mrs Pogson.

(PIPPY *sticks out her tongue as* GIRLIE *retreats into the kitchen to continue with breakfast preparations.*)

(*At the same time* HARRY KNOTT *comes into the* KNOTT *kitchen from front part of the house. He is a young man, probably younger than he looks, but responsibilities have been thrust upon him early. He is wearing his business pants, well-pressed, and beautifully-laundered white shirt. Arm-bands. There is nothing distinctive about him.*)

HARRY (*calling back into the house*) You stay there, dear. Take it easy. Can't afford to take any risks now that it's so close.

PIPPY I'm glad you came, Deedree. There's such a lot to tell you.

DEEDREE What, Pippy?

PIPPY It's the dogs....

(NOLA BOYLE *comes into her kitchen. In her forties, she is dressed in a chenille dressing-gown. Generous of figure. Tawny of head. A lioness. Stretching and yawning.*)

(BARKING *has begun again in the distance.*)

GIRLIE (*calling*) Clive? If it's *congealed* eggs you want. . . .

HARRY (*calling to his invisible wife*) A nice, light-boiled egg. Won't be a jiffy, Mave.

DEEDREE I seen the dogs, Pippy. At the bus stop.

PIPPY That's where it always begins. At the bus stop.

(NOLA, *who has been searching for something, discovers it on a shelf. Proceeds to do her lips long and lovingly in a mirror.*)

DEEDREE (*to* PIPPY) But what's up with all these dogs?

PIPPY There's a bitch in season.

DEEDREE What's that?

PIPPY She's on heat. See?

DEEDREE What's that, do?

PIPPY That's when she gets interesting to dogs. . . .

(CLIVE POGSON ENTERS *the Pogson kitchen. Round fifty. A rather thick-set business bull – a minor one, but he will probably never know that. Takes the paper, sits at the table, ready for breakfast.*)

CLIVE (*ritually*) Eggs, eh?

(GIRLIE *is above answering him. Puts plate in front of him.*)

(MAVIS KNOTT ENTERS *her kitchen. She is very pregnant under her dressing-gown. A bit miserable and fretful, though normally she would be a placid, acceptant young woman. Neither pretty nor plain. The average, decent suburban wife.*)

HARRY Arr, now, Mavis, it doesn't cost much to be *reasonable*!

MAVIS (*heavily*) I can't be reasonable, Harry, not when I listen to someone moving around in me own kitchen.

(*After some routine pottering, to uphold her rights, she sits, and lets him serve her with breakfast.*)

DEEDREE (*still in the dark, to* PIPPY) And when she gets interesting?

(PIPPY *sticks her mouth in her friend's ear, and explains very forcibly.*)

Gee! And does it last long?

PIPPY About half-an-hour.

DEEDREE Gee, Pippy! Who told you?

PIPPY (*pointing in the direction of* BOYLES') Mrs Boyle.

(NOLA BOYLE *has come out onto her back steps. She looks about her. Likes what she sees of the morning.*)

NOLA Hello, Pippy. Hello, Deedree.

CHILDREN (*enthusiastically, in unison*) Hello, Mrs Boyle!

NOLA (*descending the steps*) Doesn't it smell good, eh? I like to smell a hot day. Early. While it's still coming at you.

(NOLA *sounds hoarse, common, but comforting.* PIPPY *and* DEEDREE *sniff in sympathy.*)

(*Renewed* BARKING *from the distance.*)

NOLA Ah, there are those blessed dogs again!

DEEDREE Yes, I seen them at the bus.

PIPPY The bitch's coming on fast now, Mrs Boyle.

NOLA (*laughing*) Ah, dear! Poor thing! What can you do? They'll be treading on her, all the typists, and the ladies, as they catch the bus.

(EXIT NOLA, BACK, *to the street.*)

MAVIS (*holding her hair*) Bark, bark! What can you do? I didn't sleep one wink, Harry.

HARRY You seemed to me to be doing pretty good.

(*He kisses her hair.*)

MAVIS Bark, bark! All night. And the sheets . . . they got me tied up. . . .

GIRLIE Those dogs, Clive, are a disgrace. Surely the police . . . surely the RSPCA. . . .

CLIVE (*reading*) Something is happening in Laos.

GIRLIE Someone should complain to the Council.

CLIVE (*reading*) Something is happening in Laos, but you can never make out what. . . .

DEEDREE Would you like to be a dog, Pippy?

PIPPY I wouldn't like to be a bitch.

(GIRLIE POGSON *has come out and stood on her back step, just as* NOLA BOYLE *returns from the front gate with bread, milk and paper.*)

GIRLIE How often have I told you, Pippy, that 'lady dog' is the expression people like us use.

PIPPY But Mrs Boyle says 'bitch' is the professional word.

GIRLIE Mrs *Boyle*!

(NOLA *has started to mount her steps.*)

NOLA Yes, dear, it's me again! Always in trouble.

GIRLIE (*outraged*) Aoffhh!

(GIRLIE *retreats into her kitchen.*)

PIPPY (*humiliated*) Oh, I'm sorry, Mrs Boyle.

(NOLA *seats herself with the morning paper on her kitchen step.*)

NOLA (*tossing out her hair*) Perhaps she don't mean it all.

PIPPY Oh, but she does. Every bit.

NOLA (*laughing huskily*) One day, Pippy, you an' me'll have to pull out a couple of those loose palings. Then you can come through, and we'll comfort each other.

MAVIS (*sighing*) A hot day! When the baby's here, I'll sit around and enjoy things. It'll be nice for me to have the baby. . . .

HARRY When the baby's here, when the baby's here, I wonder if I'll know what to say. . . .

CLIVE (*reading*) It all boils down to the credit squeeze. It all boils down to what the Government wants to say. . . .

DEEDREE What'll we do, Pippy?

PIPPY Let's go under the house.

DEEDREE What for?

PIPPY For something to do.

DEEDREE Oh?

PIPPY There's a smell in there beside the chimney that's kind of grooby. As if somebody might have hidden a dead body.

(*She starts to go under.*)

DEEDREE Oh, why do we have to do that, Pippy?

PIPPY (*sticking out her head*) Arr, come on under! Nobody's going to dig and see. Only pretend.

(DEEDREE *is still hesitant.*)

Drippy Dee-*dree!* Come on! You gotta do *something*!

(EXIT CHILDREN *under the house.*)

(GIRLIE POGSON *has assumed the posture of reminiscence at* CLIVE's *elbow.*)

GIRLIE At Rosedale, when I was a girl, nobody used words. It was such a lovely property. The big verandas, and the willows round the house. . . . Nobody was in business then, everybody was on the land. . . .

CLIVE (*stuffing his mouth, speaking through food*) Yes, we know about Rosedale.

GIRLIE Girlie Pogson – Twemlow then – married in peach angel-skin and cream *shantilly....*

CLIVE Girlie Twemlow played a useful game of tennis. Neat calves standing at the net. Girlie Twemlow had a dimple in her left cheek. But Girlie Pogson closed it up....

(*A violin is heard in the other part of the Pogson house, playing something sweet and true, but with a touch that is not exactly brilliant. The piece could be the loure from the sixth Bach Sonata in E Major.*)

NOLA (*glancing through the paper, still seated on the steps*) I'd give anything to see a good picture. In which a *man* cracks a whip. (*Dreamy*) Nola Boyle – Bevan then – went to the pictures. An old bloke squeezed her knee. She got the shivers. But didn't shift....

GIRLIE When you've got the home, when you've got the kids, when you've got the wash on Monday, you forget there was a time for dimples.

CLIVE When you've been around so long, you forget running up the path from tennis ... willows tickling prickly skin. You forget bumping up against the girl on accidental purpose. You forget you could never be around enough.

GIRLIE Must remember. Oh, I must remember!

CLIVE Then ... you forget....

NOLA (*laying aside the paper*) She got the shivers in the second reel. But went on waiting for the next move. Whose move? That was always so important. More important than the picture....

(*Violin* OFF *plays a sour note.*)

CLIVE (*throwing down his paper*) If there's something I can't stand, it's a squeaky fiddle!

GIRLIE (*on the defensive*) She plays it lovely, Clive! So she ought to. Studying it at the Con. But before breakfast! A girl can't give up everything, and holidays too, for an old violin. (*Calling*) Judy! Remember your health, dear. Specially on a hot day.

(*Violin breaks off.*)

NOLA (*laughing softly, head against the doorpost*) Funny the way you keep on goin' to the pictures . . . long after you've seen them all....

(JUDY POGSON ENTERS *the Pogson kitchen. About 18. A tea-rose. Very pretty and sweet. Rather withdrawn and tentative.*)

85

GIRLIE (*to* JUDY, *without looking at her*) What'll you do when you've played your hands off on that wretched violin?

JUDY (*lightly, because she must say something*) I'll play, Mother darling, I hope.

GIRLIE Ttt! Are you hungry?

JUDY Need you ask?

GIRLIE No. Only . . . it's one of the things you go on asking.
(GIRLIE *dishes food for* JUDY)

CLIVE What I can't understand is what people think about while they sit there listening to music. Sitting, and sitting, like a lot of bloomin' mushrooms.

JUDY I'd tell you, Father . . . if I could.

CLIVE (*sighing*) Well, it takes all sorts. (*Throwing aside his paper, looking at his watch*) And this won't sell anyone a Holden Special!
(CLIVE *goes* OFF *into front part of house.*)
(*Simultaneously* ROY CHILD ENTERS *the* KNOTT *kitchen from front of house. In his early twenties. Very casually dressed. Very casual. In the course of the play his brashness should disclose a certain sensitivity underneath.*)

HARRY This won't sell the socks that keep the housewives darning.
(MAVIS *laughs too appreciatively.*)

MAVIS (*delighted, indicating her husband*) Listen!

ROY I seem to have heard!
(HARRY *puts on his coat, buttoning methodically.*)

HARRY Okay, Roy! We got to cultivate our sense of humour. Not everybody is a teacher enjoying the current holidays.
(ROY *winces.*)
(NOLA *gets up from steps, humming.*)

NOLA (*going back through her kitchen, singing softly*) Nola Bevan loved the circus. She loved the men on the trapezes best. (*Pottering, humming*) She never ever saw them fall. (*Suddenly matter of fact*) You don't if your wrists are strong enough.
(EXIT NOLA *to front part of house.*)

MAVIS Education. Ah, it's lovely! You ought to be proud, Roy, to be a teacher.

ROY (*sitting down at table, where* MAVIS *serves him with breakfast*) This teacher won't be one any longer than he can help it.

MAVIS If Mum and Dad weren't gone, it'd break their hearts!

HARRY (*patting* ROY *on back*) It's the intellectual liver. (*Concentrating on his wife*) Look after yourself, Mave. Everything that Sister tells you, dear. It's the pre-natal care that counts.

(HARRY *kisses* MAVIS *tenderly, but carefully.* MAVIS *submits, passive.*)

MAVIS Yes, dear.

(EXIT HARRY *through front of house.*)

(*Turning to* ROY) I can't understand you, Roy. After all, here's Harry and me making you a comfortable home. I can't understand you clever ones.

ROY (*cutting savagely at his breakfast*) I pay my way, don't I?

MAVIS (*unhappy*) It's not that. It's as if you wasn't one of us any more.

ROY (*in sudden outburst*) For God's sake! (*Controlling himself, quietly, appealing to her*) Don't go on about it, Mavis. People grow up different. We used to have a lot of fun together playing hoppy. Then *I* didn't want to any more.

GIRLIE (*to* JUDY) I can't understand you, Judy. I can't understand my own child.

JUDY Sometimes I can't understand myself. There are certain things I've got to do even when I don't want to.

GIRLIE But a girl can choose.

JUDY Not always.

MAVIS (*to* ROY) And whatever will you do if you give up teaching?

ROY (*desperate*) I shan't cut my throat!

MAVIS (*exasperated*) After all they spent on your education. . . .

GIRLIE But a violin, Judy! It's a man and a washing-machine that counts.

JUDY It's none of those.

GIRLIE Then what . . . ?

MAVIS (*to* ROY) What'll become of you, I'd like to know, when you've thrown away the advantages?

ROY (*furtively, with a great effort*) I'll write a book.

MAVIS A book!

ROY Not a book, Mavis. *The* book. The book I've got to write. . . .

MAVIS For heaven's sake! About what?

ROY About you, perhaps.

MAVIS (*scornfully*) Me!

ROY But I haven't looked into the pores of your skin. Not long enough, anyway.

MAVIS Sometimes I think my brother will send me round the bend....

GIRLIE You worry me, Judy. You worry me silly.

JUDY (*getting up, sighing*) Everything will always worry you, Mum.

GIRLIE A violin!

JUDY (*suddenly passionate*) Yes! Yes! A violin! I must! Even though it tortures me!

GIRLIE (*amazed and a little bit frightened at what she has stirred up*) But you *weren't* like this. (*Then, turned inward, to herself*) Perhaps if we sat for a while in the sun we could get to know each other again. Plants grow together in the sun.

JUDY (*her arm drawn momentarily to her mother's neck*) But we're not plants. Or only the human kind.

GIRLIE (*shaking her off*) And I was never a sloppy mother. My second name was always Practical.

(GIRLIE *starts to potter, fussy, but absent, while* JUDY *begins apathetically to wash the dishes.*)

JUDY Detergent's running out.

GIRLIE How many times have I told you not to squeeze it more than twice!

ROY (*slamming his hands down on the table, shouting*) Procrustes! That's what we're up against!

MAVIS Pro-what? Never heard of it.

ROY An old Greek. Used to cut his victims' legs off . . . or stretch them . . . to make them fit the bed. There they were . . . (*demonstrating with his hands on the table*) they could have been laid out in a row . . . all the same . . . all equal. . . . Normal!

MAVIS I've never known anybody who wasn't normal. Without they were real dills. (*Shuddering*) Any of those others . . . that's something in the papers. All those maniacs that murder you . . . in parks . . . or even in the home. . . .

ROY Do you think the normal don't murder in their own way? They'll knock you dead without even lifting a finger . . . without stepping out from the row in which they're bedded. . . .

MAVIS That's clever talk. All I want's a happy home.

ROY All I want is something that can't be shut up in a box. Something that blinds . . . but by which I'll see . . . or know. Some tune I've heard . . . and then forgotten. . . .

MAVIS (*dully*) I've got the beds to make. Today I'm glad I've got the beds. I don't know about Pro-what's-his name. Only that ours are first quality beds.

(MAVIS *goes into front part of house, leaving* ROY *seated at the table, stiff-necked.*)

(ENTER RON SUDDARDS *from the lane. Climbs steps to stage. Opens Pogsons' invisible back gate. He is a decent fellow. About twenty-one. Thick-set. Somewhat slow. He is wearing bicycle-clips. Mounts steps to the Pogson kitchen.*)

(GIRLIE POGSON *has moved to her back door.*)

RON Morning, Mrs Pogson.

GIRLIE (*absent-minded*) Oh. (*Recognizing, with mild signs of disapproval*) It's that Mr Suddards, Judy. From the post office.

(GIRLIE *goes back into kitchen, finally* EXIT BACK. *Judy comes to kitchen door.*)

JUDY Hello, Ron.

(*Her reception is gently cordial without being over-enthusiastic.*)

RON Hello, Judy. I got the tickets for another concert.

(ROY CHILD *has come to the back door of the* KNOTT *house.*)

JUDY (*vague, to* RON) Concert?

RON Like we said. Seeing as you're free . . . Thursday. . . .

JUDY (*embarrassed*) Oh. Yes. Yes!

RON (*suspicious*) You hadn't forgot?

JUDY No. I almost . . . (*contrite*) No, Ron, I had! (*Quickly*) But I'll come. Oh, yes, I want to!

RON If you've made up your mind, then, I'll look up the trains. And buses.

JUDY Oh, yes, it's settled, Ron. We're going.

ROY (*joining in*) By train. And bus. And the last, long lap, down the road the Board began but didn't finish.

(RON *and* JUDY *look towards him. He has seated himself on the Knott back-doorstep.*)

89

Didn't know you were interested in music, Ron.

RON (*unperturbed*) You can learn, can't you? You can learn anything if you put your mind to it.

ROY If you're lucky enough to have that sort of mind.

RON It'll be a sort of relaxation, too. From the post office. It gets you down there . . . the stamps, and the pensions, and all the telegrams about the relatives who've died. . . .

JUDY (*laughing, touching his arm*) Oh, Ron, it's not as bad as that!

ROY Could be, though.

RON (*looking at* JUDY, *shivering slightly*) No, Judy. I believe it's not as bad as that.

(RON *laughs too, and* JUDY *has to look away.*)

(*Reminded*) I'd better be going, then. See you later, Judy . . . Roy.

JUDY See you later. And Thursday. It's a date.

(RON *goes* OFF *the way he came.* ROY *and* JUDY *watch him go.*)

(*A momentary pause.*)

(*Without glancing in* ROY'S *direction, coming down steps into the Pogson yard*) Why do you look at me, Roy?

ROY (*descending the steps into the Knott yard*) You've got to look at something. And it's only natural to choose what's pleasantest in the landscape.

JUDY How pleasant you can be at times. And smooth.

(ROY *squeezes through the gap in the separating fence.*)

ROY Am I all that rough at others?

JUDY (*looking at him, candidly*) Yes!

ROY (*touching her cheek, very briefly and casually*) We've seen too much of each other. That's the trouble. We've felt each other bumping around in the next box. You've heard my thoughts trying to make sense. I've had to listen to your bloody old Bach.

JUDY As we'll have to spend the rest of our lives in boxes, we'd better get used to what's in them.

ROY Who's to say we shan't burst out, in a shower of glorious fireworks?

JUDY Fireworks are few and far between.

VOICE (*off-stage, a slight coloratura parody*) Oo-hoo-oo!

(ENTER JULIA SHEEN *from the front garden. She is glorious. Perfectly dressed. Perfectly slim. Long legs, neck. A pencil parasol.*

Any position she takes will be the artificial pose of the model.

JUDY Why, Julia!

ROY (*appreciative*) The goddess descends!

JULIA The goddess is late for her bus, and going over on her heels...
(*strikes a pose*) ... but wanted Judy to see ... this little number.

JUDY Another!

JULIA (*complacent*) The newest.

JUDY (*standing back, appraising the dress*) It's beautiful, Julia.

ROY Smashing!

(ROY's *tone and behaviour suggest he may give more active expression to his enthusiasm.* JULIA *changes position accordingly.*)

JULIA (*ignoring* ROY) But the neckline, Judy? Just a little...?

JUDY Perfect, Julia. Not half an inch either way.

JULIA Don't want to share all my secrets.

ROY Secrets are made for sharing.

JULIA Not with everyone, they aren't.

ROY Tell me, Julia, will you ever break?

JULIA I'm shattered regularly by some.

ROY Do you *hate*!

JULIA Not 'hate'. I'm cold. So you tell me. (*Catching sight of Judy*)
I love ... Judy ... (*squeezing Judy's hand*) Judy's a darling ...
only a girl could appreciate.

ROY (*ignoring all else, to* JULIA) When am I going to see you?

JULIA I've lost my book.

ROY (*as if about to move in on her again*) One day I'll help you find it.
(JULIA *moves away.*)

JULIA (*defending herself, stylishly, with the ferrule of her parasol*) One
day ... I'll have forgotten ... how to write the date.

ROY Sorry I've disarranged your stance.

JULIA (*arranging herself*) Well, I *am* a business girl. And have an
assignment.

ROY You'll carry it off in that.

JULIA Oh, not in this. Today it's bikinis. But you never know what
you'll meet in the street. And it doesn't do ... a business girl ...
in a crushed frock.

(JULIA *turns, and starts to make her way,* BACK, *towards the street.*)
'Bye, Judy. 'Bye, Roy.

JUDY 'Bye, Julia.

JULIA (*calling back to them*) I expect I've missed my bus. But there are always others. . . .

(EXIT JULIA, BACK.)

ROY If she was less brittle, she could be less stunning. But would she be less intolerable?

JUDY Aren't you prepared to tolerate as it is?

ROY Don't get me wrong, Judy. I know my Julia. (*Pausing*) *How* I know her!

JUDY And it makes no difference?

ROY Shall I drown the less for knowing I'm drowning? And only a glass rock to cling on to.

JUDY (*quite calmly, beginning to mount the steps*) I'll leave you to it, then.

ROY Oh, don't . . . *go*! Where are you going?

JUDY To my poor 'bloody old Bach'.

ROY Oh, God! On such a day! We should be lying around on some beach. Exposing our bodies to the sun. So good for the soul . . . if it doesn't dry up. In that case: just lying . . . our skins touching ever so slightly. . . .

(JUDY *returns slowly*.)

JUDY (*not in control of herself*) When you're not driving me one way, you're pulling me in another. It's quite confusing.

ROY (*taking her hand, stroking her arm*) Allow yourself to be confused.

JUDY When you're not trying to destroy what I most believe in, I can sense we share the same beliefs. (*Shaking her head slowly, like someone tormented in a dream*) But always destroying . . . destroying. . . .

ROY If you carve away, you reach the bone.

JUDY I should have thought you might have reached it. You won't even allow me my music.

ROY Judy, I don't feel it's *your* music!

JUDY In other words . . . I'm pretty lousy.

ROY Oh, who ever heard of a great virtuoso called Judy Pogson! And who wants to be a humble little fiddle?

JUDY (*wrenching herself away*) If it's names, then, is Roy Child such a shining label?

ROY (*half ironic*) Oh, Roy can stand for kings. And a child is pure enough.

JUDY And cruel. So very often, so very, very cruel!

ROY (*recovering her hand, genuinely*) I don't mean to be cruel, Judy. Or only half-mean. Half of me knows you're the truest I'll ever find. But the truth is always hardest to accept.

JUDY (*running up the steps, into the house, hiding her tears*) I give up, then!

ROY It would be so much easier if I could too.

(*He opens the invisible back gate rather viciously, and goes* OFF, *down the lane.*)

(ENTER GIRLIE POGSON *in her kitchen from front room. As* JUDY *runs* OFF, *they cross.*)

GIRLIE (*looking back after her daughter as the latter disappears in the house behind*) Whatever now? Always tears! Always secrets! When I was a girl, girls were bright. Girls were different.

(GIRLIE *goes through the motions of fetching out a broom.*)

(MAVIS KNOTT, *now in her pregnancy uniform, has come into her kitchen and armed herself with an invisible duster.*)

(NOLA BOYLE, *still in chenille, comes out from the front part of her house, and prepares to wield a feather-duster.*)

THREE WOMEN (*in unison, as they dust or sweep*) Laundry's over, thank God! Laundry's Monday. Tuesday for the Cash-and-Carry... mucking around the shops....

GIRLIE And Woolworths.

NOLA So cool.

MAVIS Woolies is lovely.

GIRLIE Got to be careful, though.

MAVIS Tuppence off tomato sauce...

NOLA ... and sixpence on the Snail Defender.

GIRLIE Specials are never special enough.

ALL (*sweeping, flicking, rubbing*) Mucking around . . . mucking around. . . . There's the pictures, too, of an afternoon. Warm as velvet on a winter afternoon...

MAVIS ... sucking a hot caramel...

NOLA ... with somebody on either side.

GIRLIE They bring the pictures close now...

NOLA ... almost into your lap. ...

(MAVIS *shakes her duster out of a window,* R.)

MAVIS (*sighing*) Oh, it's lovely at the pictures ...

GIRLIE ... for the fallen arches.

(MAVIS *takes and peels a banana.*)

NOLA Slip the stilettoes off for a while.

GIRLIE Not that we haven't our husbands' interests at heart. ...

MAVIS (*eating the banana ravenously*) The budget. ... (*Through a mouthful*) There's always the budget.

NOLA You may forget the man, just once in a while, but never the budget. ...

(THREE WIVES *have reached their back doors:* MAVIS *eating her banana and relaxing,* GIRLIE *sweeping out the dirt,* NOLA *shaking out her feather-duster.* GIRLIE *catches sight of* NOLA, *and ignores.* NOLA *catches sight of* MAVIS *beyond* GIRLIE.)

(*Calling, cheerful*) Hello, Mave! How you feelin', love?

(MAVIS *sighs, looks pathetic.*)

Like that, eh?

MAVIS Can't resist the bananas.

NOLA Yeah. They say you go for them like one thing when you're preggo.

MAVIS I'll say! I've just about eaten out the whole of Queensland. (*She turns and goes* OFF *heavily into the invisible part of her house.*)

(GIRLIE *and* NOLA *are left with each other. It is obvious they don't think much of the situation.* NOLA *is about to turn.*)

GIRLIE (*making a start*) Mrs Boyle ...

NOLA Yes, Mrs Pogson?

GIRLIE I've been meaning to have a word with you.

NOLA Okay, Mrs Pogson. What's your 'word' this time? I wonder!

GIRLIE As a matter of fact, Mrs Boyle, it's about words that I want to speak. There are words and words, you know.

NOLA You're telling *me*!

GIRLIE And some of them not very nice for a little girl to hear. It's the dogs I'm trying to refer to.

NOLA Go on! Dogs is dogs.

GIRLIE It's the female dogs, Mrs Boyle.

NOLA (*bursting*) Strike a light! Mrs Pogson, you're gunna take the stuffing out of nature! And what'll you have left? Skin! Dry skin!

GIRLIE I don't know what you mean.

NOLA Oh, yes, you do! You're picking on me again. I recognize the symptoms. It sort of gets in your nose, Mrs Pogson, that my bloke's the night-soil man. What odds! The money's good. In fact, it's better. What with the overtime. I wouldn't have thought to mention, if I didn't know it might impress. But we're human, too, Mrs Pogson. We have our worries. A sanitary lady's life is not all roses. (*Very clearly*) So, *please don't go for me in future*. I can't stick *picking*!

(MRS POGSON *is all a-flounce.*)

(*During the foregoing speech, the* BARKING *has broken out again, if anything closer to Mildred Street, and* PIPPY *and* DEEDREE *have crawled out from under the Pogson house, and are slowly climbing the steps. They are torn between listening to the argument, watching the protagonists, and concentrating on the fresh barking of dogs.*)

GIRLIE (*making as if to retreat*) Come along in, Pippy. I can find a little job for you.

PIPPY (*holding back*) Arr, gee! It's always jobs!

(ENTER ERNIE BOYLE *as from the lane, opening the invisible back gate, and coming into his own yard. He is in his forties, but very active. An obviously good-natured, innocent and generous male, who respects and depends on the 'women folk'. He is carrying his coat over his shoulder. He is happy to be free.*)

ERN How are we, eh? Morning, Mrs Pogson.

(GIRLIE *ignores.*)

GIRLIE And Deedree, it's time you ran along. Your mother will be wondering.

DEEDREE No, she won't. Mum told me to make meself scarce for just as long as I liked.

PIPPY (*desperate*) And the dogs, Mum. I gotta see the dogs! Can't you hear? They must be coming down Mildred Street.

ERN (*mounting steps of his house to where his wife leans against the door-post looking somewhat ironic*) There were dogs all right. Every mong in Sarsaparilla.

PIPPY (*shouting, almost frantic*) And the bitch, Mr Boyle . . . didn't you see the bitch?

ERN Too right I did! The bitch was leadin' the whole pack.

(*He has turned so that he faces the auditorium. Puts one arm round his wife, and with the other he assists what might be the messenger's speech from a Greek tragedy.*)

There she was. A little bit of a blessed thing. 'Er tongue almost hangin' on the ground. Lickin' the dust she was. And gunna get a whole lot drier. 'Er eyes'uv turned glassy. You can count 'er ribs. You can count the dawgs. The big, scrawny yeller fellers. The mangy reds. The woolly mysteries. That poor bitch soon won't be fit for much else but stuffin', and standin' on a bloomin' varnished board....

GIRLIE (*to* PIPPY, *piercingly*) Joy-*leen*!

(PIPPY *hangs her head, and goes inside.* DEEDREE *thinks better of it, and slinks* OFF *through the front garden.* GIRLIE *follows* PIPPY, *slams the invisible door, and they both pass through the kitchen* OUT *into the house.*)

(NOLA *laughs joyously. She and* ERN *move slowly into their kitchen.*)

NOLA I wouldn't be that bitch, not if you gave me all the money in the bank. Or perhaps I might then!

ERN Then it wouldn't be love. Love is free.

(ERN *kisses* NOLA, *rather hungrily, on the mouth. Looks at her.*)

NOLA Oh, love! Love is all right. But d'you suppose a dog like that likes it, Ernie, with a whole pack?

ERN (*sighing, serious*) 'Oo knows what 'oo likes.

(NOLA *withdraws abruptly from philosophic speculation.*)

NOLA (*almost skittish*) Won't be long with your breakfast, Ern.

ERN (*as he prepares to go into other part of house*) Had a few words with old tommy-axe next door?

NOLA (*very busy*) Words! You said it!

(ERN *goes* OFF.)

(*Calling to him*) Dog words! You know, Ernie, I don't think Sarsaparilla was ever so impressed by anything before as they are by this poor little hot bitch. In the streets, and in the homes, they're all talking about it.

(*She shakes the pan. Mimes various stages of the breakfast routine. Sings. Hums.*)

(*Calling*) How was the night business, Ern?

ERN (*off-stage*) Just the same, Nola. Just the same.

NOLA (*calling*) Fed up?

ERN (*calling back*) Nao! Money's too good.

(NOLA *goes and stands in what would be the doorway*, BACK. *In profile. Looking.*)

NOLA (*laughing, speaking to him* OFF) Gee, you look funny, Ern, with the water tricklin' down your chest!

(*Comes back, sees to the table.*)

(*Soberly, calling*) Gotta watch the fat, though.

ERN (*calling back*) Eh?

NOLA (*calling back*) You're fat!

(*Slight pause.*)

They say there's an Eyetalian going to buy that block up the street. (*Thoughtfully*) Some of those Eyetalians . . . they're all shoulders and no hips. . . .

ERN (*calling*) Saw a bloke I used to know.

NOLA (*not too pleased*) Oh?

ERN (*calling*) A good mate of mine. Rowley Masson. 'Digger' Masson. We was together in the Western Desert.

NOLA These mates! (*Pause, then calls*) What's he do?

ERN (*calling back*) Think 'e said 'e drives a truck. Somewhere up in the north-west. Or might'uv been Queensland. I didn't take it in. We had so much to say.

(*Re-enter* ERN. *He is in pyjamas now. Rubbing his wet head with a towel.*)

Mind you, I don't think Rowley ever sticks at anything for long. You'll like 'im, though. I told 'im to look in and see us.

NOLA Some dirty, no-hope truck-driver! I don't see why you're gunna let 'im bludge on *us*!

ERN (*seating himself firmly at the table*) Thought you enjoyed a bit of company.

NOLA I like to choose me company.

ERN (*starting to eat furiously*) I'd rather choose it for yer.

NOLA What do you mean?

ERN (*cutting at the plate savagely*) You didn't never used to go crook on the men.

NOLA I like. . . . Well, didn't I tell yer in the beginning: there had

97

been Stan? And you weren't all that holy before we married!

ERN (*swinging his head*) Yairs! Yairs! *I* know! But there was Stan. (*The following is performed as a kind of double soliloquy.*)

(*Thoughtfully*) How can a man ever know, where there was one, there wasn't others. . . .

NOLA (*putting her hands behind her hair, in still ecstasy*) Yes. Yes. There were others. You always knew. But what is a woman to do when she wasn't born mean?

ERN What is a man to do when his guts are twisted by his thoughts? And all the flickery pictures that he sees at the back of his eyes?

NOLA Yes. Yes. The dreadful things. The mad things. The long, velvety moments. You wonder afterwards if any of it happened.

ERN It's different in a man.

NOLA Yes. Oh, yes. Men are different. That's why we put up with them. Love them, even. Even finish up loving the most different of all.

(ERN *is not appeased. But they resume a normal naturalistic exchange.*)

(*Rather innocently*) Ernie, I believe you're jealous about a lot of silly things that happened a long time ago!

ERN (*dully, automatically, tired*) I'm . . . jealous. . . .

(*He puts his arm round her waist.*)

NOLA Then what got into yer to invite this truck-drivin' number?

ERN He would'uv give me the shirt off 'is bloody back.

NOLA Men do that, I suppose. Still. . . . What's 'e look like?

ERN (*drowsily*) Skin and bone.

(*He continues sitting, holding his arms round her waist. Buries his face in her side.*)

NOLA One of those. Probably yarns 'is head off. (*Sighs*) About the blessed Western Desert.

(*All the time she is stroking* ERN's *head.*)

ERN (*drowsily*) You'll send me off to sleep, Nola. . . . (*Looks up at her.*) What did we say to each other?

NOLA What did we say, eh? A few of those things we go on forgetting. . . .

(*Both laugh.* ERN *gets up. Runs his lips down her neck.*)

ERN You been up since early?

NOLA Pretty early. (*Remembering*) I gotta run up to the Cash-and-Carry.

(*They stand together, and he puts his arms round her.*)

ERN It's too sleepy a day to run.

NOLA (*softly, laughing*) It's sleepy all right!

(*They move slowly* BACK.)

ERN (*drowsily, spell-binding*) Hot, eh? The air lays along yer on a day like this.

NOLA (*tenderly*) Perhaps I'll go later . . . when it's cooler. . . .

(*They disappear towards the other rooms. She is leaning on him.*)

(*At same time* ROY CHILD *appears along the lane. He is looking sunburnt. Goes into the* KNOTT *yard, but instead of entering the house, leans up against the proscenium arch,* R., *lazily, thoughtfully, observing the houses. The light has changed to suggest that of later afternoon.*)

ROY (*meditating*) When summer closes the door on chalkdust, and foxy questions of forty children, the mind should find release. But it doesn't. Nobody who has been boxed is ever quite free. His thoughts home like pigeons, to roost on their familiar perches . . . with the boxed thoughts of those he has never really left.

Here I am, then . . . smelling of salt, sun, and seaweed capsules popped in the heat of the day. Wearing its glaze of summer, my body is more or less renewed . . . while my mind lurks in stuffy corners, filled with Genoa velvet and silky oak veneer. Where the body ignores, the mind reminds . . . that the radio hasn't left off playing in empty rooms . . . that the TV will continue to dissolve human personality, like gelatine in tepid water.

Of course, We-Who-Know-All-This hate it, and promise ourselves to escape to something better. But wonder if that exists . . . and depend on those twin dazzlers, time and motion, to help us believe we are doing and being. Who can resist deceiving himself when the razzle-dazzle's on?

(*A razzle-dazzle of light is played on the proscenium: the effect of a blind flapping, light flickering through its slats. While the razzle-dazzle is in action, movement is shorter, sharp, stylized, something like the motion of figures in a silent film, though less jerky.*)

(JUDY POGSON's *violin is heard* OFF *in the Pogson house, playing, something firm, gay, a trifle harsh – the* bourrée *from the second Bach Sonata in B minor – Violin accompanies the following snapshots.*)

Here they go now. That nice girl Judy Pogson can't give the violin away. She won an Instrumental Section once. At night her dreams breathe music. Its curtain hides whatever she has to discover.

(MAVIS KNOTT *has come into her kitchen. Potters about. Scrapes vegetables in obvious discomfort.*)

All the afternoon my sister Mavis will have had the wind. Her time is getting close. This evening she could kill the carrots.

(BARKING *has started again.*)

And the dogs. . . . The dogs have never really stopped barking in anybody's mind.

(PIPPY *appears in the Pogson kitchen. She has a mission. Runs down the back steps.*)

GIRLIE (*calling*, OFF) Pippy? Where are you off to?

PIPPY (*pausing, wary*) Nowhere. I'm gunna muck around the street a bit.

GIRLIE (*calling*) Not now, dear. We'll be having tea very soon.

PIPPY (*moaning*) Ohhhh!

(*She goes on, however, towards the garden.* DEEDREE *has come in from the street. She whispers into* PIPPY'S *ear. They both laugh loud. Run* OFF *into the front garden towards the street.*)

ROY Looking for something to do. Looking for something to do. A lot of it is strictly necessary, of course. But above all it is something to do.

(NOLA ENTERS *her kitchen. She is dressed for going out. Touches her hair in the glass. Smoothes her lips. Makes faces. She has a basket.*)

NOLA (*calling*) Won't be long, Ern. You oughta get yourself a nice cold glass of beer. There's plenty in the fridge. Then we'll have tea.

ROY Out and in! In and out! Direction is the least of it.

(NOLA *passes down her back steps.* CLIVE POGSON ENTERS *the Pogson block from the lane. He is carrying a parcel.*)

CLIVE (*opening his gate, catching sight of* NOLA) How are we, Mrs Boyle?

NOLA (*smiles*) Pretty good, thanks. How's yourself?

CLIVE (*laughing, rather sheepishly*) I'm good too. Yes. All things considered. Dogs and all, eh?

(CLIVE *laughs again, watching* NOLA.)

NOLA (*calmly*) Dogs'uv gotta be dogs. That's the way I look at it.

CLIVE (*laughing*) That's one way!

(NOLA *passes along the yard towards front garden and street as* CLIVE *watches from the Pogson block.*)

Provided they don't interrupt your sleep.

NOLA You can always go to sleep again.

(NOLA *goes* OFF *towards the street.*)

(CLIVE *mops his brow. Runs up steps into Pogson kitchen.*)

CLIVE (*calling*) Girl-ie!

(GIRLIE ENTERS *quickly, and at once presents her cheek for a routine kiss.*)

GIRLIE (*immediately, as a matter of course*) Don't tell me you forgot the fish!

CLIVE Who said I forgot the fish?

(*Dumps the parcel in her hands.* EXIT CLIVE, BACK.)

GIRLIE (*looking out of kitchen door, automatically calling*) Pip-py?

(*Withdraws into kitchen.*)

(HARRY KNOTT ENTERS *from garden of Knott home. He too is carrying a small parcel. Comes forward into the yard.*)

HARRY (*calling from steps as he mounts*) Hi, Mave? Everything okay? Still in one piece?

MAVIS Oh, Harry, I had such a day!

HARRY (*kissing and fussing*) What's up?

MAVIS Nothing. (*Masters her wind*) Oh, nothing that you could say. You can't explain to anybody who never had a baby.

HARRY (*offering parcel*) Brought you something good.

MAVIS (*sentimental*) Oh, Harry!

HARRY That's breasts of chicken in a sort of jelly.

MAVIS Breasts of. . . . (*Repulsion rising*) Oh, I don't think I. . . . Breasts! (*Controlling herself*) Oh, thank you, Harry dear! (*She kisses him rather nicely*) It was real sweet of you to think of that.

(HARRY *and* MAVIS *go* OFF *into front part of their house.*)

ROY (*sighing*) The lives of good, kind people seen through doorways! And those we love are always the most exposed....

(GIRLIE POGSON *scaling fish at sink.*)

(ERNIE BOYLE *has come into the Boyle kitchen, dressed now, though without his coat. Looks into fridge. Takes out bottle of beer. Pours one. Drinks. Belches.*)

GIRLIE (*scaling fish, disgusted*) Once upon a time they used to scale the fish....

ERN (*shivering*) Christ, it's empty in the home just before your tea! Christ, what can you do when you're alone...? What if you was ever left alone...?

(*Fidgetty. Goes into front part of house carrying his bottle and glass.*)

GIRLIE (*scaling*) When we were first married, Clive scaled the fish. Under the water, his hands moved so quick. They used to fascinate me. Didn't notice them all this time....

(ENTER CLIVE.)

CLIVE What's that you're saying? If you want me to hear, you know, you've got to speak up.

(*He sits down with the evening paper.*)

GIRLIE (*angry*) I was saying that fish scales.... Pfough!

(*Spits a scale out of her mouth.*)

(JUDY *has put aside the violin. Crosses the kitchen, intent on something.*)

(*To* JUDY) You might lend me a hand, and lay the table, dear.

JUDY (*absent*) Yes, Mother.

(EXIT JUDY *by the kitchen door.*)

GIRLIE (*to* CLIVE) There! You see? For what you count! Now, at Rosedale, when I was a girl, I'd lend a hand by second nature ... not only when we were entertaining ... which we did frequently, of course ... no one in the district kept a better table....

CLIVE (*continuing to read*) Yes. We know about Rosedale....

(*As* JUDY *descends the steps, the razzle-dazzle is abruptly turned off. She notices* ROY. *Stops short. He comes towards her, smiling, squeezing through the gap in the fence. They meet in the Pogson yard.*)

ROY It was a dazzler of a day.

JUDY (*as he pulls her down beside him on the step*) You smell of salt.

ROY I'm preserved in it.

(*They sit on the steps, knee to knee, looking into each other.*)
You should have come. It would have been company. We could have talked.

JUDY You would have done the talking.

ROY Well, that's so. But another person's silences are good, when they're the right silences.

JUDY (*turning aside, cupping her face, elbows on knees, looking straight ahead*) I'd like to glitter. I'd like to know what to say. Brilliant, sometimes cutting things.

ROY (*stroking her neck*) I doubt you'd ever kill.

JUDY To feel you might, at least ... if you wanted to....

ROY (*intent on his own thoughts*) You should have come, though. I'd have told you what I'm planning to do in the future.

JUDY All the afternoon I've been turning out boxes. . . .

ROY Of what, Judy?

JUDY Oh, old, useless stuff.

ROY Such as?

JUDY Letters and things. Some flowers we found one spring in a gully, and pressed. Remember?

ROY (*trying to*) Mmmmmm? Noooo.

JUDY They'd turned brown. They crumbled very easily. (*Practical, louder*) Oh, there was a whole lot I tidied up this afternoon.

ROY A girl could tidy herself away.

JUDY It's important to know what she's got.

ROY I'd burst out of so much neatness. I'll have to burst out soon. Did I tell you ... the book I'm going to write ...

JUDY Which one, Roy?

ROY ... I think I'm about to start. It might even be tonight. Night always suits me best. After that, I'm pushing off. Before, perhaps. I've been saving up towards the passage.

JUDY Where to, Roy?

ROY I haven't decided. Somewhere. Out of this.

JUDY If that's what you want . . . I ought to feel . . . glad.

(ENTER RON SUDDARDS *by way of the lane. He is a mixture of the diffident and the determined.*)

RON Hello, Judy. . . . Roy. I sort of looked in.

ROY (*brutally, bored by the interruption*) What for?

RON (*unperturbed*) Why, to pass the time, I suppose. Now that the post office is closed, I've got time on my hands. (*Producing a book*) Oh, and I brought you this, Judy.

JUDY (*reading title*) Whatever made you bring me this? *Decline and Fall of the Roman Empire.* Vol I!

ROY (*tearing his hair in mock despair*) O God of Night Classes. . . .

RON (*to* JUDY) It's terrific.

JUDY (*appalled*) But Vol I! What about the other half dozen?

RON We've got a lifetime, haven't we?

JUDY (*fingering the book*) A lifetime should be long enough. If you think . . . I can cope. . . .

RON You can cope all right!

JUDY If you think, Ron . . . I'll try. . . .

(*Bright calls are heard from the direction of the Pogson front gate.*)

JULIA (*calling*, OFF) Oohoo! Where is everybody?

(JULIA ENTERS *the back yard as exquisitely uncreased as before.*) Judy, I've come to show my hat.

(*She is followed by* MR ERBAGE, *carrying parcels. He is of the alderman type. Middle fifties. He is both self-conscious and self-satisfied.*)

JUDY (*to* JULIA) But that's . . . the one . . . you had.

ROY (*jumping to his feet, ready to do some stuff*) Never forget Pavlova Rising!

JULIA (*scornfully*) Oh, this! (*She almost touches her head*) This is not *it*! Mr Erbage is carrying *the* hat.

(MR ERBAGE *laughs, rather crazily for someone so important and respectable.*)

I want you to meet Mr Erbage. A friend. He hopes to become a councillor.

ROY That should be easy enough . . . for Mr Erbage.

RON Live around here, Mr Erbage?

ERBAGE (*shifting ground under the parcels*) In Amy Street.

ROY Known each other *long*?

ERBAGE (*embarrassed*) Well . . . I wouldn't care to say *how* long. Not to the day!

JULIA (*helping herself to a hat-box*) Poor Douggie's not to be tormented! (*Standing back, examining him*) Don't you think he's rather cute? (*To* JUDY) Judy, darling, let's go up and find a mirror. (JUDY *and* JULIA *go up the Pogson steps.*)

ERBAGE The young lady can't resist the hats!

RON Did I understand, Mr Erbage, that Miss Sheen was your fiancée?

ERBAGE (*laughing, drawing in a fat chin*) Neither was, nor is, Mr ... er. . . . You might say there are circumstantial obstacles.

ROY (*savagely*) Here's to trying, anyway!

ERBAGE (*uproarious*) No young lady ever knew her own mind! I can see you've 'ad experience of that. Eh? (*The parcels jig*) EH? (ROY *and* RON *are at a loss.*)

(*In the Pogson kitchen,* GIRLIE *has come forward.* CLIVE *no more than greets* JULIA. *The* WOMEN *have gathered at the wall-mirror for the hat demonstration.*)

(*A person appears by way of the back lane. It is* ROWLEY MASSON. *He is a handsome man in his forties. A bit seedy, battered. Good features of the hatchet variety. The Digger type.*)

MASSON (*to the group of men*) Any of you know if a cove name of Boyle lives anywhere around? Ernie Boyle. Sanitary.

(ROY *indicates the Boyle house.*)

(*Jerking his head*) Thanks, mate.

(*He opens the invisible gate, goes into Boyles' back yard.*) Pretty nice set-up. I knew Ernie Boyle in the Western Des.

ROY (*without interest*) You don't say!

MASSON Yeah.

(*Looks around. Appears to be investigating in one corner.*)

ERBAGE (*sighing*) Yes, the ladies!

ROY (*calling to* MASSON, *suspicious*) That's only the tool shed.

MASSON Yeah. Just having a squint. (*As it dawns*) 'Ere! You don't think I'd shake anything off Ern? 'E's my mate!

ROY Ern will just be waiting to have that yarn about the Western Desert.

MASSON (*looking around*) Yeah. It's that long. . . . Pretty fair set-up Ernie's got.

(GIRLIE, JUDY *and* JULIA *are grouped round the mirror in the* POGSON *kitchen.* JULIA *has put on the new hat.*)

JULIA (*preening herself in the glass*) Do you think it's *me*?

GIRLIE A bit freakish, isn't it?

JULIA I'd hoped it was *amusing*!

GIRLIE I can't say I like people to have a laugh at my expense.

JUDY (*putting an arm around* GIRLIE) Mother can't bear to look conspicuous.

GIRLIE (*scornful, warding* JUDY *off*) Pffh! I was never out of fashion. But what I mean to say is: I like a hat to look different, so long as it's what the others are wearing.

(JULIA *takes off the hat, and they put it back in its box during the following.*)

RON ... your policy as councillor, Mr Erbage?

ERBAGE Policy?

ROY Will you have the public interest at heart?

ERBAGE Here, what do you mean to signify? I'm standing for councillor, aren't I?

ROY Exactly.

(MASSON *has come across, and is leaning on the fence, listening.*)

ERBAGE And that's a position of trust, isn't it? That only a public-spirited man would undertake to fill? The public interest! Many a councillor has half-killed 'imself in the public interest. And nothing to show for it.

ROY Except the Green Belt.

ERBAGE (*nodding, very solemn*) The Green Belt is a problem no councillor can afford to ignore.

(MASSON *guffaws.*)

(JUDY *and* JULIA *converge on the kitchen door, about to come down.*)

JULIA (*to* JUDY) Long engagements allow a girl to sort out her ideas.

JUDY Has he given you a ring, Julia?

JULIA We're choosing the ring ... yes, if not tomorrow, early next week.

JUDY Anyway, what's in a ring?

JULIA Oh, quite a lot, dear, quite a lot. And Doug is so generous....

(JUDY *and* JULIA *come down the steps.*)

MASSON (*leaning on the palings, observing*) They got the dinkum oil in Mildred Street!

(*Everyone else is otherwise preoccupied.*)

JUDY (*handing back the hat-box to* JULIA, *who attaches it to* ERBAGE) Thanks, Julia. The hat's really fab.

JULIA (*looking at her watch*) Now we must fly. He's taking me out to dinner. Doug adores to dance.

(*She strikes a fleeting pose.*)

ERBAGE (*laughing madly*) It puts you on your metal!

ROY (*to* JULIA, *with a passion disguised as irony*) I left my flash-bulb behind! Seriously, though, I'd like to make a date . . . any time you say the word. . . .

JULIA (*eyes just glancing, lightly*) Seriousness was never your line!

(*To* ERBAGE) Come on, Doug. The night won't wait for us!

MASSON (*eyes glued to* JULIA) Waddaya know, eh?

(JULIA *and* ERBAGE *go out* BACK *to the street.*)

ROY I could rip every stitch off that girl, and make her eat the dust!

MASSON (*leaning on the fence*) I could do something about 'er me-self.

ROY She's all show. (*Desperately*) But what a show!

JUDY (*mastering her disgust and anguish, to* RON) It was kind of you to bring the book, Ron.

RON (*awkward*) Ah, well!

JUDY You *are* kind.

RON (*bitter for him*) That's what people say.

MASSON (*to* ROY) That little sheila might come round if you treated 'er rough, Jack. With some women you gotta be unkind, so as they can act kind.

ROY (*irritated*) Does it always take you so long to get anywhere?

MASSON (*laughing, rolling a cigarette*) I like to take me time. Look around. Have a yarn. There's time enough for everything.

(PIPPY *has come into the Pogson kitchen from front part of house. Catches sight of what her mother is preparing.*)

PIPPY (*to* GIRLIE) Arr, it's not old fish!

GIRLIE There's what is good for little girls.

PIPPY But not old fish! It sticks in my throat!

GIRLIE (*grimly*) There's too much sticks in your throat, my girl. One day there'll be nothing more to do about it. . . .

(PIPPY *runs out the back door.*)

PIPPY But old fish! It stinks!

ROY (*squeezing between the palings into Knotts' yard*) You've said it, Pippy. Shall we push off somewhere, the two of us, somewhere into the world?

PIPPY No. You're silly. Everybody's silly.

(DOGS *have begun to* BARK *again.*)

(*Dreamy*) All I want is to be left alone. To watch things.

ROY That's a disease of mine. But it doesn't get you anywhere.

(*He goes into the Knott house, passes through the kitchen, and* EXIT.)

PIPPY (*rocking on the back steps*) I don't wanta go anywhere. I just wanta muck around.

RON (*to* JUDY) Ah, well. Better be making tracks. They'll be waiting to give me my tea.

JUDY (*with an effort, to show interest*) Ron, it's terrible of me . . . I don't know . . . I never thought to ask . . . do you live with your family?

RON No. They're back at Mullumbimby. I answered an ad in the *Advertiser*. I got a room, with use of conveniences, and one meal.

JUDY (*choking*) How very, very . . . sad!

RON Oh, it's not too bad. When they go to the pictures they let me use the lounge. I study then.

JUDY What do you study, Ron?

RON Nothing special.

JUDY Haven't you any ambitions?

RON Why, to live, I suppose. Yes, I study to live.

JUDY (*at breaking point*) You're right, I expect. (*Runs up the steps of her house*) I'm sure you're right. You *know*!

(JUDY *runs through the kitchen, and* OFF, *holding her handkerchief to her mouth.*)

GIRLIE (*to* CLIVE, *significantly*) There!

CLIVE (*rustling his paper*) It looks like Dainty Bess is going to win the Handicap. . . .

RON (*distressed, to* PIPPY) Is your sister sick?

PIPPY No. Soft.

RON I thought perhaps she was taken queer.

PIPPY (*practical*) I wouldn't worry.

RON Perhaps I hurt her. . . . Will you tell her something?

PIPPY What?

RON Tell her. . . . Well . . . I suppose it's something you can't tell.

(EXIT, RON *quickly* BACK.)

(MASSON *has seated himself meanwhile on the Boyles' steps. Roars his head off.*)

MASSON Things are going on round here!

PIPPY Are they?

MASSON I'll say!

(PIPPY *has come down, and is kicking the ground in the yard.*)

What's your name, kid?

PIPPY By rights I'm not supposed to talk to men.

MASSON Yeah. But 'oo ever stayed formal?

PIPPY (*after a pause*) Are you a relative?

MASSON No, I'm a mate of Ernie's. I just come.

PIPPY I thought perhaps you was a relative, that's why you weren't going in. I thought perhaps you knew all there was to know.

MASSON No. I don't know nothun yet.

(HARRY *and* MAVIS *have come into their kitchen during the foregoing scene, and have sat down to their tea.*)

MAVIS (*calling*) Aren't you coming to eat your tea, Roy? There's a real tasty braise. . . .

(*No reply from* ROY.)

MASSON (*to* PIPPY) No. I used to know old Ernie. Like me own hand. Never knew 'is missus, though.

PIPPY My mother can't stick Mrs Boyle. But Dad says she's generous.

MASSON What do you make of her yourself?

(PIPPY *wrinkles up her face, thinking.*)

PIPPY (*slowly*) Mmmmmm! She's good. She smells good. If Mum wouldn't go crook, Mrs Boyle would let me spend all my time mucking around in her place. She kissed me once. It was lovely.

MASSON (*stroking the stubble on his chin*) Sounds a pretty good sort to me.

(MAVIS KNOTT *is doing dainty things with her fork.*)

MAVIS Gee, these breasts are beaut, Harry! (*More formal*) They're really *bee-yutiful*!

PIPPY (*to* MASSON) She knows about the dogs, too.

MASSON What dogs?

PIPPY Don't tell me you don't know about the dogs! The bitch we got in season?

MASSON Oh? I seen some schemozzle up the street....

(*Light is fading.* ERN *has come into the Boyle kitchen with his empty glass and bottle. Switches on the light.*)

PIPPY (*to* MASSON) Well, Mrs Boyle knows all about the dogs. What their habits are, and all.

MASSON I better ask 'er.

GIRLIE (*calling from her kitchen door*) Pippy! Whether you like or not, the tea is ready.

PIPPY (*running towards the front garden*) All right!

GIRLIE You'll get shut up in your room, my girl.

PIPPY All *right*! I'm gunna have one more look before I get shut up....

(EXIT PIPPY *towards the street.*)

GIRLIE (*retreating into kitchen, calling*) Judy! Tea!

JUDY (*calling,* OFF, *stifled*) I'm not hungry.

GIRLIE (*plaintive to* CLIVE) There, you see! In homes where the father leaves it all to the mother....

CLIVE (*folding his paper preparatory to eating*) The Lottery's gone to a bachelor. In Glebe. What does a bachelor want with a prize? (ERN *has come forward to his back steps to investigate the stranger.*) (*The* BARKING *up the street has swelled momentarily.*)

ERN (*at the door*) 'Ere, wotcher ... 'oo the ... well, waddaya know! If it ain't old Rowley Masson! (*He becomes explosive with surprise and pleasure.*)

MASSON (*laughing, rising, pleased, but without the demonstrative pleasure of the other*) Yairs! It's me all right!

ERN (*throwing his arm round his friend, drawing him into the kitchen*) Digger! Old Dig! Thought you'd surprise me, eh?

MASSON Told me to show up, didn't yer?

ERN (*more sober*) Yes. (*Seems to be remembering something*)

MASSON So I showed.

(ERN *gives in to his pleasure, and warms to his duties.*)

ERN Well, come on in, Rowley. See where we 'ang out.

(MASSON *looks perfunctorily round the kitchen.*)

MASSON (*rather flat*) Seems all right, Ernie.

ERN (*laughing softly*) Yes. (*Goes suddenly and shyly, touches an invisible object*) That's the Mixmaster. Got everythink now.

MASSON You got everything.

ERN Oh, we're livin' it up! (*Remembering*) 'Ere!

(*Fetches glasses and a bottle.*)

This'll wash the dust down yer gullet.

(*They drink. There is a slight pause, awkwardness.*)

MASSON Somehow I never thought of you in a set-up like this, Ern.

ERN Well, the wife, you know. . . . You gotta make a place decent for the missus.

MASSON Oh, yes. The missus. . . .

ERN Ever get tied up, Dig?

MASSON Yairs.

(MASSON *sits tossing his foot.* ERN *decides not to continue investigations.*)

ERN (*brighter*) You'll like Nola, Rowley. She'll be in soon. (*Looks at his watch nervously*) Gone out to do a bit of shopping. Nola's got a sense of humour. She's all right. Not that she don't have 'er off moments. Every woman has 'er off moments. Eh?

(*But* DIGGER MASSON *is lost in thought.*)

MASSON (*sitting forward, intent, glass between his hands*) Remember those bloody fox-holes in the old Des? Remember 'ow we lay there waitin'? An' the snipers up on the bloody escarpment? We used to lie and talk about what we was goin' ter eat. An' the sheilas we was goin' ter do. An' the sky, Ern. I never seen such an open sky. As we layed there talkin' into each other's ears. Blokes were close to each other then. An' you'd wake up with your hair full of dew and spiders. . . .

(*There is a silence.*)

(*Looks straight at* ERN) I reckon you forgot all that. You got sold on the bloody Mixmasters.

ERN (*unhappy*) Nao! I didn't forget none of that. But 'oo wants to go on harpin'? I've 'ad a crook back ever since. Lyin' in bloody fox-'oles in the dew!

MASSON (*still entranced*) Remember I once said: 'Bet there's a lot of the blokes'll remember this, and wish they could get back. Even when the dust blows.' What was it they called it? The bloody *campseen*!

ERN (*determined*) Look 'ere, Dig, there's a lot of that I'll always remember. (*Nudging with a gentle, grudging affection*) I reckon I was never closer to nobody, before or since, as I waited for the Jerries to blow me bloody 'ead off. (*Shouting*) But I'm 'APPY now!

(*Outside,* NOLA BOYLE *is returning in the fading light. She comes in from the front garden. Her shopping basket appears to be full.*)

GIRLIE (*looking out her back door, frowning*) That child! If it isn't one thing. . . . (*Catches sight of* NOLA. *Frowns harder. Calls once, for the sake of her principles*) Joy-*leen*!

(GIRLIE *withdraws into the kitchen, where she and* CLIVE *continue with their tea.*)

(*The* KNOTTS *have finished. They come out down the back steps.* HARRY *has his arm round* MAVIS. MAVIS *waves and smiles at* NOLA. *The* KNOTTS *come out of their back gate, and disappear down the lane, strolling.*)

MASSON (*getting up, defensively*) So am I! I don't say I'm not 'appy. Only that 'appiness can make a coot of a man.

ERN You wait! Nola's gunna talk you right side out!

MASSON (*mumbling*) I dunno about Nola. I gotta go outside, Ern.

(NOLA *comes on, dawdling, pulling a weed, examining a flower.*)

ERN (*to* MASSON) 'Ere, you don't 'ave to go outside, not in my place. I'm not emptyin' the cans for nothun. We're a septic area 'ere.

(*He leads* MASSON *into front part of house.* NOLA *mounts the steps,* ENTERS *her kitchen. She stands staring at* MASSON'S *hat on the table.*)

(ERN RE-ENTERS.)

NOLA (*looking at the hat*) Whose is that?

ERN That's Digger's. Rowley Masson's.

NOLA He didn't waste any time, did he?

(ERN *goes through violent pantomime to indicate* MASSON *is where he is, and might overhear.*)

ERN (*whispering*) We gotta show we're pleased to see 'im, Nola . . . tell 'im 'e'd better doss down with us for a bit. Digger seems sort of mixed up.

NOLA Everyone's sort of mixed up nowadays. There's no craze like crazy, as far as I can see.

(*She goes about emptying her apparently heavy basket.* ERN *is in agony lest their conversation should be overheard.*)

Where's he going to doss down, anyway?

ERN (*indicating sofa*) What's wrong with this?

NOLA I'd say the springs.

ERN Arr, look, Digger won't mind a spring or two. 'E's been talkin' fox'oles.

NOLA (*pausing*) Fox-holes?

ERN Where we used to lay up in the desert. Give ourselves a bit of cover like.

NOLA So the old Western Desert's begun already!

(RE-ENTER MASSON, BACK. *He has plastered his hair down with water.* NOLA *would like not to look at him, but does, if casually.*)

ERN Nola, I'd like you to meet my old mate, Rowley Masson.

(MASSON *comes* FORWARD. *He is once more confident, in fact cocky.*)

MASSON They call me 'Digger', Nola.

NOLA (*coolly*) Pleased to meet you, Mr Masson. Or any other of my hubby's old friends.

(*She goes ahead disposing of the articles from her basket.* ERN *is unhappy.*)

ERN (*finally*) Nola and me's been talkin' it over, Rowley. We reckon you'd better put in a few days here with us. Nola's gunna fix up this 'ere lounge. We hope you'll be comfortable.

MASSON I'll be comfortable. But expect we'll be yarnin', Ernie, half the night.

(ERN *looks in horror at his watch.*)

ERN Not most nights we won't! I've got me run, Digger. I told you I was on the sanitary. I've gotta make meself scarce. Late already.

We're short of personnel. The night-soil's not everybody's cuppa tea.

NOLA (*in despair*) But you haven't had a bite to eat, Ern!

ERN (*all action*) Sling us something in a paper bag. (*Reaching for his coat*) A couple of savs . . . and a hunk of bread. . . .

NOLA (*hurrying*) Oh, dear! (*Pausing, over her shoulder*) Beer?

ERN (*putting on his coat*) Yes. I can down a bottle later on.

(MASSON *has produced a packet of cigarettes.*)

MASSON (*offering*) Light one for the road. Ern.

ERN (*helping himself*) Thought you rolled yer own.

MASSON (*shamelessly*) So I do. I keep these for when I want to do a special favour.

(*As* NOLA *thrusts the snack at* ERN, *and the latter grabs*, MASSON *seems to come between them, and he and* NOLA *almost collide.* NOLA *barely disguises her disgust.*)

ERN (*running down steps, calling*) See yez some more! The springs on that lounge aren't too good. But they'll hold. . . .

MASSON (*laughing, calling back*) Okay, Ern! We done worse in our time. . . .

(ERN *goes* OFF *by way of the lane. A silence falls in the kitchen. Then* NOLA *begins to hum.* MASSON *sits – statuesque.*)

(GIRLIE *has come to her back door.*)

GIRLIE (*looking out, to* CLIVE) Mr Boyle is going on the job. Did you know a gentleman came? She'll have to give him tea. She's not too pleased either. And I *heard*, Clive, because certain people talk so *loud* – the visitor's staying the night!

CLIVE What of it?

GIRLIE But staying the night! Of course I'm not saying any more. I mind my own business.

CLIVE (*getting up*) Glad to hear it, Girlie. Ooh! (*Eases his sciatica*) I'm going in to twiddle the TV.

GIRLIE (*putting an additional shine on some articles of crockery*) There was something lovely this afternoon. Some lady telling us how to make rissoles out of practically nothing.

(EXIT, CLIVE, BACK.)

GIRLIE (*to herself*) But staying the night. . . .

(GIRLIE *follows* CLIVE, OFF.)

NOLA (*to* MASSON) Suppose I better get you some tea.

MASSON I don't wanta put anybody out.

NOLA There's ham. But some people don't like ham.

MASSON (*with a sudden sincerity*) I'll like anything you give me.
(NOLA *lowers her eyes, and moves about. Pantomime of laying a plate on the table.*)

NOLA And a termarter. (*Gentler*) It got bruised.

MASSON (*laughing*) That'll make it softer.

NOLA (*indicating his place at table*) Go on.
(MASSON *sits down, but does not begin.*)

MASSON Aren't you keeping me company, Nola?

NOLA No. Haven't any appetite.
(*Silence. She pours tea.* MASSON *starts to eat, but produces packet of cigarettes.*)

MASSON Cigarette?
(NOLA *hesitates, but accepts.*)

NOLA Thanks.
(*As he lights it, she averts her eyes. Could be fascinated by his hands.*)
(*Suddenly, jerkily, blowing out smoke*) You're not doing me a favour, mind.

MASSON (*sitting down again at table*) What you got against me?

NOLA (*mysteriously*) Nothing. I ain't got nothing, I suppose. But all these men! (*Throws back her head, laughs uproariously*) Mates!

MASSON (*cutting his meat*) Don't seem to have much of an opinion of we men.

NOLA (*contemptuously*) I know men!
(EXIT, BACK.)
(MASSON *does not realize at first.*)

MASSON (*eating and speaking, now with an air of self-conscious refinement*) Of course there's men and men. There's some'ud stink the roof off. I admit. But there's some as are pleasant ... well, pleasant sort of men. I'm not blowin' any trumpet for *myself*. I'm something. Nola, that you've got to decide about. I....
(*Looks round, sees that she is not there. Swallows. Stuffs his mouth.*
NOLA RE-ENTERS *with armful of bedclothes. Dumps them on the lounge.*)
(*Eyeing her, swallowing*) Pretty nice 'am.

NOLA (*unimpressed*) Just ham.

MASSON Pretty good.

(*He continues to eat, ravenously now.*)

NOLA (*looking at him*) You're not *starving*!

MASSON I got an appetite. That's all.

NOLA There's more if you'd like it. I hate to see even the *dog* go hungry.

(MASSON *shakes his head. Pushes back the plate. Sucks his teeth.*)

MASSON What's all this with the dogs round 'ere?

NOLA I wouldn't of thought I'd have to explain the habits of dogs to a man like you. Who's been around. Who's been on leave in Egypt.

MASSON (*laughing, showing his teeth, throwing up his head, softly*) Egypt!

NOLA It's her season. That's all. They won't stop pesterin' that poor blessed bitch.

MASSON Ever kept a dog, Nola?

NOLA No. (*Pauses*) I didn't. (*Pause*) Didn't ever have anything against dogs. Just didn't think of having one.

MASSON I had a dog.

NOLA (*glowing*) But a cat. You can cuddle a cat. A cat is soft. . . .

MASSON That dog was my shadder. It could read yer thoughts. Used to lay on me feet in bed.

NOLA (*making a face*) Good job you didn't have a wife.

MASSON I did.

NOLA And did she swaller that dog laying on your feet in bed?

(MASSON *does not answer at first.*)

MASSON She sent it to the vet. While I was away interstate. I didn't see that dog again.

(NOLA *is torn between the directions of sympathy.*)

NOLA Well. . . .

MASSON I loved that dog.

NOLA You do get fond of a pet. But. . . .

MASSON (*turning to her, as if to reveal a great truth*) The dog was honest.

NOLA I don't hold anything against the dog. But think of all those dusty blankets. Your wife now. . . .

MASSON My wife was a rotten, dishonest cow.

NOLA (*brassily, after a pause, taunting*) Are you all that honest, Rowley Masson?

MASSON I'm rotten in parts . . . too. But in different parts.

(NOLA *laughs throatily. Shakes out her hair. Explores the nape of her neck.*)

NOLA Well, we aren't half having a talk!

MASSON Passes the time.

NOLA I'd like to have seen that wife of yours.

MASSON She went on getting skinnier.

NOLA And what became of her?

MASSON There's better things to talk about. . . . I seen 'er last at Sydney Central. Buying a bag of oranges. She got shook on these vitamins they write about in the magazines.

NOLA You're not a lady's man. I can see that.

MASSON There's been women would tell you different.

NOLA That don't mean you're a woman's man.

MASSON Who can say without they find out?

(*They have both overstepped the mark.* NOLA *begins to make up the lounge.*)

NOLA Funny Ern never spoke about Rowley Masson before.

MASSON I think I meant a lot to Ernie. We were in some pretty tough spots.

NOLA That's all very well. But you *talk* about a person. . . .

MASSON Ern feels more than 'e ever lets on.

NOLA You needn't tell me about me own hubby! (*Patting the pillows*) Ern's good. Ern's the best.

MASSON (*moodily*) I wouldn't be one to contradict.

NOLA Gave me all this house. All the latest.

MASSON 'Oo else would?

(NOLA *gulps down her disgust.*)

You'll have to show me yer house, Nola. I ain't seen it. Only the bathroom. That's beaut. Everything working.

NOLA Ernie'll show you the house if you ask him. It's Ernie's house.

(MASSON *very moody at table.*)

(*Standing back from the lounge*) Well, Mr Rowley Digger Masson, I hope you'll get a good night's rest.

(MASSON *throws himself on the lounge.*)

MASSON I oughta! (*Looking at his watch*) It's early enough to please Mum!

NOLA I like to go to bed early. Always when I'm on me own. I like to curl up with a couple of nice magazines.

(*She goes out* BACK *towards the bedroom.* MASSON *starts to take off his tie.*)

(STAGE DARKENS, *and remains for a moment in total darkness. Then* ROY CHILD *is seen in a spot against proscenium arch,* R.)

ROY They're sleeping now. In the brick boxes. In the brick homes. Their dreams are rubbing on one another. There's nothing like friction, even in a dream. Sometimes they call out ... and nobody answers. It's terrible then. But is it worse than when a man forgets the language others speak by daylight? It's most terrible of all not to be able to change love into the currency of words.

I've been sitting alone in the kitchen, writing the book I've got to write. Or have I ... got to? Have I anything to say? Of course I have! Otherwise, *I* would not be *I*. It's only a question of somebody else cracking the code. And somebody must. There's no code that's never been cracked. But till they find the key there are all those torn-up pages ... so many dead intentions. Life in the brick boxes is never so dead as the ghosts of words littering the kitchen floor.

There are times, and places, when night itself is the ghost of what it's meant to be. Here where the owls no longer float, the air won't let their feathers rest. The great trees continue to spread, never quite exorcized. And soon, we can expect the dawn ... the least substantial moment of all ... here where the peewees have died of Thalrat, and teeth grind in the tumblers at thought of another day....

(LIGHT INCREASES.)

(GIRLIE POGSON *and* HARRY KNOTT ENTER *their respective kitchens simultaneously. Mad but shortened breakfast activities.*)

HARRY (*calling*) A nice egg, Mave. Lightly boiled.

GIRLIE (*calling*) The bus, Clive! You'll miss the bus!

(DIGGER MASSON *is fast asleep, almost hidden by bedclothes on the Boyles' lounge.*)

(*Intermittent dogs'* BARKING.)

ROY Turn the razzle-dazzle on!

(RAZZLE-DAZZLE *on. Movements speeded up.*)

They can't spin too fast! Turning in the boxes of the brick homes! Revving up! Revving up!

(CLIVE ENTERS *the Pogson kitchen.*)

CLIVE (*rubbing his hands, ritually*) Eggs, eh?

(MAVIS ENTERS *her kitchen. She is dishevelled, in dressing-gown, holding her hair, her face, herself.*)

HARRY Arr, Mave, I told you....

MAVIS (*sitting down dejected at table*) It's no use, Harry. I don't know any longer where to put meself. It's no longer *my* life. He won't let me alone.

(HARRY *and* CLIVE *in respective kitchens go through mad motions of eating.*)

ROY (*lounging away from his position as commentator*) So it's no use. I must put on life, as the others have been putting on their clothes....

(*He goes up steps as the* RAZZLE-DAZZLE *continues.*)

CLIVE (*eating, glancing at his unopened paper*) No time for the paper this morning. No time. No time. Read it in the train. The train....

GIRLIE As far as I can see, there's never anything *in* the paper. Unless the Queen goes somewhere in that yacht....

(ROY ENTERS *Knott kitchen.*)

MAVIS Wherever have you been, Roy?

ROY Listening to the owls.

MAVIS I never ever heard an owl here. Not since we built.

ROY That doesn't mean there aren't any.

(EXIT ROY, BACK.)

MAVIS (*holding herself*) Never another baby, Harry. Not after this.

HARRY (*laughing*) That's what we say.

MAVIS That's what we say.

(HARRY *grabs his coat.* HARRY *and* CLIVE *kiss their wives simultaneously.*)

GIRLIE (*at a loss, following* CLIVE *to the door*) Now what was it I was trying to remember not to forget?

(GIRLIE *returns to clean up kitchen.* HARRY *and* CLIVE *run down steps simultaneously, as* ERNIE BOYLE ENTERS *from lane.*)

HARRY (*calling over the fence, to* CLIVE) How are we doing, Mr Pogson?

CLIVE Cutting it pretty fine, Harry.

(BOTH EXIT *through their front gardens, as* ERN *mounts the steps and* ENTERS *the kitchen of his house.*)

ERN (*calling*) Nol ... !

(RAZZLE-DAZZLE *stops.*)

(ERN *restrains himself on realizing* MASSON *is asleep on the lounge.* MASSON *does not stir.*)

(NOLA ENTERS, *yawning, in chenille.*)

NOLA (*stretching*) Ah, dear! How was business, Ern?

ERN (*whispering*) Get on all right? (*Indicating*) With Dig, here.

NOLA (*looking for lipstick, and finding*) Oh, we had a yarn.

ERN (*gratified*) You did, eh? What about?

NOLA (*doing lips at mirror*) Mmmm. Oh, about life and things.

ERN Go on!

NOLA And dogs. And wives.

ERN Does 'e like yer?

NOLA You should be asking me whether I like *him!*

ERN Well, you know what I mean.

NOLA By now, I ought to, Ernie.

ERN I'd like yer to like each other. Because we was such good mates.

NOLA (*drily*) I'll try then. I'll try hard.

(*He kisses her carefully on one cheek.*)

Run along, dear, and sweeten up before breakfast.

ERN I was hoping I was always sweet.

(EXIT, ERN, BACK.)

NOLA (*preoccupied, but calling after him*) You are! You're lovely!

(MASSON *stirs, and wakes.*)

MASSON Must have overslept.

NOLA (*busy with breakfast preparations*) People wake up at any old time in this house.

(MAVIS *has come out into her yard. So has* GIRLIE *into hers.*)

GIRLIE (*to* MAVIS, *over the fence*) How're you feeling, dear?

MAVIS Look, I could have been hit all over. It's the kick, kick, kick!

GIRLIE They say it's always easier if it's mobile.

(GIRLIE *has fetched a watering-can, and is filling it at a tap.*)

(MASSON *has risen gingerly from the lounge, behind* NOLA's *back. He is in singlet and V-undershorts. Gropes after his pants, which are lying on a chair.* NOLA *humming and singing. She half-turns, glances, during her work.*)

MASSON Sorry about this.

NOLA (*laughing*) Everybody knows what to expect. (*Pause*) You're better covered than you look, though.

(*She continues with her work.*)

MAVIS (*indicating Boyles', to* GIRLIE) They got a visit in there.

GIRLIE (*holding can firmly*) So it seems.

MAVIS A relative perhaps?

GIRLIE (*swishing her can*) I don't know. And am too discreet to ask.

(MASSON *buttons up his trousers.*)

MASSON (*to* NOLA) I'm gunna make meself scarce today.

NOLA Why?

MASSON Don't wanta impose on anybody.

NOLA That's up to you.

MASSON Later on this arvo I'm gunna take Ernie out and buy him a good time.

NOLA Oh, Ernie's got the money to buy anything he wants. If he wants it.

(MAVIS *has squeezed through the gap in the Pogson-Knott fence.*)

MAVIS You know, Mrs Pogson, I get worried at times.

GIRLIE About what, Mavis?

MAVIS About myself. And this baby. It's getting on my nerves.

GIRLIE (*swishing the can*) Pouff! Plenty of people had a baby!

MAVIS Oh, I know. I know I'm wrong. But I imagine things. Of course, they say everything's only mental.

GIRLIE Oh, go on, Mavis! You've got the evidence to prove some of it isn't!

(GIRLIE *goes off into a thin shriek.*)

(MASSON *has strolled out onto the Boyle back doorstep.*)

MASSON (*to everyone and no one*) Good air! The exhausts haven't taken over in Sarsaparilla. . . .

(GIRLIE *stops laughing when she sees* MASSON. *She is interested, but embarrassed.*)

(*To* GIRLIE) Bit of a gardener.

GIRLIE (*unwilling*) A garden never leaves you alone.

MASSON (*coming down steps, very relaxed, well-built in his singlet*) Old weeds grow like smoke.

GIRLIE (*dashing the water from her can*) Always water, water! (*Primly*) But I'm almost finished. I've got to be.

(GIRLIE *returns to tap to re-fill the can.*)

MASSON Done some gardening meself in me day. Carried off a prize for charm dahlias.

GIRLIE (*almost sentimental*) I like zinnias.

MASSON Give me dahlias. Zinnias are dry.

GIRLIE There's nothing common about zinnias.

(*Finds she cannot turn off the tap.*)

(*Wailing*) Ohhh!

MASSON What's up?

GIRLIE Tap's . . . stuck! It's the washer . . . the thread . . . or some blessed thing. I asked Mr Pogson. . . . (*Struggling with the tap*) But some . . . times . . . you can ask . . . and ask. . . .

(MAVIS *has retreated through the fence to avoid something which might upset her.*)

MAVIS You'll get your feet soaked, Mrs Pogson.

GIRLIE (*wrestling with tap*) What's a person to do? And the rates . . . Mr Pogson says the rates are something crook. . . .

(MASSON *drags off a couple of loose palings from the Boyle-Pogson fence. Scrambles through.*)

MASSON Fix that for yer! Quick and lively!

(*He turns the tap smartly off.*)

(*Laughing*) 'Ow's that for service?

GIRLIE (*grudgingly*) Some men are born handy. . . . (*Looking at the palings*) But I don't know what Mr Pogson will say about the fence.

MASSON Makes it more friendly like.

(ENTER PIPPY *from front garden.*)

(*To* GIRLIE) Fine, sturdy kiddy you got.

(*He tries to pat* PIPPY *on the head, but she frowns, sticks out her lower lip and recoils.*)

GIRLIE I wouldn't know, Mr ... er. ... I see so little of her. Now that you're here, Pippy, you're jolly well coming in to eat your breakfast.

(GIRLIE *starts to mount the steps.*)

(ERN *has come into the Boyle kitchen, rubbing his wet hair with a towel, dressed in pyjamas.*)

NOLA (*calling from the back door*) Digger! (*Noticing her neighbours*) Your breakfast is ready when you are, Mr Masson, and my hubby's waiting.

(GIRLIE *continues on into her kitchen, and prepares to get Pippy's breakfast.*)

MASSON (*squeezing through the fence, shouting*) Okay, Nola! Shan't keep anyone waiting when the *mungareer's* on the table!

(*Runs up the steps and into the Boyle kitchen.*)

You wouldn't stop me with a camel steak....

(PIPPY *remains kicking the ground in the Pogson yard.*)

MAVIS (*leaning on fence*) What's upsetting you, dear?

PIPPY Nothing.

MAVIS You're changing, Pippy. Always running around the streets. A real little larrikin.

PIPPY I've got to run *some*-where! (*After a pause*) It's the dogs, Mrs Knott. I had to go and look at the dogs.

MAVIS (*tossing her head*) The dogs!

PIPPY She's at her hottest now.

(BOYLES *are seated with* MASSON *at their kitchen table. Eating. Talking in undertone. Laughing. Hearty. Happy.*)

MAVIS (*to* PIPPY) That's no way for a big girl to speak. You're growing up. You're different now.

PIPPY (*pausing, looking up, almost frightened*) Different? I'm not any different.

MAVIS Yes, you are. You're a big little girl. Big girls don't talk about things like that.

PIPPY But if things like that happen?

MAVIS They notice them, perhaps. But don't talk.

PIPPY There's too much you don't talk about. You'd pretty soon blow up.

(MAVIS *mounts the steps.*)

MAVIS (*sighing*) Well, that's the way it is. (*Sententious*) Girls've got to learn to be nice. Then they marry some nice man. And have a lot of little babies. . . .

(MAVIS *crosses her kitchen with stolid tread, and* EXIT BACK. PIPPY *is left looking panic-stricken.*)

(*There is an intermittent* BARKING, *punctuated by the snarling of one dog.*)

ERN (*standing, one arm round* NOLA, *one round* MASSON) I know this is the sort of thing a man says when 'e's drunk, but 'ere I am, stone cold sober. This is one of the happiest days. . . . 'Ere we are, all three . . .

NOLA (*embarrassed*) How you carry on, Ern!

MASSON Let's 'ave it, Ernie.

ERN . . . the best of wives . . . and the best of mates . . . and a bugger like me. . . .

(NOLA *extricates herself. Goes about her work.*)

NOLA You're downright soft at times.

PIPPY (*alone in the yard*) Why do they always know? I don't believe they know . . . anything at all . . . or . . . do they?

GIRLIE (*calling*) Pip-py! Come and have your breakfast. Here's your kedgeree.

PIPPY (*her throat contorting*) Kedger-*ee*!

(*She turns and drags up the steps towards the unavoidable.*)

NOLA (*grumbling, at the sink*) . . . sentimental!

MASSON I don't say no to a dose of sentimental . . .

ERN . . . when the organ rises out of the ground . . .

MASSON . . . and the coloured lights are turned on.

NOLA Pffh! You are the men!

(EXIT NOLA, BACK.)

(PIPPY *is stuffing the food down.*)

GIRLIE (*watching*) If you eat like that, you'll swallow a bone, and choke.

PIPPY It didn't ought to have any bones, not if it was made proper.

GIRLIE Grammar, dear! Don't they teach you any grammar? That is as good a dish of kedgeree as you're ever likely to sample. At Rosedale, when I was a girl, it was too far for fish. I would have given my hair for a dish of kedgeree.

(PIPPY *swallows down a glass of milk.*)

PIPPY (*breathless*) Finished!

(*Runs out through the back door.*)

(*To herself*) Now I'm free! I got the whole day. Now I can muck around. And watch the. . . .

(*Remembers, and changes her tune. She continues down the steps, slowly, disconsolate.*)

(*Slowly*) No, I can't. Not now.

(*She reaches the bottom step.*)

If only school would begin. But it won't. Deedree come. But Deedree's backward. Deedree's stupid. I don't know why I put up with Deedree, except we've gone and got used to each other.

(EXIT PIPPY *dawdling into the front garden.*)

(SCENE DARKENS *for a moment.*)

(*In the next picture,* NOLA *is walking in her back yard, in a light of late afternoon. She is dressed in something intended to be summery and gay. It is, in fact, a bit off, without appearing altogether grotesque.*)

(GIRLIE *is ironing in her kitchen.*)

NOLA (*strolling, picking at this and that in the garden, smelling here and there at a flower, soliloquizing*) This is the best time of all. Before the men come. (*However, she looks at her watch*) Even in summer, at the end of the day, when you feel you could have been spat out, when the hair is stuck to your forehead, it is best, best. A time to loiter. The flowers are lolling. The roses are biggest. (*Stoops to smell*) The big, lovely roses, falling with one touch. .

(*Laughs*) I could eat the roses! Dawdling in the back yard. If there was none of these busybodies around (*glancing at the Pogson home*) – thin, prissy, operated women – I'd take off me clothes, and sit amongst the falling roses. I've never felt the touch of roses on my body. (*Examining her bare arm*) Green in the shade. Green for shade. Splotchy. You can imagine the petals, trickling, trickling, better than water, because solid. . . .

(*She looks again at her watch, irritation rising.*)

But the men don't come! They gotta come! When you expect them. Now, or then, it's the same. They gotta come. The men. Standing in bars, with arms round one another's shoulders, faces running together, to tell a bluer story. . . . Men are dirty buggers! But they oughta come. They're expected.

(ERNIE *and* MASSON *appear from the lane. Arms round one another's shoulders. They are fairly drunk. Apparently very happy. They are singing in unison the tune, though not the regrettable words of 'Up Your Pipe, King Farouk. . . .' They open the gate, squeeze through it abreast, into the yard.*)

(*Coldly*) Thought you'd drowned yourself in it.

ERN What can yer do? We just got caught up with some of the boys.

NOLA Oh, I'm not criticizing. It's the steak will criticize. It got itself shrivelled up waiting. A nice piece of topside boot, with black onions. . . .

(NOLA *mounts the steps, and* ENTERS *the kitchen, colder than ever.*)

ERN (*nudging* MASSON, *but less happy now*) Good old Nola!

(*The men proceed to follow her.*)

NOLA (*talking back at them, enunciating very clearly*) I never criticize. I believe in letting the facts explain themselves.

ERN (*stupidly*) Facks. . . .

(*All three have* ENTERED *the kitchen.*)

NOLA (*to* ERN) And you'd better throw it down your throat quick and lively, 'cause you've got the run.

ERN (*very quietly, more sober*) Yes, the run!

(ERN *and* MASSON *sit at table.* NOLA *produces two plates from the oven, puts them in front of the men with scorn. They look at it for a moment, but tuck in with simulated enthusiasm.*)

MASSON (*attempting a kind of professional charm, looking at* NOLA, *more sober than* ERN) I reckon we done you pretty wrong, Nola.

NOLA It don't trouble *me*! A woman might have a whole *bunch* of kids running in late and acting silly.

MASSON Never had any kids?

(*A pause.*)

NOLA (*sullen*) No.

MASSON You ought'uv had a few kids, Ern. Five. Or seven. Seven's lucky, ain't it?

ERN Cut it out!

MASSON Why did you have no kids, Nole?

NOLA (*grimly, quietly*) We tried. But they wasn't in our line.

MASSON (*chanting*) All of us tried! But none of us has anythink to show!

ERN Oh, Gawd! Stuff yer mouth with some of this bloody steak, Dig. (*Turning aggressively*) What's wrong with you, Nola? Aren't you gunna join the banquet?

(NOLA *marches and pulls open the fridge very firmly.*)

NOLA No. I'm going to help myself to a drink.

ERN (*in amazement*) What's bitten . . . ? I never ever seen you have a drink. . . . (*Quietly, remembering*) Once, perhaps.

(NOLA *has taken a bottle from the fridge.*)

NOLA (*pouring*) There's a few things left for you to see me do. (*Downs a good half-glassful*) And it's not bad. It's not bad! Nothing's bad when you're in the right frame of mind.

ERN (*unhappy*) She's not like this, Digger.

NOLA Nobody's like what they're supposed to be.

ERN (*getting up*) Oh, Gawd! The run! I'm gunna reach before the night's out.

NOLA Somebody else's going to reach if you tip the truck into somebody's nice suburb. (*Laughs loud and brassy*) All those cans! (GIRLIE POGSON, *who has been ironing in her kitchen, slams the window shut.* EXIT, BACK.)

MASSON Look 'ere, Nola, give the poor bugger a go!

(NOLA *does not answer. Starts clearing table.*)

ERN (*sad*) Well, good-night. Good-night . . . all.

(*He goes out, down the steps, and* EXIT *by the lane as usual.*)

(MASSON *and* NOLA *are silent at first. When* MASSON *speaks he appears to have sobered up a lot.* NOLA *is still flamboyant with rage and unaccustomed drink.*)

MASSON (*playing with what could be a fork left on the table*) It's my fault, you know.

NOLA There's usually more than one to make a fault.

(*She begins to sing at the sink, wordlessly, rather tuneless, tremolo, but loud.*)

MASSON You're a real tiger.

NOLA (*defiant*) I gotta be a tiger!

MASSON But always were. From the beginning. I can guess that. You was born with stripes on.

NOLA I wouldn't hurt a fly ... if the fly acted decent.

MASSON Ernie ain't a fly.

NOLA (*choking*) No kidding!

MASSON Ernie's just about the most decent bloke alive.

NOLA You know what Ernie means to me. Do you have to go on about it?

MASSON I was just tellin' yer.

(*A silence.* NOLA *flings the water off her arms. Blows her nose.* MASSON *begins to hum, fluctuating, vibrating.*)

(*During this silence* PIPPY *is seen coming in from the street. There is a whine, a whimpering howl, and one or two* BARKS *from under the Pogson house.* PIPPY *runs to the place near the back steps where she usually crawls under.*)

NOLA (*to* MASSON) You seem to bring out the worst in me.

MASSON I'd say it don't look too bad.

NOLA What are you getting at?

MASSON The way you look at blokes. . . . It's turned me to jelly once or twice.

(NOLA *laughs contemptuously.*)

(PIPPY *peers under the family house. There is an isolated* BARK, *then the sound of a* DOG-FIGHT.)

NOLA (*to* MASSON) My trouble is: I've never really liked men. I only needed them.

MASSON My trouble is: I never had a woman I liked. But tried often enough.

NOLA Are you going to get out of Ernie's house tonight?

MASSON (*getting up, looking at her straight*) No.

(EXIT NOLA *to front of house.*)

PIPPY (*watching activities under Pogson house*) It happened then. She's all ... caught up. . . .

(NOLA RE-ENTERS *the kitchen with the pile of bedclothes. Throws it on the lounge.*)

NOLA (*looking at* MASSON) It would be better for everyone if you cleared out.

MASSON It would be better. . . . A lot'ud always be better. . . .

(*He goes towards her, takes her bare arm, examining it as though it were an inanimate object.*)

(*Slowly, remembering aloud*) There was a place near Sidi Haneesh. We drove there once. Pinched a jeep. Me and a bunch of cobbers. There was a sort of oasis in the desert, that the Wogs had left, when the war come their way. There was the mud houses. But deserted then. On the edge of the sea. We took off our clothes, and swam in the sea. I had a slight wound in the groin. The water was that clear, you could see yourself standing in it. From the chest down. Naked.

(*He drops her arm. But she is staring at him and continues, fascinated.*)

PIPPY (*turning her head frantically from side to side, getting up from her knees*) But it's wrong! It's all wrong! I mustn't look any more. It's wrong....

MASSON (*looking at NOLA, entranced*) We lay in the shade. In our skins. And we ate the fruit we found. Because there was fruit growin' there. Vines. (*He takes her breasts and begins to fondle them*) There were juicy, black figs. And yellow melons. I can smell the smell of those melons in the heat. The juice running out of our mouths....

(*He stoops and grinds his mouth on hers.*)

(PIPPY *has run forward* CENTRE *of the Pogson yard.*)

PIPPY (*distraught*) Gee, I wanta talk to somebody. I wanta be with somebody. If Mrs Boyle....

MASSON (*coming up for breath*) ... running ... over ... ripe....

(*He and* NOLA *look at each other, embrace with equal passion, as* PIPPY *catches sight of the new gap in the fence, squeezes through, mounts the Boyle steps.*)

(*To* NOLA) Well?

NOLA (*eyes closed*) You are a bastard. I've known from the start. A plain bastard!

(*She takes him by the little finger, beginning to lead him,* BACK, *into the house.*)

But what does that make *me*?

(*She continues slowly to lead him.*)

(*Sleep-walking, yet bitter*) I was always this kind of a bitch....

The Season at Sarsaparilla

(PIPPY *has been standing against the doorpost, watching the end of the foregoing scene. When* NOLA *and* MASSON *disappear, she trails back down the steps, gets through the fence. Bursts into tears in the Pogson yard, runs up the steps into the kitchen, and through, trying to suppress her sobs.*)

ACT TWO

MAVIS KNOTT *is sitting alone in her kitchen, in the armchair, wearing her nightdress. She looks exhausted. Her head is heavy. She is fanning her face with her hand.*
The other kitchens are empty. The pile of bedclothes on the Boyle lounge has not been disarranged.
There is a BARKING, *but intermittent, and distant now.*
HARRY ENTERS *the* KNOTT *kitchen, apparently from the bathroom. He is wearing his usual well-pressed business pants, but a singlet up top. He is lathering his face.*

HARRY (*anxiously*) Make you a nice cup of tea, Mave?
   (MAVIS *slowly shakes her head. Tragic.*)
MAVIS I could float off in all the cups of tea I drunk. I got up twice in the night and made meself a pot of tea. It's the dogs, the dogs! Bark, bark!
   (*Swaying her head in time*) Under the homes, too. Under your own home.
HARRY But the dogs have gone now. They ran up Ethel Street, the whole mob, after I chased them from under here.
MAVIS The dogs have been going for days. But don't. It's up to the authorities. . . .
HARRY It'll be over soon, Mave. It can't last for ever. Nothing can last for ever.
MAVIS (*sitting up, holding herself*) No. You're right. (*Frightened*) Harry I got a feeling it's going to be today.
   (HARRY *puts down his shaving brush rather jerkily.*)
HARRY (*coming to her, kneeling, holding her, trembling*) Are you sure, Mave? What makes you think?

MAVIS I got a feeling I'm going to be swallowed up by an awful big wave.

HARRY Yeah? Feelings! But is it what the Sister told you?

MAVIS I don't know what the Sister told me. Everybody's been tellin' me so much, I don't know any more what anybody's been tellin'.

(HARRY *gets up, determined.*)

HARRY I'm going to run into Pogsons'.

(*Prepares to go, lather and all.*)

(*As an after-thought, on the kitchen step*) Have a banana?

MAVIS (*shaking her head, wan*) No more bananas.

(HARRY *runs out, down the steps, through the gap in the fence, up the Pogson steps. Loud knocking.*)

HARRY (*calling*) Mrs Pog-son?

(*After a pause,* GIRLIE ENTERS. *She is dressed, but is wearing butterfly clips. Could be without her teeth. Anyway, she averts her face.*)

GIRLIE Whatever is it, Harry? You gave me a fright.

HARRY It's Mavis.

GIRLIE (*eagerly*) Is it the pains?

HARRY I dunno. We don't know. It might be.

GIRLIE Oh, dear! Poor thing!

HARRY Could we use the 'phone? If necessary? Only in an emergency, of course.

GIRLIE Oh dear, yes! I was never one not to co-operate with any neighbour.

HARRY Thanks, Mrs Pogson.

GIRLIE Night or day, Harry, you can use the 'phone. I wouldn't refuse assistance. . . .

(MAVIS *has risen. She is starting to prepare breakfast.*)

HARRY (*to* GIRLIE) I'll be getting back, then.

(*He is already running down the steps.*)

GIRLIE (*at the door, calling after him*) Anything to help a neighbour. . . .

(HARRY *does not reply. Squeezes through the fence, returns to his own kitchen.* GIRLIE *starts to prepare breakfast in hers.*)

HARRY (*entering the kitchen*) Here, what you up to? Lay off!

MAVIS There's your breakfast, isn't there? You'll miss the bus.

HARRY I'm not going to catch the bus today. I'm gunna stay with my wife.

MAVIS (*bursting into tears*) Oh, Harry!

(*They clutch at each other.*)

HARRY (*passionately*) Not today!

MAVIS What'll they say when you don't clock in?

HARRY Whatever they like to. (*Calmer, softer*) I'll ring them later on. (*Soothing her*) Say it's out of the question. My wife.... We're all we've got, Mave!

(*They cling together.*)

MAVIS (*crying, softly*) I used to think you was so awful as a boy.

HARRY (*stiffening*) Eh?

MAVIS Such a streak! All those pimples!

HARRY Lots of boys have pimples before they settle down.

MAVIS (*sighing*) It's marvellous what you have to go through.

(MAVIS *and* HARRY *go* OFF *into the other part of the house.*)

(*At the same time* ENTER CLIVE POGSON *in the kitchen next door.*)

CLIVE (*looking over* GIRLIE's *shoulder*) Eggs, eh?

GIRLIE (*shaking the pan*) Pah! That's what they're sold as. One thing we always had was eggs. Warm from the nest into the pan. And shells! The Rosedale eggs didn't break if you dropped them on the floor.

(*Without paying further attention,* CLIVE *has sat down and opened his paper.*)

CLIVE (*studying paper*) Something is happening in Laos. But what?

GIRLIE If you ask me, the hens are fed on chemicals today ...

CLIVE (*reading*) ... sixteen men shot in Cuba ...

GIRLIE ... and that's what we build the kiddies on.

CLIVE (*reading*) ... revolution in Algeria ...

GIRLIE Poor Mavis! She's for it! I wouldn't mind betting her time is close. It'll be today as near as anything....

(GIRLIE *puts a plate in front of* CLIVE.)

CLIVE (*grimly, throwing paper aside*) ... and the Congolese have violated twenty-seven Belgian nuns.

GIRLIE Ah, the women! It never pays to be a woman.

CLIVE (*grimmer*) If it's any consolation to you, Girlie, they did a Pakistani colonel, too.

(GIRLIE *recoils.* CLIVE *starts to eat.*)

GIRLIE Clive, there are certain things that . . . in the home . . . are not, well . . . nice.

(*She stands twisting the pot-holder, almost crying.*)

When we were girls at Rosedale, we were taught just how far a person may go, in conversation, or . . . life. We were educated, you might say, to look at things *ethically*. All the young fellows who visited us at Rosedale were hand-picked country stock. . . .

CLIVE You've said it!

GIRLIE (*wound up, so that she does not hear*) Mother wouldn't have tolerated horseplay . . . or words. With the result that, when it came to choosing partners, Kath and Isa both paired off with decent, steady graziers. I was allowed to marry you, because . . . because they gave in to me.

CLIVE (*pushing back his plate*) Girlie, I never told you that I've *had* Rosedale, and all you girls! All the borer activity in the veranda posts and flooring, to say nothing of the three-legged cedar furniture. I've had my two-no-hoper, cow-cocky brothers-in-law, and might have had that bullocky, my father-in-law, as well. But he died, at least, before the mortgages caught up with him, belting hell out of his team, two miles the other side of the Railway Hotel at Mungindribble.

(GIRLIE *is punctured.*)

GIRLIE (*tearful*) Sometimes I think you've changed, Clive . . . that you don't care for me any more.

CLIVE Your trouble, Girlie: you think a honeymoon can be made to last twenty years.

GIRLIE Sometimes I think it's since my operation.

CLIVE Your operation! (*Moments of perception*) Perhaps I had an operation, too! Only it wasn't by the knife. A man can't stand up to the cheese-grater for twenty years, without he loses a bit of himself.

(GIRLIE *wipes her eyes.*)

GIRLIE Nice thoughts for two people to have! Before breakfast's finished, even.

134

CLIVE (*easing off*) Yairs. (*Clearing his throat*) Yairs. (*In more normal, mechanical vein*) You've got February to look forward to.

GIRLIE (*unnaturally bright, equally mechanical*) The rented cottage on the coast. The same work in a different setting.

CLIVE You've got your own home. Everything paid off.

GIRLIE We've got our health. And Medical Benefits in case....

CLIVE And a life insurance policy besides.

BOTH (*looking at one another, in unison*) What more can anyone expect?
(*Here they return to a more naturalistic delivery.*)

GIRLIE And so much happening. There's always something going on. Clive, do you know what?

CLIVE No. What?

GIRLIE (*jerking her head towards the Boyles' side*) Something's going on in there.

CLIVE How do you know?

GIRLIE I don't. But smell it. It has a really very nasty smell.

CLIVE Grease trap?

GIRLIE (*sucking her teeth, contemptuously*) Tathh! It's the friend! The friend that came. And stayed. Something not at all above board is happening over there.

CLIVE It's no business of ours.

GIRLIE It's no bus . . .! We're the parents, let me remind you, of two young and impressionable girls.

CLIVE They don't go round expecting to catch every second man with his pants off. Not unless you teach them to.

GIRLIE Clive, I . . .!
(GIRLIE *sweeps into a position of protest which promises to become tearful, only* JUDY ENTERS *from front of house, forcing her to disguise her feelings.*)
(JUDY *proceeds to get herself tea and toast. She is very detached.*)
Clive, I wonder whether you would see that Miss Dickerson at Farmers' Corsets, and fetch my bra that they were doing the alterations on.

CLIVE (*outraged*) Catch *me*! Carrying a parcel with a bloomin' brazeer inside!

JUDY Oh, go on, Dad! Mr Boyle carries flowers.

CLIVE Mr Boyle is Mr Boyle. He couldn't get any lower if he tried.

GIRLIE (*sighing, resigned*) Your father is difficult this morning.

(PIPPY *comes in from bedrooms. Her hair is very carefully done. She is carrying a book. Sits down. Starts her cereals. Spreads book beside her on table.*)

CLIVE (*heavily paternal, to* PIPPY) Haven't you got 'good-morning' for your old dad?

PIPPY Hello.

(*She kisses him casually from where she sits. Starts eating and reading.*)

(*More stylized delivery from* ALL *during the following thought sequence.*)

GIRLIE Wonder whether I ordered the three lambs' fry, wonder whether blue is right for Elvie's wedding, whether the shoes, whether the thread, whether the radio licence is due. . . .

JUDY Now that the music has died in me, I wonder whether the silences will grow any less intense. I wonder whether I shall find a meaning, standing behind the counter, or sitting at the desk.

(ROY ENTERS *the Knott kitchen from bedrooms as* JUDY *begins her piece. Potters about, getting himself coffee and bread, sits down finally with book propped in front of him.*)

CLIVE (*looking at his watch*) Time to go. Time to go. At least it's time to bugger off. Get in the train. Burrow in with a lot of men. Smell of papers. Smell of smoke. You can relax along with a lot of blokes. Men, on the whole, ask the questions you expect. . . .

PIPPY (*reading, to herself, in same tone as the others who have spoken in this thought sequence*) 'After the death of Galerium, Valeria's ample possessions provoked the avarice, and her personal attractions excited the desires of his successor, Max . . . (*carefully*) Max-im-im. He had a wife still alive; but divorce was permitted by the Roman law, and the fierce passions of the tyrant demanded an immediate gratification. . . .'

GIRLIE (*as a matter of course*) What ever are you up to, Pippy?

PIPPY (*with cold logic*) Reading.

GIRLIE Well!

CLIVE (*tickling the back of Pippy's neck*) I wouldn't strain yourself, sweetheart. You won't be your father's girl.

(CLIVE *takes his hat.* GIRLIE *offers her cheek. He goes down steps, and* EXIT *through front garden.*)

GIRLIE Now there's something I meant to say to your father. To say . . . or ask. . . . What was it? But in the end, of course, you never do say to people half the things you mean to. Pippy, the sausages are keeping warm. Judy, are you happy? I no longer hear you practise on that violin.

JUDY Yes, Mother, I'm happy. But. . . .

GIRLIE I often wonder whether everyone is happy. Everybody ought to be. There's nothing to make them *un*-happy. But the violin, Judy. Why don't you play your piece . . . do your scales?

JUDY I've decided, Mother, I'm not very good. I shan't go back to the Con. when term begins.

GIRLIE (*aghast*) Nonsense! After all we've paid? Your father's going to be ropeable!

(ENTER DEEDREE *from front garden.*)

JUDY (*to* GIRLIE) I could pay the money back . . . when I've made it . . . in some job.

GIRLIE (*sucking her teeth*) First one thing! Then another! You never know what's going on in a person's mind.

JUDY I expect there's usually rather a muddle. But in mine the muddle no longer exists. (*Standing up, coolly*) Now that I've decided. (*In an uncertain, breaking tone*) I'm quite empty.

GIRLIE And the violin? But I suppose there'll be a buyer for the violin. Like anything else. There's always someone for everything.

(DEEDREE *has climbed the steps, and now stands at the door.*)

DEEDREE Morning, Mrs Pogson. Morning, Judy. Morning, Pippy. (ALL *greet her, though without ceremony, and* PIPPY *does not look up from her book.*)

What's up, Pippy? I never ever see you now.

PIPPY (*continuing to read*) Nothing. (*Looking up in annoyance*) Saw me yesterday! Anyway, what's up with *you*? You look queer.

DEEDREE I don't feel good. I been drinking ink.

PIPPY (*contemptuous*) Whatever for?

DEEDREE Monica Jeffreys dared me to.

PIPPY (*snorting*) Monica Jeffreys!

DEEDREE Said it would show up in me veins, like I was one of those dyed flowers.

(JUDY *gets up, descends steps, goes* OFF *towards street. Preoccupied.*)

(*To* PIPPY) What you doing?

PIPPY (*superior*) Studying.

DEEDREE Ah! (*She is too mystified to say more immediately. Tentatively*) Why?

PIPPY (*looking up*) I'm different now.

GIRLIE Different I would like to think!

(GIRLIE *goes* OFF *into other part of house.*)

DEEDREE (*to* PIPPY) What's happened to yer?

PIPPY (*in a wistful trance*) Everything's changed. Everything's different now.

DEEDREE Aren't you gunna come and find the dogs?

PIPPY They've gone away.

DEEDREE But not right away. I seen them early. She's started to bite them when they try it on.

PIPPY That means it's going to be over soon.

DEEDREE Well, anyway, aren't we gunna muck around at something?

PIPPY No.

(RE-ENTER GIRLIE, BACK.)

GIRLIE Pippy, dear, come and help me turn the mattresses. Some mornings they get that heavy.

PIPPY (*flat*) Yes, Mum.

GIRLIE (*looking at her closely for a moment*) There's nothing wrong with you, is there?

PIPPY No. Why?

GIRLIE I just wondered.

(PIPPY *and* GIRLIE EXIT, BACK.)

DEEDREE (*calling, sad*) 'Bye, Pippy!

PIPPY (*calling, OFF*) 'Bye!

(DEEDREE *turns, goes down the steps.*)

DEEDREE Everyone turns funny at times. I wonder if there's anything wrong with me. I wonder whether I got a smell. . . .

(ROY *is no longer reading the book he had started. He has laid his head on a castle of fists, on the kitchen table, and is sorting out his thoughts.*)

ROY (*dreaming*) . . . not if I hung around here . . . slaving and scratching . . . saving up in a hundred years. . . . Better to cut now. Work my passage. . . .

(DEEDREE *is crossing the Pogson yard, preparatory to going out through front garden.*)

(ENTER JUDY, *apparently from letter-box, with a handful of letters, and a parcel from which she is unknotting the string.*)

DEEDREE (*to* JUDY) You got a parcel.

(JUDY *continues unwrapping. Preoccupied. Smiling, but to herself.*)

JUDY (*vague, noticing* DEEDREE) Oh, yes. Yes, Deedree!

(*She continues to unwrap.*)

DEEDREE (*glum*) No one ever sends me a parcel . . . without I send a coupon. . . .

(EXIT DEEDREE *to street.*)

ROY (*in same position, dreaming*) . . . Mauritius, Réunion, St Helena . . . Samoa, Pitcairn, Galapagos. . . . All the world . . .!

(JUDY, CENTRE *of Pogson yard, finally tears off the wrappings.*)

JUDY (*wryly, tenderly, laughing, but sadly, looking at a book*) Volume Two!

(*She starts to go up steps into the Pogson kitchen.*)

(ROY *throws aside his book.*)

ROY (*in motion, oppressed by his surroundings*) . . . get involved in something! Wars and revolutions are laid on in each hemisphere for those who want to let their blood! Or someone else's. Perhaps it's necessary to kill a man in order to live. . . .

(*He comes out of the kitchen onto the step.* JUDY *has been hesitating.*)

JUDY Roy?

(*Puts the mail down on a step. Descends.*)

ROY (*absent*) Hello, Judy.

JUDY Do you think Mavis wants any help?

ROY (*shrugging*) Oh . . . Mavis. . . .

(JUDY *comes through gap in fence.*)

JUDY Or anyone?

ROY Or anyone! The trouble is: when it comes to the point, you've got to help yourself.

(*He joins her in the Knott yard.*)

JUDY Roy, I came to tell you I decided to take your advice.

ROY That's rash! On what?

JUDY The violin. I've decided to give it away.

ROY (*sincerely, as if he has forgotten about all advice given*) Oh, but isn't that foolish? To throw away your talent?

JUDY My little talent!

ROY I mean, such as it was, of course. (*In nostalgic vein*) You could have played your piece...

JUDY (*catching the same tone of faintly ironic, yet wistful, nostalgia*) ...to entertain the relatives...

ROY ...as they sit on Sunday afternoon...

JUDY ...waiting for the scones to appear...

ROY ... and the fluffy sponge. (*Reverting to naturalistic delivery*) What will you do, Judy, instead?

JUDY I shall become a tier-up of parcels. Or I may even aim higher. A business career. I dare say my touch will learn to adapt itself to the machine, and my shorthand will give up some of its secrets.

ROY Oh, God! And what about life?

JUDY That is life. The way I begin to see it, it has a fascinating regularity.

ROY But it's just from that that we're trying to escape!

JUDY And then there's marriage. I suppose one can reasonably expect....

ROY You're touching, Judy!

JUDY (*wincing*) There are others.

ROY And will you write to me?

JUDY Write?

ROY When I've gone.

JUDY (*laughing*) Oh yes, when you've gone!

ROY Because I'm going.

JUDY When?

ROY Today...tomorrow...I don't know when. But soon. I'll work my way. I've got to, got to go....

JUDY But what will you find?

ROY That is what I must find out.

JUDY It's difficult to understand the things I don't want to happen.

ROY With women, perhaps it's different. They're more vegetable than men. Provided the bed's well-dug, they take the shapes that are expected of them.

(*He looks closely at* JUDY.)

But you're not all that vegetable, Judy. My pretty Judy! Can you resist coming along?

JUDY Just like that?

ROY A stewardess, perhaps. You'd look smashing. So obviously disguised.

JUDY And in the streets of great cities, I'd need every bit of every possible disguise . . . as I listened to you learn the language of the diamond women.

ROY Well, a few phrases, certainly. Everyone should learn to communicate.

JUDY And what about Julia?

ROY (*shouting*) Julia!

JUDY But I thought you were in love with her?

ROY Julia's hell!

JUDY And I thought you loved her!

ROY Oh, I could always burn with Julia. She's pretty cold fire, though. (*Indicating*) Talk of the devil!

(JULIA SHEEN *appears from the lane. She is wearing something very simple. She is changed. Pale. White lips. Hatless. Hair even a bit unkempt. She comes in at the Knotts' gate.*)

JULIA (*looking from* JUDY *to* ROY) I came to see . . . someone. . . .

JUDY (*suspicious*) But what is it, Julia? Are you ill?

JULIA Not really. Stocktaking.

ROY No assignments today?

JULIA None. Or none that I didn't cancel. It's not a job that matters very much. Perhaps that's even why I chose it.

(JULIA *sits down on the steps.*)

(*Laughing rather hysterically*) So here I am. Craving for company. Languishing for conversation.

(ROY *and* JUDY *look at her.*)

Tell me something. I'm all agog. Who is the sanitary man's wife sleeping with this year? Or is it week?

(*She laughs again, and claps her hands to her face, holding them very stiff and straight.*)

JUDY (*compassion rising, going and sitting beside* JULIA) Something's happened! Do tell us!

JULIA (*taking* JUDY'S *hands*) Darling Judy, whose only fault is that she's a human being!

JUDY Tell us, Julia!

JULIA Oh, nothing. Nothing that can't be put right.

(RON SUDDARDS *has come in from the Pogson front garden. He approaches the Pogson steps. Climbs. Finds the book which Judy has abandoned there earlier on. On this occasion his dress shows an attempt at the casual.*)

Roy is no doubt ruthless enough to be able to devise the quickest way.

JUDY Of course. . . . It was Roy you came to see. Of course. . . .

(JUDY *gets up, hiding a renewed unhappiness.*)

Roy will advise some . . . thing.

(*She goes towards the fence. Realizing the others are in the next garden,* RON *begins to take notice.*)

ROY (*not altogether happy at being left alone with* JULIA) Here, steady on! Three heads are better than two.

JUDY (*with a trace of cynicism*) When one is off its form?

(*She gets through the fence.*)

RON Hello, Judy.

(*He comes down to her, still holding the abandoned book.*)

JUDY Hello, Ron. Not at the post office?

RON I'm on holiday.

JUDY I thought it was still some way off.

RON I managed to arrange it. Seeing as . . . so many others . . . are on holiday now.

ROY (*with* JULIA) Well, Julia, aren't we telling?

JULIA That's what I came here for.

RON (*with* JUDY) I see you got the book.

(*He and* JUDY *go towards the Pogson steps.*)

JUDY Oh, the book! Yes, I'd forgot. . . . Yes, that was sweet of you, Ron.

RON I dropped it in early. Then I thought I'd come around . . . and see. . . .

(RON *and* JUDY ENTER *the Pogson kitchen.*)

JULIA (*to* ROY) . . . and obviously must. It's not very difficult to
tell. I'm in a spot of trouble.

ROY Trouble? What sort . . . of . . .?

JULIA Oh, the old-fashioned kind! Quite uncomplicated really.
I've known for some time now. It didn't seem to matter. Was
even a kind of *gesture*. Then, one morning, you wake up. Dogs
are barking. The sky is ablaze. People are asleep in other rooms.
The furniture is so . . . wooden. . . . It is suddenly TERRIFYING!

ROY Was it Mr Erbage?

JULIA It could have been. Or it could have been his double. In my
carelessness, I was always careful to choose a man of substance.
It's the wives who spoil everything.

ROY And what do you expect me to do?

JULIA (*laughing and crying*) I don't . . . really . . . know.
(JUDY *and* RON *have sat down at Pogson's kitchen table.* JUDY *has
opened the book, but her mind is obviously not concentrating on it.*)

JUDY (*letting the pages drift*) You're so kind. But I'm afraid I'm not
the person you think me to be.

RON You're the person I know you are.

JUDY But so superficial. *Volume One*, Ron . . . it kills me just to
look at it.

JULIA (*to* ROY, *quieter*) But hoped you might find an answer of
some kind.

ROY (*scratching his head*) To such a very personal question?

JULIA Because I thought you were fond of me.

ROY Fond? Yes, fond.

JULIA Fond is a cool word.

ROY Because that's what I imagined you wanted.

JULIA (*jumping up*) Yes! Oh, yes! You are right!

ROY Can you expect me to be more?

RON (*to* JUDY) I didn't expect you to read that book. Not exactly.

JUDY Then why did you lend it to me?

RON I dunno. It's hard to say. I thought, I suppose, that if you had
it, it would help to bring us closer.

ROY (*to* JULIA) Don't get me wrong. I do genuinely sympathize.

JULIA (*sighing*) Yes. After your fashion. I suppose you do. After
all, we're two of a kind. We've never given ourselves to any extent.

ROY I should have thought you've had a pretty good try.

JULIA (*coldly*) I have never given myself. Any more than you have ventured down . . . off the fence . . . into life.

(JULIA *starts to leave.*)

ROY And what about the child?

JULIA He won't be the first child who hasn't had to suffer.

(*She goes out the gate the way she came.*)

ROY (*calling*) Julia! If you're going short in any way. . . .

JULIA (*brutally*) One thing I'll never do is go short.

(EXIT JULIA *down the lane.*)

RON (*very awkward, to* JUDY) I could bring you as close as it is possible to get. If you'd let me.

JUDY Oh, Ron, Ron, how do you know what is possible?

RON Anything is possible if you want it.

(ROY *has entered the Knott kitchen. He turns for a moment, facing the audience.*)

ROY Did Julia hit the nail! She drove it in right up to the head! (*With an expression of amazed horror*) And I'm not even hurt!

(EXIT ROY, BACK.)

JUDY (*to* RON) If I could love you. . . .

RON (*clenching his fists on the table, very awkward, but determined*) I'll make you, Judy. I'm going to make you. . . .

(ROWLEY MASSON ENTERS *the Boyle kitchen from front part of house. Dressed in trousers and shirt. Throws his coat on back of the lounge.*)

(GIRLIE POGSON ENTERS *from front of her house, interrupting the scene between* RON *and* JUDY.)

GIRLIE (*to* RON) Oh, Mr Suddards, I didn't recognize you. All dressed up. Or quite *un*-dressed, you might say. For you.

RON Getting the smell of post office ink out of me nose. The air hits you when you start to breathe it again.

GIRLIE Has Judy told you she's leaving the Con? Quite the independent young lady. A business career.

RON No, she didn't tell me.

GIRLIE You don't seem at all surprised. Perhaps guessed.

RON No. I know nothing. I only know that Judy will always decide what is best.

(MRS POGSON *looks at him with some interest but does not comment.*)

(MASSON *has come out onto the Boyle steps. He is ill at ease. Unhappy.*)

GIRLIE (*to* RON) I won't say my girls will grow up unable to make up their minds. That is something they'll have from their mother.

JUDY (*ashamed*) Oh, dear! *Mum!*

GIRLIE Competent! Even little Joyleen can run up a batch of fairy cakes. And Judy. . . . That reminds me, Judy, you promised to cut out the yoke, dear, for the dress I'm going to wear to Elvie's wedding.

(RON *gets up.* GIRLIE *fusses her way* OFF, BACK.)

RON When you're ready to say it, Judy. . . .

JUDY (*distracted*) I'm struck dumb!

RON Give it time. Give it time. You'll find your voice.

JUDY But shall I be able to learn to speak . . . all over again?

(EXIT JUDY, BACK. RON *comes out, and down the Pogson steps.*)

RON (*catching sight of* MASSON) Enjoying your holiday?

MASSON To tell the truth, I'm wonderin' whether to cut it short.

RON Not bad news?

MASSON Nah. Not yet, anyway.

(RON *continues on his way.*)

Got the time on yer, mate?

RON (*looking at his watch*) Twenty-to-ten. Or must be near enough. I set it yesterday arvo. By the P.O. clock.

MASSON (*unhappier*) Late. He's late.

RON Expecting someone.

MASSON Ernie Boyle. Should be comin' in from 'is run.

RON Ah! Overtime perhaps.

(EXIT RON *through the Pogson front garden.*)

(NOLA ENTERS *the Boyle kitchen. She is looking awful. Chenille, as usual, but this morning she does not look for the lipstick to do her lips. Slops about getting breakfast.* MASSON *apparently realizes she is there. Looks round casually, and discreetly looks away. Starts to whistle: 'Up Your Pipe, King Farouk. . . .' Leaves off. Goes down into the yard, mooning around.*)

MASSON I reckon it's time I got going. Down this way you can smell the frost even when there's a heat wave on. Get back north. They're easy-goin' up there.

(PIPPY *comes out of the Pogson house. Marching primly, as though on an errand.* MASSON *catches sight of her over the fence.*)

(*Calling*) How're you doin', sis?

(PIPPY *looks at him. Ignores. Continues* OFF *through front garden.*) Christ! Even the kids! (*Pauses*) And the dogs. . . . (*Listening*) I never heard a dog in Sarsaparilla this last half-hour.

(NOLA *calls from the kitchen without coming to the door.*)

NOLA There's breakfast if you want some.

MASSON (*turning, unenthusiastic*) I suppose a man's gotta keep body and soul together.

(*Goes up the steps.* NOLA *is moving about. Takes no notice of* MASSON. *He sits down. She might be a waitress in a railway refreshment room. It is as if they both agree it should be that way.*)

NOLA (*shoving a plate in front of* MASSON) It's cold this morning.

MASSON It's not warm.

NOLA I mean I couldn't be bothered cooking a lot of stuff.

MASSON You've gotta draw the line somewhere.

NOLA I got a head.

(*She helps herself to Aspro. Swallows with the help of water. Coughs open-mouthed.* MASSON *begins to eat. Detached.*)

(*Coughing huskily*) Like a termarter with it?

MASSON No, thanks.

NOLA (*rummaging*) Just as well. I don't think there is any.

(*He continues to eat, she to sniff and slop as if on her own. Gets herself a cup of something. Lights a cigarette. Blows smoke out of her nostrils.* NOLA *comes and sits at the table, but sideways. Sipping. Tossing the slipper on her toes.* NOLA *looks at her watch, calmly though.* MASSON *appears increasingly unhappy. Pushes his plate back.*)

(*Flat, without malice, and without looking at* MASSON) You didn't like your breakfast much.

MASSON I didn't say so.

(NOLA *blows smoke.*)

I got no appetite. (*Rubbing the back of his neck*) I got twinges in me neck.

NOLA Must of twisted it.

MASSON Yeah. We're not as young as....
(Breaks off with distaste. NOLA remains expressionless.)
(After a pause) Expect you'll be glad to see the end of me.
(NOLA continues to sip, thoughtful.)

NOLA That's a pretty difficult question.

MASSON Well, I mean . . . it won't look so bad . . . when I'm off
the place.

NOLA *(bitterly)* Nothing can make things look any better than they
are.
(MASSON gets up.)

MASSON *(touching the back of her chair)* Sorry, Nola.

NOLA I'm not one that's due for pity.
*(She has turned round, and is sitting with her elbows on the table,
holding the cup in both hands, drinking in great animal gulps.)*

MASSON *(indicating neat pile of bedclothes on the lounge)* Aren't you
gunna muck up these blankets a bit?
(NOLA shakes her head. Continues to brood over her cup.)

MASSON There's no point in asking for it.

NOLA I'm not asking for nothing. You can't hide a pumpkin in a
bed, even when you've gone and messed up the blankets.

MASSON *(distracted)* But you're gunna make it worse for Ern.
(NOLA turns her face aside.)

NOLA *(taut, speaking parrotwise)* The best mate you ever had!
(Quieter) Don't start that Ern stuff. He's my husband.

MASSON You acted like it!

NOLA *(beating the table with her fists)* Yes! Oh, yes! Yes, yes, yes!
(Calms down as quickly as she flared up.)
(Passive) I know how my joints are greased. *(Getting up, groggily)*
I am what I am. Just about the dishonestest cow. *(Fingering the
pile of bedclothes, thoughtful)* But don't you think a person can act
a bit honest in dishonesty?

MASSON *(not quite ironic)* If you're goin' in for the finer points. . . .
*(NOLA has suddenly bustled into activity. Getting another break-
fast.)*
But I'm not a bloke to start advisin' a woman on moral issues. No
more than you're a woman as can take advice.

(NOLA *continues with her work.*)

NOLA (*tersely*) Choke yourself, Rowley. Ern's here.

MASSON (*glancing about, very uncomfortable*) Where?

NOLA In the lane.

MASSON How d'you know?

NOLA I heard 'im. I've not been listening for Ern all these years and not know when he's at the gate.

(*A listless* BARKING *of dogs, ending in a whining, and a long howl.*)

(ERN *comes up to the back gate. He is in his shirt sleeves, carrying his coat as usual, but lacking in his customary buoyancy.* NOLA *works.* MASSON *fidgets.* ERN *comes up the steps into the kitchen.*)

ERN (*low-pitched, to* MASSON) How are yer?

MASSON (*rather high*) Okay, Ernie! Okay!

(ERN *throws down his coat. Stands for a moment staring at the pile of undisturbed bedclothes on the lounge.*)

NOLA (*at the stove, tentatively*) Gunna have your shower, Ern?

ERN Nah.

NOLA (*without looking up*) Oh! *Why?*

ERN (*sitting down heavily at table*) I'm tired. (*Wiping his face with his hand*) Tired.

NOLA (*very kind and gentle, coming forward with a plate of something*) I warmed up some of the brown stew. (*Coaxing*) Remember how you used to like stew for breakfast?

(ERN *looks at it dully.*)

(*Very contrite*) You used to say you never liked nothing better.

(ERN *takes his knife and fork.*)

ERN Sometimes you get sick of things. If they're dished out too often.

NOLA (*choking*) Well, that's what it is. Stew. (*She retires to back of kitchen*) It's sometimes hard to think of things. Day after day....

(ERN *eats.*)

Well, I'm gunna turn out the front of the house. If there's anything you want, Ern....

(*She takes the pile of bedclothes.* EXIT NOLA, BACK, *without looking at either of the men.*)

(ERN *continues eating.*)

MASSON (*after a pause*) Reckon I've outstayed my welcome.

ERN I didn't say it.

MASSON Reckon I'll catch the evenin' train to Brizzy.

ERN Pretty hot up there by now.

MASSON That's right.

(*Pause.* MASSON *has something he can't quite get off his chest.*)

(*At last*) Oh, Christ, Ern!

(ERN *messes his stew about, listens very intently.*)

I was thinkin' in the night. . . . Remember it was just before Christmas . . . that Jerry that sneaked up on us outside Capewzo? He would'uv got me. Only you stuck 'im first.

(ERN *has stuffed his mouth.*)

ERN (*through full mouth, staring ahead*) Yeah.

(*Pause.*)

MASSON Well, see yez some more, Ernie!

ERN (*staring ahead, chewing*) See yer some more.

(MASSON *puts on his coat, crosses towards door into yard.*)

ERN (*as the knife of realization twists again*) 'Ere!

(*He jumps up.* MASSON *turns.* ERN *socks him one.* MASSON *half-falls against the edge of the table. They look at each other just for a moment.* MASSON *gets up.* EXIT *the way he arrived.*)

(NOLA *comes in just before this.*)

NOLA Want some more, Ernie?

ERN No. I've had enough. Of everything.

(*He turns.* EXIT ERN *to front part of house. He is walking slowly, unsteadily, his shoulders hunched.*)

(NOLA *continues on through the kitchen, and down the steps, like a sleep-walker.*)

NOLA The terrible thing about a conscience is it don't stay with you all the time. It walks out, and lets you down. When you're weak.

(*She reaches the bottom of the steps. Twists off a flower.*)

I'm weak. (*Tearing the flower. Walking and meditating*) There are times when the flesh lies too easy on your bones. When even the air tickles your skin, in the places where it can get at you most. I can't help it if I want to dance at odd moments. Or if somebody else joins in. After all, I'm only half-wanting what I can't help. (*Throws away the flower she has been tearing, disgusted*) I would like to be left in peace with what I respect most, and love. Not kill. (*In a panic of shivers*) I don't wanta *kill*! Thank Gawd, I never ran the knife all that far. Or did I! (*Holding her head, in agony*) Have I? You do if you keep at it! (*Throwing up her head in a blaze of protest*) Whether you like it or not. (*After a pause, choking, running her hands down her flanks*) It's this blasted body! It's put together wrong. If your hips was to work different. . . . Or there weren't none of those pulses in your throat. (*Looking up at the Pogson house, bitterly*) I bet some women aren't all that good. They just haven't got the kind of glands it takes to make a person go to the pack.

(PIPPY *returns from her errand. Approaching from front garden, she* ENTERS *the Pogson yard. Quickly realizes* MRS BOYLE *is in hers. Advances cautiously, hoping to make the back steps without becoming involved in conversation.*)

(*Looking over the fence, immense relief*) Is that you, Pippy?

PIPPY (*embarrassed, cautious, mincing slightly*) Yes.

NOLA Oh, I'm so glad to see you! I haven't seen you, Pippy, since I don't know when.

PIPPY It was only yesterday, Mrs Boyle.

NOLA Was it? Well, a lot has happened. I mean . . . I've been sort of busy. Had a few problems on me mind. . . .

(PIPPY *has continued standing, out of politeness, but remains silent. A look of isolation about her.*)

NOLA Then you begin to miss the faces you haven't noticed.

(PIPPY *silent.* NOLA *senses something.*)

NOLA (*in desperation*) You remember once we said how good it would be if only there was a hole in that fence, so as you could crawl through, and we could comfort each other? Well, there! (*Pointing*) Somebody's made the hole!

PIPPY Yes. That was Mr Masson.

NOLA Oh, I don't care who *did* it!

PIPPY Dad says Mr Masson is liable. He went real crook.

NOLA (*sighing*) Ah, we can put it back then. If it'll make anybody feel safe. (*Pause*) You'll never cure some people of being afraid.

(PIPPY, *after seeming to hesitate, accepts a challenge.*)

PIPPY I'll come through, if you want me to.

NOLA (*snooty*) I don't want you to do anything your parents wouldn't want.

PIPPY (*squeezing through*) Oh, them!
(*She seems to recover something of her old form at mention of her parents.*)
I do what I want, you know. I only let them think I don't.

NOLA (*putting an arm round* PIPPY) That's all right, so long as you don't do too much of it.
(*They stroll a little, describing an arc in the yard before approaching the steps.* PIPPY *walks very stiffly inside the encircling arm.*)

NOLA (*encouraging*) Well now, it's quite like old times.

PIPPY I dunno.

NOLA No. You got something. It's not. It's never the same again.
(*Pause, as they mount the steps.*)
(*Hopefully*) Aren't you gunna tell me something? What about those blessed dogs you was always talking about.
(PIPPY *is embarrassed. They stand together on the steps.*)

PIPPY I'm not all that interested in dogs any more.

NOLA Oh?

PIPPY Anyhow, they're going away. I think it's going to be over soon.

NOLA Could be. They was at it long enough.

PIPPY Anyway, I don't like dogs. Dogs are dirty.

NOLA (*surprised*) You were such a one for dogs before.

PIPPY But they're dirty. You didn't ought to take any notice of them when they carry on like that.

NOLA They're teaching you fast! (*Sadly, nodding her head*) Well, perhaps it's all for the best.
(NOLA *goes on up the steps.* PIPPY *remains half-way up.*)

PIPPY I mean, you can notice, but you mustn't look.

NOLA (*laughing softly, sadly*) That's the way it is! (*In the doorway*) Aren't you coming in, Pippy?

PIPPY What ... in there?

NOLA It won't give you leprosy!
(PIPPY *glances over her shoulder at her own home.*)
But if your mum and dad are in any way....
(PIPPY *marches up the steps, and enters the kitchen behind* NOLA.)

(*Delighted, expanding again*) There! (*Fussing around*) I'm gunna give you a treat.

PIPPY (*doubtful*) What?

NOLA (*searching for something*) If I can find it. . . . (*Searching*) I got a box of marshmallers stuck away somewhere.

PIPPY (*wrinkling her nose, but politely*) Oh.

NOLA Don't you like marshmallers, Pippy? I've always liked marshmallers. (*Finding*) There! They're that soft. Scenty, too. (*She offers, and* PIPPY *takes unenthusiastically.*)

PIPPY I like paddlepops best.

NOLA (*stuffing her mouth*) That's all right! But how am I gunna produce paddlepops out of me fanny adams for every little casual girl?

PIPPY (*laughing her head off*) Fanny adams!

NOLA (*laughing too*) Well?

PIPPY (*choking*) It's funny.

NOLA What's true is often funny too. (*Sighing*) Ah, dear!

PIPPY (*frowning at the marshmallow*) This has got a sort of funny smell.

NOLA That's the scent. (*Surprised*) Don't you like it?

(PIPPY *wrinkles her nose again. Does not answer. Takes small, careful bites.*)

(*Through full mouth*) I think it's lovely.

PIPPY (*thawing, looking about her*) It's lovely in here.

(*She walks around, examining things. Carefully puts her marshmallow down somewhere.*)

NOLA What's so different about it?

PIPPY (*prowling*) Oh, I dunno. You can be natural in it.

(NOLA *looks glum.*)

(*Landing on the sofa*) This lounge!

(*She wriggles about on it.*)

NOLA (*contemptuously*) That old thing! Springs are gone.

PIPPY (*trying to bounce*) No, they're not. Not this end. All our furniture's stuffed too full. And Mum won't let us do anything on it.

NOLA (*quietly*) I hate that old lounge. (*Glances towards other part of house, listening*) And you could disturb Mr Boyle. He's trying to get some sleep after the night run.

(PIPPY *remembers something. Cautious again. Starts prowling around.*)

PIPPY (*carefully*) Are you lonely when you're all alone at home at night?

NOLA (*equally careful*) Other women have the daytime to be lonely in. It amounts to the same thing.

PIPPY One night I was feeling lonely. I wanted to come in.

NOLA You ought'uv.

PIPPY I did. (*Quickly*) I didn't, I mean! (*Tracing something on the furniture*) I was afraid.

NOLA (*suspicious, nostrils dilating*) Are you your mother's daughter?

PIPPY (*surprised and suspicious in turn*) Me mother's daughter?

NOLA (*quickly, shrugging it off*) It's a way of speaking.

PIPPY We got somebody like that at school. Only it's the father.

NOLA Oh, Gawd! You're your mother's daughter, *and* your father's, if that's what you wanta know. Only you're not. See?

PIPPY (*rather dismal*) Mum's all right. She can't help it. (*Pause*) I like you, Mrs Boyle.

NOLA (*going to* PIPPY, *half-tearful*) That's the first blessed thing I've liked hearing today!

(NOLA *puts her arms round* PIPPY, *who submits, but is embarrassed, and shy.* NOLA *draws her down on to the sofa.*)

(*Dreamy*) The first thing!

PIPPY (*submitting, but very careful*) I love you. I love the way you smell.

NOLA Eh?

PIPPY You smell good.

NOLA What of?

PIPPY Of bread.

NOLA That's harmless enough to please anybody!

PIPPY And tinned peaches.

NOLA Well, waddaya know!

PIPPY Those big yellow ones.

NOLA (*trying to trap the child's head*) Pippy, don't say any more, dear. You'll spoil it!

(*A short silence, in which their composition remains rather awkward.*)

PIPPY (*tentatively*) About those dogs....

NOLA (*withdrawing*) We're on to that subject again!

PIPPY The bitch. . . . What'll happen to her . . . when the dogs can't get any more, and go?

NOLA (*unhappily*) That's one way of putting it! (*Pausing*) Well, she'll go away and have pups.

PIPPY Pups!

NOLA Yes. Don't you like them?

PIPPY Oh, yes. They're lovely. But do all bitches have pups after ... after it's happened?

NOLA (*sombre*) Some bitches are lucky enough to escape. Some of the time. I mean, it's lucky for those street bitches. What'd they do with a lot of pups? Just roaming around. After they're turned out.

PIPPY Are they?

NOLA Some of them are. Their owners can't take what's been happening. And it happens again.

PIPPY What, all over again?

NOLA Yes. Every six months. That's nature.

(*She breaks down.* PIPPY *is at first surprised, then horrified.*)

PIPPY (*shaking* NOLA, *frightened*) Mrs Boyle! Don't, Mrs Boyle! We're not going to talk about it.

NOLA (*blowing her nose*) But it happens ... that way....

(ENTER ERNIE BOYLE *from* BACK. *He is rubbing his head with a towel. Dressed in pyjamas.*)

(*Realizing without turning, repairing the damage*) Aren't you gunna get your sleep, Ern?

ERN Sleep! (*Does not look at* NOLA. *Struts about, drying his hair.*) Haven't seen you, Pippy.

PIPPY I've been here.

ERN Must'uv been keeping yourself dark. (*Sits down on the doorstep with his back to the others*) What'uv you been up to?

(*Both* ERN *and* NOLA *are clinging desperately to* PIPPY's *presence.*)

NOLA She's been studyin'.

ERN No kiddin'!

NOLA She's been reading books.

ERN What about, eh? Science? That's what they all go for now.

PIPPY No. Emperors and empresses. And murders. *Decline and Fall of the Roman Empire.*

ERN I never read a book like that. I wouldn't know about that.

NOLA Sounds dry to me. Even with the murders.

PIPPY (*getting up*) There are the dry bits. But there's the other bits as well.

ERN But emperors and empresses! They wouldn't make sense today. Only on the pictures.

(PIPPY *approaches the back door, wondering how she can get by.*)

PIPPY Oh, they're the same. Everybody's the same. Even dogs are.

(ERN *and* NOLA *realize she wants to leave. Their horror grows.*)

ERN (*to* PIPPY) You ain't goin', are yer?

PIPPY Yes.

ERN We like to have yer talk, Pippy . . . tell us things. An educated girl. And you're gunna walk out. . . .

PIPPY (*very quiet*) I've said all I've got to say.

NOLA (*looking at her lap*) That's a pretty good reason.

(PIPPY *squeezes past* ERN *on the step. She goes down, gets through the fence, and disappears into her own house. All of it she does very smoothly. Her thoughts are for the moment totally disguised.*)

(*The following short reverie of the* BOYLES *should be spoken as if from an inescapable nightmare.*)

ERN When you're left alone together, that's when the trouble begins.

NOLA You can't cut the silences anyhow.

ERN You're surrounded by bloody furniture.

NOLA And thoughts.

ERN I remember the Sunday at Manly. We got half boiled by the sun. There was hairs on your wrist I'd never noticed before. The sand tricklin' down the little blonde hairs. . . .

NOLA I remember 1948. I thought I'd copped it at last. I was carrying *you*! YOU. And we tore the cold chicken apart. And we toasted him in real wine, like the social set do. But it was only another false alarm. . . .

(*Here they resume a naturalistic delivery.*)

NOLA You ought to lie down, Ern. Try to get some sleep.

ERN (*jumping up irritably, ignoring her*) Nao.

155

NOLA You'll be dog tired.

ERN I can get bloody well flogged for all I care.

NOLA (*avoiding looking at him*) Sit on the front veranda, then. It's nice and cool.

ERN Sit on the front veranda, and watch 'em saying: 'He must be the only one who doesn't know!'

(EXIT ERN *to front of house, avoiding her.*)

(*A distinct, sharp moan is heard from* OFF *in the Knotts' house. At Pogsons'* GIRLIE *comes running out from the front rooms to her back door.* NOLA *gets up, and comes, slower, but anxious, to hers.* GIRLIE *and* NOLA *both crane in the direction of Knotts'.*)

(*Another stifled moan as* HARRY KNOTT *appears in his kitchen. Very agitated. Runs down the steps.*)

GIRLIE (*calling*) Is it the pains, Harry?

(GIRLIE *starts down her own steps, equally agitated, to meet him.*)

HARRY It's the pains all right! It's begun! We didn't ought of . . . I was all for . . . Mrs Pogson, can I use the 'phone?

(HARRY *gets through the fence.*)

GIRLIE (*spinning round*) Oh, dear! Yes!

(GIRLIE *gets through fence into Knotts'.*)

HARRY (*mounting the Pogson steps*) If she'd only done what Sister told her. . . .

(GIRLIE *is all of a dither. After approaching the Knott steps, she thinks better of it.*)

GIRLIE (*undecided*) Oh, dear! Some women don't like . . . (*Deciding, calling*) Harry, I'd better come and show you. There's a little trick . . . (*gets back through the fence*) . . . in dialling. (*Running back towards her own steps*) Everybody's 'phone has something special that you've got to learn. . . .

(HARRY *has disappeared into the front of the Pogson house,* GIRLIE *following.*)

(NOLA *has leant against her doorpost, facing away from Knotts', but not from lack of sympathy.*)

NOLA (*rubbing her head against the doorpost, swaying very slightly*) The pains have got her. It's happening to Mavis Knott. Always a decent, dumb cow. One of the lucky ones. She'll settle down to it like shelling peas. Wonder whether I could have stood that pain.

(*Closing her eyes, gritting her teeth*) Tearing me in half. Tearing. But, oh God, what lovely . . . lovely . . . *relief.* . . . (*Opening her eyes, savagely*) Of course I could'uv stood it! It's nothing to what you bear in your mind. . . .

(HARRY REAPPEARS *in Pogson kitchen, looking rather dazed. He is followed by* GIRLIE, JUDY *and* PIPPY.)

GIRLIE (*assuring him*) If there's anything I can do for Mavis, Harry. . . . Always oblige a neighbour if I can. . . .

(MAVIS *has meanwhile* ENTERED *her kitchen, walking very slowly, heavily, holding herself, supported by* ROY. *She is wearing her overcoat. She seats herself carefully in the armchair, waiting in a trance.* ROY *squats beside* MAVIS, *holding her hand.* HARRY *runs back to his own house.* THREE POGSONS *all gather at their back door.*)

PIPPY I'm never gunna have a baby if it hurts like that! Ugh!

(JUDY *shushes her.*)

(HARRY *arrives in his own kitchen.*)

HARRY I rung, dear. You oughta wait. They'll fetch a stretcher.

(MAVIS *does not answer. She sits supporting her head. Pale.*)

(DEEDREE ENTERS *from the Pogson front garden. Comes on at a skipping pace into the yard.*)

PIPPY (*to* GIRLIE) But doesn't it hurt?

GIRLIE Pippy, my nerves won't stand any more! (*Glancing, realizing* NOLA BOYLE *is at her door*) It's something, Mrs Boyle, that only a woman can understand. Take the husband. . . . Harry is good. . . .

NOLA (*vigorously*) Harry is good!

GIRLIE But poor fellow . . . it's not the same. . . .

NOLA It's never the same.

(GIRLIE *and* NOLA *seem to have discovered each other, and to have formed an alliance.*)

NOLA (*looking at the sky*) And on such a day!

GIRLIE It's hot all right.

NOLA And will get hotter.

MAVIS (*stirring*) I'll be all right. I got a fright. (*To* ROY) Roy, dear, I want to be with Harry a little. I'm silly. That's all. But with Harry . . . till the ambulance. . . .

(ROY *pats her. Goes down into the yard. Walks about. Lights* cigarette. *Ends up leaning against the proscenium arch.*)

GIRLIE (*to* NOLA) Already at six o'clock I said to Mr Pogson: 'Clive,' I said, 'already I feel I'm going around under the lid of a big copper. Pressing down . . . down. . . .'

(NOLA *shakes her head, sucks her teeth in sympathy.*)

(DEEDREE *has approached, and mounts the lower steps.*)

DEEDREE What's up, Pippy?

PIPPY Shut up, silly!

MAVIS (*to* HARRY) There's something I want you to remember, dear. You must always take the bus. Never get carried away. Taxis'll drain you dry. From Sarsaparilla to Barranugli. Take the bus to the hospital. We'll need every penny now. It's the pennies that count.

(HARRY *puts his arms round her, comforting.*)

GIRLIE (*to* NOLA, *indicating* ROY) There's the brother. Blood, maybe. But never so close as a woman. Even the neighbour is closer than a brother.

(NOLA *nods her head.*)

(THE AMBULANCE *is heard in the distance, approaching always closer.*)

DEEDREE (*to* PIPPY) Is somebody sick? Has there been an accident?

PIPPY Get *her*!

(GIRLIE *gives* PIPPY *a push.* JUDY *is unable to remain where she is any longer. She goes down to* ROY. *He holds out his hand to her, draws her into the shadow of the Knotts' yard.*)

MAVIS (*very serious*) There's something I want you to know, Harry.

HARRY What?

MAVIS I'm glad I'm not having this baby with anybody else.

HARRY (*glad, helpless, comforting*) I should hope so, dear!

(AMBULANCE *apparently comes to a stop.*)

MAVIS For instance, I can't think what it'd be like to have it with Mr Pogson.

HARRY No. Clive Pogson's a decent enough cove. But not to go having babies with.

(ENTER TWO AMBULANCE MEN *from the Knotts' front garden. They have a stretcher.*)

GIRLIE (*excited, to* NOLA) The ambulance!

(AMBULANCE MEN *advance*)

FIRST MAN (*to* ROY) Home of Mr H. Knott?

ROY That's right. (*Calling*) Harry, the ambulance!

GIRLIE (*simultaneously, pointing*) In there! I bet she'll be relieved.

NOLA Yes, poor thing!

(AMBULANCE MEN *ascend.*)

DEEDREE (*to* PIPPY) Is somebody having a baby?

PIPPY You'll kill me!

(AMBULANCE MEN ENTER *the Knott kitchen.*)

FIRST MAN Mrs Knott? We'll have you there before you know you've left your own home.

MAVIS But I'm all right now. I'm *not*. But you know.... It comes and goes. It puts the wind up you at times.

(AMBULANCE MEN *arrange the stretcher.*)

HARRY (*hoarse*) There you are, dear. Do everything they say.

SECOND MAN (*asserting himself, jovially*) How are yer for weight, Mrs Knott?

MAVIS (*drawing back*) Oh, but I don't wanta go on a stretcher! I can leave home on me own feet. If I take it slow.

FIRST MAN (*a bit dry*) It's up to you.

HARRY I'd do what they say, dear. After all, we suscribe to it.

MAVIS (*thoughtful*) Yes.... Well.... If we've paid for it....
(*She allows herself to be helped to lie down.*)
(*Fretfully*) Only I never thought I'd leave me own home on a stretcher. All the neighbours waiting for a body....

GIRLIE (*craning, to* NOLA) Do you think anything can have gone wrong?

NOLA They do say those men are very capable.

GIRLIE Can deliver at a pinch....

MAVIS (*on the stretcher*) Harry, you'll have to stop the milk.

HARRY (*going round in circles*) The milk? The milk. . . . Yes, the milk!

GIRLIE (*frustrated, to* NOLA) Well, I dunno....

NOLA Could be remembering what to take. Or what to leave. A girl friend of mine lost some costume jewellery at the Mater.

GIRLIE (*hissing*) You can't be too careful! You can't call your teeth your own once you get inside a hospital.

NOLA Mind you, I'm not suggesting that the nuns.... There are all sorts that come and go.

GIRLIE (*craning*) There are all sorts....

MAVIS Harry, what am I.... The over-night, Harry!
(HARRY *disappears to fetch the bag.*)

FIRST MAN You can relax, Mrs Knott.
(AMBULANCE MEN *lift her.*)

MAVIS (*tearfully*) My husband....

FIRST MAN (*taking the weight, grimly*) Ladies are having babies every moment of the day. You'll find it monotonous yourself after the first half-dozen.
(HARRY REAPPEARS *with the over-night bag.*)

MAVIS (*to* HARRY) Oh, dear! What are you gunna do? There's the cold mutton....

GIRLIE (*getting angry*) What are they *doing* in there?
(AMBULANCE MEN *emerge. Carry* MAVIS *down the steps.* HARRY *follows with the bag.*)

NOLA (*sucking her teeth*) Poor soul!
(ROY *and* JUDY *move* FORWARD, *murmuring good-byes. They touch* MAVIS *as she passes.*)

ROY See you soon, Mavis. (*Patting*)

JUDY (*bending, softly*) ...over...soon...Mrs Knott.

MAVIS (*protesting*) You're no longer a person. You're a sack!

NOLA (*calling*) Keeping me fingers crossed, love!

GIRLIE ...any little thing. Just you tell Harry. A cold baked custard.... Some of those hospitals leave it all to the relatives and friends.

MAVIS Oh, dear! Harry? I can feel...I got the....

FIRST MAN Take it easy, Mrs Knott. Try not to rock the....

HARRY Here I am, dear. Right beside you. I'm coming in the ambulance.

MAVIS (*wearily*) I wonder what you're gunna do when that alarm doesn't go off in the morning?

PIPPY (*calling*) 'Bye, Mrs Knott! We'll come and see the little baby!

(MAVIS *is carried* OFF *through the front garden accompanied by* HARRY. *As this happens,* GIRLIE, PIPPY *and* DEEDREE *run through the front part of the Pogson house.* NOLA *disappears to the front of hers.*)

GIRLIE (*calling, angry,* OFF) Mind that jardineer, Deedree! You'll have it over!

(JUDY *and* ROY *remain* CENTRE *of the Knott yard.*)

JUDY (*upset*) I'm so sorry for her!

ROY What's so terrible about the natural occurrences?

JUDY It's more than that. Can't you see? This house . . . all of a sudden it's empty. All of a sudden all the little things . . . that meant something to somebody . . . don't mean anything any more. It was the owners who gave them their importance. It's pitiful!

ROY Possessions!

JUDY They're part of you till you go. Then they're nothing.

ROY But can never die right out. Upholstery breeds like man . . . as often and as ugly.

(*A silence.*)

JUDY (*moodily*) We shall never see anything through each other's eyes.

ROY Nobody does . . . really. That doesn't make it tragic.

(*He takes her hand.*)

JUDY (*insisting*) Oh, but they do! Some people do! I'm convinced!

ROY (*turning her face towards him*) I would like you to see me through *your* eyes.

JUDY (*bitterly*) Would you take the risk? Would you dare to be seen as you really are? (*With scorn*) I might even 'possess' you! Then where would you be?

ROY We'd sort ourselves out in time. Two people have to develop a way to love.

JUDY (*shaking her head free*) Now it's 'love'! (*Sullenly decided*) I'm not the intellectual type. I couldn't *talk* to you enough about it.

ROY If it's a practical demonstration . . . (*passionately*) . . . I can show you! (*Embracing her*) . . . Convince . . . you what it is I . . . need . . . most!

JUDY (*fiercely, whispering, between her teeth*) Need! (*Wrenches her-*

self away) You've worked it out on paper! Along with the notes for the books you never write!

ROY Can't you believe in lightning?

JUDY If it struck me dead . . . then, perhaps, I'd begin to believe in it.

ROY (*sincerely, gentler*) Darling Judy! (*Again kissing her passionately*) Now I see . . . know . . . feel. . . .

JUDY (*stiffly, from behind closed eyes*) And I . . . feel . . . nothing. . . . (*Opens her eyes.*)

(*He might have intended to caress her, but her manner repels him.*)

ROY This is the moment one hopes may never happen!

JUDY (*sadly*) Once I wanted love. Oh, it seems as though for years . . . years longer than possible . . . I've sat around dreaming of nothing else. Somebody to fall in love with. Then I wanted a real person. I wanted *you*, Roy . . .

(*Turning to him, looking at him, but her manner continues to hold him off.*)

. . . wanting you so badly, I'd almost bang my head against the wall at night. So helpless. Then, quite suddenly . . . quite recently . . . was it in the last few minutes? . . . I found I no longer wanted love.

ROY (*exasperated*) But. . . . (*Laughing*) No one's desirable all of the time!

JUDY This isn't a question of desire.

ROY (*flip*) If not . . . what?

JUDY It sounds very silly. What is simple . . . obvious . . . but true . . . can be made to sound ridiculous . . . by clever people.

ROY Let's have it, though! What's to take the place of this wild beast, which not even you will persuade me to leave off hunting.

(JUDY *scarcely dares.*)

JUDY (*diffidently*) Kindness. Affection. That's all that really matters.

ROY Kindness? Spaniels!

JUDY (*unswerving*) Loving-kindness!

ROY That follows. After people have stopped loving. When they've begun to put up with each other.

JUDY I hope to find it in the beginning. It's more convincing . . . valuable . . . when it already exists.

(RON SUDDARDS *has* ENTERED *the Pogson yard from the front* garden. *Rather breathless. Runs up the steps. Is about to knock. But catches sight of* JUDY *and* ROY *in the next yard. Stands looking down at them as they stand looking up.*)

RON (*slowly*) Hello, Judy. . . . Saw the ambulance turning out of Mildred Street. . . . Came along to see. . . .

JUDY (*answering slowly, coolly*) It was Mrs Knott. She's going to have her baby. Didn't my mother tell you? She was out in front.

RON Didn't see a soul. The whole street's dead.

(*He appears a little dazed.*)

ROY Excitement dies very quickly. (*Briskly, to* JUDY) Well, I'm going up into this house which you've shown in such a pathetic light . . . (*slower*) all emptiness and furniture.

JUDY (*turning, impulsively*) Oh, Roy, you make me feel I've done and said the most horrible things!

ROY (*running up the steps, recovering his steely self*) Don't let charity make you do, or say, anything you might regret more. That would be the worst sell of all.

(ROY ENTERS *the Knott kitchen. Crosses it quickly.*)

ROY (*singing, raucous, in authentic pop tones*) 'You ob-vi-ously do not adore me. . . .' (*Speaking, very sober*) Was there any reason why you should?

(EXIT ROY *into front part of house. At same time* RON *descends the Pogson step.*)

RON (*slowly*) Judy, I interrupted . . . something important.

JUDY (*squeezing through the fence*) No, you didn't, Ron. What you interrupted was nothing. Do you see? Of no importance at all.

(*They look at each other.*)

RON I see.

JUDY (*approaching him*) I know now . . . (*taking his hands*) . . . what I think . . . (*holding his hands to her cheek*) . . . you've always known.

RON (*laughing, softly, happily*) I'm the one should be holding hands!

JUDY We'll hold each other's . . . equally.

(*They cling to each other in the shadow of the fence, kissing freely, in joyful relief.*)

(DEEDREE *and* PIPPY *have* ENTERED *the Pogson kitchen from front of house.*)

GIRLIE (*calling*, OFF) Don't you go far now, Joyleen. I've got some things for you to do.

PIPPY (*calling back*, *making a face*) May not go anywhere, anyways.

DEEDREE (*giggly*, *chanting*)   'Oily Joly

Ate a doily.

Spewed it up

In her cup. . . .'

(DEEDREE *continues to giggle inanely at her own wit.*)

PIPPY (*loftily*) That isn't funny.

DEEDREE 'Tis!

PIPPY 'Tisn't!

(*They fall silent.*)

DEEDREE (*putting out a feeler*) I got a secret I'll share with you.

PIPPY What?

(DEEDREE *approaches and whispers to* PIPPY *behind her hand.*)

PIPPY (*contemptuous*) That's not much of a secret.

DEEDREE (*whining*) Oh, why?

PIPPY It's not worth having.

DEEDREE Why's nothing worth having without *you* think of it?

PIPPY Because I have better ideas.

(DEEDREE *drifts wretchedly to the back door.*)

DEEDREE Aren't you coming out, then?

PIPPY What for?

DEEDREE Muck around.

(*She looks out. Beckons wildly to* PIPPY, *who acts superior.* DEEDREE *beckons ever more frantically.* PIPPY *cannot resist.* DEEDREE *reveals* RON *and* JUDY.)

PIPPY Oh, that! Thought she was going soft on him.

DEEDREE That's that Mr Suddards.

PIPPY Ron Suddards 's a drip.

DEEDREE I think he's nice.

PIPPY Wears brown socks.

(PIPPY *and* DEEDREE *descend the steps, looking and not looking.*)

DEEDREE Nice colour hair.

PIPPY Not bad.

DEEDREE Nice in his sweatshirt.

PIPPY (*deciding grudgingly*) Mmmmmm.

(CHILDREN *prepare to depart for the street. Looking back openly now, from corner of the house.*)

PIPPY She's pretty soppy, though. Isn't she soppy?

(DEEDREE *whispers feverishly to* PIPPY *behind her hand.*)

PIPPY (*shrieking*) That's different! That's with dogs! And empresses....

(PIPPY *and* DEEDREE *go* OFF *towards the street, screaming their heads off.*)

(JUDY *and* RON *have come forward into the* CENTRE *of the Pogson yard. They have a kind of quiet serenity.*)

JUDY It's so peaceful....

RON (*tweaking her ear*) Dull is what they call it!

JUDY In the whole of Sarsaparilla, nobody knows as much as us.

RON That's how it ought to be for a little.

JUDY Until we sound a trumpet. (*Becoming more ambitious, visualizing, indicating with her hands*) Or masses. Desks and desks! Of massed brass!

RON (*laughing happily*) Get that old What's-his-Name . . . that *Handel* to blow his head off for us. Split the sky open at last. He's the one. He would have been glad....

(*They go* OFF *hand in hand, down the lane.*)

(*At the same time* ERNIE BOYLE ENTERS *the Boyle kitchen. He is sprucely dressed, shaven. Looks at himself gloomily in the wall-mirror. Opens his mouth. Makes a despairing face at himself, stands staring after it has faded.* NOLA ENTERS. *Also dressed for going out. But obviously has not realized* ERN *was in the kitchen.*)

NOLA Didn't know you was thinking of going out, Ern.

ERN (*aggressive and defensive*) I wasn't goin' out. Not exactly.

NOLA You're all dressed up, anyway. Don't often put on your gun-metal flannel.

(*A pause.*)

ERN (*more aggressive*) Well, if you'd like to know, I'm gunna drive down to the Bull. Get meself a beer or two.

NOLA In that suit!

ERN You dress up, don't you, when you're gunna celebrate?

NOLA (*faintly*) Celebrate?

(*But* ERN *does not attempt to explain.*)

What are you going to . . . celebrate?

ERN The day my eyes was well and truly opened.

(NOLA *sits down abruptly on the lounge. Fetches out her handkerchief. She has grown rather soggy.*)

ERN (*without turning*) And what are *you* up to? Goin' on the streets?

(NOLA *breaks down.*)

NOLA (*crying*) I was going up to Woolie's. Move around a bit. I can't stay here . . . listening to the clock. A clock in an empty house can send a person barmy.

ERN (*wildly*) Invite some of 'em in, then! Make 'em comfortable in the home! We got the furniture!

(NOLA *sits looking at her hands and her miserable handkerchief.*)

NOLA I know about meself, Ern. You don't have to rub it in.

ERN Sometimes it looks as if you don't know. Or perhaps it's just that you forget too often.

NOLA (*controlling herself*) I think it's best if you go off and get shickered as you planned.

ERN Shickered! That's a nice sort of word for a lady to use!

NOLA That's a word I learned from my dad, and I used it because no other word says so good what it's supposed to. Dad only used it under provocation, though. He was not one for the booze, or anything else.

ERN He handed on a pretty good line in morals!

NOLA (*quietly*) Dad's not to blame if I grew up with a blistered heel.

ERN (*ferociously*) Thought it was supposed to be the parents.

NOLA (*averting her face*) Nobody's going to hold that against *us*!

(*There is a silence.* ERN *suddenly turns away as though he has been slashed. He is trembling. Walks about in great agitation, making inarticulate noises.* NOLA *does not look at him at first.*)

(*Not looking at him, blurting*) I didn't suggest that you. . . .

(*Wearily*) We know I'm about as barren as an old boot.

(ERN *is desperate. He stands* CENTRE. *He could be about to break down.*)

(*Wearily, quietly, going to him, to protect*) Ernie, we seem to 'uv been accusing each other all our lives. And we don't even think of something new!

(*She reaches him just as he appears to break up. They stand,* C.,

*clutching at each other. His head is against her shoulder. He is not
exactly crying, but has broken out in a kind of dry rasping.*)
(*Softly, soothing, a little shocked, though she had half expected it*)
Ernie! Ernie!
(*She caresses him.*)

ERN (*panting*) It's me that's weak, it seems. I'm the weak one.

NOLA (*willing him*) No more than most. Ern, dear! D'yer hear?
D'you know why I loved you? Because you was never dismal.
You always stood up to things better than the others. 'That little
fat bugger,' I said, 'he's cheerful. I'm gone on him for that before
anything else.'
(ERN *has quietened, but remains passive in more or less the same
position, listening.* NOLA *is warming to the past, or her own performance, or both. The emotional flood is gathering strength.*)
So I've always waited. I've waited for you to come in. My life's
been set by you, Ern. By your coming in and going out. Even in
the days when we had no more than that bloody old black lounge
suite that we swapped for the Wilton square, I wouldn't'uv
waited for nobody else. (*On dangerous ground*) Not regular.
(*Suddenly bursting into tears*) None of those! (*She slides down
against him*) I know I'm lost, Ern . . . (*kissing his thigh*) . . . but I'd
be more lost without you. I'd finish it . . . without. . . .
(*She grasps his ankles, crying, paddling her hair in his feet.*)
(ERN *has been wrung dry.*)

ERN (*dully*) Better get up, Nola. Somebody might come in. (*Tries
to free his ankles by motions of the feet, very stiff*) Go on! That
prissy old cow from next door. . . .

NOLA (*still crying, spasmodically*) She don't need to come in. She
was born with imagination. And a thousand ears.
(*She sits up sniffing. Awful.* ERN *goes and looks out of the back door.
He is shattered.*)

ERN We both showed up pretty well.

NOLA D'you know, Ernie, sometimes I lie and watch you when
you're asleep. (*Blowing her nose*) There's some men you can't
bear to watch when they're sleeping.
(*She gets up, blowing her nose.*)

ERN That bloody Masson!

NOLA I hated him from the start.

ERN So you did.

NOLA All those mates! The desert gives me the creeps. I wonder what a woman would do in the desert. And those fox-holes! All those men ... lying in fox-holes ... and talking about things. ... (*Fiercely*) I hated all that!

ERN (*sadly*) It's just something that happened in some part of a man's life. If it happened at all. ...

(*There is a short silence.* ERN *walks about, shakily, distracted.* NOLA *looks at herself in the glass.*)

NOLA I've never looked so bloody awful.

ERN (*without looking at her to confirm*) You look awful all right. Like a soddy scone.

(NOLA *purses up her mouth in the glass.*)

NOLA Some day it comes to you, they say ... to stay. ...

ERN I'll never believe in that day.

(ERN *is going towards the door,* BACK. *Tired out.* NOLA *pretends to be intent on making up her mouth.*)

NOLA (*too bright*) What are you gunna do, Ern?

ERN What am I gunna do? I'm gunna get out of this suit. Dressed up like a sore finger. ...

(EXIT ERN *to bedroom.*)

(NOLA *buries her face in her hands. She is taking the deep breaths of somebody returning to life.*)

(*calling,* OFF) You might bring that cold bottle. And a couple of glasses. We can sit a while in front.

(NOLA *goes to the fridge. She is exhausted, but wearing an expression of restored happiness.*)

NOLA (*taking the bottle, fetching glasses*) Might as well get undressed meself. Don't know whatever persuaded me I could wear an orange blouse.

(EXIT NOLA, BACK.)

(*Simultaneously* CLIVE POGSON *returns.* ENTERS *smartly from his own front garden, carrying the rolled evening paper. Whistling.* GIRLIE POGSON ENTERS *her kitchen.* CLIVE *and* GIRLIE *meet on the steps.*)

GIRLIE Where's the melon?

CLIVE The melon?

GIRLIE That we spoke about.

CLIVE Oh.

(*He hesitates, goes on in, hangs his hat.*)

GIRLIE You didn't get the melon?

(CLIVE *shoots his cuffs, draws his chin in.*)

CLIVE No.

GIRLIE When I was relying on the melon!

CLIVE (*baleful*) Well, I didn't get it. I forgot it. See?

(EXIT CLIVE, BACK, *followed by* GIRLIE *complaining unintelligibly.*)

(*At the same time* MR ERBAGE *comes into Knotts' yard from the street. He is obviously very put out. Runs up the steps pretty briskly for a fat man. Knocks loudly. No reply.*)

ERBAGE (*calling*) Mr Child?

(*Waits. Knocks again.* ROY ENTERS *the kitchen.*)

(*Relieved*) Ah, Mr Child. . . . (*But upset*) I come around. . . .

(ROY, *all attention, leads* ERBAGE *slowly down into the yard.*)

(*Embarrassed*) I came. . . . Something has happened.

ROY Something in the Council?

ERBAGE Wish it was! You can manage public affairs. They're open to influence. It's the private ones. . . .

(*They have arrived at bottom of the steps.*)

I've come to advise you *re* a friend of yours . . . Mr Child.

ROY A friend?

ERBAGE (*mopping himself*) That Miss Julia Sheen.

ROY I always thought, Mr Erbage, you and she were closely acquainted . . . not to say connected.

ERBAGE Not on your life! That is, we were, I suppose, *technically*.

ROY Technique should clinch the matter.

ERBAGE Eh?

ROY All right. Let it pass.

(ERBAGE'S *anger gets the better of his mystification.*)

ERBAGE Look 'ere, I came around for pretty important reasons.

ROY Yes? Yes? Let's have it.

ERBAGE Your friend, Miss Julia Sheen, has taken her father's car, and driven it against a wall.

ROY Good God!

ERBAGE We hope so. 'Cos the young lady's ... passed on.

ROY (*moved, half to himself*) Then, brittle Julia did break at last.

ERBAGE (*puzzled*) Eh? (*He is sweating at every pore, and mopping constantly*) The point is: there's to be an enquiry. The father's an enquiring man. Who knows who and what will come out of it whole.

ROY (*genuinely, if not deeply concerned*) Poor Julia! Her legs were perfect.

ERBAGE I'm not one to disagree that she had what it takes.

ROY (*prepared for sentimental recapitulation*) Her neck....

ERBAGE 'Er neck? Yes, it was 'er neck. She can't 'uv known much about it.

(BOTH *are silenced for a moment.*)

ROY This is horrible! Did you know Julia was expecting a child?

ERBAGE I did hear something. Something. But Julia was an excitable girl. You might say hysterical. (*He looks at* ROY *pointedly*) She might have imagined things. But I won't say more. She's a goner.

ROY Can't defend herself from her mistakes.

ERBAGE You've said it! It might have been one. But more likely it was many. (*Looking at* ROY) Eh, Mr Child?

ROY I wouldn't know. I was never there. (*Looking at* ERBAGE) I should have been, of course. Then none of this might have happened.

ERBAGE In the circumstances, I don't see who's to blame.

ROY Everybody is always a little to blame.

ERBAGE Well, I only thought I'd tip you off. (*Mopping himself again*) A man's reputation can suffer. Particularly in the public service. (*Preparing to leave*) If I can ever do anyone a favour ... (*mopping*) it's no trouble, I'm sure.

(ERBAGE *is making for the street.*)

ROY (*calling*) Thank you, Mr Erbage, for telling. I'm sorry about the scare you had.

ERBAGE (*turning*) Eh? Well, I mean to say. . . . I worked pretty hard to get where I got, and it don't seem fair if a little bit of pleasure goes wrong....

ROY It'll pass. Don't worry, Mr Erbage. We are not the kind that suffer. That's our trouble.

ERBAGE There we're coming into country where I've never been before. I never saw the necessity for getting clever. (*Nodding*) Good-evening, Mr Child.

(EXIT ERBAGE, BACK.)

(*During the foregoing,* CLIVE POGSON *has* ENTERED *their kitchen from front part of house, and seated himself with his evening paper.*)

CLIVE (*studying paper*) Some girl has run herself against a wall. Wonder what gets into them. Suppose the usual. You're up against that sort of thing with girls. (*Thoughtfully*) Now if we had had boys. . . . (*More cheerfully*) But boys don't pay when the parents grow old. A girl will bring you a billy of soup. . . .

(HARRY KNOTT *has* ENTERED *the Pogson yard from the street. He is very tired, but satisfied. Climbs the steps, is about to knock, but catches sight of* CLIVE.)

HARRY I passed by, Mr Pogson . . . thought you might like to know. . . .

CLIVE (*coming to door, lethargic*) Yairs, Harry?

HARRY It's a boy, Mr Pogson.

CLIVE I'm real glad! It's a satisfaction to have a boy.

HARRY (*sighing*) I'll say!

CLIVE She was quick, though.

HARRY (*as he turns away*) Oh, I got a taxi home.

CLIVE (*watching his neighbour*) I'll tell the wife . . . (*slower, quieter, frowning at the front rooms*) tell the wife. . . .

(CLIVE *re-seats himself with his paper.*)

(HARRY *goes on through the fence, catches sight of* ROY.)

HARRY It's a boy, Roy.

ROY (*sympathetic, but absent*) I'm glad, Harry. It had to be.

(HARRY *goes up the steps. Very exhausted.*)

HARRY She told me something . . . something I had to do. . . .

(EXIT HARRY *towards the front rooms.*)

ROY So they die. So they are born. And are the sins of the watchers forgiven, in the backyards, at dusk?

(EXIT ROY *down the lane.*)

(*At same time* ERN *and* NOLA ENTER *their kitchen.* ERN *is wearing his work clothes, carrying his coat.* NOLA *is comfortable in her usual chenille dressing-gown.*)

NOLA Have to get you a bit of tea.

ERN Nah.

NOLA But you gotta eat.

ERN I feel good. I feel warm.

(*He kisses hungrily – bite-kisses – down her neck.*)
I ate!

NOLA (*giggling, withdrawing*) You're a trimmer! You'll leave bruises for everyone to see.

ERN Trademarks.

NOLA (*serious, drawing her gown close*) But wrap up warm, Ern. One of those southerlies come. I felt it as we were laying on top of the bed.

ERN (*putting on his coat*) You don't have time to feel cold.

NOLA (*laughing*) Don't get yarning to all those ladies! In the small hours. In the homes.

(ERN *starts feeling his coat.*)

ERN 'Ere, what's all this?

NOLA What?

ERN Me coat?

NOLA I gave it to the dry-cleaners.

ERN Me old coat!

NOLA We agreed, didn't we? We agreed to give it to the gentleman who's started calling regular with the van.

ERN Didn't know....

NOLA Well, we did. (*After a pause*) He's ever so polite.

(ERN *is listening.*)

D'you know ... that man's wife has had eleven operations. She's had practically the whole of her insides taken away from her. She's practically all plastic now.

ERN (*gloomy*) She would be.

(*Another pause.*)

NOLA (*laughing*) He's a funny sort of bloke.

ERN (*gloomier*) 'Ow?

NOLA Oh, I dunno. He's red. (*Shuddering*) Ugh, I don't like the red, freckly men!

ERN Don't go much on the blueys meself.

(*He goes out down the steps, thoughtful, and sad.*)

NOLA (*calling*) Aren't you gunna kiss me?

ERN (*looking back*) I did!

NOLA (*giggling, softly*) That's right! You did!

(ERN *goes on, turns again, waves, but sad.* NOLA *blows him a couple of fruity kisses. He turns for the last time, then* EXIT *down the lane.*)

(NOLA *sighs, withdrawn inside the kitchen. Rubbing her arms.*)

(*Sighing*) Ah, dear! Pippy was right. It's lonely when you're on your own. What can you do? Look at the TV.... (*Grimacing*) A lot of grey tadpoles....

(EXIT NOLA *into front of house.*)

(ROY *has* ENTERED *from the lane. He has returned to the Knott yard, and is standing against the proscenium arch in his characteristic attitude for observing.*)

ROY In Mildred Street there's practically no end to the variations on monotony. The Iceland poppies replace the glads, the dahlias take their turn with the chrysanths. At weekends, Pogsons are painting their house a shade of French-grey they've seen on someone else's. Boyles are indulging in a daring splash of red. Nothing stands still. Not in the razzle-dazzle of time.

(RAZZLE-DAZZLE *turned on.*)

People are spattered and splashed by it, of course. But for the most part, not very dangerously. So the men of Mildred Street continue on their way ... out, in ... in, out....

(HARRY *and* CLIVE *march out through the razzle-dazzle of light, dressed for business, as* ERNIE *returns from work via the lane.* ALL *greet one another — conventional gestures — as the commentary continues.* HARRY *and* CLIVE EXIT, BACK, ERNIE ENTERS *his kitchen, and* EXIT *to the unseen rooms.*)

Supported by Hire Purchase, the splendid climate, and their Australian extrovert temperament, they are able to lead the Good Life. Some of them have even sent the population up....

(MAVIS ENTERS *her kitchen, and is hanging out nappies.*)

My sister Mavis has been home ... is it two ... three ... how many weeks? She had her boy easily enough, and for some unknown reason chose to call him ... Kev-on. Mavis is the cornu-

copia. Mavis must spill, and in that find her purpose, her contentment.

(JUDY *and* RON *have* ENTERED *the* POGSON *yard by way of the
lane. They are holding hands, courting. They moon around the
yard.*)

Here's my girl, Judy Pogson. She seems to have struck it pretty
good. Whether she's struck the best, only time, that lovely and
distorting razzle-dazzle, will show . . . as the price of things goes
up, but never down . . . as the men of Mildred Street continue
marching . . . in, out . . . out, in . . . through the sunny Australian
climate, and the rain of politicians' promises. . . .

(CLIVE *and* HARRY RE-ENTER, BACK. ERN ENTERS *his kitchen
from inner rooms, followed by* NOLA. CLIVE *and* HARRY *step inside
their homes as* ERNIE *leaves his. Conventional greetings.* NOLA
stands and waves.)

The sanitary man's wife is sad. She's between her times. Something has ended, and nothing has begun.

(NOLA *turns back into her kitchen.* GIRLIE ENTERS *hers.* HARRY
and CLIVE, EXIT, BACK, *after kissing their wives.* EXIT ERN *down
the lane.* JUDY *and* RON *have seated themselves on the Pogson steps,
absorbed in each other.*)

(MAVIS *and* GIRLIE *busy themselves at their stoves with conventional gestures.* NOLA *has seated herself on the lounge, looking
through a magazine, licking her thumb liberally from time to
time.*)

MAVIS Food, food . . .

GIRLIE . . . food is always the question. . . .

NOLA . . . meals to shove in front of men.

GIRLIE Steak, chops, chops, steak. . . .

NOLA Meat is a must for men . . . with the juice running out . . . and
a nice piece of fat to get their tongues around.

MAVIS Eggs are livery in the end.

GIRLIE I always say: Educate them in daintiness. A nice spaghetti
on toast. Or beans. All this meat! They'll complain at first. But
settle down. Daintiness pays. . . .

ROY . . . and food is so nourishing. Not to say necessary. How else
to resist being blinded by the razzle-dazzle of time?

(RAZZLE-DAZZLE *gives way to normal evening light.*)

(ROY *goes up into the Knott's house.* CLIVE *and* HARRY *have come out into their respective kitchens. The wives serve their husbands with food.*)

HARRY (*to* MAVIS) Would you say they were grey, or blue?

MAVIS (*without hesitation*) Oh, blue! There's no mistaking when he opens them at you.

(HARRY *and* MAVIS *are too absorbed to notice* ROY, *who passes them, and* EXIT *to the rooms beyond.*)

RON (*to* JUDY, *as they sit looking into each other*) You know, when I first met you, I thought your eyes were blue. Then I saw they were grey.

JUDY (*laughing*) They're really a kind of dirty green.

(*Pause, as they continue looking at each other.*)

(*Gently touching his eyes*) There's no mistaking brown. Brown eyes are for faithfulness.

(PIPPY *has* ENTERED *the Pogson kitchen from the bedrooms. She sits at table with a book. Absorbed.*)

(NOLA *hums and vibrates, looking through her magazine.*)

CLIVE (*pauses in eating, looks out through doorway*) It's a lovely evening all right.

GIRLIE When I was a girl, at Rosedale, oh, the evenings were lovely then! Playing rummy on the mosquito-proof veranda. With the young fellers who would come in. Off the neighbouring properties. Oh, the light beneath the willows! Oh, the lamplight at Rosedale, when I was a girl!

CLIVE Yairs. Rosedale! We know all about that.

(NOLA'S *humming stops. She throws aside the magazine. Sits with her face cupped in her hands, staring out into the evening.*)

NOLA Perhaps if I had a cat. A little, white, fluffy cat. . . .

GIRLIE (*to* CLIVE) It's peaceful enough in Mildred Street. Nowadays, at least. Remember all those dogs? How disgraceful! I'll never forget. Anyway, its finished.

PIPPY (*raising her head*) But it's gunna begin again.

(CLIVE *and* GIRLIE *look at her aghast.*)

CLIVE AND GIRLIE (*together*) When?

PIPPY In six months time.

GIRLIE (*almost crying*) But it shouldn't be allowed!

PIPPY Every six months. For ever and ever.

CLIVE How d'you know all this, Pippy?

PIPPY Mrs.... (*Thinking better of it, cold and superior*) I learned it. (*She turns away to her book.*)

MAVIS (*to* HARRY) The whole thing with a baby is to give it affection. I read that in a magazine. Look, when little Kevon.... (ENTER ROY *from front part of house. He is carrying a pack.* MAVIS *and* HARRY *both notice him this time, and stare.*)

HARRY What's... what's got into you, Roy?

ROY I'm going away.

MAVIS You never said you was going away.

HARRY What, up the Coast somewhere?

MAVIS Some say the air's nicer down the South.

ROY No. I'm going away ... London ... Paris ... the Galapagos Islands.... It doesn't much matter where.

MAVIS (*laughing*) Aren't you a caution! Send us a postcard, then. (*Recovering her real interest*) Look, I was telling Harry tonight, you'd never guess what that kid did. When I went in after his sleep, he looked at me ... and winked, Roy!

HARRY (*pushing back his plate*) You can tell that kiddy's got a sense of humour even now....
(ROY *continues out.*)

ROY 'Bye, Mavis. 'Bye, Harry.
(*But* MAVIS *and* HARRY *have forgotten about him. So he continues slowly down the steps.*)

MAVIS Look, Harry, I tell you who he's like. It isn't Dad after all. It's my Uncle Will. A big, happy sort of man....
(*A desperate outburst of humming from* NOLA, *as she sits tossing the slipper on her toes.*)

GIRLIE (*to* PIPPY) But I shan't be able to stand it again!

PIPPY (*beating time remorselessly with her head*) Over, and over, and over. For ever, and ever, and ever. That's nature!
(ROY *has reached the lane. Stands* CENTRE *of stage.*)

ROY (*looking back at the rear view of Mildred Street*) Listen to them, the poor sods! They'll still be at it when I get back.... (*Slower, more thoughtful*) Because ... of course ... I *shall* get back.

(*Exasperated*) You can't shed your skin . . . even if it itches like hell!

(*He goes* OFF *down the lane, as if to avoid emotion by speedy departure.*)

(*Lights dim. When they go up again, other characters have removed themselves.*)

A CHEERY SOUL

Robyn Nevin as Miss Docker and Pat Bishop as Mrs Custance in the Sydney Theatre Company production of A Cheery Soul, 1979. Photo by Branco Gaica.

A Cheery Soul was first performed by the Union Theatre Repertory Company at the Union Theatre, Melbourne, on 19 November 1963 with the following cast:

MRS CUSTANCE	Doreen Warburton
MR CUSTANCE	Sydney Conabere
MISS DOCKER	Nita Pannell
HIRE CAR MAN	Simon Chilvers
REMOVAL MEN	Eric Hoek, Paul Eddey
MAID	Elspeth Ballantyne
MRS LILLIE	Sheila Florance
MISS DANDO	Dorothy Bradley
MATRON	Bettina Smeaton
MR WAKEMAN	Brian James
MRS HIBBLE	Moira Carleton
MRS TOLE	Jane Casson
MRS WATMUFF	Louise Homfrey
MRS ANSTRUTHER	Christine Calcutt
MISS PERRY	Wyn Cunningham
MRS JEBB	Helene Jacoby
YOUNG MRS LILLIE	Jane Bertelsen
TOM LILLIE	Simon Chilvers
MRS PINFOLD	Bettina Smeaton
VIOLET PORTEOUS	Gerda Nicholson
MR LICKISS	Eric Hoek
CHILDREN	Dawn Wright, Cherie Martini, Paul Float, Henry Drazak, Heather Charles
MR BLEEKER	Paul Eddey
MRS BLEEKER	Bettina Smeaton
MR FURZE	Simon Chilvers
MRS FURZE	Jane Bertelsen
VOICES	Jane Casson, Paul Eddey
SWAGGIE	Sydney Conabere

Directed by John Sumner
Designed by Desmond Digby

CHARACTERS

MRS CUSTANCE

MR CUSTANCE

MISS DOCKER

HIRE CAR MAN

TWO FURNITURE REMOVAL MEN

MAID

MRS LILLIE

MISS DANDO

MATRON

MR WAKEMAN

MRS HIBBLE, Leader of chorus

MRS TOLE

MRS WATMUFF

MISS PERRY

MRS ANSTRUTHER

MRS JEBB

YOUNG MRS LILLIE

TOM LILLIE

MRS PINFOLD

VIOLET PORTEOUS

BABY PORTEOUS

MRS WAKEMAN

MR LICKISS

MR BLEEKER

MRS BLEEKER

MR FURZE

MRS FURZE

FIVE CHILDREN

TWO VOICES

SWAGGIE

SETTING

Sarsaparilla, a fictitious outer suburb of Sydney.

182

ACT ONE

KITCHEN AT THE CUSTANCES': *A summer evening.*
A pleasant room, obviously lived-in. Door R. *to rest of house. Door* L. *to drive. Stove against wall* R. FORWARD. *Sink against wall* BACK R. *Dinette* BACK L. *Window behind, opening on veranda. Double doors* BACK C. *open on veranda. The* CUSTANCES' *veranda room is behind the wall against which the dresser stands. Veranda room door, when ajar, is visible from the kitchen. Steps from veranda lead down to garden and rows of over life-size tomato vines. The light through their spires reaches the kitchen greenish and slightly mysterious.*
(Painted, stylized furniture where practicable, and mime whenever possible.)
MRS CUSTANCE *is preparing a meal. She is in her forties. An agreeable, fresh-looking housewife, rather thin, at times given to seriousness, even anxiety. She is standing at the kitchen table. Goes to stove* R., *opens oven, looks inside, returns to table.*
ENTER MR CUSTANCE, *her husband,* L. *About* 50. *A bank teller. Grizzled. Nietzschean moustache. Still a fairly active and not unattractive male, although he can turn surly. He is carrying his hat and evening paper.*
At first CUSTANCES *act as though taking each other for granted.*

MRS CUSTANCE (*at table, preparing something*) You got back.
MR CUSTANCE I got back.
   (*He crosses to sofa* R.C. *Throws hat and paper on it. Starts to take off his coat, which he lays on arm of sofa.*)
MRS CUSTANCE (*preoccupied*) Have a good day?
MR CUSTANCE The same.
MRS CUSTANCE (*acceptant*) It's often the same.
   (MR CUSTANCE *half turns his shirt sleeves.*)
   (*Suddenly remembering*) Oh, Ted, I saw an accident! A fellow in a little cream car was tossed up against the Dingles' fence. Oh, it was awful! It was one of those lorries. Tip and run. Only it was more

183

than tip. The poor fellow was almost a corpse. Mrs Dingle was wiping the blood off his face with a towel.

MR CUSTANCE (*grunts*) He'll get something out of it.

(MRS CUSTANCE *frowns in sympathy, sucks her teeth.* MR CUSTANCE *goes towards door* BACK.)

MRS CUSTANCE Has a wife and two kiddies.

(MR CUSTANCE *returns as an after-thought, kisses his wife from behind, in the angle between neck and shoulder.* MRS CUSTANCE *almost recoils, almost giggles.*)

MR CUSTANCE What's wrong?

MRS CUSTANCE It tickled!

(MR CUSTANCE *continues out* BACK. *Strolls amongst his tomatoes. Begins to breathe again after the day.*)

(*Calling without looking*) I didn't say it wasn't nice, though!

(*Finishes her work at table. Goes to dinette, to check. Brings additional crockery and cutlery from dresser.*)

I didn't complain. Just that your chin was a bit rough. (*Standing back, looking at dining table*) You expect that at the end of the day. Specially in summer. (*Laughs softly*) It makes things grow.

(MR CUSTANCE *has grown contemplative amongst the tomatoes. Pinches out a shoot or two.*)

No letters. Not even a bill. I put my feet up and had a read. (*Brings dish from oven.*) Ought to feel bored. (*Realizing*) Funny thing . . . I never was!

(*Sets hot dish on dining-table.*)

(*Looking, calling*) Ted, what are you doing out there?

MR CUSTANCE Nothing.

MRS CUSTANCE It's ready. Tea!

(MR CUSTANCE *comes in.*)

Sometimes I think those blessed tomatoes will block the light completely.

MR CUSTANCE They alter it. That's all.

MRS CUSTANCE Yes, it does alter. Green. Green, they say, is restful.

(*As they sit down she takes his hand for a moment.*)

Aren't you going to wash them, Ted? They're stained.

MR CUSTANCE A bit of clean green?

MRS CUSTANCE Yes, I suppose it's clean. (*She serves*) You haven't got a bank teller's hands.

MR CUSTANCE Didn't ought to have been in a bank.

MRS CUSTANCE You're handy, of course. (*Pauses*) What would you be, Ted, if you weren't with the bank?

MR CUSTANCE I've forgotten.

MRS CUSTANCE Are you ever bored?

MR CUSTANCE What's the use?

MRS CUSTANCE That's true. But I never am bored. (*Pauses*) I mean . . . I don't have to make the effort not to be. (*Pauses*) Sometimes I wonder if it's right to feel always happy.

MR CUSTANCE Why not, while you've got it good?

MRS CUSTANCE That's so.

MR CUSTANCE Next moment someone might toss you up against the Dingles' fence. Like the fellow in the cream car.
(*He laughs, eats.*)

MRS CUSTANCE (*remembering, sucking her teeth*) Oh, dear! There, you see, it's not right to feel so happy . . . when that fellow with the wife and kiddies. . . .
(*While he eats, she finnicks with her food.*)
We're not selfish, are we?

MR CUSTANCE What's got into you?

MRS CUSTANCE Nothing.
(*They eat in silence.*)
(*At last*) Ted, I ought to tell you. I've got a plan.

MR CUSTANCE (*frowning, suspicious*) What sort of plan?

MRS CUSTANCE Well . . . (*dainty work with fork*) . . . it's that Miss Docker.

MR CUSTANCE That old ratbag!

MRS CUSTANCE Somebody ought to do something about her. Such a cheery soul, Ted. Always so helpful.
(MR CUSTANCE *grunts*).
And now she's going to be turned out. Since old Miss Baskerville died. Since the niece decided to sell *Lyme Regis*.
(MR CUSTANCE *looks very sulky.*)
Miss Docker won't have a roof.

MR CUSTANCE What do you reckon on doing?

185

MRS CUSTANCE (*cautiously*) Well . . . I'll tell you. What I'd like to do is to ask Miss Docker to accept . . . (*pausing, choosing words with particular care*) . . . to come and live in our little glassed-in veranda room. She could pay us back by helping with the chores. (*Quickly*) Not *rigidly*. I wouldn't make a slave of her or anyone else.

(MR CUSTANCE *stirs tea, does things to his teeth with his tongue. Above all sceptical.*)

MR CUSTANCE Yeah?

MRS CUSTANCE She'd be free to come and go. And she's in such demand – baby-sitting – mending – we'll hardly notice she's here.

(MR CUSTANCE *continues to stir his tea, too loud.*)

Poor soul! Nobody in Sarsaparilla ever did so much good.

MR CUSTANCE Provided it's not you who's having a fly at doing good, I shouldn't worry all that much.

MRS CUSTANCE Oh, Ted! (*Pause, then slowly*) You've got to justify yourself in some way. You can't just take, take, without you show a little gratitude.

MR CUSTANCE (*getting out his pipe, moving away from table*) Here, are you sick?

MRS CUSTANCE You know I'm never sick. But I'm getting on for forty-seven.

MR CUSTANCE Insurance, eh?

(*Fills his pipe, amused and stolid.*)

MRS CUSTANCE (*passing it off*) It would have been different if we'd had some kids. I wonder if people ever think we didn't because we couldn't be bothered? That'd be awful!

MR CUSTANCE Want us to go around with a placard: VICTIMS OF THE ABSENT-MINDED SURGEON?

MRS CUSTANCE Ah, Ted! We've been through all that before. It wasn't his fault. I was on the wrong trolley.

MR CUSTANCE (*lighting his pipe*) We could have sued.

MRS CUSTANCE Wouldn't have been decent. And the reporters. Imagine the reporters!

(*She starts to clear away. He smokes stolidly.*)

MR CUSTANCE (*suddenly*) When do you think of asking her?

MRS CUSTANCE Asking . . . ? Oh, Ted . . . you mean . . . then, we can tell poor Miss Docker? As a matter of fact, I was going to suggest to her that she moves in on Thursday.

(MR CUSTANCE *shrugs. Strolls towards veranda.*)

(*Bustling cheerfully*) Only I wanted to tell you first. (*Pausing, almost apprehensive at the thought*) Of course we mustn't expect our lives to remain unchanged. . . .

(MR CUSTANCE *hunches his shoulders.*)

MR CUSTANCE She may be a tippler. One of the wardrobe jobs.

MRS CUSTANCE I tell you she's the soul of goodness. (*Scraping plates*) Oh dear, I'm quite excited! At last we're doing something!

MR CUSTANCE Has your life been all that empty?

(*He moves* OFF, BACK, R., *into what is the veranda room.*)

MRS CUSTANCE What a thing to ask!

MR CUSTANCE (OFF) You asked for it!

(MRS CUSTANCE *pauses, with a particularly cautious air.*)

MRS CUSTANCE I told you I'm happy. Too happy. And I never seem to . . . thank anybody for it. (*Embarrassed*) People like us live such quiet lives we're not in the habit of doing and saying. But we're not vegetables. Not in the eyes of God!

(*She becomes more embarrassed, even angry. Busies herself with work.*)

There, you see! That's what I feel. Even if you don't like it. (*Pause*) I wonder if Miss Docker's a one for puddings. (*Pause*) What are you doing, Ted?

(*No answer.* MRS CUSTANCE *goes* BACK, *looks through the door of the veranda room.*)

Ted?

(MR CUSTANCE *emerges. Shoulders her back.*)

MR CUSTANCE Having a look to see whether I could put up some sort of shelf. Stick her old books on.

MRS CUSTANCE (*terribly grateful*) Then you're not selfish!

(*He pushes past her.*)

MR CUSTANCE (*embarrassed*) Oh yes, I am! When you've got to be!

MRS CUSTANCE But supposing she doesn't read? At least I've seen her *sitting* with a book. And then I expect she's inherited a few. She'll like to have them about.

(MR CUSTANCE *grunts.* MRS CUSTANCE *goes to him quickly, takes his hand.*)

Thank you, Ted. You were always clever with your hands. Always doing something. (*Examining his hand as if for first time*) How rough they are! I wonder they can count out the notes.

MR CUSTANCE (*dragging away his hand*) Want me to sleep in gloves, eh? Like the film actresses do.

MRS CUSTANCE (*very quietly*) I wouldn't want you altered. Not a bit of you.

(*He flicks at her ear. Then kisses her with an unexpected display of passion. She would like to enjoy and return it, but restrains herself.*) (*Rather weakly, then extricating*) There's the ... washing-up. (*She goes to the sink.*)

MR CUSTANCE (*sighing, stroking his nose*) Yairs.

(*He takes towel and follows.*)

MRS CUSTANCE Better get it over. Then we can sit and enjoy the peaceful evening.

(*Together they wash and wipe.*)

This is the time of day I enjoy most. When you've come. When the light begins to fade the other side of the tomato plants.

MR CUSTANCE Doesn't seem to cost any effort.

MRS CUSTANCE When you're together it's so peaceful. People were meant to go in pairs.

(SCENE FADES.)

(*While* STAGE IS IN DARKNESS *a car is heard approaching, very loud and menacing, then pulling up. Loud blast on the horn. Then* MISS DOCKER'S VOICE.)

MISS DOCKER (OFF, L.) You'll think I'm acting bold, tooting your horn like that. But to me it's friendly. Let's them know you've arrived.

HIRE CAR MAN (OFF) You've arrived all right!

(LIGHTS ON SAME SCENE *as before, bit earlier in the afternoon, the following Thursday. Empty stage.*)

MISS DOCKER (OFF) Isn't it lovely to be amongst friends! What would we do without them? (*Pause*) Neat place they've got. (*Pause*) As a matter of personal taste, I'd have painted it cream and green.

(ENTER MRS CUSTANCE *very hurried and breathless,* R., *from front of house. Rushes towards door,* L. *Hesitates, and gets into position from which she can take an unobserved, long-range peep.*)

(OFF, *to* HIRE CAR MAN) Here! Help yourself to a lolly. Don't tell me there's a man hasn't got a sweet tooth.

(ENTER MISS DOCKER, L., *followed by* HIRE CAR MAN. *He is a big, jolly type in tight blue shiny suit. Young. Will laugh a lot, but not know what to say. He is carrying an enormous heavy port, and an old-fashioned luggage basket with a strap round it.* MISS DOCKER *is about 60. Although not particularly large, she gives the impression of being over lifesize. She is dressed up. Beige powder and plenty of purple lipstick. Probably a dark brown woman underneath. She is carrying: a hat in a paper container; a dress-box tied with string; a transistor (silent); and the open paper-bag from which she has offered the lolly.*)

(MRS CUSTANCE *hesitates to approach and welcome* MISS DOCKER.)

MISS DOCKER (*looking around, ignoring* MRS CUSTANCE) Ah dear, it's lovely! Must catch the morning sun.

HIRE CAR MAN (*dumping luggage*) There's yer stuff, then.

MISS DOCKER (*absently, glancing over her shoulder*) Cheeri-bye... Fred, isn't it? See you later.

(HIRE CAR MAN EXIT L., *and is heard driving away.*)

(*Now ready for* MRS CUSTANCE) You're looking peaky, aren't you? What've you been up to?

MRS CUSTANCE (*shocked and embarrassed*) Me?

MISS DOCKER Who else? Fisher's Ghost?

(MISS DOCKER *shrieks.*)

(*Nudging* MRS CUSTANCE *with her elbow*) It's me sense of humour. You and I'll have a laugh together. Oh, not all laugh. Wait till I get me sleeves rolled up. I was never one to avoid showing gratitude.

(*She begins to walk around, humming.*)

MRS CUSTANCE (*tentatively*) I do hope, Miss Docker, you'll be able to feel this is your home.

MISS DOCKER (*continuing her inspection*) Don't worry about *me*. I can always feel at home. You've got to! (*Peering through door* R.) Don't some people have the luck!

MRS CUSTANCE (*proud, though ashamed*) There are still things we have to do.

MISS DOCKER It all takes time.

MRS CUSTANCE Ted does it at weekends. He's a real handy man. (MISS DOCKER *turns away from door*.)

MISS DOCKER Well, I was never a nuisance to anyone. I'll take what's offered, whether garage, or shed.

MRS CUSTANCE (*hurt*) Oh! Surely you understood you were to have the little glassed-in veranda room?

MISS DOCKER (*moody*) If that was *agreed*, then.

MRS CUSTANCE Oh, yes, yes! It was agreed.

(*Noise of a motor vehicle approaching.*)

MISS DOCKER (*listening*) One thing I didn't mention, dear. . . . Or did I? There's a few sticks – all my wordly goods – unimportant – but it's what you've got, isn't it? – What you love.

MRS CUSTANCE Oh, yes, what you love!

MISS DOCKER A rocker that's just about part of my own body. A chest . . . real mahogany. . . . Can stand outside somewhere. Of no value except to me.

(*Noise of vehicle pulling up* L.)

MRS CUSTANCE Oh, we'll find *room* for them!

MISS DOCKER Provided they're inspected regular for white ant. . . . (*Peering out*, L.) Why, I believe it's the little van I made the arrangement with. Yes, it's the little van already.

MRS CUSTANCE Wouldn't you like to see the room?

MISS DOCKER Yes. We ought to get that over. I mean, we can enjoy a yarn then.

(MRS CUSTANCE *picks up the port and basket. Staggers with them to veranda, and* EXIT R. *into room.* MISS DOCKER *follows.*)

MRS CUSTANCE (OFF) There, you see, it's small, but nice.

MISS DOCKER (*peering in, gloomily*) Nice and airy.

(RE-ENTER MRS CUSTANCE *to veranda.*)

MRS CUSTANCE Oh yes, it's airy!

(EXIT MISS DOCKER *into room.* MRS CUSTANCE *remains visible on veranda, watching* MISS DOCKER'S *operations inside.*)

MISS DOCKER (OFF) Is the bed hard?

MRS CUSTANCE I hope not!

MISS DOCKER (OFF) I like a hard bed. I mean, it's healthier and all that. That's obvious, isn't it? But it helps remind you. . . .

MRS CUSTANCE (*her doubts ascending*) Mmmmmmm. . . ?

(A FURNITURE REMOVAL MAN *appears* L. *with a big old rocker.*)

FURNITURE REMOVAL MAN (*to* MRS CUSTANCE) Mrs Custance's place? (*As she nods*) Miss Docker's rocker.

(*He places rocker* CENTRE. *Starts it rocking violently.* EXIT FURNITURE REMOVAL MAN.)

MISS DOCKER (OFF) I mean, you've got to study the ethical side of life. Otherwise you'd be no more than animal.

MRS CUSTANCE (*sadly, staring at the rocker*) I don't think Mr Custance would ever stand for a hard bed.

MISS DOCKER (OFF) Don't tell me the rooster rules the roost!

(*Noise in the veranda room, as though* MISS DOCKER *is slamming the door of a bedside table, and opening and closing drawers.*)

MRS CUSTANCE He's my husband.

MISS DOCKER (OFF) Bet he crows, though! (*Shrieks with laughter*) Never been able to make up me mind about husbands. Though I can't say I'm not partial to the men. (*Sound of squeaky furniture in veranda room*) Look at this ricketty little thing! We'll put a chock under that. Or perhaps we'll put it out altogether.

MRS CUSTANCE (*glancing in*) That was my mother's pot-stand.

MISS DOCKER (OFF) Well, now don't think I have anything against your poor mother. Nor against her pot, neether. It's just that I'm practical.

MRS CUSTANCE (*regretfully*) Perhaps it *is* a silly little thing.

MISS DOCKER We'll call it dainty if you'd rather . . . out of respect for poor Mum. . . .

(MISS DOCKER'S *behind appears momentarily through doorway of veranda-room, as though she is stooping.*)

(TWO FURNITURE REMOVAL MEN *appear* L., *staggering awkwardly as they carry a tallboy.*)

FIRST FURNITURE REMOVAL MAN Miss Docker's tallboy.

MRS CUSTANCE Tallboy? I thought it was going to be a chest!

(RE-ENTER MISS DOCKER. *She has left the things she was carrying, and discarded her coat, but is still wearing a hat.*)

MISS DOCKER But a tallboy's a sort of chest, isn't it?

MRS CUSTANCE (*reluctantly*) I suppose it is . . . a sort of chest.

MISS DOCKER No one could object to the tallboy, at least in my own room. There's not that much furniture. In fact, it's fairly bare. You men will move the tallboy in, won't you?

(*She motions them towards veranda.*)

(*As men manoeuvre into veranda-room*) Easy does it, boys! Bet you men can put away the steak. Strong-looking fellows, aren't they?

(EXIT MEN *into veranda-room, followed by* MISS DOCKER.)

(OFF) There! Right here, Jack. Snug little room, isn't it? Good job I've got me corsets on! (*Shrieks with laughter*).

(MRS CUSTANCE *watches dubiously from veranda.*)

MRS CUSTANCE Oh, but Miss Docker, don't you see, it'll be standing in front of the louvres!

MISS DOCKER (OFF, *gloom descending*) You can't have it all ways.

MRS CUSTANCE You won't get any air.

MISS DOCKER (OFF) If Mrs Custance knows, she knows. We'll give it an extra shove.

(*Brief sound of splintering wood.* FURNITURE MEN *come backing out.* EXIT *very impersonally* R.)

(OFF) What's that?

(MRS CUSTANCE *darts suddenly* OFF *into veranda-room.*)

MRS CUSTANCE (OFF) Nothing really.

(RE-ENTER MRS CUSTANCE. *She is carrying some pieces of wood with an air of tenderness.*)

(*Upset*) Nothing of importance. Just a little bookshelf.

(RE-ENTER MISS DOCKER *hatless*).

MISS DOCKER I'm sorry. But accidents will always happen.

(MRS CUSTANCE *drops the wood reluctantly into dustbin.*)

(*Cheerfully, reviving her hair*) Anyhow, I've arrived!

(*Sound of van driving away.*)

And here's me old rocker. (*Goes to it*) You could say: Here's Me!

(*Looks around*) We'll put this out on the veranda, where I expect we'll often sit and yarn. (*Carries chair* BACK *to veranda*) A lady left me this when she died. (*Puts chair in position* C.) Yes. (*Sits*) Aren't we lucky?

(MISS DOCKER *rocking*, MRS CUSTANCE *watching her amazed.*)

(SCENE FADES.)

(SAME SCENE. *Same evening a little later.* MRS CUSTANCE *standing at kitchen table preparing a dish. Loud strains of vibrant humming* OFF R.)

MRS CUSTANCE (*slightly irritated, calling*) Don't you think you ought to settle down?

MISS DOCKER (OFF) I *am* settling down.

(ENTER MISS DOCKER R., *looking rather gloomy.*)

Everybody has their own methods.

MRS CUSTANCE You're all right, are you? Not depressed?

MISS DOCKER I was having a look to see what luck other people have.

MRS CUSTANCE (*abashed*) I never thought of it as ostentatious.

MISS DOCKER It's what you're used to. (*Snapping out of it*) Look here, I'm not like this! Everyone'll tell you I'm the cheerfulest person. Normally. But there are moments in life which aren't normal . . . when you're dislocated, so to speak. Won't you agree?

MRS CUSTANCE (*feebly*) Yes.

(*She continues with her work.* MISS DOCKER *comes and stands over her.*)

MISS DOCKER (*observing*) Macaroni cheese. Remind me to tell you of a trick I learned with that.

MRS CUSTANCE Yes. I'll remind you.

MISS DOCKER And a nice piece of rump. Tender, I bet. Good and thick.

MRS CUSTANCE That's for my husband. After a hard day's work, I consider a man needs meat.

(MISS DOCKER *throws back her head and laughs.*)

MISS DOCKER I'll say!

N

MRS CUSTANCE (*embarrassed*) I mean . . . they burn more fuel than us.

(MISS DOCKER *roams around.*)

MISS DOCKER (*sighing*) Ah, the men! One day I'm going to tell you all about the men in my life. There's some won't believe, but I'm not forcing anybody to accept the truth. It's like religious faith. Take it or leave it, I say. (*Sighing again*) Yes, the men! (*Gazes out of window above sink.*) Would that be a hydrangea? That staggy, sickly thing over by your rotary clothes-line?

(MRS CUSTANCE *goes to look.*)

MRS CUSTANCE (*apologetic*) Yes.

MISS DOCKER (*disapproving*) I bet you didn't prune in July – leaving two pair of eyes – like we're told.

MRS CUSTANCE I never prune it.

MISS DOCKER What? You're not one of those who're *afraid* to prune?

MRS CUSTANCE It's useful for drying things on. When they overflow from the line.

MISS DOCKER But that's not a hydrangea's purpose.

(*Seems depressed again. Roams and hums.*)

(*Humming*) Hy-der-range-y
            hy-der-range-y
            hy-der-range-y-*er*!

(MRS CUSTANCE *almost collides with* MISS DOCKER *mid-stage as she goes to put macaroni-cheese in oven.*)

Whatever will you think of me? No one can say I'm helpless. Here, give us a towel!

(*She takes one herself. Slings a couple of plates about at sink.* MRS CUSTANCE *continues with other work.*)

Cheerful's in my horoscope. What are you?

MRS CUSTANCE (*absent*) Ohhh . . . Virgo, I believe.

MISS DOCKER Virgo? That's bad! A Virgo's always put upon.

(MRS CUSTANCE *does not reply. Continues absent and busy.*)

(*Losing interest in dishes*) Where does the tea live?

MRS CUSTANCE (*exasperated*) But it's far too late and still too early.

(MISS DOCKER *finds canister and pot on dresser.*)

MISS DOCKER (*sententiously*) It's never too early for a cuppa tea.

(*Fills pot, spilling dry tea copiously.*) No one is installed till after their first cuppa tea. (*Fills pot from kettle on stove*) That's as clear as charity. And warmer too. (*Spills plenty of sugar as she helps herself at dresser.*)

MRS CUSTANCE (*sharp for her*) Charity's often not as bad as she's supposed to be. (*Pause*) I'm glad you're making yourself comfortable, Miss Docker.

(MISS DOCKER *brings her cup of tea down* FORWARD *as* MR CUSTANCE ENTERS L. *carrying hat and evening paper.*)

MISS DOCKER Well! Here he is! (*To* MR CUSTANCE) And this is Me!

MRS CUSTANCE (*desperate*) Yes. This is Miss Docker, Ted.

(*He looks quite frightened, nods, walks past in a round-about way, lifting up his feet as he crunches over spilt tea and sugar.*)

MISS DOCKER That's a little bit of spilt tea and sugar that I'll sweep up when I'm feeling more relaxed.

(EXIT MR CUSTANCE R. *as quickly as possible.*)

Yours Truly won't deny it makes all the difference having a man in the house. (*She sits on sofa.*)

(*Singing*) 'Where skies are blue,

And hearts are true. . . .'

Wouldn't know I had a voice. Only amateur, of course. Chorus work. But there has to be a chorus too.

(MRS CUSTANCE *continues with her work.*)

Ever done any acting?

MRS CUSTANCE I couldn't act.

MISS DOCKER 'Ts easy. You've just got to be yourself. That's the secret.

MRS CUSTANCE Provided you know what you are.

MISS DOCKER Eh? Who's going to know if you don't yourself?

(MRS CUSTANCE *does not answer. Takes cutlery from dresser.*)

Here! (*Gets up*) Allow *me*! (*Takes cutlery from* MRS CUSTANCE.)

Tea in the dinette, I presume, when we're *ong fameel*.

MRS CUSTANCE (*with an effort*) That's it!

(MISS DOCKER *lays and hums.* MRS CUSTANCE *switches light on.*)

MISS DOCKER (*squinting in disapproval at light*) I say, do you people really go for these hard lights?

MRS CUSTANCE (*exasperated*) We have nothing to hide.

MISS DOCKER Now! Now! Sharp tongues give unkind answers.

(MISS DOCKER *and* MRS CUSTANCE *exchange hard glances for a moment.*)

Besides, do you think I'm the kind of person to hide things?

MRS CUSTANCE No! No! Not for a moment!

(*She goes desperately to stove, inspects oven and hot-plate.*)

MISS DOCKER I was always frank in everything.

(MRS CUSTANCE *goes to door* R.)

MRS CUSTANCE (*calling, making it sound an awful confession*) Tea is ready, Ted.

(*Returns to stove for macaroni-cheese.*)

MISS DOCKER In fact, I'm going to admit you and me just had words, and I'm sorry for it.

(MRS CUSTANCE *places dish on table.*)

MRS CUSTANCE (*standing with head bowed, as though about to say grace*) When I was a little girl I hated macaroni-cheese. Then I found I'd got used to it. Or I just didn't care.

(MISS DOCKER *flops down at table.*)

MISS DOCKER (*sighing*) There's a lot you've got to get used to.

(ENTER MR CUSTANCE R. *Walks straight to his place at table. Sits.*)

(*Extra loud and hearty*) Ha! The master at his own board!

(MR CUSTANCE *manages not to wince. Does not answer.* MISS DOCKER *serves bread in great hunks.* MRS CUSTANCE *brings steak for* MR CUSTANCE.)

Whenever I cut into a loaf of bread it makes me thankful. It makes me feel how much we've got.

(*She chews a big, virtuous lump of it.* MRS CUSTANCE *hands her a plate of macaroni cheese.*)

(*Protesting through mouthful of bread*) Not all that much. Just a teeny weeny bit for me!

MRS CUSTANCE Don't you like it?

MISS DOCKER God gave me bread.

MRS CUSTANCE *And* macaroni-cheese.

MISS DOCKER You see, I have to resist gluttony. Oh yes, you wouldn't believe. There was never such a glutton, and worst of all for meat.

(*She eyes* MR CUSTANCE *as he eats his steak. Receives back her reduced helping of macaroni. Continues staring at* MR CUSTANCE.)
Is it tender, Mr Custance?
(MR CUSTANCE *grunts but does not answer.*)
Not very talkative, is he?

MRS CUSTANCE Some people aren't. (*Almost tenderly to her husband*) Ted, dear, you haven't got your mustard!
(*She is about to fetch it.*)

MR CUSTANCE (*shaking his head, eating quickly*) No, no. Doesn't matter.

MISS DOCKER Well, it takes all kinds. Personally, I like a good discussion, amongst friends, on a metaphysical theme.

MRS CUSTANCE (*apologetic*) We're inclined to be book-worms.

MISS DOCKER Oh, I'm not above having a read! A lady lent me the *Tanglewood Tales.* Once I read the Bible from cover to cover. That was when I was at the end of me tether. A whole fortnight it took me. I lay in bed, and read, and read. It was raining cats and dogs. Never stopped. Before that I was pagan. But suddenly I saw.

MR CUSTANCE (*fiercely, glaring at her*) What did you see?

MISS DOCKER Don't be silly! You can't say what you see. But *see*. See?
(MR CUSTANCE *tries to outstare her.*)
He's like somebody, isn't he? Now, who is it? Somebody in a moustache. Somebody historical.
(MR CUSTANCE *pushes his plate away.* MRS CUSTANCE *takes it quickly.*)

MRS CUSTANCE (*soothing, for him alone*) There's your Lemon Delicious, dear.

MISS DOCKER (*to* MR CUSTANCE) You know what's the matter with you, don't you?
(*He doesn't answer. Messes about with his pudding.*)
(*Hunching her shoulders, lowering her eyelids*) Your posture is all wrong. And posture is nine-tenths. According to Indian philosophy. Mind you, there's a lot of that isn't altogether healthy, but you can pick up a wrinkle here and there. Now posture. . . . Remind me to show you, some other time. (*Pauses*) I've got to be without me corsets.

(MISS DOCKER *nearly bursts*. MR CUSTANCE *gets up, goes out* BACK *looking rather tense*.)
Moody type.

MRS CUSTANCE Ted is the most even-tempered of men. (*Controlling herself, but speaking coldly*) Here is your Lemon Delicious, Miss Docker.

MISS DOCKER When you only want to help a person. When there are so many people waiting to be helped. So much love waiting to be poured out on those who are unwilling to accept it. The world would be a wonderful place. . . .

(MRS CUSTANCE *has gone to the sink. Measures something into a glass of water*.)

(*Watching*) Not sick, are you?

MRS CUSTANCE I'm taking a little bi-carb. (*Drinking*) Just so much as will fit on a sixpence. (*Turns to the sink*)

MISS DOCKER So long as you're not sick. Though you wouldn't want for a nurse. (*Brightening, as a thought enters her mind*) By the way, guess what I'm doing tomorrow. I'm going up to the butcher's to buy a couple of mutton shanks.

MRS CUSTANCE (*incensed*) You'll have no need to buy food in *this* house!

MISS DOCKER It's that Mrs Apps. Pernicious anaemia! If you ask me she's starved for love. Well, I'm going to make Mrs Apps a basinful of broth.

MRS CUSTANCE (*genuinely impressed, though at the same time humouring a child*) I think that's a wonderful idea, Miss Docker.

MISS DOCKER (*smiling, childlike*) Eh? (*Growing serious*) There are so many professing Christians. . . . Mind you, I think a lot of things just don't cross their poor minds. (*Her voice rising almost hysterically to a note of desperation*) But you can't leave people to starve. Can you? Now, can you?

(SCENE FADES.)

(LIGHTS UP. *Same scene. Night.* MR CUSTANCE *is lying back in a corner of the sofa,* R. MRS CUSTANCE *is in much the same position, resting against his chest. Marriage has obviously left them very much in love.*)

MRS CUSTANCE But you've got to admit, Ted, Miss Docker is a dedicated soul.

MR CUSTANCE Dedicated, my foot! The soul of a bulldozer, and we're the ants!

MRS CUSTANCE Perhaps we're the ones who are to blame.

MR CUSTANCE (*mimicking woman's voice*) She's so helpful, so good!

MRS CUSTANCE We mustn't just *put up with* her. We must learn to love her. Then it will be different. (*Wondering*) Or perhaps we don't understand love.

MR CUSTANCE (*chuckling, then with a kind of gruff tenderness*) Thought we did!

MRS CUSTANCE (*laughing, equally tender*) Of course we do! (*Again anxious*) Only . . . there are the different *kinds.*

MR CUSTANCE (*sighing*) Ah yes, there's the different kinds.

MRS CUSTANCE We've got to learn.

MR CUSTANCE Anyway, we'll try!

MRS CUSTANCE (*blissfully*) Listen!

MR CUSTANCE What?

MRS CUSTANCE So peaceful. When I lie and listen to the frogs croaking like that after rain, it's as if we were alone on an island. Our island.

MR CUSTANCE Are you serious?

MRS CUSTANCE Oh, I know! But she's gone to bed now. She's asleep.

MR CUSTANCE Even when she's asleep, you can seem to hear her rubbing against the wall.

MRS CUSTANCE Don't, Ted! That isn't what I want to hear.

MR CUSTANCE Sometimes when we're in bed I could swear we've got a third person with us. . . .

(*A stream of radio music is turned up from the veranda-room. The* CUSTANCES *listen, horrified.*)

199

MISS DOCKER (OFF, *calling drowsily above the music*) You ought to invest in a transistor.

MR CUSTANCE (*calling back*) We don't need to!

MISS DOCKER (OFF) Ah, the lovely music it does you good. And talks. Always something to learn. Though what I go for most of all is the man saying goodnight. So friendly.

(*Music ends.* RADIO VOICE *is heard closing down.* MISS DOCKER *begins to snore.* MR CUSTANCE *starts pinching at his wife's arm in wild glee, in time with the National Anthem.*)

MRS CUSTANCE (*dragging her arm away, jumping up, speaking in a loud whisper*) Oh, do stop it!

MR CUSTANCE She's asleep, isn't she?

(MR CUSTANCE *moves after* MRS CUSTANCE, *embraces her passionately. She drags away her mouth, resists.*)

MRS CUSTANCE (*guiltily*) It makes me feel embarrassed.

MR CUSTANCE (*grimly*) The Presence, eh? Never absent!

(SCENE FADES.)

(SAME SCENE. *Sunday morning before midday dinner.* MISS DOCKER *amongst tomato vines,* BACK. *She could have been pruning. Lets fall a couple of shoots.*)

MISS DOCKER (*looking around*) Sunday middle of the day you can relax . . . can't you? (*In a gust of apprehension*) You've been forgiven . . . haven't you? You've sung your best. Sin has shot off on a motor-bike. . . . (*More relaxed, inhaling deeply, beaming*) I love midday Sunday. I love its smell. Fat spitting in the pan . . . I love the lamb's tail, the parson's nose . . . even when they don't give them to you. . . .

(*She goes and sits in her rocker, on the veranda, facing* R.)

(*Waving, calling to invisible passer-by*) Oohoo! Miss Sutch! He gave me a lift . . . Mr Custance. Wasn't it nice? . . . No, they're slightly Baptist. I mean, they don't always remember. . . . Still, wasn't it nice of him. People *are* nice! (*Pause*) (*Calling*) How're you doin', Mrs Buckingham? . . . Yairs. . . . He's looking peaked,

though. You can see the kiddy's in need of iron. . . . Oh, but you
can't go by what a doctor tells you. . . . (*Pause*) (*Tentatively*) Mr
Lickiss. . . . (*Shouting, waving*) Mr Lick-iss! (*Despondent, muttering*) Some people won't know you. . . .

(*During the foregoing,* MRS CUSTANCE *appears from* R. *Looks in
the oven. Suddenly notices the thermostat.*)

MRS CUSTANCE (*turning on* MISS DOCKER) Miss Docker?

(MISS DOCKER *comes into kitchen, all Sunday smiles.*)

Did you turn the oven off?

MISS DOCKER (*pleased*) Yes! Finish it on stored heat.

MRS CUSTANCE (*almost crying*) But I never trust the stored heat!
(*She obviously turns the oven up pretty high.*)

MISS DOCKER Silly girl! It's practical. It's what it says to do.

MRS CUSTANCE What *what* says?

MISS DOCKER Why, the book of rules.

MRS CUSTANCE (*petulant for her*) I didn't think *you* ever went by
the book of rules.

MISS DOCKER (*piously*) Look, it's Sunday. I'm not going to quarrel
on a Sunday.

MRS CUSTANCE No. We mustn't quarrel. It was just that you provoked me.

MISS DOCKER Only thought to help a person.

(ENTER MR CUSTANCE, R.)

MR CUSTANCE (*friendly for him, rubbing his hands*) . . . eat a horse!

MRS CUSTANCE Well, it's not ready yet. We're not quite certain.
(*A meaningful pause.* MISS DOCKER *looks righteous.*)

MRS CUSTANCE So you'll have to . . . talk.

(MRS CUSTANCE *immediately horrified at what she has said.* MR
CUSTANCE *ironical.*)

MR CUSTANCE Oh, Miss Docker and I'll keep the ball of conversation rolling. Did she tell you about the crisis at the Church of
England?

MISS DOCKER It's that woman. That Miss Scougall has something
against me. She can't bear me to use my voice. She won't allow me
to improvise. And of course her sister sides with her. She plays
flat. (*Pauses*) Oh, dear, why are people like they are?

MR CUSTANCE Because they're people, I suppose.

MISS DOCKER That reminds me. There's something that's been grieving me. Here in the home.

(*The* CUSTANCES *tense themselves to receive a blow.*)

For some time I've wondered why . . . amongst good friends . . . why there seems to be a ban on Christian names.

(MR CUSTANCE *could be warding something off.*)

I was christened Gertrude. But everybody calls me Gee. Gee would feel she really was your friend to hear her name occasionally.

MRS CUSTANCE (*hanging her head*) I expect we're not the kind. . . . We're not exactly cold, not formal . . . (*awkwardly*) . . . stiff perhaps. (*Making the greatest effort*) Yes, I suppose, too, we're shy.

MISS DOCKER But it's not mature! Ted's Ted, we know. But I'd never ever have known Mrs Custance had a name if I hadn't seen it written in a book.

(MR CUSTANCE *is near to bursting with distaste.*)

(*Coaxing* MRS CUSTANCE) Come on, Gwen! A name is friendship's sweetener.

MR CUSTANCE (*very quiet, very quick*) I'm buggered if I'll come at this.

(*He walks out firmly into the garden,* BACK.)

MISS DOCKER (*sitting down*) Ah well, it was only a suggestion. *Nemo* will remain *Nemo*. That means *Nobody*.

MRS CUSTANCE (*as if going to bring her husband back*) Ted! (*Returning*) Oh, dear! Why does everything happen at once? (*Looks in oven*) It's . . . I believe . . . the shoulder's *burnt!*

MISS DOCKER I shouldn't say, but Temper turned the oven up too high.

(MR CUSTANCE *has picked up the couple of tomato shoots* MISS DOCKER *let fall earlier. Runs up the steps and into kitchen.*)

MR CUSTANCE (*congested, shouting*) Miss Docker!

(*Showing the tomato shoots.*)

MISS DOCKER (*calmly*) What's up, Mr Custance? What if I did give you a hand with the tomatoes? Those couple of shoots needed pinching out.

MR CUSTANCE (*incredulous, trembling with rage*) You meddled with my tomatoes?

MISS DOCKER What I did, Mr Custance, was scientific. It's what I learned from an approved manual.

MR CUSTANCE (*throwing shoots on floor*) But this is the scientific end!

MISS DOCKER Oh, all right, all right! I'll leave you to judge yourselves and enjoy your dinner.

(*Stamps* OFF *tearfully into her room.*)

MRS CUSTANCE (*exhausted, putting her arms round her husband*) Ted, oh, Ted, I always thought we were cool!

(*They stand* C., *arms round each other.*)

MR CUSTANCE (*stroking her*) Cool, vegetable flesh . . .

MRS CUSTANCE . . . made to twine together in silence.

MR CUSTANCE But that doesn't mean the vegetable kingdom can't act. I've seen roses tear a roof off.

MRS CUSTANCE Yes. Something, something must be done!

(SCENE FADES.)

(LIGHTS UP *on same scene.* MISS DOCKER *seated on veranda, monumental in her rocker. The kitchen is empty. After a moment* MISS DOCKER *gets up, steals across kitchen to door* R. *The door is shut.* MISS DOCKER *listens intently. From her expression of frustration, she probably just can't hear enough. Suddenly runs and composes herself on sofa before door opens.* ENTER MRS CUSTANCE, R. *She notices* MISS DOCKER, *starts to cough nervously.*)

MRS CUSTANCE Got a frog in my throat.

MISS DOCKER It's convenient having a 'phone in the home. (*Pauses, then pointing in direction from which* MRS CUSTANCE *has entered*) By the way, did you see the little notebook I hung beside it on a string? That's to enter up my calls.

(MRS CUSTANCE *looks unhappy.*)

MRS CUSTANCE (*making an effort*) Miss Docker, I might as well tell you. . . .

MISS DOCKER Yes?

MRS CUSTANCE (*agitated*) We have decided . . . Mr Custance and I

. . . that at our time of life, we're too set in our ways . . . too *selfish* perhaps . . . to share our home with a third person. It's dreadful, I know, *dreadful*!

MISS DOCKER (*smiling, almost serene, as though she has been prepared from the beginning*) People can't help theirselves.

(*Suddenly bursts into a dramatic, though dry, sobbing.*)

MRS CUSTANCE (*desperately*) You know what a privilege it is to be accepted by the Sundown Home at Sarsaparilla. You should see the waiting list. Many of them well-connected couples. To say nothing of single ladies. . . .

(MISS DOCKER *continues to sob.*)

. . . Well, to cut it short, I know somebody who not exactly knows, but is acquainted with Bishop Agnew, and the Home has decided to accept you . . . overlooking prior claims. . . .

(MRS CUSTANCE *exhausted and distraught. But* MISS DOCKER *could have been through it all before. Sits up. Blows her nose.*)

MISS DOCKER (*quite collected*) Will Thursday suit?

MRS CUSTANCE (*feigning vagueness*) Thursday? Yes, Thursday.

(SCENE FADES.)

(LIGHTS GO UP *on same scene. Thursday.* MISS DOCKER *in hat and coat strolling pensive amongst tomatoes.* TWO FURNITURE REMOVAL MEN ENTER *from veranda-room, stagger across kitchen with tallboy.* EXIT L.)

(ENTER MRS CUSTANCE *from veranda-room to kitchen. Goes back to veranda, brings rocker, and stands it firmly, though not vindictively, by door* L.)

MISS DOCKER (*mounting veranda steps*) I was having a last look around familiar scenes.

(*She pauses to gaze sentimentally into veranda-room.*)

MRS CUSTANCE (*in kitchen, avoiding something she ought to face*) The tallboy, Miss Docker. . . .

MISS DOCKER You know . . . however short a time you spend in a place, you leave part of yourself behind.

MRS CUSTANCE When the men were moving the tallboy. . . .

MISS DOCKER (*entering kitchen, rather languid*) It's sad, but true. We've got to face it.

MRS CUSTANCE You know the tallboy wasn't in the best condition, and. . . .

MISS DOCKER Even the railway waiting rooms . . . the waiting rooms you've waited in . . . sort of take something from you.

MRS CUSTANCE That *tallboy*. . . !

MISS DOCKER Ever listened to a sheep train pulled up in a siding . . . at night? I reckon that's the loneliest sound on earth.

MRS CUSTANCE (*turning on her, gasping*) Miss Docker!

MISS DOCKER (*innocent*) What was it you was saying about the tallboy, Mrs C?

MRS CUSTANCE (*hurrying*) When the men were moving it, I heard a sound of . . . (*hesitates*)

MISS DOCKER Yes?

MRS CUSTANCE . . . of something happening . . . of wood tearing . . . coming apart. . . .

MISS DOCKER Those old bits of furniture . . . the bits we *love* . . . act quite human, don't they? . . . in the end.

MRS CUSTANCE (*discreetly using her handkerchief*) Oh, I'd hate anything to happen to it!

MISS DOCKER (*watching her effects with half an eye*) Didn't you say it had happened? Or was my ears deceiving me?
(*She turns to go into veranda-room.*)

MRS CUSTANCE (*tormented*) . . . something else . . . to tell you. There's something you've forgotten to pack.

MISS DOCKER (*blandly*) What is that, Mrs Custance?
(*She turns for a moment, a monumental sight* CENTRE *of veranda.*)

MRS CUSTANCE A little china shoe I noticed on the dressing table.

MISS DOCKER That is not forgotten, Mrs Custance. That is a little memento I left for my friends to remember me by.
(EXIT MISS DOCKER *into veranda-room.* MRS CUSTANCE *in some distress.*)

MRS CUSTANCE You do make it difficult!

MISS DOCKER (OFF) My only thought is to make it easier for other people. There must be *some* pleasant memories, and the little shoe will bring them back.

MRS CUSTANCE I hope you're right!

(FIRST FURNITURE MAN *appears in doorway*, L.)

FURNITURE MAN (*nodding at* MRS CUSTANCE) All serene, eh?

(*He takes rocker, and* EXIT. *At same time van is heard starting up.*)

MISS DOCKER (OFF) Oh, I don't want to make it look as though I'm in the right! I know only too well I'm usually in the wrong. See?

(MRS CUSTANCE *looks battered. Van is heard driving away.*)

(OFF) If I was comfortable . . . I mean to say, if I was a lady of means, I might atone for it in some way. It's so much easier for the wealthy. They can pay the people they haven't meant to hurt.

(*A car is heard approaching.* MRS CUSTANCE *quite distraught.*)

(OFF) Don't you agree?

MRS CUSTANCE (*in agonies of distress*) I expect *you*, Miss Docker, will be received into the Kingdom of Heaven.

MISS DOCKER (OFF) I wouldn't presume . . . I mean, who are you and me to decide?

(*Car is heard pulling up outside.*)

(OFF) In any case, all Yours Truly asks is a crust of bread and a sound roof over her head. . . .

(HIRE CAR MAN *appears at door* L.)

HIRE CAR MAN (*very respectful and subdued*) Miss Docker's car.

(MISS DOCKER ENTERS *from veranda-room. She is carrying the dress-box, the paper bag containing a hat, and her transistor – now in action.*)

MISS DOCKER (*to* HIRE CAR MAN) Well, Fred, you can fetch my things from the . . . (*motioning with her head*) . . . guest-room.

(HIRE CAR MAN *quickly crosses kitchen, fetches port and luggage-basket from veranda-room, and* EXIT L. *during the following.*)

MRS CUSTANCE Miss Docker, I hope you and I will be able to meet without bitterness.

MISS DOCKER One thing I never was is bitter.

MRS CUSTANCE Yes. But some things rankle.

MISS DOCKER Only in a rankler, Mrs Custance. (*Pause*) (*Formally*) I'm not going to speechify, only to say that Christian kindness is a rare thing, and never too easy learned, even by those of other virtue.

MRS CUSTANCE (*wounded*) Goodbye, Miss Docker.

MISS DOCKER Cheerio, Mrs Custance.

(EXIT MISS DOCKER, L.)

(OFF) Okay, Fred. Drive on in this lovely car . . . that you've spat on extra hard, I see . . . for me. Some men claim that face-powder polishes good. Ordinary face-powder. Did you know? (*Car door heard to bang.*)

MRS CUSTANCE (*propelled to doorway,* L., *by guilty conscience, calling*) It's only next door, Miss Docker! We shall be practically neigh-bours!

(*Car heard driving away.* MRS CUSTANCE *goes* BACK *into veranda-room. Returns at once with an expression of extreme guilt, holding what must be the little china shoe.*)

(ENTER MR CUSTANCE *stealthily* R., *carrying hat and evening paper.*)

MR CUSTANCE Is it done?

MRS CUSTANCE It's done.

(MR CUSTANCE *throws hat and paper on sofa.*)

MR CUSTANCE (*whirling through kitchen*) Wotcha, Lady Macbeth! (*He grasps* MRS CUSTANCE, *and completes the whirl with her in his arms.*)

MRS CUSTANCE (*half laughing, half crying*) Oh, but we're bad, Ted! We're bad!

MR CUSTANCE What odds! We're bad!

(*He drags her down with him on the sofa, kissing her, laughing.*)

MRS CUSTANCE (*resisting*) Ted! Whatever would people say!

MR CUSTANCE (*suddenly sober*) Listen!

MRS CUSTANCE Yes. It's ours now.

(MRS CUSTANCE *gets up, moves away.*)

But I shall always stand condemned in any trial by goodness.

(MR CUSTANCE *goes after her. Sees that she is holding something.*)

MR CUSTANCE What's that?

MRS CUSTANCE A little china shoe she left us to remember her by.

(MR CUSTANCE *takes the shoe, and pitches it into the garden. They stand, supporting each other, looking out at the spires of the tomato vines.*)

MR CUSTANCE She'll be there any moment now. It's only a stone's throw. She'll have started the next round. Poor devils! They haven't a hope in hell!

MRS CUSTANCE You do tempt me, Ted, to think we're in the right. (*They embrace tenderly.*)

ACT TWO

Vast and dusty-dark. An impression of former splendour. Once sumptuous, now worn furniture. Disintegrating hangings. Double doors, BACK, in a wall which will grow transparent at times. Behind the wall, three rostra, R., C., and L. (Little scenes will be enacted on these, and they must be high enough for the action to be visible above the furnishings in the foreground.) Against the wall, on either side of double doors, are twin consoles, lacquered, with twin cloisonné vases. (Tables and vases painted to fade with the scrim walls.) Telephone (public installation with box for pennies) L. corner. Dilapidated lacquer cabinet against wall, L. Suggestion of fireplace C. against footlights. Around this the furniture is more or less grouped: two armchairs, R., separated by a fringed standard-lamp. Sofa C. Armchair L. Behind the sofa a table with a few upright chairs. Fringed lamp hanging C.

When CURTAIN RISES MRS LILLIE *is discovered in the armchair* R. *The lamp beside her illuminates. She is a distinguished old lady in her eighties. In her youth she has been a great beauty, but the beauty has disintegrated, and she suffers from a palsy. (As this role is largely static the actress who plays it should have a fine voice and commanding presence.)*

ENTER MAID. *She is carrying a large tray with coffee pot and cups. A sturdy fresh-faced girl in her early twenties. She puts the tray down on table.*

MAID (*noticing somebody in chair*) Who's that? Mrs Lillie?
MRS LILLIE (*shaky, rousing herself*) Yes. It's I, Meg.
  (MAID *laughs.*)
  What is it?
MAID (*kindly*) You ladies sound so funny at times.
MRS LILLIE I don't *feel* funny.

MAID *Sound*, I said. You talk different. Like books.

MRS LILLIE (*as if echoing a frequent preoccupation*) I'm old.

MAID (*looking around, helplessly*) It's all old. Makes more dust than you can dust. (*Looking to* MRS LILLIE *for agreement*) So there's no point, is there? Whatever Matron says.

(MRS LILLIE *lost in her own thoughts. Does not answer.*)

Didn't you go in for your tea?

MRS LILLIE (*fretfully*) No. I didn't feel like it. What was there?

MAID (*gaily*) Mince collops, and bread pudding. Oh, lovely!

MRS LILLIE Always the same.

MAID That doesn't mean the same isn't lovely. (*Laughs*) Ask Miss Docker.

MRS LILLIE Who?

MAID Miss Docker.

(BOTH *fall silent.* MAID *shakes up the ancient cushions.*)

She knows.

MRS LILLIE She hasn't seen me yet.

MAID She will.

MRS LILLIE Oh, yes. She will. She's only been here three days.

MAID Her? She's been here always! She knows where the damp patches are, and where that bad smell comes from.

MRS LILLIE I shouldn't be surprised.

MAID Cheer up, Mrs Lillie! Let me help you to a delicious cup of coffee essence. Like you was in the Hotel Australia.

MRS LILLIE I'm too tired. Turn this lamp off, Peg.

MAID It'll be ever so dismal without.

MRS LILLIE I'll have the fire.

MAID But there isn't one! It's still summer.

MRS LILLIE Is it? Well, there'll be light enough.

(MAID *switches off standard, leaving light from above.*)

I'll take a nap.

MAID Aren't you a caution! It's all nap at the Sundown Home . . . exceptin' the carpets.

(*She stamps* OUT *of the room.*)

(*After a moment* MISS DANDO RUNS IN. *A small, frail, elderly maiden. She pockets the sugar from the coffee table. Drops a lump. Retrieves it. Runs* OFF *again.*)

MATRON (OFF) Take your time, Miss Dando. You won't miss anything.

MISS DANDO (OFF, *giggling*) Oh, yes, Matron.

(ENTER MATRON, *a large, firm woman, middle-aged, kindly cynical. Her dress a compromise between the normal and the institutional. She is followed by* MR WAKEMAN, *a muscular, youngish clergyman. Handsome. Experiences some difficulty in giving expression to his earnestness.*)

(*On no account must he become the stuttering stage clergyman.*)

MATRON Miss Dando is always on the run. She fell down last Friday.

MR WAKEMAN Are there many falls?

MATRON Oh, all the time. All of them. Let me tempt you to a cup of coffee, Mr Wakeman.

(*He almost accepts.*)

MR WAKEMAN No . . . thank you, Matron.

MATRON Perhaps you're right.

MR WAKEMAN I just looked in. To see whether she'd made herself at home.

MATRON Miss Docker will never need assistance.

MR WAKEMAN Such a . . . (*searching for the expression*) . . . such a cheery soul.

(MATRON *smiles a slow, ambiguous smile.*)

MATRON Yes.

MR WAKEMAN They're not all so appreciative.

(MATRON'S *smile is fixed. Stares at something invisible in the fireplace. Does not comment.*)

Although I feel that perhaps . . . inwardly they are.

MATRON Old people have too many things to remember to find time for gratitude in the present.

MR WAKEMAN (*with genuine admiration*) How well you express it! (*Thoughtfully*) Yes. (*Rousing himself*) At least it must be gratifying to Mr Etchell to know that the house he left behind is put to such good use.

MATRON (*frowning, preoccupied*) Always dusty! (*Shaking a cushion*) It's as if the cement he made his millions from strayed into his house and won't be got rid of.

MR WAKEMAN Cosy, though.

MATRON *Inwardly*, Mr Wakeman, we *hope* we are cosy.

MR WAKEMAN (*earnestly*) Matron . . . do you allow prayer to help you?

MATRON There are the ones who pray, and the ones who are prayed for. By the time I get my collar off at night I only hope I'm prayed for.

(LADIES *begin to trickle in*: MRS HIBBLE, MRS WATMUFF, MISS PERRY, MISS DANDO, MRS TOLE, MRS ANSTRUTHER, MRS JEBB. *All dressed in black of varying design.*)

MRS HIBBLE Mr Wakeman! Our first surprise since when I wouldn't like to calculate!

(*She is bent, arthritic, walks with a stick, yet gives an impression of toughness. She makes at once for the armchair next to* MRS LILLIE'S. MRS LILLIE *remains impassive.*)

MRS WATMUFF It's always such a delight to have our rector with us.

(OTHER LADIES *murmur agreement, though* MISS DANDO *sniggers.*)

MR WAKEMAN (*pleased, but overwhelmed*) Thank you, ladies!

MRS ANSTRUTHER Saw you in the street. But you didn't notice.

MRS JEBB He always notices *me*!

MISS DANDO (*showing* MR WAKEMAN, *trying to attract attention*) My finger's sore. Do you think I'm developing a whitlow?

MR WAKEMAN (*torn between one and the other*) What does Matron say, Miss Dando?

(MISS DANDO *shrugs and pouts.*)

MISS PERRY Perhaps you've come to give us an interesting talk.

MRS TOLE (*hovering round coffee table*) Ooh, mumma, mumma, mumma!

(MATRON *shepherds* MRS TOLE *and pours coffee for her.*)

MR WAKEMAN I only wish I had the time.

MATRON (*to* MRS TOLE, *as if to a child*) Careful! Careful! Careful! Remember how you spilled it down your front last night.

MRS TOLE Ooh, mumma, mumma, mumma!

MISS PERRY (*to* MR WAKEMAN) You always put things so beautifully, Rector.

MR WAKEMAN (*laughing, and perhaps genuinely surprised*) I'll have to engage Miss Perry to stand at my elbow while I write my sermons.

MISS PERRY Beautiful sermons.

MR WAKEMAN Words are. . . . (*Almost stammering*) I wish I. . . .

MRS HIBBLE You mean to say: Words are the devil!

(ALL *laugh gaily and innocently, except* MRS LILLIE, *who remains withdrawn.*)

(ENTER MAID. *Hovers.*) (*This is the same maid who has been addressed by* MRS LILLIE *as 'Meg' and 'Peg'.*)

MAID (*in loud whisper*) Matron!

MATRON What is it, Edna?

MAID Mrs Chambers won't get up from table.

MATRON Is she ill?

(MATRON *moves towards door.*)

MAID I think she's had an accident. It's Miss Docker. Kept her there too long. Talking at her.

(MATRON *and* MAID EXIT.)

MR WAKEMAN (*to* LADIES) Actually, I came to see Miss Docker.

MISS DANDO (*disappointed*) Oh!

MRS WATMUFF She'll come.

MRS HIBBLE (*laughing*) Oh, yes! She'll come!

(ALL *fall silent.*)

MR WAKEMAN (*glancing at watch*) Otherwise . . . I'm afraid I'll . . . have to go.

MISS PERRY (*shyly*) Perhaps if you can't give us a talk . . . perhaps you'll say a prayer for us.

MRS TOLE Ooh, mumma, mumma, mumma!

MR WAKEMAN I'd like to leave you with a prayer. (*Pause while he gathers his thoughts*) O Lord of mercy . . .

(MR WAKEMAN *could be distressed by his search for words.* LADIES, *whether seated or standing, are frozen into informal attitudes of prayer.* MRS HIBBLE *perhaps a bit of a sceptic.*)

. . . O Lord, put into our mouths the words of praise . . . soothe us with memories of our fruitful lives . . . fulfil Your promises of everlasting peace. This night and always . . . Lord . . . in gratitude . . . we pray. Amen.

LADIES Amen.

MISS PERRY (*genuinely uplifted*) Lovely!

(MRS TOLE *chuckles very low.*)

MR WAKEMAN And now I must really leave you.

MISS DANDO Miss Docker will be sorry.

MRS WATMUFF She'll be sorry.

MR WAKEMAN But after all . . . I shall be seeing Miss Docker. I see her all the time.

(EXIT MR WAKEMAN.)

(MRS HIBBLE *puts her hand momentarily on* MRS LILLIE'S. *The latter stirs, but does not respond appreciably.*)

MISS DANDO I don't pray any more. My room's too cold to pray in.

MRS HIBBLE You ought to be warm enough on all that stolen sugar.

MISS DANDO Don't be nasty, Mrs Hibble!

MRS ANSTRUTHER Do you know what Miss Docker told me . . . she has a list of people she prays for, thirty-seven in all.

MRS WATMUFF I can quite believe it. I've heard her at it through the wall.

MISS PERRY She's organizing weeding parties.

MISS DANDO She's going to take us down to the village to buy sweets.

MRS JEBB Miss Docker. . . .

MRS HIBBLE (*wagging her head from side to side*) Miss Docker! Miss Docker! Miss Docker! She's only been here a couple of days, and her name beats in my head like a gong. Miss Docker!

(ENTER MISS DOCKER. *She is dressed in brown, in contrast to the others, who are all in black. She is carrying a shoe-box.*)

MISS DOCKER Did I hear my name?

MRS HIBBLE You did! And you missed the parson!

MISS DOCKER (*disappointed*) Ohhhh! (*Stands for a moment* C. *pawing the ground like a horse*) Something else I've missed!

MISS PERRY He said a prayer for us.

MISS DOCKER Has trouble in finding words. But I ought to be able to fix that in time. (*Brisker*) Anyway, where are the men?

(*Nobody answers.*)

There are several men, aren't there? Where have the old boys toddled off to?

MRS HIBBLE To their rooms. To die. Perhaps.

MISS DOCKER What a thing to say! And in a Church Home! We're here by the grace of God.

MRS HIBBLE Do you think God will have room for an agnostic?

(MISS DOCKER *sucks her teeth*, *and* SEVERAL LADIES *look frightened.*)

MISS DOCKER If I'd thought it was going to lead to this, I wouldn't have mentioned the gentlemen. I'm only trying to organize a spot of recreation. We could have played a game, but I saw from the start we're not exactly a gamey lot.

MISS DANDO (*appalled*) I was never good at games!

MISS DOCKER Still, Animal-and-Vegetable helps to pass the time. Or the Truth Game. Only some object to that.

MISS PERRY Oh, yes!

MISS DOCKER Some are afraid of the truth.

MRS TOLE Ooh, mumma, mumma, mumma!

(MISS DOCKER *sits in chair facing* MRS LILLIE *and* MRS HIBBLE.)

MISS DOCKER So I fetched down my box of photos. Maybe a few of us could look through those. Though mind you, it isn't compulsory.

MRS JEBB (*reminiscing, without expression*) I had a Box Brownie. I used to get under the bed to change the film.

MRS ANSTRUTHER (*expressionlessly*) All my snaps were lost in a fire. . . .

MISS DOCKER (*fumbling with the box*) I won't bother you. . . .

(*Tears a strip off the lid as she stares at* MRS LILLIE) Is that a face I haven't met? (*Opening box*) I don't want to thrust a lot of pictures on people unacquainted with the subjects, but thought you might be amused to take a squint at Yours Truly at different stages.

(MISS DOCKER *hoots with laughter, and several photos shoot out on the floor.*)

Oh dear, clumsy Me!

(MISS DANDO *and* MRS JEBB *help retrieve them.*)

(*Re-seated, breathless*) No doubt you'll be bored, Mrs Hibble. And your friend, perhaps, who I haven't met.

MRS HIBBLE (*laughs*) We shall see.

(*Glances at* MRS LILLIE, *who remains staring at the fireplace.*)

MISS DOCKER (*brandishing photo at a cluster of* LADIES) There! You wouldn't believe! Now would you? I ask! Or would you?

MISS DANDO (*snatching the photo excitedly, doing a few twirls of a girlish dance*) So young! So gentle! And a butterfly bow in her hair. So *velvety*! (*Shows photo to* MRS HIBBLE) Isn't that a tasteful crocheted collar?

MRS HIBBLE It *could* be Miss Docker. One can see. One can see the way life gets hold of us.

(MISS DANDO *returns photo to* MISS DOCKER.)

MISS DOCKER There must have been a great deal we didn't understand, young girls like that. We must have been real ignorant. (*Shrieks at the thought*) Well, we were! A lot of silly young things! Age has its compensations.

MRS LILLIE (*half to herself*) Youth didn't need compensation.

(MISS DOCKER *is torn between* MRS LILLIE *and the photo.*)

MISS DOCKER (*squinting*) Can everybody see in this dim light?

MRS HIBBLE Oh, yes. (*Bitterly*) Well enough!

(MISS DOCKER *skips over and switches on standard-lamp between* MRS HIBBLE *and* MRS LILLIE.)

MISS DOCKER (*returning to her chair*) Shouldn't think any of us have much to hide.

(MRS LILLIE *has put up her hand for a moment, but lets it fall.* MISS DOCKER *sits on the edge of her chair.*)

(*Staring across at* MRS LILLIE) Well! Waddayaknow! Isn't that Mrs Lillie? Mrs Millicent Lillie?

MRS LILLIE (*staring, evasively*) I am Mrs Lillie.

MISS DOCKER Well, now, what a contrary thing! Not to make yourself known to a friend!

MRS LILLIE It didn't occur. . . . I thought there would be time enough.

MISS DOCKER In a place like this, never leave undone. . . . Wouldn't you agree? (*She looks to the company*) Time can play tricks.

MRS TOLE Ooh, mumma, mumma, mumma!

(MRS LILLIE *looks to* MRS HIBBLE.)

MRS HIBBLE (*looking straight ahead*) Friends can do nothing in the end.

MRS LILLIE (*sighing*) No. Nothing.

MISS DOCKER Who would believe it's two – or is it three? – years since your poor hubby passed on?

MRS LILLIE (*weakly*) I forget.

MISS DOCKER (*rummaging in box*) Wait! As a matter of fact. . . . It couldn't be coincidence, could it? There's a snapshot. . . . Somewhere. There!

(*Brandishes a photo. Then settles down to devour.* MRS LILLIE *moistens her lips. Her palsy becomes more noticeable.*)

Tom and Millie Lillie!

(*Again* MRS LILLIE *wets her lips.*)

MRS HIBBLE I don't believe those who *called* her by her Christian name ever called her that.

MRS WATMUFF Oh, names are *in*!

MISS PERRY And getting shorter.

MISS DOCKER (*contemplating the snap, sentimentally*) And there's Me! Holding his hand. He had begun to need attention. That was after the first stroke. (*To* MRS LILLIE) Remember how I'd come? Voluntarily. I was never one to refuse assistance to anybody who needed it. Now was I?

MRS LILLIE (*faintly*) No.

MISS DOCKER Later on I used to help you turn him. I don't know how you'd have managed. He was that heavy. A big man.

(*Wall* L. BACK *becomes transparent, and the* FIGURE *of* TOM LILLIE *is seen standing on a rostrum, dressed in Edwardian evening dress. Half-turned away at first, he reveals himself more fully during* MRS LILLIE'S *speech. He is a man in his magnificent prime, the ideal of male beauty.*)

MRS LILLIE (*soliloquizing*) A no-hoper, they called him. I loved him! We drained a fortune to the dregs, and I loved every penny of it. I loved my Roman plaque, I loved his copper-coloured hair. He was the rudest man, but kind too. I loved, I loved him!

MISS DOCKER (*meandering*) I was afraid at first, I have to admit, Mrs Lillie. Your aristocratic nose put me off. Do you care for it yourself?

MRS LILLIE (*honestly*) I never thought about it.

(*Wall* R. BACK *dissolves, and the* FIGURE *of* YOUNG MILLICENT LILLIE *appears. She is the feminine counterpart of* TOM LILLIE'S *ideal beauty. Dressed in pure white,* décolletage, *a single-strand choker of diamonds, an aigrette.*)

MISS DOCKER A nose can cut, you know.

MRS LILLIE I never thought to ask the glass. There was no need. Everything was given me without. Nobody human contradicted my face. I was not proud, though. You might even have said I was humble. I could afford to be . . . to press notes into beggars' hands.

MISS DOCKER He, though, he was *bluff.* I think I heard them call it. Yes. A lovely man! His speech went in the end. But does speech make all that difference?

(MRS HIBBLE *throws back her head, and lets out a long, raucous laugh. She glances at* MRS LILLIE, *but her friend does not notice.*)

(THE TWO FIGMENTS *on the rostra* FADE.)

Towards the end I used to turn him on my own. Like he was a baby.

CHORUS OF LADIES (*awed*) Her hands, her hands touched the man. Her freckled, her muscular hands. . . .

MISS DOCKER (*to* MRS LILLIE) You, my dear, never had the strength.

MRS LILLIE No, indeed. *Your* strength rocked the fibro . . . the sordid little house to which we were reduced. How I remember! I remember the smells and stains of sickness. . . .

MISS DOCKER I loved that log of a man. So dependent on me.

(*The two* FIGMENTS REAPPEAR *on rostrum* C. – *united.* YOUNG MRS LILLIE *is leaning against* TOM. *They proceed to mime the more concrete details of the following.*)

MRS LILLIE (*reverie*) I was dependent too. But afraid. Even in our beginning I was haunted by our end. What would come to our rescue if the flesh lost its divinity? We travelled, of course . . . Europe . . . the Nile. . . . As the dahabyiah carried us deeper into Egypt, I looked for answers in the stone hieroglyphs. It puzzled Tom. It was too perverse . . . irrational. . . . So I joined my mouth to his. His kisses smelled of claret. I grew gratefully drunk on them. But, as the boat rocked us into deeper moonlight, sometimes the dust would reach out from the eroded shore . . . and I would taste . . . the desert . . . on my lips. . . .

(FIGMENTS FADE.)

MISS DOCKER (*realizing*) But you haven't seen!

MRS LILLIE Oh, but I have!

(MISS DOCKER *runs to* MRS LILLIE'S *side to show the snap.*)

MISS DOCKER You want to take a proper look. You're the one. It's not all that much to *me*.

(*She holds the snap under* MRS LILLIE'S *eyes.*)

MRS LILLIE (*to herself*) Shall we ever suffer a knout more brutal than the truth?

(MISS DANDO *hangs over the other side of* MRS LILLIE'S *chair.*)

MISS DANDO Is that Mr Lillie in the tweed cap? That Miss Docker's got her arm around?

MISS DOCKER (*proudly*) That's him!

MISS DANDO He isn't taking much notice, though.

MISS DOCKER (*sharply*) That was on account of his stroke.

MRS LILLIE (*serenely, to herself*) Tom was like a rock. He could ignore. (*Smiling*) But rocks will open at a touch.

MISS DOCKER Oh, we understood each other.

MRS LILLIE Miss Docker putting out an arm. . . . It was Tom, though, who always put out an arm for *me*. Horses' nostrils, for instance, used to terrify me. . . .

MISS DANDO (*examining snap*) But Mrs Lillie is a blur. She's moved.

MRS LILLIE A ghost by then!

MISS DOCKER It's her affliction. (*To* MRS LILLIE, *menacing*) Would you like to keep it? As a memento?

MRS LILLIE No. (*Pause*) Thank you.

MISS DOCKER It was only a thought. You can only offer. (*Returning to her chair*) And we've lots of other pictures to get through.

CHORUS Yes! Yes! Show us the pictures!

MISS DOCKER (*shouting*) Oh, this! This will kill you!

(*She flies at* MRS HIBBLE. SEVERAL LADIES *group around.*) This is Me! As Aladdin! At a ball!

MRS HIBBLE (*very detached*) Her legs were quite remarkable.

MISS DOCKER (*screaming*) I could kick up me heels with the best! At the Charleston . . . and all that!

MISS DANDO (*clapping her hands*) Oh, the Charleston!

MISS DOCKER (*executing a few grotesque steps*) Here we go! Oh-de-doh!

(TWO *or* THREE LADIES *attempt very briefly to swing a leg.*)

CHORUS Oh, the fringes, the fringes of the Charleston! Oh, the sequins of our beige bandeaux! Oh, the mirrors of the sequins at the Charleston!

MRS LILLIE (*dreaming*) On seas of music . . . of amethyst music . . .

(TOM *and* YOUNG MRS LILLIE *are shown gravely dancing on rostrum,* L. Valse noble et sentimentale. *Her dress rose-to-amethyst, long floating sleeves, spray of diamonds in her hair. They mime the following.*)

(*almost singing*) . . . swelling, and swirling in rosier shawls . . . of light . . . of music. . . . (*Recitative*) Once, I remember, his shirt-front broke open, and there we were together on our knees . . . laughing for the unimportance of a vanished pearl.

(FIGMENTS FADE.)

(MISS DOCKER *is back in her chair rummaging in the shoe-box.*)

MISS DOCKER (*rummaging, muttering*) This? Not that one!

MRS JEBB (*as though her life suddenly depends on it*) What about that one?

MISS DOCKER (*firm, afraid*) That's private! Somebody who died. . . .

MRS LILLIE (*bitterly, almost laughing*) Death can be the least private act of all!

MRS TOLE Ooh, mumma, mumma, mumma!

(SCENE FADES.)

(CHORUS *of* OLD LADIES *forms up* FORWARD *in a frieze,* LEADER MRS HIBBLE. MISS DOCKER *and* MRS LILLIE *absent.* CHORUS *lit from footlights.*)

MRS HIBBLE Nothing to get worked up about, however.

CHORUS So ordinary, everyday. It comes in with the morning tea. It goes out with the supper tray. It comes and goes as quick and light as you spill the egg on the sheet.

MRS HIBBLE Sometimes the sheet tightens and twists. But it's nothing to get worked up about.

CHORUS Nothing to get worked up about. Nurse is so kind, the doctors love her. One's thoughts are worse than the touch of her hand. But the sound of brass will drown one's thoughts at twilight if one lets it.

MRS HIBBLE Mercifully we are often deaf. We can lie and watch the pictures . . .

CHORUS . . . the flicker of the silent pictures.

(CHORUS *disperse* L. *and* R. *They line sides of the stage.*)

(MISS DOCKER *and* MRS LILLIE *are shown on rostrum,* C., *either side of a bed,* MISS DOCKER *seated,* MRS LILLIE *standing. The* FORM *of* TOM LILLIE *in bed.* MRS LILLIE *trembling in her palsy.*)

MISS DOCKER (*explaining to* MRS LILLIE, *though absorbed in the patient's face*) I'm talking to him. You never know with a stroke. You might get through to them. (*Looking directly at* MRS LILLIE) You don't mind, now do you, dear? I have what they call an intuition. I've been telling him about the process of digestion, which I read about in a medical journal, in a doctor's home, where I was invited recently.

(*She is fanning the patient with a rolled-up newspaper.*)

MRS LILLIE (*helplessly*) I must do . . . *do!* I can see the hate in his eye. Only *I* can see.

MISS DOCKER (*fanning*) Humour the sick. Keep their interest alive. Only I know how to do it.

MRS LILLIE (*helpless*) If I could only act. . . . It was Tom who always acted for me.

MISS DOCKER (*fanning*) A norrible fly is threatening to land on the patient's nose.

(MISS DOCKER *in her enthusiasm is hitting the tip of the patient's nose.*)

MRS LILLIE (*in distress*) Fanning and hitting. . . . Hitting! Hitting! And all I can do is smile. Mine is the kind of face on which the smile gets fatally stuck.

MISS DOCKER (*fanning and hitting, to* MRS LILLIE) You, dear, are the kind that dispenses passive charm. I am the practical one.

(*Laughing*) Perhaps there should be *two* women in the life of every man. . . .

MRS LILLIE (*smiling and trembling, fascinated by the patient*) Oh, my darling . . . my breath . . . my life-blood . . . is flowing out of me!

MISS DOCKER (*laughing*) . . . one to bear the brunt, the other to radiate . . .

CHORUS . . . one to bludgeon, the other to close the eyes. . . .

MRS LILLIE (*in great anguish*) Because love . . . love is dead!

(*She brushes the dead man's eyes with her fingertips.* MISS DOCKER *stops fanning.*)

MISS DOCKER Eh?

(MRS LILLIE *hangs her head in grief.*)

(*Wringing the dead man's hand*) Don't tell me your hubby's passed on? (*Furious*) But he gave me no indication!

(PICTURE FADES.)

(CHORUS *grouped* FORWARD *as before, in a frieze.*)

MRS HIBBLE (*very matter of fact*) Not horrible, only natural.

CHORUS Oh, yes. Death is the least of living. Death is tiddly-winks to living. How do we know? We've had a peep or two by now. We've watched the canary-coloured light, from under the door. We've heard the silence with half an ear. So cool. . . .

(MISS DOCKER *appears from* BACK. CHORUS *grouped behind her in half-circle.*)

MISS DOCKER (*haranguing audience in hectoring, naturalistic tone of voice*) If there's anything I object to, it's people slipping away without saying goodbye. I ask you! It was a long time before I could forgive Tom Lillie his manner of dying. I could have been a comfort to him. Tom wasn't all that keen, but you've got to teach people to take their comfort along with their medicine. Tom gave me the slip. That was bad. The funeral, though, that was worse . . . worst of all. I'll never forget it. Not even the widow suffered worse at Tom Lillie's funeral.

(EXIT MISS DOCKER *and* CHORUS *as rostrum* R. *is revealed.*)

(MRS LILLIE, MRS PINFOLD, *and* VIOLET *and* BABY PORTEOUS *are seated at a small table.* MRS PINFOLD, *a sister of* MRS LILLIE'S, *is quite colourless. The* PORTEOUS' *are two elderly, well-*

bred, spinster sisters. All are discreetly dressed in some kind of black, relieved here and there by white – spots and stripes. All wear black straws. MRS LILLIE'S *mouth is distinguished by a scarlet cupid's bow.*)

MRS LILLIE (*to* MRS PINFOLD) It was good of you to come, Agnes dear.

MRS PINFOLD (*faintly*) But the sister. . . . I thought a sister *had* to come.

MRS LILLIE And Violet and Baby. Always so reliable. Even after one's fortune went.

VIOLET Friendship is friendship.

BABY We just can't help being sympathetic.

MRS LILLIE So silent now that it's over. Listen to the starlings on the roof. Who ever thought one would end up living under corrugated iron!

VIOLET (*disapproving*) Black thoughts! (*Looks at* BABY)

BABY (*opening her bag*) I think we should take a good strong nip. Don't you? In the circumstances?

(MRS PINFOLD *murmurs unintelligibly.* BABY PORTEOUS *produces the smallest-size brandy flask and a tot measure. She solemnly pours a tot for each.*)

MRS LILLIE *My* hands would tremble.

MRS PINFOLD Baby was always so capable.

VIOLET I hope it won't make us tipsy. I should hate to look tipsy.

MRS LILLIE (*drinking*) On the contrary, it will lead us to the heart of the labyrinth, and there we shall find . . . who shall say? . . . but let us hope.

MRS PINFOLD (*drawing attention to tot measure*) Do you think it's the right shade?

(ALL *look at the measure.*)

VIOLET (*giggling*) Millicent has left lipstick on it! (*Wipes it off with her handkerchief.*)

(OTHERS *drink in course of following.*)

MRS LILLIE Oh, that was Miss Docker. She told me lipstick strengthens the morale. I accepted, because it pleases her. (*Suddenly realizing*) You know . . . her goodness is a disease. She's sick with it. One must try to be kind to her.

VIOLET I think I should feel afraid of Miss D.

BABY She sounds so . . . brown.

MRS PINFOLD I once saw her from behind.

(MRS LILLIE *has taken the mirror from her bag. Looks in it.*)

MRS LILLIE (*trembling, to herself*) Horrible! Horrible! Even marble will melt into soft, palpitating, white *kid*! (*Puts away her mirror as quickly as she can.*)

(MISS DOCKER *climbs on the rostrum, hatted, breathless. A car toots at the same time.* MRS LILLIE'S VISITORS *jump.*)

MISS DOCKER (*shouting*) Expect you'd given me up! But I wouldn't let a person down. Beat the car by a toot of the horn!

BABY (*craning*) Such a splendid car! It couldn't belong to anything but a . . . business firm.

MISS DOCKER Well, we're going to arrange ourselves. . . .

(MISS DOCKER *shepherds* MOURNERS *from rostrum,* R., *to rostrum,* L., *which is now illuminated, and where five chairs have been arranged as for car seats.*)

MISS DOCKER Careful now, the lady in the spotted voile. . . .

(MOURNERS *totter with grief and brandy.*)

Had a nip . . . well, there's no harm done. Only if you fall.

VIOLET We're not tipsy. Or I don't think so.

(*At rostrum* L., MOURNERS *arrange themselves according to* MISS DOCKER'S *directions.*)

MISS DOCKER (*commanding*) Mrs Pinfold get in first. (*To* MRS LILLIE) Then you, dear, in this nice, comfy corner. The two ladies – sisters, I'd say, at a guess – will take the collapsibles.

(ALL *seat themselves.*)

Little Me will squeeze into the middle of the back. (*To* MRS PINFOLD) You see, your sister is used to leaning on me. I've seen her through so much. And understand. Understanding is everything. (*Loudly*) Thank you, driver. (*To her companions*) Seems a polite young fellow, doesn't he?

(MISS DOCKER *grasps both* MRS LILLIE'S *hands. The frailer* MOURNERS *nod gravely with movement of the car.* MRS LILLIE *trembles.* MISS DOCKER *immovable. They are suddenly jolted as the car apparently stops.*)

(ENTER MR WAKEMAN *in surplice.*)

MR WAKEMAN (*putting his head in, smiling to* MRS LILLIE) Everything all right?

MISS DOCKER (*sternly*) Why shouldn't it be, Mr Wakeman? I've seen to it.

MR WAKEMAN Just a short service in the church. Then we'll form up for the drive to the crematorium. You must look to your friends, Mrs Lillie. You have a fair share of them, haven't you?

MISS DOCKER There's friends and friends, you know. Some don't always stick.

MR WAKEMAN I shall be just in front, Mrs Lillie. (*Pointing*) In my car . . . look . . . the little Morris. You'll only have to follow. (EXIT)

(MRS LILLIE'S *car apparently starts, for the occupants have begun to rock again.*)

VIOLET (*looking after* MR WAKEMAN) Unnecessary . . . but nice!

MISS DOCKER (*laughing bitterly*) Oh yes, Mr Wakeman's quite the charmer! Helpless, though. You'd be surprised.

(PICTURE FADES.)

(CHORUS ENTERS. *Positions taken up* FORWARD.)

CHORUS So they rode to the funeral in the hired car. Their grief was ever so gently, ever so expensively sprung. The wreaths were lovely, as might have been expected. *And* sheaves . . . a sheaf is less suggestive. Miss Docker, of course, counted every floral tribute, and found less than there should have been. So they rode. So they trickled. So they drove. The man in gloves pointed where. Some of Sarsaparilla said: Funerals are nothing for women, leave it to the men. Others decided: We have not read about it in the *Herald*. But those whom habit, or a sense of duty, would not leave in peace, drove . . . and drove . . . and drove . . . in the funeral procession.

(PICTURE *of* MOURNERS *in the widow's car, rostrum* L., *occupants rocking gently as* CHORUS *lines the stage* L. *and* R.)

MISS DOCKER (*looking out*) There's Mrs Stapleton. Thought she might have come . . . seeing you were customers.

(*Pause.*)

(*Looking out*) There's that blue cattle-dog. Get run over if it isn't careful. Some people aren't fit to keep dogs.

MRS HIBBLE Some people can't bear their grief. Others, it fits like a glove. Some people smile because they cannot bear it. Others weep for their emptiness.

CHORUS So they drove. And they drove. And the dust came in at the windows.

MISS DOCKER (*to* MRS LILLIE) Are you comfy, dear?

MRS LILLIE (*smiling*) Yes. (*For herself*) Only that the knife is stabbing my side.

MISS DOCKER You can depend on me, dear. At all times. Even in the middle of the night you can give me a tingle on the 'phone. That's what the alcoholics do.

MRS LILLIE (*smiling and trembling*) Even if she tears my hands off their wrists, that will be better, that will be best. To kiss the eyes of my young, my beautiful husband ... *again*. ... I couldn't bear it!

CHORUS So they drove. And they drove. The brick boxes were thinning out. On that side of Sarsaparilla the scrub grows sour. They throw their bottles into the scrub. And empty tins. And old shoes. And mattresses.

MRS HIBBLE (*business-like*) But Tom Lillie will be treated hygienically. No paspalum and jam jars for *him*!

CHORUS So they drove. And they drove. The widow and the mourners, in their balibuntals and their spotted scarves ...

MRS HIBBLE (*very dry*) ... when the most extraordinary thing happened.

(PASSENGERS *in car are thrown together as it stops.*)

MISS DOCKER (*angry*) What is it? Eh? Want to break a person's neck? (*Reaching across* MRS LILLIE *she winds feverishly at a window*) Don't mind me, dear. Where'd we be if we had to escape by a window? That *handle* ... looks so *bright* ... but the thing's *rusted*! (*She cranes out, obscuring* MRS LILLIE) There's Mr Wakeman. He's got out. And that fellow from the funeral establishment. The one in gloves. Now what are they up to? Looking at a signpost. ... (*Pause*) You can see Mr Wakeman's every inch an ex-army padre! Can't give up those service boots. A proper man's man. (*Pause*) But a signpost! Don't tell me they've lost their bearings! I'd have thought a professional funeral establishment would know the way from anywhere to *There*!

CHORUS There was certainly some uncertainty.

MRS HIBBLE They had halted in the scrub . . .

CHORUS . . . and were trying to read the names . . .

MRS HIBBLE . . . which time and the weather had rubbed off.

MISS DOCKER (*craning, irritated*) But I can tell them. Everybody ought to know the way to the Northern Suburbs Crematorium. We're going there every other week.

CHORUS Perhaps we just don't remember.

MRS HIBBLE There's always so much to chat about at other people's funerals.

MISS DOCKER (*calling through car window*) I say! Mr Wakeman! Mr Wake*murrn*! (*Furious*) Ohhh! How stupid can some men get! (VIOLET *and* BABY PORTEOUS *withdraw themselves as far as is physically possible from a scene.*)
(*exasperated*) I can't take it any longer!
(*She leaps out. Begins to march downstage, towards proscenium arch,* L., *easing her clothes, butting the air.*)
(*calling*) I don't want to interrupt. Perhaps you gentlemen are holding a council of war.

CHORUS It was suddenly so peaceful in the widow's car.

MRS LILLIE (*staring at her own skirt, entranced*) A bee has flown in. It's pinning itself to my skirt. My jewel. . . .

MISS DOCKER (*calling into the distance*) Perhaps us women aren't included. I don't know. . . .
(MISS DOCKER *disappears* L., *at proscenium arch.*)
(OFF) . . . I'd just like to point out. . . .

CHORUS When just as suddenly as *she* had jumped out, the two men jumped back . . . in.

MRS HIBBLE Their strings had jerked them.
(RE-ENTER MISS DOCKER, *laughing heartily, backing towards the widow's car.*)

MISS DOCKER (*shouting in direction of the invisible men*) Okay, the joke's against *me*! At least I *meant* well!
(*She continues laughing, and gulping air.*)

FIRST CHORUS For a moment she stood . . .

SECOND CHORUS . . . alone.

THIRD CHORUS The empty sky . . .

FOURTH CHORUS ... distorted ...

FIFTH CHORUS ... inflated her.

ALL Huge ...

MRS HIBBLE ... but not huge enough!

(MISS DOCKER *stops laughing.*)

MISS DOCKER (*muttering, as doubts rise*) They don't hear. They never ... *listen*!

FIRST CHORUS The procession gathered itself ...

SECOND CHORUS ... to begin ...

THIRD CHORUS ... to thin. ....

(MISS DOCKER *turns towards the widow's car.*)

MRS HIBBLE The widow's car, of course, was only part of a procession.

MRS LILLIE (*in a dead, mechanical voice*) What is happening? We shall never know.

CHORUS The door shut ...

MRS HIBBLE ... or slammed.

(*Noise of car door slamming.*)

MISS DOCKER (*halted, staring*) They can't ... have forgot. ....

MRS LILLIE It can't have been the polite young chauffeur ...

MAN'S VOICE Too distant!

MRS LILLIE ... or the Porteous girls ...

VIOLET and BABY Too discreet!

MRS LILLIE ... or Agnes. ....

MRS PINFOLD Too helpless!

MRS LILLIE Certainly *I* am much too weak.

MISS DOCKER (*astonished*) They can't ... they can't. ....

CHORUS But the door shut ...

MRS HIBBLE ... or slammed ...

CHORUS ... and the faultless young chauffeur drove. ....

MISS DOCKER (*calling, gesticulating to group in car*) Hey! Wait a mo!

CHORUS Smoothly drove the young chauffeur ...

MRS LILLIE (*looking away*) There is her face ... outside the window. ....

MISS DOCKER There is her face ... and that lipstick I thought of getting her from Woolie's. ....

(GROUP *on rostrum* FADES.)

(MISS DOCKER *is left alone in a white spot.* CHORUS *will no longer be seen, only heard.*)

CHORUS . . . and drove . . . and drove. . . .

MISS DOCKER (*frantically, running a few steps in direction of vanishing car, i.e. towards proscenium arch,* L.) Hey! Have a heart!

CHORUS The enormous car slipped slowly out of her control . . .

MRS HIBBLE . . . others knew better than to run the risk.

MISS DOCKER (*looking in direction of escaped car*) What do you take me for? One of those Olympic atherletes?

(MISS DOCKER *turns back, as if along the line of cars.*)

(*calling*) Mr Gartrell, then. . . .

CHORUS Other cars were gathering speed . . . gathering speed. Some of them sounded hostile . . .

MRS HIBBLE . . . to judge by the grinding of metal teeth.

MISS DOCKER (*calling, waving to an invisible car*) Mr Custance?

CHORUS Several drivers seized on difficult handbrakes . . .

MRS HIBBLE . . . as an excuse for bowing their heads.

MISS DOCKER (*waving helplessly*) Mrs Fitzgibbon!

CHORUS It was so important to preserve a continuity.

MISS DOCKER (*waving*) Mr Galt!

FIRST CHORUS Curious, but . . .

SECOND CHORUS . . . in the grip of procedure . . .

THIRD CHORUS . . . or grief . . .

FOURTH CHORUS . . . nobody recognized Miss Docker . . .

FIFTH CHORUS . . . although, it is true, all examined the object by the roadside . . .

MRS HIBBLE . . . the clown's face at the curve of the road.

MISS DOCKER (*in a renewed burst of energy, running and calling*) Commander Clapp. . . . Colonel Ogburn-Pugh. . . !

(*She* DISAPPEARS *momentarily* L. *at proscenium arch.*)

(*Calling,* OFF) Mr Thomp-*surn*! Remember that cake I iced for the kiddy's birthday. . . .

CHORUS But the cake had turned to stone . . .

MRS HIBBLE . . . with cherries and angelica of glass.

(MISS DOCKER REAPPEARS *disconsolate,* L., *at proscenium arch. The top of one of her stockings has fallen down, so that on one leg she appears to be wearing a musketeer's boot.*)

MISS DOCKER (*following cars with her eyes, from footlights, as if on the curve of a road, calling, waving, sometimes running a few paces.*) Mrs Jones! Miss Ethel Jones . . . you, Miss Dora! . . . Mr Lickiss. . . .

CHORUS But the cars were dedicated to their mission.

MISS DOCKER (*calling and waving desperately to what could be the last car*) Mr Lickiss! For God's sake! (*Not quite whimpering*) Mr Lick-iss!

(*She stumbles and falls to her knees.*)

(*Hanging her head, unemotionally*) Looks as though I mucked up me best nylongs. . . .

(*Makes an effort to get up.*)

(*On her feet again*) But it might have been worse. . . . They throw their empties out on the roads. . . . You could tear your knee on a broken bottle.

CHORUS When at last she was alone, with the dust, and the blow-flies, and the dead heads of the banksias . . .

MRS HIBBLE . . . not to mention the hoarding which says: TWO MILES TO SARSAPARILLA, THE FRIENDLY SUBURB . . .

CHORUS . . . Miss Docker turned.

(MISS DOCKER *turns.*)

MISS DOCKER I'd better be making tracks then. . . . It's not all that far . . . and mostly downhill. . . . (*Wearily, starting to walk* BACK) I'll be home before you can say knife. (*Trudging*) Make meself a . . . cuppa . . . tea. . . .

(MISS DOCKER FADES.)

CHORUS (*without* MRS HIBBLE *lined up along footlights.*)

CHORUS Was it necessary? Was it kind? She did so want to watch Tom Lillie's polished casket stagger down the ramp towards the curtain. She would have wrung the widow's hands. She would have cried professionally. So was it necessary? Was it kind? Who can say? Or what is kindness? At least she has her pension. She has her health. She has her cup of Ovaltine at bedtime. She has her awfully cheery nature – her goodness which can only be escaped by car. So what is good? What is kind? Is it fair to answer questions? Who knows? Why, *she* does, of course. She knows. She knows. She knows the distances and heights. She knows who went, who came, who stayed. She knows what is good for *you*.

She knows what is *good*. Then what is wrong? Or bad? (*Suddenly oracular*) Ask the piebald cat!

(LIGHTS *on the Chinese Room at the Sundown Home.* MRS LILLIE *and* MRS HIBBLE *in their same chairs.* MISS DOCKER *in hers, rummaging in the shoe-box. Members of the* CHORUS *take up positions in a natural context. They become again a group of old ladies looking at photographs.*)

MISS DOCKER Ah, look, say if you're sick of seeing photos. You'll tell me won't you?

MISS PERRY Sometimes they're sad.

MISS DANDO They're funny too . . . silly. . . .

MRS ANSTRUTHER I think I was really glad when all my photographs were lost in the fire.

MRS JEBB Why?

MRS ANSTRUTHER I think I felt I was no longer responsible.

MISS DOCKER What a trick you are! Responsible for what?

MRS ANSTRUTHER For anything I had been, I suppose. For anything I had done.

MISS DOCKER (*sorting*) I wouldn't like to lose all my photos in a fire. I'd feel a real sense of personal loss.

MISS DANDO (*impatient*) Aren't you going to show us some more? Or are they finished?

MISS DOCKER Oh dear, no! Or if they were, we could always begin again.

(MRS LILLIE *extricates herself from her chair. There is a silence, though nobody exactly watches. She begins to walk slowly and infirmly towards door.*)

(*Truculently*) What's up with her?

MRS HIBBLE I expect she's turning in. The past has been too much for her.

MRS LILLIE (*turning at the door, smiling sadly*) Goodnight, ladies. Yes. It is time. . . .

(EXIT MRS LILLIE.)

MISS DANDO (*fretfully, looking towards door through which* MRS

LILLIE *has disappeared*) Oh, dear! The stairs are so threadbare! I'm afraid of them!

MISS DOCKER (*pouncing on a photo in her box*) Ha! Ha! Here's something to put the wind up the nervous. This is really it! (*Flourishing the photo*) Will anybody recognize the true portrait of Little Me?

(LADIES *cluster.* MRS HIBBLE *rises with difficulty, advances till she is able to examine the photo. She is in the shape of a half-open knife.*)

MRS HIBBLE (*rather disgusted*) I never saw such an enormous baby.

MISS PERRY Lovely rug.

MRS HIBBLE (*fascinated by photo, to* MISS DOCKER) You look as though you'd . . . swallowed the world.

(*She returns the photo.*)

MISS DOCKER (*looking at it complacently*) I was a bed-wetter, too, they say.

(SOME *of the* LADIES *straighten,* OTHERS *recoil.*)

(*Very grave*) Somewhere I read . . . in a medical journal, I believe . . . I read that bed-wetting is a sign of parental discord.

(SOME *of the* LADIES *shake their heads in disbelief.*)

MRS WATMUFF (*earnestly*) Isn't that what you'd call psychological?

MISS DOCKER (*exploding*) The funny part of it is . . . if it isn't a joke, you'll tell me . . . I was a . . . I was a *norphan*!

(*She shrieks with laughter.*)

MRS TOLE Ooh, mumma, mumma, mumma!

(MISS DOCKER *continues shrieking, and brings the* CURTAIN DOWN *on her laughter.*)

ACT THREE

SCENE ONE

GARDEN OF THE SUNDOWN HOME. *Time: The following spring. A gauze suggestive of espaliered trees, blossom, weathered brick wall.* ENTER *in file from* L. *and* R. CHORUS OF OLD LADIES (*minus their leader,* MRS HIBBLE).

CHORUS (*blinking, protesting*) The glare . . . is like glass. . . . The sun is a rocket . . . shooting . . . too soon.
(*They take up positions in front of gauze, singly, in pairs – anyhow, provided the grouping is not too formal.*)
Who would have thought that the spring. . . . But it is. Again. Listen! Dribbling. Trickling. Breaking open. *Bursting!* It moistens our skins . . . under the talcum powder.
(LADIES *explore their own skins, one a hand, one an arm, a face, and so forth.*)
Sticky spring!
(ONE LADY *laughs gaily, rather high and girlish.*)
Wool is full of the funniest prickles! It is still the season of wool. Daren't put away yet. With greater care this time. Last year the moth got into the interlock. The wind still bashes. Jokey. But dangerous. The ice cracks in the tumbler. Teeth smile bravely, but trapped . . . under the ice . . . in the tumbler. Chilblains fumble with cruel buttons. But spring breaks. Burbles. Stickles for the convention of blossom. Violets swoon. Narcissi bend under the load of it. All for a fortnight. Before we burn. Brown.
(LADIES *clutch themselves, hold their cheeks, draw scarves tightly about their throats. One puts up a rusty black parasol.*)
We are burnt at the edges in spring. We are too white . . . white. And frail. Our pagoda topples easily. Old, dusty, thumbed cards. . . . It is almost time we returned to the Chinese Room.
FIRST CHORUS Oh, there are other rooms, too.

A Cheery Soul

SECOND CHORUS There's the billiard room.

THIRD CHORUS Still smells of cigars.

FOURTH CHORUS There's the ballroom.

FIFTH CHORUS Too slippery.

FOURTH CHORUS There's the library . . .

THIRD CHORUS . . . the wooden books put by the man who made cement . . .

SECOND CHORUS . . . where, we are told, we may write letters . . .

FIRST CHORUS . . . from which we should send postcards to those we can no longer remember.

FIFTH CHORUS Spring is the season of postcards.

ALL But we all prefer the Chinese Tomb!

FOURTH CHORUS It echoes the thoughts we want to hear.

THIRD CHORUS It's nice and fuggy.

SECOND CHORUS It has the telephone . . .

ALL . . . the telephone!

FIRST CHORUS It might ring. . . .

THIRD CHORUS Somebody we had forgotten.

ALL The telephone.

FIFTH CHORUS It doesn't.

FOURTH CHORUS But might!

(LADIES *begin to drift.*)

CHORUS Prayers and doubts ring like glass on spring afternoons. (*Shivering, trying to extract warmth from their scarves and shawls*) It is too soon cold. The night is tightening, tightening on us. O Lord, be kind to us at night. We have not meant any of it. . . .

(LADIES *drift* OFF *to* L. *and* R.)

(GAUZE RISES.)

SCENE TWO

THE CHINESE ROOM. *Evening. Firelight from the grate.* MRS HIBBLE *and* MISS DOCKER *seated in same chairs as before.* MRS HIBBLE *is looking methodically through a magazine.* MISS DOCKER *has a couple of shoe-boxes in which she is sorting stamps and putting them in envelopes.*

MISS DOCKER (*suddenly shouting*) Oh, the unimportant countries have the pretty stamps! The smaller, the poorer – the prettier!

MRS HIBBLE (*looking at her magazine*) I wonder whether the Duchess of Windsor knows. . . .

MISS DOCKER (*rejecting a stamp*) Golly, some are ugly!

MRS HIBBLE I'd like to know whether the Duchess of Windsor. . . .

MISS DOCKER (*rejecting another stamp*) Terrible ugly! (*Pouting*) I can't go for the British.

(*Telephone rings and rings. They let it.*)

(*Shaking it off*) Makes you nervous at times.

MRS HIBBLE (*turning pages*) Why don't you answer?

MISS DOCKER I bet that's some poor woman standing in a public box – aren't they *red*, those public boxes? – standing and trying to reach her niece.

MRS HIBBLE Better answer and find out.

MISS DOCKER Then she'll lose her pennies.

MRS HIBBLE It's all in the game.

MISS DOCKER Poor thing, she might be short.

(*Telephone stops ringing.*)

That's better. People don't realize how nervous they make you.

(ENTER MRS JEBB.)

MRS JEBB Did I hear the telephone ring?

MISS DOCKER (*looking through her stamps, quietly*) I wouldn't say it didn't ring some time today. I haven't been sitting here all today. You wouldn't expect that of me, would you? Much as I like to be of assistance. . . .

MRS JEBB (*looking suspiciously at phone*) I thought I heard it ring. I thought it might have been my niece at Grafton.

(*Neither* MISS DOCKER *nor* MRS HIBBLE *answers. Continue*

with their occupations. MRS JEBB *drifts disconsolately* OFF.)

MISS DOCKER (*waving stamp daintily between finger and thumb, girlish voice*) Tiggy-tiggy-tiger! (*Blows at stamp, then suddenly contrary*) I think I'm just about sick of collecting stamps. (*Sighs*) But they tell us we ought to collect *something*.

MRS HIBBLE (*turning back to a page in her magazine, looking closely*) Do you know what they say about a woman whose face is covered with tiny wrinkles?

MISS DOCKER Search *me*! She's an old bag, I suppose.

MRS HIBBLE They say that in her lifetime she's been a very passionate woman.

MISS DOCKER (*impressed*) Go on! Waddayaknow!

(*They continue with occupations. Then* MISS DOCKER *steals a glance at* MRS HIBBLE'S *face. Continues sorting.* MRS HIBBLE *has a surreptitious look at* MISS DOCKER'S. *Continues reading.*)

(*Jumping up, shouting*) Know what I'm going to do?

MRS HIBBLE I have no idea.

MISS DOCKER (*rummaging in shoe-box, producing a chink of pennies*) I'm going to ring Mr Finlayson the butcher.

MRS HIBBLE Do you want to order something?

MISS DOCKER I want to hear his voice.

MRS HIBBLE It's too late.

MISS DOCKER I'll ring him at his home.

MRS HIBBLE He won't be very pleased.

MISS DOCKER (*going back to phone box*) He's that handsome. (*Dialling*) That nice! I think I've got a crush on Mr Finlayson. (*Listens*) I may even find the courage to speak.

MRS HIBBLE (*slowly, looking through her magazine*) Do you think you will?

MAN'S VOICE Hello?

(MISS DOCKER *jumps. Presses button.*)

MISS DOCKER (*hand over mouthpiece, to* MRS HIBBLE) I pressed, anyway.

MAN'S VOICE (*louder*) Hello, there!

(MISS DOCKER *smiling esctatically. Removes hand from mouthpiece. Holds up a finger to* MRS HIBBLE.)

What are you playing at?

MISS DOCKER (*hand over mouthpiece, in loud whisper to* MRS HIBBLE)
He's so *manly*!

(*Removes her hand. Pause, while she listens.*)

MAN'S VOICE Well, if you won't answer, stop breathing down my
ear!

(*Sound of subscriber cutting off.*)

MISS DOCKER (*to* MRS HIBBLE) Of course I'm silly. But it's
human, isn't it?

(MISS DOCKER *replaces receiver, and returns to her chair.*)
Provided you're human, I say, it doesn't matter. That reminds
me, I ought to go up to Mrs Chambers. But I always seem to have
so much to do. Ought to ring the Reverend Wakeman. Do you
know I think Mrs Chambers is preparing to pass on?

MRS HIBBLE (*looking at her magazine*) I shouldn't be surprised.

MISS DOCKER When I keep her company she closes her eyes. I
can't seem somehow to pep up her spirits however hard I try.

MRS HIBBLE No. Poor Mrs Chambers. I'm afraid there's very little
hope.

MISS DOCKER Poor thing. But I do try.

(MISS DOCKER *rummages in shoe-box for pennies. Goes to phone.
Business of making call.*)

VOICE OF MR WAKEMAN Hello?

MISS DOCKER The Reverend Wakeman, is it?

VOICE OF MR WAKEMAN Yes.

MISS DOCKER (*giggling*) Silly of me! I ought to have known. This
is Miss Docker. Gee Docker on the line.

VOICE OF MR WAKEMAN (*patient*) Oh yes, Miss Docker.

MISS DOCKER I wanted to tell you I mightn't be able to come and
mow the lawn Thursday. Not as usual.

VOICE OF MR WAKEMAN Oh, that's all right. I must cope. You've
taken it off my hands long enough.

MISS DOCKER It's that Mrs Chambers. She's sick. In fact, I think
she's seriously ill. Thought I'd inform you. All my available time
I'm sitting with her. I'll continue to do so while I have the
strength. . . .

VOICE OF MR WAKEMAN I recommend . . . I mean, I *commend* you,
Miss Docker, for your charity.

MISS DOCKER (*hand over mouthpiece, addressing* MRS HIBBLE) Never was able to express himself. Fatal in a parson.

VOICE OF MR WAKEMAN Do you think she'd like me to visit her? Would it be any comfort to her?

MISS DOCKER (*sternly*) I doubt there's more comfort than what I'm able to give.

VOICE OF MR WAKEMAN Let me know if there's anything. . . .

MISS DOCKER Yes, yes. 'Bye for now.

VOICE OF MR WAKEMAN Goodbye, Miss Docker.

MISS DOCKER 'Bye!

(*She replaces receiver.*)

(*Returning to her chair*) Words stick in that fellow's mouth like stones.

MRS HIBBLE (*without looking up from her magazine*)

'Sticks and stones
Will break my bones,
But words will never hurt me!'

MISS DOCKER (*sentimental*) That old kiddies' rhyme! There's a lot of truth in the old rhymes.

MRS HIBBLE (*thoughtful*) I was taught to believe that one. But now I think I no longer do.

MISS DOCKER You know, you're the only person in this place that you can have an intellectual conversation with. Not to say . . . spiritual. (*Remembering something*) I have half an idea it's Bible Study tonight. (*Agitated*) Or is it?

MRS HIBBLE (*without looking up*) He didn't say.

MISS DOCKER He didn't say. No. (*Suspicious*) But I'm going to give him another tingle. (*Rummaging in shoe box for pennies*) Some people act funny at times. (*Going again to phone*) Good thing pennies don't buy anything nowadays. There wouldn't be enough for the phone.

(*Business of telephoning. Telephone heard ringing.*)

GIRL'S VOICE Hello?

MISS DOCKER (*taken aback, pressing button*) Oh! (*Pause*) Is that the rectory, Sarsaparilla?

GIRL'S VOICE (*hesitant*) Yes.

MISS DOCKER Can I speak to the Reverend Wakeman, please?

(*Pause.*)

GIRL'S VOICE No, I'm afraid you can't, Miss Docker.

MISS DOCKER Oh. Well. . . . Is it the night for Bible Study?

(*Pause.*)

GIRL'S VOICE No. It is not, Miss Docker.

MISS DOCKER (*relieved*) Then I wasn't out in my calculations. Though if I was, thought I might still have time to toddle along.

(*Pause.*)

GIRL'S VOICE It might be far too late.

MISS DOCKER (*inquisitive*) Who *is* that?

(*No answer.*)

Is it Charmae? Is it Glenyse?

(*No answer.*)

(*To* MRS HIBBLE) Doesn't it get you down when they breathe in your ear!

(*Sound of other person disconnecting.*)

(*Replacing receiver*) Some young girls are that uncivil. (*Returning to her chair*) It was only sociable to inquire. But at least Bible Study is not tonight.

(MRS HIBBLE *does not answer, continues to look through magazine.*)

(*Fretfully, pushing aside the shoe boxes*) Stamps!

MRS HIBBLE (*slowly and significantly, without looking*) Have you given up the choir?

MISS DOCKER (*taking deep breath, as though preparing for something long and complicated*) I haven't given up the choir. The choir has given up me. To be more exact, there's no choir any more. (*Pauses*) It's those women. That Miss Scougall's a ball of ego. (*Snorts*) Called herself a choir mistress too! Of course when she walked out, Mrs Knight – she was the organ – could only follow suit, depending as she did for a lift in her sister's car. *So* . . . we are disbanded.

MRS HIBBLE (*languidly*) I hope it isn't a *tragic* situation?

MISS DOCKER (*exalted*) Oh, no! *I* shall sing! How I shall sing! I shall be the whole choir. Nothing should prevent you praising God. Now should it?

MRS HIBBLE (*quietly*) I never had a voice. (*Exerting herself*) But you are such a pillar of the church. *The* pillar, I should say.

(MISS DOCKER *smiles with joy. Her smile fades, though.*)

MISS DOCKER (*frowning, suspicious*) That young girl. . . . There was something funny. Why was she at the rectory? Mrs Wakeman doesn't encourage casuals. She could have gone for guidance, I suppose. Perhaps she did. But I believe it *was* Bible Study!

(MRS HIBBLE *raises her head. She looks straight at* MISS DOCKER *for the first time during their scene.*)

MRS HIBBLE (*deliberately*) I think perhaps I ought to tell you. Mrs Watmuff and Miss Perry left for the rectory immediately on finishing their tea.

MISS DOCKER (*incredulous, staring, protesting*) Without telling? (*Punctured, almost crying*) I can't believe!

(ENTER MRS WATMUFF *and* MISS PERRY *in hats and coats. They look refreshed and meek. There is a silence.*)

MRS WATMUFF (*approaching fire, holding out her hands*) So cold! I should say it's still freezing at night.

MISS PERRY (*ostentatiously*) Oh, yes! I've been following the temperatures in the *Herald*.

(*Pause.*)

MISS DOCKER (*too hurt to accuse*) I hope you enjoyed it.

MISS PERRY (*embarrassed, laughs*) Oh. . . .

MRS WATMUFF (*more composed and hypocritical*) The discussion was most refreshing.

MISS DOCKER Were there many? Was there some young girl?

MISS PERRY There were several.

MISS DOCKER But the one who cheeked me on the phone?

MRS WATMUFF I can't think. (*To* MISS PERRY) Can you?

(MISS PERRY *shakes her head conscientiously.*)

MISS DOCKER Did you have the savoury boats?

MRS WATMUFF Yes. Mrs Wakeman handed round the savoury boats. Afterwards.

MISS PERRY With a pot of tea.

(MISS DOCKER *does not comment. She sits staring ahead.*)

(SCENE FADES.)

SCENE THREE · GARDEN

DARKNESS *at first in which* VOICES *are heard*: MISS DOCKER *and* MRS WAKEMAN.

MISS DOCKER'S VOICE Thursday's my day for the rectory. That is to say, it's Mr Wakeman's day. There's Mrs Wakeman, too. But Mrs Wakeman hasn't forgiven me yet.

MRS WAKEMAN'S VOICE (*very stern*) Miss Docker, do you know you have pruned *Crimson Glory* to death?

MISS DOCKER'S VOICE I only pruned the rose as a gesture. And nobody knows for certain it didn't die a natural death.

MRS WAKEMAN'S VOICE We don't know by scientific proof.

MISS DOCKER (*thoughtfully, as* LIGHT *goes up on* GARDEN GAUZE) Bit unorthodox in a parson's wife. . . .

(MISS DOCKER *alone in front of gauze wearing a grotesque stocking cap, and carrying another knitted article.*)

MISS DOCKER (*cheering up*) But him! He has that kind of adam's apple the words can't get over. Once or twice I've smelt him just after shaving. Sometimes he cuts himself . . . thinking. (*Tenderly*) I love those finger joints . . . handing the chalice. . . . (*Hurriedly*) Of course, it's nothing sinful. There's spiritual love, too. I'll understand it. I'll understand it in time. Anyway, this is Mr Wakeman's day. I go there Thursdays to mow the grass. My labour of love. . . .

(SCENE FADES.)

SCENE FOUR · THE RECTOR'S STUDY

Large office desk, L.C. *Wastepaper basket beside it. Window frame,* BACK. *Doors* R. *to garden,* L. *to house.* MR WAKEMAN *seated at his desk, occupied with parish matters. Tired and discouraged.*

MRS WAKEMAN *is seated beside the window. She is intermittently peeling rhubarb and looking out. In her thirties. An earnest young woman, devoted, dowdy, rather humourless.*

MRS WAKEMAN Surely the freewill offerings have improved the situation?

MR WAKEMAN That's what humiliates most. They give their money, but they won't come to church.

MRS WAKEMAN (*gently*) To do neither might be worse.

MR WAKEMAN But the books don't balance ... not when the spirit's absent. And the more they give, the less they come. They're buying their way out. (*Holding his head*) That is what distresses. (MRS WAKEMAN *bites her lip, looks down into the bowl of rhubarb. Because he is distressed, so is she.*)

MRS WAKEMAN We must give more time to winning them over. If I get up an hour earlier. I shall go from house to house.

MR WAKEMAN If you get up an hour earlier, you'll drop.

MRS WAKEMAN I'm strong.

MR WAKEMAN There are limits.

MRS WAKEMAN (*attacked by other doubts*) But I'm not inspired. Oh ... I'm often ... dull. ...

MR WAKEMAN You give me words when I'm in need of them.

MRS WAKEMAN Words are from God, surely?

MR WAKEMAN By devious ways.

MRS WAKEMAN Then I am the most devious of ways!

MR WAKEMAN (*possessed of an idea*) *I* know!

MRS WAKEMAN What?

MR WAKEMAN We'll send out Miss Docker to bring souls to God!

MRS WAKEMAN The souls may resist.

MR WAKEMAN Such a pillar of the church?

MRS WAKEMAN Almost its surviving one. And the pillar may bring it down.

MR WAKEMAN What do you mean?

(*Pause.* MRS WAKEMAN *hangs her head.*)

MRS WAKEMAN Nothing. I'm prejudiced.

MR WAKEMAN She's so good. We can't expect more of her. She does so much already.

MRS WAKEMAN Oh, she does *everything*!

MR WAKEMAN Is that kind?

MRS WAKEMAN Gregory . . . I am not kind!

MR WAKEMAN Two such imperfect beings as we to counsel souls!

(*She would like to help him, but can't. On an impulse she brings him the bowl of rhubarb.*)

MRS WAKEMAN (*standing the bowl on his desk*) Gregory . . . look! (*Running her hands through the peeled rhubarb*) This is perfection. The original crimson! And we have been given it!

MR WAKEMAN You say you're not inspired, Mary.

(*He puts out his hand. She takes it, appears about to kneel and kiss it, but resists.*)

MRS WAKEMAN (*humbly*) You know I married you for wrong reasons? (*Putting his hand tenderly away from her*) But discovered true ones.

MR WAKEMAN My dear, gentle Mary! The last to be moved by base reasons!

MRS WAKEMAN (*going away from him impetuously*) Oh, I'm not gentle! (*Leaning against window*) My name is not Mary!

MR WAKEMAN It's what your father christened you.

MRS WAKEMAN Not Mary! (*Looking out*) And here is Miss Docker. Did you know it was her day?

MR WAKEMAN Yes. No. I had forgotten.

MRS WAKEMAN She's brought you something. Something brown. I can see it dangling from her hand.

MR WAKEMAN Something she can't afford.

MRS WAKEMAN Or made. That would please her better. (*Tossing her head*) Oh, I mustn't! I must learn! I must learn to love her.

MR WAKEMAN You must let her teach you.

MRS WAKEMAN (*with repugnance*) Yes.

(*She takes her bowl, as though preparing to leave him.*)

MISS DOCKER (*Calling,* OFF) Anyone in? . . . Mrs Wake-*murn*? . . .

243

I can come in, can't I? Aren't I at home here?

(MRS WAKEMAN *is at a loss, hesitates, puts her bowl down again on desk. Moves towards door,* R.)

(ENTER MISS DOCKER, R., *carrying the something-brown-and-knitted.*)

Thought I'd act informal. Thought I'd show meself before getting out the mower.

(*She breathes loud and smiles wide.*)

MR WAKEMAN If you really *insist* on cutting the grass week after week.

MISS DOCKER It's the least I can do, isn't it? Wouldn't you agree, Mrs Wakeman?

MRS WAKEMAN (*stiffly, with an effort*) You're very kind and thoughtful, Miss Docker.

MISS DOCKER (*looking at* MRS WAKEMAN) Don't you look cold and peaked! Don't tell me you gave away your winter undies? I wouldn't put it past you. Anyone in need. You're so good.

(MRS WAKEMAN *looks as though she may well have given them away.*)

MRS WAKEMAN Underclothes are one's own private affair.

MISS DOCKER But we've got to wrap up warm. Eh, Mr Wakeman? As a matter of fact, I brought you something. Something I made.

(MRS WAKEMAN *looks coldly and sideways at the object* MISS DOCKER *has brought.*)

See? A balaclava cap. Perhaps you don't know what it is?

MR WAKEMAN (*laughing*) Oh, I do, Miss Docker! Truly.

(MRS WAKEMAN *takes the bowl of rhubarb.* EXIT L., *without further ado.*)

MISS DOCKER Bet you don't know how to wear it!

MR WAKEMAN I do, Miss Docker! I do! (*He puts it on to prove.*)

MISS DOCKER (*addressing audience*) Men are all boys really. Silly at times. They'd be lost without a woman's subtlety to get them by.

MR WAKEMAN (*showing himself in the balaclava*) There!

MISS DOCKER We'll miss seeing your chin. But these hard spring mornings . . . you want to wrap up good when you walk from the rectory to the church.

MR WAKEMAN (*a bit weary*) Now I shall be able to.

MISS DOCKER Well, I'd better get out the old push mower.

MR WAKEMAN Since you're so kind, I'll be able to compose my sermon.

(MR WAKEMAN *sits down at desk.* MISS DOCKER *has moved towards door,* R., *but now hesitates.*)

MISS DOCKER Those sermons!

(*She still hesitates.* MR WAKEMAN *looking out papers on desk.*)

Wish I could write one for you.

MR WAKEMAN (*absently*) Don't you approve of those you get?

MISS DOCKER Mr Wakeman, can I tell you something. . . . I mean, as a friend?

MR WAKEMAN (*unwilling, though resigned*) Yes.

MISS DOCKER I can only be frank. That's the worst of *me*! I can only see the naked truth. And tell. But it isn't so bad coming from a friend. Now is it?

MR WAKEMAN If a friend can't advise, who else can?

MISS DOCKER That's correct. (*Coming to the point*) The trouble with you, Mr Wakeman, and a serious one in a clergyman, you can't seem to learn to preach.

(*Silence.* MR WAKEMAN *moves one or two things on his desk.*)

MR WAKEMAN (*with an effort*) I'm sorry . . . you should feel like that.

MISS DOCKER Somehow you don't give yourself to it.

(*A short awkward pause.*)

MR WAKEMAN I can't argue with you, Miss Docker, on that point. Naturally, you must be the . . . better judge. I am only the preacher of my own sermons.

MISS DOCKER But they're *corny*!

(MR WAKEMAN *breaks the pencil he has been resisting.*)

I see I've touched on a raw nerve. Don't think I'm not sorry for it.

MR WAKEMAN (*with an effort*) Don't be sorry. I'm open to criticism. In every way. Otherwise, should I be fit to serve our Lord?

MISS DOCKER But inspiration . . . where is inspiration?

MR WAKEMAN I can't answer that.

MISS DOCKER A clergyman should have the answers.

(MR WAKEMAN *smiles a taut smile.*)

MR WAKEMAN I agree. Oh, how I agree with you, Miss Docker!

MISS DOCKER (*relenting*) You don't mind me telling the truth. Someone has to.

MR WAKEMAN (*struggling*) It's just that . . . the truth we know already is always hardest to bear.

(MISS DOCKER *catches a glimpse of something which begins to cause her pain.*)

MISS DOCKER (*her face working*) It's in my nature! A person can't always resist her nature. That's something that's given to her . . . too.

(MR WAKEMAN *drags off the balaclava, drops it on the desk.*)

(*As gently as she dares*) I see you've been cutting yourself again.

MR WAKEMAN (*laughing, puts his hand to his cheek, absently*) Have I? There's always so little time.

MISS DOCKER (*businesslike*) Well, I'd better start on the grass. (*Goes to door,* R.) That thing I knitted for you, that balaclava, it was supposed to be heather mixture, but it seems to have turned out brown. (EXIT R.)

(MR WAKEMAN *immediately appears deflated.*)

MR WAKEMAN (*covering his eyes*) O Lord, where am I to go from here? Teach me . . . show me the impossible.

(MRS WAKEMAN ENTERS L., *too hurriedly for the unimportance of her mission.*)

MRS WAKEMAN (*in an assumed voice*) Oh, Gregory, I forgot to tell you . . . (*notices his attitude, and falters*) . . . the Challenors . . . (*approaching the desk, her voice softer*) Mrs Challenor rang to say the boys will have to miss their confirmation class. (*Her voice positively tender*) They're down with the . . . German measles. (*She has reached the desk. Picks up the balaclava, holds it for a moment, but lets it fall back on desk.* MR WAKEMAN *uncovers his eyes.*)

MR WAKEMAN (*looking ahead*) I am writing my sermon, Mary.

MRS WAKEMAN (*gently*) Of course.

(*She almost touches him, but tiptoes* OUT, *closing the door very softly, as she does on sermons. At the same time the clatter and slash of a push-mower is heard outside.*)

(SCENE FADES *for a moment.*)

(LIGHTS UP *on same scene later in the afternoon.* MR WAKEMAN *sitting hunched at his desk, hands over his eyes. Continuous sound of lawn mower outside.*)

MR WAKEMAN (*without moving*) In a world of light, I am darkness. The *ghosts* of ideas struggle to escape out of this obscure mind. If they would put on flesh. . . . If I could kindle truth into a fire that no one would mistake. . . . Now that it is spring the black wattles blaze on the hillside. I walk in the grove of black wattles . . . to learn by example . . . to lighten darkness. My mind gropes inside its aching skull. I dawdle in the grove of wattles. The black trunks ooze an insipid, colourless gum. At most the bark scores my forehead, and underlines impotence. (*Pauses, his mouth working to express*) Or I pass through my wife's kitchen. A vision of crimson rhubarb is more articulate in praise than the chaos of a dark mind. I have nothing, nothing, it seems, to offer my Divine Love.

(*Takes away hands from in front of his eyes. Noise of mower stops.*)

(*Desperately*) *Nothing* is perhaps the truth!

(*His eyes are drawn to the balaclava on his desk.*)

Or is truth a perverse and ugly rag made by man to throttle with?

(*He picks up* MISS DOCKER'S *present and throws it violently into wastepaper basket. Walks round the desk in a state of great agitation. Goes and leans against the window-frame.*)

(*Door,* L. *opens softly.* MRS WAKEMAN *appears.*)

MRS WAKEMAN (*although possibly she knows*) What is it, Gregory?

MR WAKEMAN (*turning, laughing*) Why . . . nothing. *Nothing*! What else should there be?

(MRS WAKEMAN *advances. Catches sight of the balaclava in wastepaper basket. Stoops, and returns it to the desk. She goes to her husband, crying softly in spite of her efforts not to. Puts her arms round him. Rests her face against him.*)

(MISS DOCKER'S VOICE *is heard.*)

MISS DOCKER (OFF) Enough for today, Mr Wakeman. I've put the mower in the shed. Hope I've done a decent job.

(*The* WAKEMANS *stand as before. He does not answer.*)

(OFF) 'Bye for now!

MRS WAKEMAN (*eyes closed, to her husband, very softly*) You know I would suffer for you if you would allow me.
(*He unties her arms. Kisses her very tenderly.*)

MR WAKEMAN (*gently, pushing her away from him*) We must be stronger than our bodies . . . even when we imagine the spirit has abandoned them. . . .

MRS WAKEMAN (*looking at him, as if to compel him to see*) . . . even when we *imagine* we are dumb . . . and our words illuminate another's darkness.

(SCENE FADES.)

SCENE FIVE · THE WAY TO CHURCH

Dark stage, empty except for the three rostra. A spot picks up MISS DOCKER, R., *near proscenium arch. Dressed for church. Fitting her gloves.*

MISS DOCKER (*forcing fingers into gloves, feverishly bright*) Gloves for church! Nice for church! Sixpence is cheap for what you get. Sing! Sing your heart out, and it comes back new. I like the hymns best, because they're cheerful. Psalms are a bit leathery. . . . But the hymns! I can sit alone and sing. In fact, I do sit alone. You can concentrate all the better. (*Pauses*) Now can't you?
(GROUP OF OLD LADIES *is shown on and against rostrum,* R.: MISS DANDO, MRS WATMUFF, MISS PERRY, MRS ANSTRUTHER, MRS JEBB. *As they are revealed a burst of tinkly laughter falls from the* OLD LADIES' *mouths. Quickly control themselves.* MISS DOCKER *has turned, and makes her way towards them.*)
You girls ought to come along. Do you good. Accepting asylum from them, too . . . at a nominal rate.
(OLD LADIES *snigger, and only one or two bother to hide it.*)

MISS DANDO Too draughty!

MRS WATMUFF My good coat went to the cleaners, and didn't come back.

MRS ANSTRUTHER I'm too deaf by now.

MISS PERRY I have trouble with my water.

OLD LADIES (*in unison*) Our joints click, our voices won't carry, our eyes look inwards for what they have to see. . . .

MISS DOCKER Well, you're a nice collection of crocks. Where are the others? There must be someone.

OLD LADIES Gone! Gone! Some found nieces who were willing to take them. Others simply . . . died . . . of something.

MISS DOCKER If that's the way it is. . . .

OLD LADIES Oh, yes . . . it is!

(OLD LADIES *laugh faintly as they* FADE FROM SIGHT. MISS DOCKER *alone in spot.*)

MISS DOCKER If I'm a mug it looks as though I'm the only one. (*Pauses*) But anyway . . . (*growing aggressive*) . . . wasn't it the mugs that burned the brightest?

(MRS CUSTANCE *is disclosed standing on rostrum,* BACK C. *Workaday but neat in a clean apron. Amiable expression as she stares into distance. Does not at first notice* MISS DOCKER.)

(*Approaching*) Why don't you give us a trial, Mrs Custance?

MRS CUSTANCE Oh . . . Miss Docker! You startled me!

MISS DOCKER You can show appreciation of your blessings, you know, in any shape of church.

MRS CUSTANCE Yes, yes!

MISS DOCKER So come along.

MRS CUSTANCE I must.

MISS DOCKER Join your voice.

MRS CUSTANCE I will.

MISS DOCKER How's Mr Custance keeping?

MRS CUSTANCE He's . . . (*guarded, rather dry*) . . . the same, thank you, Miss Docker.

MISS DOCKER Bring him along.

MRS CUSTANCE I'll try.

MISS DOCKER We want the men.

MRS CUSTANCE Of course. He must.

MISS DOCKER I'll hold you to it, then.

MRS CUSTANCE (*with mounting shame for her own hypocrisy*) Yes, Miss Docker! Oh, yes, yes, yes, yes, yes!

(MRS CUSTANCE *hangs her head as* LIGHT FADES *from rostrum.* MISS DOCKER *walks on.*)

MISS DOCKER (*sadly*) God sent the plagues on Egypt. Today I reckon *He*'s all ten rolled into one. . . .

(LIGHTS *discover rostrum* L. MR LICKISS *appears, a sturdy, elderly, thickset, working man, dressed in work-clothes, carrying an extension ladder.*)

Are we all so intellectual, and not intelligent enough, Mr Lickiss?

MR LICKISS (*frightened*) Eh?

MISS DOCKER Sunday is the Lord's day.

MR LICKISS It's the only day I got to clean the gutters.

MISS DOCKER (*supercilious*) God can wait?

MR LICKISS God don't wait to send the rain. And what if a man's got a full gutter?

(MISS DOCKER *snorts. Continues on her way.* MR LICKISS *begins to extend the ladder.*)

WOMAN'S VOICE (OFF, *loud and angry*) Was it Her?

MR LICKISS (*loud, awed whisper*) It was Her all right!

(LIGHT FADES *from rostrum,* L.)

(MISS DOCKER, L., *in spot against proscenium arch.* GAUZE FALLS *behind her.*)

MISS DOCKER I can pray for a certain number. But you've got to draw the line *some*-where. I mean . . . the day wouldn't be long enough.

SCENE SIX · STREET

ENTER FIVE CHILDREN, R,: *two boys, three girls, between* 10 *and* 5, *neatly dressed, carrying prayer and hymn books.* CHILDREN *brake hard on seeing* MISS DOCKER.

FIRST BOY (*to* OTHER CHILDREN) It's Her!

MISS DOCKER (*rejoiced*) The kiddies! At least you can rely on the children.

(CHILDREN *remain where they are, silent.*)

(*approaching*) Hello, Vince. . . . Les. . . . Berys. . . . Narelle. . . . And isn't this little Zola?

(*Slight pause.*)

FIRST GIRL (*simpering, putting her arm round youngest*) Yes!

MISS DOCKER You can't pretend you don't know me.
(*Pause.* CHILDREN *bite their lips, cast their eyes down.* YOUNGEST GIRL *picks her nose, and stares.*)
Well, who am I?

FIRST BOY Dad says you're . . . the scoo-*erge*. . . .
(FIRST GIRL *pushes him.*)

MISS DOCKER (*not understanding*) Eh? What did your dad say?
(*Silence.*)

FIRST BOY Dad said he's gotta take down the carburettor. . . .

MISS DOCKER Got the rest of the day for that. No reason why he shouldn't come to church.

SECOND BOY My dad says the church isn't big enough. . . .

MISS DOCKER What about the mothers then? Haven't they the souls of women?

FIRST GIRL (*righteously*) Mum's gotta baste the joint.

SECOND GIRL (*swinging her handbag*) There's always the Sunday dinner.

MISS DOCKER (*moved and outraged*) So the children stand proxy for the parents! Lord reward the innocents!

FIRST BOY (*practical*) We don't do it for nothing, you know.

SECOND BOY My dad gave me a shilling.

FIRST BOY (*contemptuously*) A shilling! I said it wouldn't be worth me while this side of five bob.

MISS DOCKER Haven't your parents heard of hell?

FIRST GIRL They talk about it enough.

LITTLE GIRL They say She'll ferret them out even if they hide under the house.

MISS DOCKER (*most unhappy, thoughtful*) She? Hell is how you see it, I suppose . . .
(*She turns away.*)
. . . how you see it.

LITTLE GIRL (*to* SISTER) Is she mad as well as a scoo-*erge*?

FIRST GIRL (*shaking her*) Ssh! She's only a bit funny.

MISS DOCKER We'd better all go into church. Love one another while we can. . . .
(*She shepherds* CHILDREN *as* GAUZE RISES.)

SCENE SEVEN

NAVE AND VESTRY OF ALL SAINTS, SARSAPARILLA

North and East walls of church converge BACK *of stage to make a corner. Altar suggested on East wall,* L. *Free-standing pulpit,* L.C., *as skeletal as possible so as not to obstruct. Corner of vestry* L. FORWARD. *Small deal table and chair. Three or four choir pews backing on North wall, facing pulpit. Organ and board for hymn numbers suggested on wall behind choir pews. Three or four pews facing altar,* R.C. *Entries as from church's West door should be made from behind proscenium arch,* R. *Entries to vestry as from outside, to be made from behind proscenium arch,* L. *Wall between vestry and body of the church is an open screen or transparent wall with door-frame set in it.*

MR *and* MRS BLEEKER *and* MR *and* MRS FURZE *are discovered seated in rear pew,* R.C.: *two elderly couples, one shop-keeping, the other poultry-farming.*

MISS DOCKER *and* CHILDREN *advance into church as* GAUZE RISES. CHILDREN *push ahead. Shove and jostle. Seat themselves in row in front of adults. Kneel ostentatiously, but very briefly, to pray. Look around afterwards.*

MISS DOCKER *pauses at pew occupied by adults.*

MISS DOCKER (*loud whisper*) Morning, Mrs Bleeker. . . . Mr Bleeker. . . . Mrs Furze. . . . Got your books everybody?
(BLEEKERS *and* FURZES *grunt and murmur, sidle in their seats.*)
There's lovely hymns. I know, because I chose them.
(*She goes on to seat herself alone in one of the empty choir pews.*)

MR BLEEKER (*to* MRS BLEEKER, *in voice of deaf person*) What did she say?

MRS BLEEKER A lovely day.

MRS FURZE (*to* MR FURZE, *in deaf person's voice*) Can't you shut the door, Stan? The wind's cruel down my neck.

MR FURZE (*also deaf, in reply to* MRS FURZE) They say it'll hardly play no more. And the dry rot's got into it.
(MISS DOCKER *kneels to pray.*)

MISS DOCKER (*praying*) O Lord, help me to help the helpless . . . even while their number makes me dizzy. While I have the strength, inspire me to use it for purposes of good. . . . (*Looking around*) Ah dear, forgot to change the flowers. Church is smelling of dead flowers. The dust . . . the dust has got me beat. Mrs Furze has a cold, I'd say. Tell her Vitamin C. . . .

(*Gets up from her knees, and settles herself in pew.*)

(CHILDREN *whisper and giggle. Drop books.* LITTLE GIRL *begins to cry, whispers to* FIRST GIRL.)

FIRST GIRL (*angry*) You ought to of done it earlier!

(EXIT FIRST GIRL *with* LITTLE GIRL, R., *as through West door.*)

(MR *and* MRS WAKEMAN *have* ENTERED *vestry,* L. *He is dressed for service in his surplice. She wears her usual dress, and a cheap-looking little hat.*)

MR WAKEMAN (*concealing nervousness*) How many this morning, Mary?

(*Stamps a few times, beats his sides to restore circulation to his hands.*)

(MRS WAKEMAN *goes to doorway leading from vestry into church.*)

MRS WAKEMAN (*peeping at body of church*) Oh, the Furzes. And the Bleekers. And three children.

(MR WAKEMAN *is waiting to hear.*)

MR WAKEMAN (*suspicious*) That all?

(MISS DOCKER *and* MRS WAKEMAN *stare across at each other.*)

MRS WAKEMAN (*to* MR WAKEMAN) Oh, Miss Docker is there, of course.

MISS DOCKER There's Mrs Wakeman. Must be her only hat.

(MRS WAKEMAN *withdraws into vestry.*)

MR WAKEMAN (*tensely*) Aren't you going in, then?

MRS WAKEMAN (*looking at him, smiling, touching his arm*) Yes. I'll go in.

(*He tries to return her smile, but fails.* MRS WAKEMAN ENTERS *church through vestry door, trying to efface herself as much as possible. Makes her way to front pew of those occupied by congregation. Kneels and prays. She will remain on her knees until the hymn.*)

MR WAKEMAN (*kneeling in vestry*) Forgive me, Lord, that I should have dispersed Your flock. Fill me with words . . . to enlighten . . . to enlighten . . . (*his voice has stuck*) . . . those who remain.

(MR WAKEMAN *gets up, enters the body of the church. Congregation rises, with exception of* MRS WAKEMAN, *who remains on her knees.* MR WAKEMAN *stands at prayer desk,* R. *of altar.*)

(*Reading*) Dearly beloved brethren, the Scripture moveth us in sundry places to acknowledge and confess our manifold sins and wickedness. . . .

MISS DOCKER (*loud and rather nasal*) Amen! Amen!

MR BLEEKER Where's the place?

MRS BLEEKER Where's the place?   } *Scrambled voices.*

MR FURZE What's he say?

MRS FURZE What's he say?

(FIRST GIRL RE-ENTERS *as from West door during foregoing, leading* LITTLE GIRL. *They take their former places.*)

MR WAKEMAN (*kneeling and reading*) Almighty and most merciful Father . . .

ALL (*kneeling, praying in traditional tone used for the confession*) . . . we have erred, and strayed from Thy ways like lost sheep. . . . (*At this point the clear white Sunday light deepens into the golden glow of inwardness.* ALL *raise their faces in supplication, and take part in the following litany of their personal hopes and fears. As each individual supplicant speaks, he or she rises to feet, with exception of* MRS WAKEMAN, *and strains forward imploringly.*)

ALL (*imploring*) . . . we have erred and strayed, Lord, but don't tell us we are lost. We are afraid of unfamiliar places, and our own darkness most of all.

MR WAKEMAN (*rising*) Good Lord, hear us, we pray You, even when the words stick in our mouths.

ALL We beseech You, Lord, to hear us!

MRS WAKEMAN (*on her knees, looking at her husband*) Give him, dear Lord, not the strength of lions, but that of ordinary, callous men. Break me, Lord, if You will, but leave him straight and beautiful.

ALL O God, hear us, we pray! We are so much in need!

MR BLEEKER (*rising*) Send us honest customers, O Lord, who will pay on the first of the month . . . or better still, over the counter. Preserve us from mortages. Favour, I pray You, all small enterprise.

ALL O Lord, good Lord, do not withhold Your mercy.

MR FURZE (*rising*) O God of poultry farmers, I'm not a mean man
. . . not by any means . . . but ask You to prevail upon the Egg
Board to treat us good. . . .

ALL O Lord, dear Lord, even though the faces that love us are blank,
You will understand.

MRS FURZE (*rising*) O Lord, may those persimmons not drop before their time, may the white butterfly not get in amongst the
cabbage.

ALL O Lord, O Lord, we are Your miserable servants, searching and
searching for what we cannot always find.

MISS DOCKER (*rising*) O Lord, I know! I know! I *know*! That is
the awful part of it. Why is it they can't see what I tell them?

CHILDREN (*rising*) Please God, let it be quickly over. We've
always said the prayers they tell us . . . but pray You let us out of
here.

MRS BLEEKER (*rising*) O Lord, stop up our leaking roof. Inspire
us with a few new lines in hardware. Spare us those sleepless
nights, and the terrors of a hidden cancer.

ALL Good Lord, we beseech You, hear!

MR WAKEMAN If I am shortly to be judged, O Lord, I only ask that
You have mercy on the instrument of judgment.

MISS DOCKER If I am about to judge, O Lord, it is because You
have shown me who. And anyway . . . it hurts me to!

MRS WAKEMAN (*on her knees*) If I love immoderately, O Lord, it is
because You are in his image. Do not blame me, dearest God, I
do not mean to blaspheme.

MISS DOCKER (*impatiently*) O Lord, why are the strong weak, and
the weak strong? Particularly when he has such a handsome
face. . . .

ALL Forgive us, Lord, we are sometimes fools. But dare we say:
You made us!

MR FURZE O Lord, the Egg Board. . . .

MR BLEEKER O Lord of justice, Woolworths and the supermarkets
are driving us out!

MRS BLEEKER and MRS FURZE (*in unison*) Dear Lord, we cannot
talk like our daughters-in-law. Do not let them laugh at us.

255

LITTLE GIRL Please God, why can't we sit down more often in church? I pray there's ice-cream pudding for dinner.

MRS WAKEMAN (*looking at her husband*) As his ordeal approaches, Lord, may I send him winged words. Without denying Your divine love, let me offer him mine . . . perhaps he'll find it easier to grasp.

MISS DOCKER Lord, I beg You make him understand the words I speak are those of God. This isn't vanity, Lord, is it? Nobody's vain who expects an end . . .

MR BLEEKER . . . how ever it comes . . .

MR FURZE . . . in a crunchin' of bones . . .

MRS WAKEMAN . . . or an opening of eyes . . .

MRS BLEEKER . . . or . . . Oh, no!

(ALL *drop to their knees in a gust of terror. With the exception of* MISS DOCKER, *who stares straight ahead,* ALL *look back terrified over their right shoulder.*)

ALL . . . or the great mushroom . . . growing . . . and *growing.* . . .

MISS DOCKER (*staring ahead, comparatively tranquil, as though she sees something clear and personal*) . . . or just a tap on the shoulder any cold morning.

(ALL *resume the conventional attitude of prayer, heads bowed above their hands.*)

ALL Your will be done, O Lord, but do not break our hearts. So we pray . . . on this, and every other day . . . humbly . . . hopefully. . . .

(*The brooding light of inwardness is lifted in favour of the clear white light of Sunday morning.*)

MR WAKEMAN (*reading*) Hymn Number . . . 240.

MISS DOCKER (*annoyed, loud whisper*) 54! I *told* you!

MR BLEEKER What's he say?
MRS BLEEKER What's he say?   } *Scrambled voices*
MR FURZE Where's the place?
MRS FURZE Where's the place

MR WAKEMAN (*glancing at board, correcting himself*) Hymn Number 54.

(MRS WAKEMAN *gets to her feet.*)

(*The following hymn is sung to a slight parody of a Victorian hymn tune.*)

(BLEEKERS *and* FURZES *search for the place throughout.* CHILDREN *hang their heads over their books, and mumble.*)

MISS DOCKER, MRS WAKEMAN *and* MR WAKEMAN (*singing, unaccompanied*)

> I do not ask for jewels or gold,
> The truth, O Lord, is all I seek.
> I'll die convinced that all is told,
> If I may hear You speak. . . .

MISS DOCKER (*solo, improvising*)

> . . . if I may hear You speak.

(MR WAKEMAN *gathers notes, and approaches pulpit.*)

MISS DOCKER, MR WAKEMAN *and* MRS WAKEMAN (*singing*)

> I do not ask for pastures green,
> I'll trudge along the stony ways. . . .

(MR WAKEMAN *misses a step in mounting the pulpit, almost falls, but rights himself.* CHILDREN *giggle.* MISS DOCKER *almost rushes to his side.* MRS WAKEMAN *holds book to her breast, lowers her eyes in pain.* MR WAKEMAN *continues, but without singing.*)

MISS DOCKER (*continuing to sing, solo*)

> . . . if faith will guide me, tho' unseen,
> I'll bear the burden of my days,
> the burden of my days.

(MR WAKEMAN *in pulpit sorts his notes. Somewhat shaken.*)

(*triumphant, solo*)

> I'll bear the tumult of my heart,
> If I may see the light at last,
> If I may hear the trumpet blast
> Outside the gates!

(*Silence.*)

(CONGREGATION *seats itself.*)

MR WAKEMAN (*addressing* CONGREGATION) This morning it isn't my intention to preach to you on any text. At the time I wasn't able to think of one. And texts . . . at best . . . sound cut and dried. Whereas life remains . . . remains . . . (*clenches his fist, raises his head as words elude him*) . . . contradictory. (*Shuffles his notes, then continues, head down*) I am going to speak to you this morning about sin . . .

R

MISS DOCKER (*to herself*) Why not? It's always with us.

MR WAKEMAN . . . no ordinary sin, however. But the sin of goodness. That is to say, of . . . of . . . of *militant* virtue. . . .

MISS DOCKER (*fidgeting, mouth open*) Not only is that man a
terrible preacher, he's all mixed up besides.

MR WAKEMAN (*fiddling with notes*) How often do we pride ourselves on virtue? How often do we *luxuriate* in our own good
deeds until they turn grotesque and ugly in other people's eyes?
You might liken us to a penful of pigs, wallowing in the mud
of . . . of our own deception, the stink . . . stench of which enters
every nostril but our own. . . .

(CHILDREN *giggle*).

MISS DOCKER What's got into him?

MRS FURZE (*to* MR FURZE) What's he say?

MR BLEEKER (*to* MRS BLEEKER) You can always rely on the rector
to give us a sermon. He preaches a *fine* sermon.

MR WAKEMAN Let me take another example . . . a humble one . . .
because the simplest picture will often illustrate most tellingly.
Take a pumpkin. . . . (*Leans over the pulpit, offering his symbol with
both hands.*)

(MISS DOCKER *groans. Sits forward.* A CHILD *drops a book.*)
No doubt every one of you has noticed an ordinary pumpkin
from time to time. Some of you have watched your mothers bak-
ing it for Sunday dinner. Some of you have tilled the soil and
sown the seed in your own orchards. (*Taking a deep breath*) As
I was saying, there is nobody amongst you who isn't acquainted
with the pumpkin. . . .

(MISS DOCKER *cannot restrain herself any longer.*)

MISS DOCKER (*leaning forward, addressing* MR WAKEMAN *without
qualms*) You're right there, Mr Wakeman. But why pick on the
poor pumpkin?

(MR WAKEMAN *refuses to hear.*)

MR WAKEMAN (*mouth struggling for words*) If, as I say, we take a
pumpkin. . . .

MISS DOCKER But why? But why? Don't be so unreasonable. Not
when sin comes up for consideration. If you had shown us a
gramma. . . . Ugly shapes! Or choko. . . . All those prickles! But

not a pumpkin. You picked the wrong one there.

MR WAKEMAN Take the pumpkin. . . .

MISS DOCKER Oh, dear! Take one! Take two! But must we? And anyway, sin is more of a summer subject. Not all the sin in the world will persuade me that the pumpkin. . . .

(MR WAKEMAN *is leaning over the edge of the pulpit. A ghastly smile.*)

MR WAKEMAN Take the leaves . . . (*attempts to demonstrate with his hands*) . . . on which the telltale spores of mildew and blight will settle in the best of seasons . . .

(MISS DOCKER *sputtering.*)

MR FURZE (*to* MRS FURZE) Interesting sermon all right! We'll never have peace while they go on piling up those bombs.

MR WAKEMAN . . . in a single day you can watch the leaves shrivel and wilt. . . .

MISS DOCKER (*leaning forward, addressing* MR WAKEMAN) Not if you spray, Mr Wakeman. But people won't take the trouble. If *I* gave the time to planting pumpkins, I'd also take the trouble to spray.

MR WAKEMAN (*raising his eyes, speaking for himself*) O Lord, I have failed again!

MISS DOCKER (*inspired*) Spray! Spray! Spray and pray! It is prayer that saves pumpkins, as every clergyman should know and teach.

(CHILDREN *shriek with laughter.*)

MRS WAKEMAN (*leaning forward, clenching her hands, in anguish*) O Lord, show him, I pray, that pumpkins light lamps of splendour perched on iron roofs.

MISS DOCKER (*shouting, preaching*) Of course it's a personal matter. Everything's personal. For and against. Take prayer, for instance. Or sin. And God. Your God is not my God. I am God if I think I am. (*Hastily*) Only I wouldn't be so bold. And sin. To return to sin. Sin is what you make it. Or *un*-make. On the cold winter evenings I am knit up, knit, yes *knit*, in my warm jacket of prayer. That, that is prayer. No one is closer to You, Lord, on the cold winter nights. Don't you see, everybody, prayer is protection?

MR WAKEMAN (*reeling*) Then nothing . . . in the end . . . protects?

MISS DOCKER (*almost bursting a blood vessel*) Oh, I could tell, if I could tell! All of you! But failure is not failure if it is sent to humble. The only failure is not to realize. . . .

MR WAKEMAN (*falling on his knees in pulpit*) Am I illuminated? (*Crying out*) I am blinded!

(*He collapses, head and arms lolling over the edge of the pulpit – one of the conventional figures of the Punch and Judy show.*)

MRS WAKEMAN (*falling to her knees, praying in a piercing voice*) O Lord, save us! O Lord, protect us from the powers of darkness!

MISS DOCKER (*coming to her senses*) Hey! Someone! Mrs Wakeman! The rector's taken a turn!

(CHILDREN *frightened*. LITTLE GIRL *begins to cry*. ALL CHILDREN *scamper away, and* OFF R.)

(*Distracted*) I read somewhere . . . if you breathe into their mouths. . . .

(MISS DOCKER *and* MRS WAKEMAN *both rush to pulpit, arriving simultaneously at its foot.*)

MRS WAKEMAN (*very quiet and stern*) Miss Docker, you have killed my saint. (*With an effort*) Only time will show whether you have killed my God as well.

MISS DOCKER Eh?

(MRS WAKEMAN *turns and races* OUT *of church through vestry.*)

(*Looking after her, brushing something aside*) Expect she'll give Doctor a tingle . . . (*confused, looking at* MR WAKEMAN'S *lifeless arms*) . . . but people turn to dough . . . under your eyes . . . (*she moves into body of church*) . . . and those of us who act in all good faith . . . get no thanks.

MRS BLEEKER (*to* MR BLEEKER) What's he saying?

MR FURZE (*to* MRS FURZE) Instructive, isn't it? Nothing does you more good than to listen to a sermon that makes you think.

(BLEEKERS *and* FURZES *continue to listen*. MISS DOCKER *moves towards West door,* R., *and reaches proscenium arch.*)

MISS DOCKER (*rallying*) We know, though, WHO appreciates us. (*Breathing deeply, exalted*) My thoughts could light a fire! I could breathe love into the dead . . . if they was only willing. . . .

(GAUZE FALLS *behind* MISS DOCKER.)

SCENE EIGHT · STREET IN SARSAPARILLA

Same as scene six.

MISS DOCKER *alone, holding down brim of her hat.*

MISS DOCKER (*gasping, recoiling*) This wind would freeze you. . . .
Only thing that saves you is your thoughts.

(TWO VOICES *heard in this scene are spoken parts.*)

SOPRANO VOICE The wind blows along the Northern Road. . . .

BASS VOICE The wind blows. . . .

MISS DOCKER Never saw a windier, emptier street.

SOPRANO VOICE The wind *always* blows along the Northern
Road . . .

BASS VOICE . . . windiest, emptiest on Sundays after twelve.

MISS DOCKER Everybody sitting down to dinner. Better be getting along myself. (*Starts to walk* R.) But the wind . . .
(*straining*) . . . the wind is *against* you!

(ENTER TWO BOYS *previously seen in church. Running and
laughing. They skid to a stop on seeing* MISS DOCKER.)

Thought I was the last soul alive. And here's you two boys. Bet
you're running home to eat a good Sunday dinner.

FIRST BOY (*surly*) I'm not hungry.

MISS DOCKER Well, I'm glad to see you, anyway. There's nothing
cheers like another Christian face. (*Noticing something along street,*
R.) And there's that blue cattledog. I've noticed him several
times before. Know who he belongs to?

(BOYS *glance back along the street.*)

FIRST BOY Nah.

SECOND BOY Perhaps it don't belong to anyone.

MISS DOCKER That's not possible. Everyone belongs to someone.
(*Pause*) Eh? Don't they?

(BOYS *don't answer. Could be contemplating a way of escape.*)

(*Facing up the street, calling*) What do *you* say, Bluey? Here!
Blue? Blue? Blue?

(BOYS *look same direction.*)

FIRST BOY (*discouraging*) It's got the mange.

MISS DOCKER That's something he hasn't got! You can't tell me that dog's got mange.

(ALL *continue looking in* DOG'S *direction.*)

SECOND BOY It'll probably bite yer. They're savage.

MISS DOCKER He won't! I won't let him! (*Calling*) *There*'s a fine dog! Come and have a yarn with a poor old woman who never did anything without she was certain it was for someone's good.

(ALL *follow the invisible* DOG *with their eyes as it approaches, somewhere along the line of footlights.*)

(*Looking somewhere just in front of her*) Nose is a bit dry. Ah, but you're good, Bluey! You're good!

(BOYS *eye the invisible* DOG *without enthusiasm.*)

SECOND BOY (*laughing callously*) You're not game to touch it!

MISS DOCKER (*ignoring him, speaking to* DOG, *though without attempting to touch*) Would you come with me, Blue, and share my mince collops and bread pudding . . . at an old persons' home?

FIRST BOY Ugh! Mince!

MISS DOCKER (*addressing* DOG, *which must be very close by now*) I'd allow you every licence, Bluey. You'd sleep on my bed. We'd keep us warm . . . on nights when everything else had failed.

FIRST BOY Gee, hasn't it got yeller eyes!

SECOND BOY I don't like yeller eyes in a dog.

FIRST BOY (*chanting*) Yeller yeller

Bite a feller. . . .

SOPRANO VOICE The dog with eyes the colour of pumpkin seeds. . . .

BASS VOICE But pumpkin seeds germinate.

SOPRANO VOICE (*sighing, high*) Will these?

MISS DOCKER (*ignoring* BOYS, *to* DOG) Will you come along, Bluey? After you've sniffed me?

(*Steps back suddenly with exclamation of disgust.* BOYS *shriek with laughter.*)

FIRST BOY He's wet 'er!

SECOND BOY He's done it on 'er leg!

(BOYS *run* OFF L., *laughing.*)

MISS DOCKER (*looking at her right leg*) On my good nylons!

SOPRANO VOICE The wind, the wind . . .

BASS VOICE . . . the wind is circular . . .

SOPRANO VOICE . . . and cuts . . .

BASS VOICE . . . with little invisible knives.

SOPRANO VOICE It slashes with razor blades!

(ENTER SWAGGIE, R., *humping his bluey. A man with hollow, burning eyes. Very unprepossessing. Probably a bit drunk. Glances at invisible* DOG *as it passes.*)

MISS DOCKER (*looking in direction of departing* DOG) See that dog?

SWAGGIE (*turns and looks back* R. *along street*) Not a bad sort of a dawg.

MISS DOCKER He lifted his leg on me. He wet me.

SWAGGIE Wot'd yer done to *'im?*

MISS DOCKER I offered him a home. What'd he have against me?

SWAGGIE (*laughing*) That's somethun you should of asked the dawg.

MISS DOCKER (*distressed*) But I'd just come out of church. I felt so well disposed. . . . I could have loved that dog. And then. . . . (*Almost crying*) It was a judgment! Judged by a dog!

SWAGGIE Why should Gawd judge yer?

MISS DOCKER I said 'dog'! Not 'God'! See? (*Suddenly appalled*) Why did you say that?

SWAGGIE (*pitilessly*) It's what I heard.

MISS DOCKER (*slowly*) I never knew before . . . but 'dog' is 'God' turned round.

SWAGGIE Wot of it?

MISS DOCKER If you can't see . . . I can't tell.

SWAGGIE Wot's a drop of dog's piss? If Gawd was goin' to judge yer, 'E wouldn't use a bloomin' dawg. Not as I see it. Not from readin' the newspapers. 'E'd rustle up a stroke of lightnin' . . . or stick yer out in the middle of a level crossin'. . . .

MISS DOCKER (*deflated*) I . . . don't . . . know. . . .

(SWAGGIE *sizes her up.*)

SWAGGIE 'Ow about 'elpin' a bloke stock up on 'is groceries, etc? Times are 'ard.

MISS DOCKER (*looking in her bag, angrily*) Here's a shilling. I'm poor, you know.

SWAGGIE Everybody's poor.

MISS DOCKER And you're drunk, I s'pose. From what you say.

SWAGGIE Drunk! 'Oo was actin' drunk just now?

MISS DOCKER But a dog! A dog! (*She bows her head, wipes an eye.*)

SWAGGIE You're not lettin' it get yer down?

MISS DOCKER No. It's my conjunctivitis. Been a martyr to it ever since I was a girl. I reckon I'd better ... bathe my eyes ... if the little eyebath hasn't got lost. (*Pulling herself together*) Oh, I'm not going to make a song and dance about it! I was never ever one to cry. Never ever. . . .

(*Pause.*)

(*Aggressively*) Well, my friends will all be wondering where I am. They'll be waiting to dish up dinner.

(*Starts on her way.*)

(*Again in doubt*) There's prayer, too. I'll pray ... and if it isn't answered ... then, I'll ... pray. . . .

(*She goes* OFF, R., *old, shattered, holding down the brim of her hat.*)

SWAGGIE If that's wot yer need. . . . (*Tosses up the shilling, catches it, laughing*) Every man to 'is own poison. . . .

(EXIT SWAGGIE, L.)

CURTAIN

NIGHT ON BALD MOUNTAIN

Nita Pannell as Miss Quodling in the Adelaide University Theatre Guild production of Night on Bald Mountain, *1964.*

Night on Bald Mountain was first performed by the Adelaide University Theatre Guild at the Union Theatre, Adelaide, on 9 March 1964 with the following cast:

MISS QUODLING	Nita Pannell
STELLA SUMMERHAYES	Barbara West
DENIS CRAIG	Robert Leach
HUGO SWORD	Alexander Archdale
MIRIAM SWORD	Joan Bruce
MRS SIBLEY	Myra Noblet
CANTWELL	James Hind
TWO HIKERS	Laurie Davies
	Don Barker

Directed by John Tasker
Designed by Wendy Dickson

CHARACTERS

MISS QUODLING, a goatkeeper
STELLA SUMMERHAYES, a nurse
DENIS CRAIG, a university lecturer
HUGO SWORD, Professor of English
MIRIAM, his wife
MRS SIBLEY, a housekeeper
CANTWELL, a grocer,
TWO HIKERS

SETTING

The action takes place over twenty-four hours, on Bald Mountain, beyond Sydney.

ACT ONE

SCENE ONE · OUTSIDE MISS QUODLING'S SHACK AND GOATYARDS, BALD MOUNTAIN

The shack, R., is of untreated slab. One chimney. Behind the shack an ancient apple tree in flower. A rudimentary front veranda, one or two steps to ground. A piece of clothesline stretched between two of the veranda-posts on which MISS QUODLING *will dry her rags. At* L. *is a goatyard made of saplings lashed together with wire and patched with rusty corrugated iron. Two gates are visible. It is, in fact, a double yard, in which* MISS QUODLING *keeps her does* R., *and a buck* L. *A third gate will open outward from the back, so that, when necessary, the audience will be able to see it ajar from the* BACK R. CORNER *of the yard. It is through this back gate that* MISS QUODLING *lets out her does to browse on the mountainside. (Goats heard, but not seen.) A staggy old gumtree rises out of, or at back of, the yard. Between the shack and the yard there is a view: a suggestion of vastness – rock colours at the ground, thinning out into greys and blues. It must be possible for the actors to move between this 'illusion' and the shack and yard in making occasional exits and entrances.*

CURTAIN RISES *on a colourless dawn. Shapes only just visible. Traces of mist. A faint feather of smoke from the shack chimney. Light will increase, and the sun rise* OFF R., *during the scene. Goat-bells are heard intermittently from the yard, and a bleating of does. There is an occasional grunting and stamping from the buck in his individual yard,* L. *The sapling fence is occasionally seen to shake. Sound of a tin billy striking on an iron can as* MISS QUODLING *goes about her business in the does' yard. Her voice is heard, abusive and tender by turns. At times her head is visible above the fence as she straightens, and more of her when she climbs to a higher level at the back of the yard. She will turn out to be a large old woman made larger by all she is wearing on a chilly morning: a stiff, dirty old tweed skirt, several cardigans, over them a bag worn as a cape. Gum boots. A man's hat. She has a large, leathery-brown face.*

MISS QUODLING (*shouting*) Fair-*ee*! If you put yer foot in the milk *again*, I'll dong *you*! ... What d'yer think we're after? ... Flavour?
(*Sound of bleating and metal from the yard.*)
(*Tenderly*) Dolores! My Dolores! You're the wisest goat that ever.... You're my darling *thing*!
(*Bleating.*)
(*Matter of fact*) Finished with you, Fairy. Never ever saw such an ugly-lookun udder. Trailun all over the ground. Don't know why we don't scrub yer. And such a little mingy pair of tits ... a person can't get 'er hand around....
(*Sound of metal and pouring.*)
(*Sighing*) We're sentimental, I s'pose, when it comes to the point.... Sentimental! ... Ah, dear ... goats!
(*Grunting, stamping. Buck shakes his yard fence.*)
And you ... you big bugger in there, you Samson ... want to get at 'em, eh? Well, it's not your time. (*Laughs*) You've had 'em! Only the visiting ladies now ... if you're lucky....
(*Stamping and grunting from the buck.*)
(*Almost exalted*) Nature, it's something, it's ... something. ...
(*Admonishing*) You be careful, Jessica, with that bellyful you've got. Triplets ... I'd bet a bale of hay.... Gone an' slipped yer bell, too! ... Arr, you would!
(*Sounds of metal.*)
(*Coldly*) Now, Elspeth, I don't fetch out all that good lucerne, prices rising all the time, for you to do it on.
(*Pause, silence.*)
(*Screaming*) Dolores! You leave Jessica alone! (*Sound of blows, bells and commotion*) If there's anything I hate, it's a goat with horns. You're a cow of a goat at times. Think you can run the yard. Wall-eyed, cow-hocked thing! I *hate* you, bloody Dolores!
(*Pause. Silence.*)
(*Softly, tenderly*) No, I don't. Dolores? You're the best. The best! Eh? My Dolores! (*Genuinely remorseful and enraptured*) You've got the face of a regular Christian. (*Pause. Silence.*)

(*Sun begins to rise,* OFF R., *and flood the stage. Strands of mist still visible.* MISS QUODLING *comes* FORWARD *through yard gate. Over one shoulder she is carrying a dirty, wet teat-rag, in one hand a tin billy, and in the other a medium-sized iron milk-can which weighs down that shoulder.*)

(*Wincing*) Got into me shoulder again. It's the mornuns. The mornuns 'ud freeze the snot on an old man's nose. . . .

(*She crosses to shack. Goes inside. Comes out again almost at once after depositing can and billy. She is carrying the teat-rag.*)

Oughta chop a bit of wood when I get the time. One thing about a man . . . at least he'd chop the wood . . . or wouldn't. . . .

(*She proceeds to wash the teat-rag in a bucket on the veranda.*)

(*Contemptuously*) Or wouldn't. . . . (*Pause*) Nip up later on and pinch one of Sword's fence-posts. . . . They'll never notice. . . . Stick it in the fire. . . . A fence-post burns good and long. . . .

(*She hangs the teat-rag to dry on the little veranda line.*)

(*With a note of satisfaction*) There! Bet there's a lot of women don't even wash their tit-rags.

(*Chorus of bleats from does' yard.*)

(*Calling*) All right! All right! Don't you girls be so impatient. I got a soul of me own, haven't I? . . . (*grumbly*) . . . to consider. . . .

(*She hobbles back into does' yard to the gate* BACK R. CORNER *through which the goats will escape down the mountainside.*)

I'm comun, aren't I? . . . as always? . . . Born to everybody's beck and call. . . .

(*She flings open back gate of yard, and stands holding it, watching, as invisible goats pour down the mountainside.*)

(*An urgent, pattering music to accompany the following speech.*)

(*Shouting*) There, now! Run! Jump! My little beauties! My little darluns! What would a woman do without her goats? Scamper, kids! Listen to the pellets patter on the rocks! Oh yes, mornun is wonderfullest when the goats burst out of the yard. I lay all last night with that nag nag nag in me off-side shoulder, but mornuns . . . you forget the nights.

(*Pause.*)

(*Admonishing*) Dolores? Don't you dare! Do you hear me, Dolores? You've got the world, but want to butt the hell out of that poor Jessica's full belly. I never saw anything like goats. . . . (*She turns, comes down and leans on front fence of yard. The risen sun hits her, and her hymn should be accompanied by a music, at first prickly, icy, then dissolving, as the mists disperse, and objects take on complete shape.*)

Mornun. . . . I love it even when it skins yer! Oh, yes, it can hurt! . . . When the ice crackles underfoot . . . and the scrub tears the scabs off yer knuckles . . . and the spiders' webs are spun again . . . first of all . . . out of dew . . . it's to remind that life begins at dawn. Bald Mountain! I wasn't born here. Oh, no! But know it, how I know it! I've learnt to understand the silences of rocks. Only the barren can understand the barren. I came, because I couldn't help it. I tasted the little, runty apples . . . and sour apricots . . . that somebody planted before they died. On Bald Mountain, nobody else has survived. Nobody else. I've lived here so long, I've forgotten now. (*Pause*) I don't go down . . . (*pointing behind her*) . . . not down there . . . though I watch the lights . . . at night . . . that glitter too much to be trusted. In the end, you can't trust anythun but goats and silence. Oh, yes, I know now! I've seen the mountain from a distance, too . . . moisture glist'nun on its bald patch . . . on bare rock. Sun on rock . . . that's the kiss that never betrays . . . because it doesn't promise nothun. . . .

(ENTER STELLA SUMMERHAYES, L., *towards the end of* MISS QUODLING'S *speech. About thirty. Small. Pretty. Fresh. Firm. There is something of the sound apple about her. She is wearing a dark cloak over clothes which should match the simplicity and direct-ness of her character.*)

(STELLA *looks around her. Delighted with all she sees. Catches sight of* MISS QUODLING. *Music stops as she speaks.*)

STELLA (*friendly*) Oh . . . is all this yours?

MISS QUODLING (*coolly proud*) Nobody else's.
(*Pause.*)

STELLA (*smiling, sniffing*) And do I smell goats?

MISS QUODLING (*firmly*) Goats don't smell. (*Pause*) But if there's goats . . . you can always tell . . . there's goats.

STELLA (*genuinely enthusiastic*) I once knew a little goat. A kid. She was lovely. She'd spring into the air, and toss her head . . . like a little dancer. Once she landed for a moment in my lap. Oh dear, she was a darling! Such pink little teats!

MISS QUODLING (*mollified*) I see you know and understand the goats.

STELLA Not really. I was born and lived in a Melbourne suburb. Hardly ever left it till now.

(MISS QUODLING *draws* STELLA'S *attention to something her side of the fence.*)

MISS QUODLING There! Take a look at these.

(STELLA *peeps over the fence.*)

STELLA (*delighted*) Oh! . . . When were they born?

MISS QUODLING The wrong side of midnight.

STELLA What *perfect* little things!

MISS QUODLING (*complacent*) There's nothun beautifuller than newborn twin does.

STELLA (*tentatively*) Babies?

MISS QUODLING (*closing the gate*) Babies!

STELLA Babies are beautiful, too. When they're all washed and powdered. But older than newborn. I admit *that*! When they look at you . . . their little trembly heads. . . .

MISS QUODLING I don't go nap on the human beings.

STELLA It's difficult to avoid them.

MISS QUODLING I avoid them.

(*Sound of stamping and grunting in the buck's yard.*)

STELLA (*a bit nervous*) What's in there?

MISS QUODLING (*laughing*) That's me buck. (*Calling*) Eh, Samson? Now don't you start creatun . . . even if she *is* pretty! (*To* STELLA) Samson always smells the ladies.

(STELLA *frowns slightly. Moves away from the buck's yard. Immediately discovers something which can give her pleasure.*)

STELLA Oh, look! An old apple tree!

(*She goes and fingers a branch of the tree growing behind the shack.*)

MISS QUODLING (*unmoved*) Little, runty, played-out apples. . . . (*Scratching herself*) Sweet enough to chew on, though. Sometimes of a hot day I carry one around in me mouth like a marble.

STELLA (*drawing her cloak around her with quiet pleasure*) I love it here . . . on the mountain.

S

MISS QUODLING It's hard at times. On winter nights, when the frost falls, Bald Mountain is hard as iron.

(*She comes out of the goatyard.*)

STELLA Who *are* you?

MISS QUODLING You may well ask. (*Pauses, scratching again*) I'm me, I suppose. (*Laughs*) Mr Abercorn . . . he was the bloke who built the house up there . . . and died . . . Mr Abercorn once called me the original wombat of Bald Mountain.

STELLA (*twirling round, delighted*) Original wombat!

MISS QUODLING (*suddenly formal, taking off the bag she has been wearing as a cape*) My name's Miss Quodling.

STELLA Mine is Stella. Stella Summerhayes.

MISS QUODLING (*folding the bag*) Yairs. You're the new nurse up at the house.

STELLA How did you know?

MISS QUODLING You can't help findun out a thing or two from a mail-box.

STELLA (*thoughtfully*) Strange house . . . I'm going to love it . . . I think. . . .

MISS QUODLING They come an' go up there. Only someone like Mr Abercorn would'uv built a house like that in the first place . . . and 'e died of it. He was a nut.

(*Goes and lays her bag-cape on the veranda.*)

STELLA And why did all the other owners leave?

MISS QUODLING Different reasons. Too lonely. Some thought they was gunna find *love*. Well, love flew outa the window pretty quick. Then there was the ones . . . they was mostly dentists . . . who was gunna raise hell growun vegetables an' things. (*Furious*) But a coupla weekends and they found out they wasn't the farmers they thought they was. (*Smiling*) Anyway, the soil round the house is sour. And who wants to live at the end of the world?

STELLA You wanted to.

MISS QUODLING (*tossing her head*) I'm different.

STELLA And Professor Sword.

MISS QUODLING Well, we all know why *he* bought the blinkin' house on Bald Mountain. To lock his wife up in!

STELLA Oh, but she's not a prisoner! She's sick. An invalid.

MISS QUODLING You needn't tell me. Once or twice I took 'er up a can of sweet goats' milk after she'd had the jim-jams. She could hardly drink it. Spilled it down 'er front. There were times, you know, when they had 'er in a straitjacket. There was one nurse....

STELLA (*quickly*) But she's better now. Much better. And will be better still. I feel I've ... gained her confidence.

MISS QUODLING That's all very well.

STELLA It's half the battle.

MISS QUODLING But I *warn* you ... though you oughta need no warnun ... a *nurse* ... there's nothun so cunnin' as a dyed-in-the-wool *dipso*.

STELLA That's a word the Professor wouldn't let you use.

MISS QUODLING Oh, the Prof!

STELLA Don't you like him?

(MISS QUODLING *snorts*.)

MISS QUODLING (*echoing*) Don't you like him?

STELLA I think he's ... distinguished.

MISS QUODLING (*malicious*) Did somebody tell you?

STELLA No. From what I see ... for myself.

MISS QUODLING How long have yer been here?

STELLA Five ... or is it six days?

(MISS QUODLING *laughs*.)

MISS QUODLING Ah, 'e's not a bad stick. (*Pause*) But stuck-up. If there's anythink I can't stand, it's a stuck-up man. Now with a woman, you can let 'er see that you know. (*Pause*) (*Laughing again*) But a stuck-up *man*!

STELLA (*with quiet detachment*) He has a wonderful head.

MISS QUODLING It's full of self-*importance*.

STELLA (*embarrassed*) I was thinking of his features.

(MISS QUODLING *shrugs this off. The buck stamps, grunts, shakes the fence of his yard.*)

MISS QUODLING (*addressing the buck*) Shut up, Sammy. Silly old thing! (*Indicating* STELLA) Her trouble is: she's simple! (*She comes up close to* STELLA, *looks into her eyes*) You're good. You're kind. You're as good as a sound apple. But somebody's gunna cut inter *you*, as sure as sure.

275

STELLA (*laughing, but recoiling*) I'm tough, really. I couldn't have got through my training. . . .

MISS QUODLING Some people are not as tough as they think. Not at the core.

STELLA (*with unusual, but slight sarcasm*) You're not psychic, I hope?

MISS QUODLING I dunno what you call it. Could be. When you live alone . . . on a mountain . . . for long enough.

(*Pause.*)

(*Gently*) I can see it in yer eyes.

(*Pause.*)

STELLA (*firmly*) Look, Miss Quodling, I'm here to do a job that I'm paid to do.

MISS QUODLING I should hope so. Money's there, even if you don't see it in cash. 'E won't let *her* have a penny . . . case she blows it on the grog.

STELLA (*ignoring*) I mean . . . the Swords don't mean anything to me. I mean . . . they're not close to me. She's my patient.

MISS QUODLING They're not yer mum and dad. How's yer mum and dad makin' do without yer?

STELLA My mother died. I was eight, I think.

MISS QUODLING Well, yer dad?

STELLA I had to see the world.

MISS QUODLING You didn't come too far.

STELLA (*raising her face, tenderly*) You're right. Something could happen while I'm away.

MISS QUODLING There, you see, you're soft!

STELLA Oh, I'm not, Miss Quodling! Don't be silly!

MISS QUODLING But this gentleman, your father, won't let yer go. Isn't that soft, I'd like ter know . . . on your part?

STELLA It's something I choose to accept. (*Pause*) My dad, by the way, isn't what you'd call a gentleman. Not what they'd want for the social page. He's getting on, too. And when you're fond. . . .

MISS QUODLING How old?

STELLA He's . . . let me see. . . .

MISS QUODLING Old as that old Professor Sword?

STELLA (*surprised*) Professor Sword? Oh . . . my dad's older . . .

yes, I think . . . older. But he's a working man. And work ages quicker.

MISS QUODLING Depends. What does your dad work at?

STELLA (*with a sudden glow*) He's a cabinet-maker. Nobody's a greater craftsman than Dad. He's almost the last of them. But at least what he makes will last for ever. (*With a quiet, dreamy nostalgia*) You know . . . often when I wasn't on duty, I'd go out into the workshop . . . with some knitting, or something . . . or shell a dish of peas . . . I'd sit there while he finished a commission. The wood smelled so sweet. . . .

MISS QUODLING So you left . . . to see the world.

STELLA Yes. You've got to make the break.

MISS QUODLING And what about the young men? I bet you had a boy or two. Anyone pretty enough is usually silly enough when the boys bring 'em to the point. Eh?

STELLA (*quietly, embarrassed, not wishing to hurt*) Isn't that my own business, Miss Quodling?

MISS QUODLING Oh, I was only takun an interest like. (*Shrugging away her guilt*) I'm gunna get meself a bite of breakfast.

(MISS QUODLING *goes towards the shack.* STELLA *has moved towards the view, where the mountain distances shimmer in a blue haze. She stands* C. *looking towards the east, where the sun has now risen above the shack.*)

STELLA (*breathing deeply, rising on her toes*) I could love it here! It's so vast . . . after the streets and the rows of little houses. Sometimes when I came off night duty, I'd wander through the wet streets . . . all those windows sealed tight. . . .

MISS QUODLING (*pausing on steps of shack*) Don't you start wanderin' around. It's slippery there, all along the edge. As sure-footed a little goatling as ever I had slithered over last December . . . just the other side of the cottage. (EXIT MISS QUODLING *into shack.*)

STELLA (*peering over what could be the edge of a cliff, drawing back*) I'll be careful. I'm the soberest, most careful person.

(MISS QUODLING *is heard banging about inside the shack.*)

MISS QUODLING (*calling back,* OFF) Ain't a matter of taking care. Nothun's gunna stop the lightnun from throwun yer to the other side of the room ... not if you're meant to be throwed.

(MISS QUODLING *is seen through a window, stooping and straightening as she fills a handleless jug from a dipper.* STELLA *comes down forward, looking determinedly in another direction.*)

STELLA There are the gentler influences, too.

MISS QUODLING (*slight contempt*) Ah, gentle!

(*She is seen through the window stuffing her mouth with bread.*)

STELLA Yesterday I went for a walk. I came across a whole patch of little ground orchids. ...

MISS QUODLING *emerges from the shack, carrying the handleless jug and an irregular hunk of bread.*)

MISS QUODLING (*through full mouth*) Don't know about the orguds. ...

(*She sits down on the steps, continues to chew bread, and drink from the jug, which is old and dirty as well as handleless.*)

STELLA I don't know about orchids either. That's what Professor Sword told me they were.

MISS QUODLING He'll tell yer, all right. He'll tell you anything.

STELLA That's beside the point. All this is what is important. Anyway, to me. The silence ... the peace. ... Suddenly to discover it! (*Remembering, at first in the same grateful strain*) Do you know, the day I came ... after I'd got to know them ... after I'd unpacked my things ... I trudged about for an hour or two. ...

MISS QUODLING (*chewing and gulping*) Where?

STELLA I don't know. Everywhere. Through the scrub.

MISS QUODLING Nuts!

STELLA But you love it too. You've as good as told me. ...

MISS QUODLING (*shrugging, mumbling, turning away*) Ah, what I ... love. ...

STELLA I know ... it's very, very private!

(*Silence.*)

MISS QUODLING And what did yer find that day? More orguds?

STELLA (*smiling*) No. Nothing. Or everything. It was too much. In the end I became so drowsy ... (*laughing*) ... I lay down in the sun ... in some tussocks of grass ... and fell asleep.

MISS QUODLING Yeah, it can get hot even as early as this. It starts yer sweatun sometimes ... at every pore. ...

(MISS QUODLING *proceeds to drag off one of her several cardigans.*)

STELLA ... but changes. (*Her expression changes to one of annoyance, even disgust, on remembering something she has experienced*) When I woke the mists had come. (*Drawing her cloak close*) The grass seemed quite cold and damp....

MISS QUODLING Oh, the mists'll come at yer on Bald Mountain before you can say knife. There's tourists and people often lose themselves in the mist....

(MISS QUODLING *looks at* STELLA *rather severely.*)

Didn't lose yer way, did yer?

STELLA (*abruptly*) No... It wasn't so very ... far from the house.

(MISS QUODLING *satisfied. Slaps her thighs, gets up.*)

MISS QUODLING You'll learn yer way in time. (*Throws the cardigan over the veranda clothesline*) I'll show you the tracks. I'll show yer better than Professor Sword. *Orguds!* I'll show you a cave across the gully where no one's ever been ... at least I'd bet nobody has. I'll show you a lyre-bird's nest, before the eggs has hatched.

STELLA (*touched*) Aren't they your secrets?

MISS QUODLING Secrets? Don't know about.... Yes ... perhaps ... secrets. (*Looking at* STELLA) But you're honest....

STELLA (*looking down*) Thank you, Miss Quodling. I'm touched.

MISS QUODLING ... perhaps too honest to be around amongst human beings.

STELLA I'm steel, you know, in any emergency.

MISS QUODLING (*laughing*) I *said* you was simple! – Steel don't cut with human beings. Not when they come over all soft and woozy. Steel gets blunted then ... or cracks. (*Pause*) 'Ere! Why didn't I think? Not very oss-*pitable*, am I! What about a drop of milk ... warm from the goat?

STELLA (*realizing*) Another time. I must be getting back to my patient. Mrs Sibley will have my breakfast for me.

MISS QUODLING Yairs. They'll be wonderun if you didn't break yer neck already.

STELLA Oh, but I had to get up and look at the sunrise.

MISS QUODLING They'll think you're a moony sort of nurse. (*Pointing* OFF L.) Looks as if they sent that young buck to find out if you're in yer right senses.

STELLA (*looking in direction indicated*) Who? (*Hiding annoyance*) Oh, Mr Craig.

MISS QUODLING (*looking at* STELLA) Yairs. It's unusual for Prof Sword to ask anyone up to the house.

STELLA (*off-hand*) He thinks very highly of Mr Craig. He's a lecturer. Of the same Department. So I understand.

MISS QUODLING Go on. Well, I suppose the Prof wants an audience now and again.

STELLA I find the Professor silent on the whole.

MISS QUODLING Oh, he's bottled up all right. But suddenly he pours out. There's nothun'll stop 'im then. Even I'll do then ... to gas at. And I expect a clever young feller like this makes the *better* audience.

STELLA (*vaguely*) I couldn't say.

MISS QUODLING (*nudging*) Go on! Don't be silly!

STELLA How can I? I hardly know him.

MISS QUODLING (*almost to herself*) If there's ever anythink worth knowun, why, you know it before you've even met it....

(ENTER DENIS CRAIG. *About thirty. Attractive. Manly. Perhaps a bit aggressive and callow on first acquaintance, but his deeper nature will predominate in time.*)

DENIS (*nodding*) Hello, Miss Quodling. (*With slight irony*) I've come to fetch the Sister.

STELLA (*very level, a bit expressionless*) There was no necessity. I was on the point of coming.

MISS QUODLING Refused me her company at a spot of nice breakfast.

DENIS Your patient's been asking for you, I believe.

STELLA (*making haste*) Splendid! We must go at once.

(*She crosses* L., *arranging her cloak.*)

DENIS How ... splendid?

STELLA It means she needs me. It's so important for Mrs Sword to need ... and to be needed.

DENIS Sounds to me like the first stages of a dangerous love affair.

STELLA (*ignoring*) I think we'd better hurry, Mr Craig.

(EXIT STELLA SUMMERHAYES, L.)

MISS QUODLING (*nudging*) Here, this girl's honest, you know.

DENIS Don't tell me! (*Follows* STELLA OFF, L.)

MISS QUODLING (*disgruntled, goes and kicks at the buck's gate*) I never went nap on the bucks! (*Sighs*) But you've gotta have 'em. (*Pause*) Even when you don't want 'em.

(*She has gone into the does' yard and climbed to the gate on the gully side.*)

(*Calling*) Now then, Dolores, you can't leap like that, not any more! You'll break yer blinkin' neck, and then what am I gunna do without yer? Kids! Pink little scuts! There's nothun prettier than a kid's behind . . .

(*She moves across towards the shack, fingers a branch of the apple tree. From now until the end of her speech there is an accompaniment of faint nature music.*)

. . . and apple blossom . . . (*looking round, secretively*) . . . and orguds. . . . Course I know about orguds . . . better than anyone . . . any professor. No one's looked into an orgud, not deeper than me. (*Slouches down* FORWARD) She's right. There *are* the secret things. (*Takes off her man's hat*) Ah, dear! (*Tizzing out her hair with stiff fingers, smiling into space*) *My* secrets! Long before any of the others came I used to lie on Bald Mountain, and listen to the rocks crack in the frost, on hard nights. (*Absently, looking in the direction the others have taken*) Wonder if there's any life inside of a rock. . . . For all we know . . . waitun to be hurt . . . like anythink else. . . .

(LIGHT FADES.)

SCENE TWO · PART OF THE BUSH

A rock, with track winding round it and trailing OFF R. *Overall a blur of yellow sunlight.*

ENTER STELLA, L. *She is panting, moving slowly, head down, as though the climb has been a stiff one.*

STELLA (*throwing up her head at once, looking* OFF R., *pausing*) Do I see the house?

(ENTER DENIS, *who has been following close behind.*)

281

DENIS (*absent, breathless*) Yes . . . the house. . . .

(*They pause together for a moment. Both wear an expression of contentment, although somewhat exhausted.*)

(*Panting*) All things come to an end, you know. That's one of the great mercies.

STELLA (*recovering breath*) Oh, I'm not . . . complaining . . . only glad of a breathing space . . . on this little . . . level bit.

DENIS (*exhausted*) I expect I'm headed for a slow and pursy middle age.

STELLA I can't imagine you old . . . any more than I can imagine myself. . . . (*Looking ahead at the climb which remains*) If it wasn't for other things, I could climb and climb until I was swallowed up, in some . . . oh, something . . . the sun, perhaps . . . or dropped. . . .

DENIS (*allusively*) Asleep?

(STELLA *immediately lowers her glance, though she is still with her back to him.*)

(*Taking her hand, from behind*) Stella! May I forget the Sister?

(*His hand persuades her to face him.*)

STELLA The sort of thing I didn't believe you'd bother to ask. . . .

DENIS But when I saw you there . . . that first day . . . in the grass . . . asleep . . . there was no way out. I *had* to kiss you!

STELLA You hadn't even seen me before.

DENIS I'd thought about you.

(STELLA *drags her hand away. Tears off an invisible twig.*)

STELLA (*stripping and examining the twig*) It frightened me . . . to see your face. It seemed to me I'd never been so close to any other face . . . except in the worst kind of dream.

DENIS But I took nothing worse than a kiss!

(*She does not answer at first.*)

STELLA (*at last*) I saw your face, though . . . and you might have. . . .

DENIS (*angrily*) What of it? Is the body something to be ashamed of . . . (*sarcastic*) . . . in a nurse's world?

STELLA (*distressed*) Oh, don't . . . don't! (*Pause*) Do you want to give all of yourself in the beginning, so that there's nothing of value left for the future?

DENIS We can be sure of the present. We've got it more or less in in our hands. (*Pause*)

(*Taking her hand again, forcing her to face him.*)

Stella! Can't you feel the sun on your skin?

STELLA (*holding herself rigidly, her face upturned, eyes candid*) Yes. I trust the sun.

DENIS (*dropping her hand, going away*) Oh, God, you're not religious, or something?

STELLA No. Never thought about religion. My father brought me up to respect what he considers right and wrong.

DENIS Then your father's the spoiler of all time!

(*She does not answer at first.*)

STELLA (*evenly*) My father's a poor, uneducated man. But he's as near to being perfect as anyone will get.

DENIS (*rather scathing*) Preserve me from ever becoming an exalted old man! (*Pause*) Old Sword's religious, you know . . . or tries to be. He finds it a bit of a struggle, I guess.

STELLA (*looking at him*) I thought you had a tremendous respect for Professor Sword.

DENIS So I have . . . only . . . respect is never completely intact. (*Pause. Slowly, thoughtfully*) Sword is a jealous man. . . . The creative daemon won't let him alone . . . and he brings forth dry . . . (*kicking at the ground*) . . . sticks! At least, that's what I suspect.

STELLA Are you a poet?

DENIS Am I a poet! The Department of English in every Australian university is littered with them . . . spawning . . . hoping . . . and deploring.

STELLA Then you ought to be able to pity.

DENIS Didn't you know? The frustrated artist can only pity himself.

(ENTER PROFESSOR SWORD, R., *at top of the incline. He stands looking down at the two figures on the level below. He is a man in his late fifties. Grey. A magnificent head, bearing, but at most times repressed in manner. For one of seeming authority his speech is inclined to invite corroboration, except on those occasions when emotion forces itself to the surface, and he is carried away.*)

SWORD Sister Summerhayes . . .

(STELLA *and* DENIS *look towards him.*)

... we'd begun to worry about you. . . . Mrs Sibley has already given notice because she can't put your breakfast on the table.

STELLA I'm sorry, Professor Sword, we'll come as quickly as we can.

SWORD But what possessed you?

STELLA I got up to watch the sunrise.

SWORD You were right perhaps. . . . Not since a boy. . . . To watch the sunrise. . . Mrs Sibley. . . .

STELLA And Mrs Sword, Professor? She's the one I have on my conscience.

SWORD Mrs Sword? Oh, yes. Mrs Sibley has been with her. (*Almost in doubt*) She's well. . . . At least . . . yes, she's well.

STELLA (*approaching the last lap of the climb*) I'll go straight to her.

SWORD (*pointing an authoritative finger*) Denis, run on ahead, and tell Mrs Sibley Sister Summerhayes is on her way.

DENIS (*disguising resentment*) Yes, sir.

(SWORD *has come down to the same level as the others.* DENIS *runs past him up the incline, and* EXIT R.)

SWORD She's a stupid woman. But we can't afford to accept even her *false* notices.

STELLA (*cheerfully*) If I've put her out, my horrible appetite's going to get her right back in.

SWORD (*looking at her, thoughtfully*) I wonder whether you aren't too young for the job . . . whether you won't be . . . oppressed by your surroundings?

STELLA Perhaps I should wear my uniform, Professor . . . to convince you of my authority.

SWORD (*suddenly furious*) No, no! We don't want any of that! We've had too many dressed-up battle-axes of nurses . . . (*pauses, lowering his voice*) . . . to remind us why we need them. . . . (*Pause*) I wouldn't ask you, Sister, to alter yourself in any way. I think, perhaps, you may be our salvation. (*Pause*) Now, shall we go in to breakfast? Mrs Sibley . . . we are *all* . . . expecting you.

STELLA Yes, Professor!

(*She walks past him up the incline. He follows.* BOTH EXIT, R.)

SCENE THREE · INTERIOR OF THE
HOUSE ON BALD MOUNTAIN

The structure itself could have been ugly, something of a folly, but the rooms as they are now furnished suggest civilized tastes in the present owner — contemporary paintings, sculpture, pots, handsome rugs, full book-cases. Rooms of the upper-storey, as well as those of the ground-floor, are exposed. The ground-level is divided into: study, R. BACK, a living area BACK C. expanding into the whole of the FORWARD stage, and an entrance hall, L. In the study, R., there is a window, C., opening onto a view. Under window PROFESSOR SWORD'S desk. Table C. Both the desk and the table are littered untidily with papers and books. Various other furniture, such as easy chairs, at least one upright chair, book-cases. A small fireplace, R. CORNER. BACK CENTRE of the living area huge glass doors opening onto the undefined mountain view. Along the wall separating this glassed-in area from PROFESSOR SWORD'S study, there is a long upholstered seat. In front of this a low table with magazines and papers. Dining table and chairs slightly FORWARD in CENTRE of main stage. In the wall R. FORWARD a large fireplace set with logs, but not burning in ACT I. Between fireplace and study, a door communicating with kitchen quarters. Against the wall separating the glassed-in area from the hall, a staircase curves round to the upper floor. Against the wall L. FORWARD in the main living area, there is a large and conspicuous sideboard. The hall or ante-room, L., has a window BACK C. Pieces of occasional furniture, including a small table with telephone and directory, and a small, low-built chair beside it. Cutting across the L. CORNER of the hall there is the front door. It is open. Upstairs three bedrooms open on to the landing: MRS SWORD'S R., PROFESSOR SWORD'S C., STELLA SUMMERHAYES' L. At the end of the landing, R., a door communicates with the other rooms on the upper floor. In each room a window, C., shares the common view of the mountain landscape. In STELLA'S room the curtains are drawn back. The bed is not yet made, but the room otherwise tidy. Bedhead against the wall, L. Dressing-table against wall, R. Small table C., with bunch of native flowers in vase. Upright, and small easy chairs. In PROFESSOR SWORD'S room the window is curtainless. A minimum of furniture, and what there is very austere. An air of asceticism. An iron stretcher is so placed that its head is between the window C. and the wall separating the Professor's room from his wife's, the frame of the bed lying along the wall. On either side of the window there are paintings of a religious nature. In MRS SWORD'S room the curtains have not yet been drawn. Against the wall L., separating her room from her husband's, a dressing-table. A small oblong table against wall BACK to accommodate mainly medicine bottles. The bedhead stands against the wall R. Beside it, FORWARD, a bedside table and lamp. Rather an elegant chair of the Victorian era, grandmother type, stands CENTRE.

As the scene is revealed, ENTER MRS SIBLEY, R., from kitchen. About sixty. A stupid, grumbly, but conscientious body. She crosses the living-room, pausing at dining-table, C., to rearrange a jam-pot, continues into the hall, L., glances through the front door. Turns back, frowning and muttering.

MRS SIBLEY (*sucking her teeth*) Tt-tt-tt! (*Almost under her breath*) When they won't come for their breakfast....
(*She mounts the stairs. Approaches the room of* MIRIAM SWORD. *Knocks on the invisible door.* MIRIAM *is still in bed.*)
(*Calling, listening*) Are you awake, Mrs Sword?

MIRIAM (*stirring, speaking in a low, apathetic voice*) Yes.
(MRS SIBLEY *goes in.* MIRIAM *does not move. When finally she becomes visible she will appear to be a woman of about forty-five, of chalky, ravaged face, but with the remnants of sensitivity, even beauty. She displays the apathy which long illness and suffering bring. The expression of the eyes is now vague and dull, except when she is possessed by her daemon. Her clothes are individual rather than fashionable, subdued in colour, inclined to trail untidily, her greying hair trying to escape from control.*)

MRS SIBLEY It's a fine day ... if it stays with us....
(*She goes* BACK *to window as if to draw curtains.*)

MIRIAM (*suddenly anxious*) No. Leave them.

MRS SIBLEY But ... let a bit of light in....

MIRIAM *She*'ll draw them.

MRS SIBLEY (*put out*) Didn't think it mattered who draws the curtains.

MIRIAM (*listless*) It gives me pleasure to watch her do it.

(MRS SIBLEY *grunts. Hesitates.*)

MRS SIBLEY I'll bring up your tray then. What about a nice fresh egg . . . lightly boiled?

MIRIAM (*moving her head from side to side*) *She*'ll bring it when she comes.

MRS SIBLEY (*unable to restrain it*) *Her*! It's all Her nowadays!

(MIRIAM SWORD *is silent.* MRS SIBLEY *leaves her. Goes downstairs. Appears most discontented.* ENTER DENIS *briskly through front door.*)

DENIS (*hearty*) Well, here we are, Mrs Sibley . . . or almost. I've been commanded to tell you.

MRS SIBLEY I bet you were! It's all commands in these parts. (*Moving towards the kitchen*) I 'ad a nice dish of sowty kidneys. It's looking that sad by now. . . .

DENIS Mountain air will brighten it up.

MRS SIBLEY (*inconsolable*) You've got to fight these days to get a kidney out of the butcher. . . .

(EXIT MRS SIBLEY, R. DENIS *pauses a moment. Goes back to hall, glances through front door, returns, goes quickly into study. Searches for something amongst papers on the desk. Fails to find. Goes to the littered table,* C. *Quick search through papers lying there. Apparently finds what he has been looking for. Quick glance through a certain sheaf of papers – could be a typed manuscript. Lays the sheaf on top of the litter as* PROFESSOR SWORD *and* STELLA SUMMERHAYES ENTER *the house through front door.* STELLA *is by now carrying her cloak.*)

STELLA (*to* SWORD) . . . and when you followed the tracks to the cliff, what happened? Did they just disappear?

SWORD (*vaguely*) Yes. . . . No, I think he went into a cave.

STELLA But didn't you go inside to find out? I mean . . . it's not every day, surely, that you track a wombat on your walk. I'd have wanted to *see.* . . .

SWORD Precisely.

(DENIS *has come to the study door. He is watching and listening without being noticed.* STELLA *waits for* SWORD *to continue.*)

Sister Summerhayes, are you ever aware of the moment when a

287

lie takes over? You realize, but you follow it wherever it leads . . .
there's no holding back.

STELLA (*puzzled*) I . . . don't think so.

SWORD I don't think I ever tracked a wombat on any of my walks
. . . until this morning, in our conversation, I was compelled to do so.

(STELLA *shrugs, still uncertain of the point.*)

Forgive me.

STELLA (*laughing*) Certainly.

SWORD I didn't intend. . . .

STELLA Well . . . it's time I went to my neglected patient.

(*She runs up the stairs.* SWORD *turns and notices* DENIS.)

SWORD (*half to himself*) I wonder why I was compelled to follow
that imaginary wombat?

DENIS (*with a faint malice*) Only you can tell. (*Follows* SWORD *into
the study*)

(STELLA *has reached the landing. Goes into* MIRIAM'S *room. Tiptoes towards the bed.*)

SWORD (*giving the mountain of papers on the table an angry shove*)
Essays . . . poems . . . (*with the greatest distaste*) . . . even a . . .
symbolic novel. I'm paid to cope with the essays . . . but why must
they write their poems? And why send them to *me*?

DENIS First, to express . . . then to impress, I expect.

SWORD (*peevishly*) Curse all adolescent poets and intense, middle-
aged females!

(MIRIAM *stirs in her bed.* STELLA *drawing the curtains.*)

STELLA I hope you're feeling well, Mrs Sword, on such a glorious
morning?

MIRIAM (*shielding her eyes*) Well? Oh, yes . . . . I suppose *well* . . . in
a horribly decontaminated way.

(STELLA *proceeds to tidy one or two things.*)

DENIS (*to* SWORD, *cautiously*) There must be the odd grain amongst
the chaff.

SWORD (*snorting*) The same welter of words . . . the same bodies
interlocked . . . the same search for God and self. Oh, I don't read
the stuff, of course, but my nose can detect the authentic stench.

(STELLA *brings tablets and a glass of water to* MIRIAM, *who winces
but swallows.*)

DENIS I like to think I'd make an *attempt* to read what I was sent.

SWORD Oh, one does, one does. Here and there a line ... a phrase.... (*He picks up the manuscript* DENIS *has arranged on top of the tableful.*)

(STELLA *brings second lot of tablets to* MIRIAM.)

STELLA Here's the second lot. Then I'll leave you alone. (MIRIAM *swallows automatically.*)

SWORD (*to* DENIS) Take this fellow, for instance. (*Reads from manuscript with emphatic distaste*)

> 'Dawn reproaches the murderers
> with evidence of unwanted sperm
> on greying sheets....'

DENIS (*suddenly appalled*) I understand what you mean!

SWORD Only youth could adopt such an attitude of prim licentiousness. (*He throws manuscript on the table*)

DENIS I have known a few elderly, academic hacks....

STELLA (*to* MIRIAM) Didn't Mrs Sibley bring you your tray?

MIRIAM No. I didn't let her.

STELLA You didn't let her?

MIRIAM (*stealthily*) No. I ... (*guiltily*) ... I'd like ... you ... always to bring me my tray, Sister.

STELLA But....

MIRIAM No. I know it isn't part of the nurse's duties. (*Rudely*) But we pay you well, don't we?

STELLA (*hiding annoyance, perhaps also hurt*) It isn't a question of payment. I was surprised. That's all.

(STELLA *tidying the dressing-table.*)

DENIS (*to* SWORD) You can send up Shakespeare himself if you pick bits out of their context.

SWORD (*wearily*) This context is all bits.

MIRIAM (*supporting herself on her elbow, eagerly, to* STELLA) Won't you do me this kindness?

STELLA (*restored to good humour, laughing*) How silly you are at times!

MIRIAM Allow me the luxury of being silly.

STELLA If it's going to give you any pleasure.

MIRIAM You won't believe me ... half the things people say are

T

lies . . . but it's brought me great happiness . . . having you here in the house.

STELLA (*touched*) Thank you, Mrs Sword. (*Pause*) I'll fetch the tray then.

(*She leaves* MIRIAM'S *room. Goes to her own for a moment. Leaves her cloak. Brushes and quickly arranges her hair.*)

(DENIS *has been fingering the manuscript. Takes it up finally.*)

DENIS (*to* SWORD) Shouldn't we destroy this one at least?

SWORD That's a privilege we should allow the author.

(DENIS *tears up the sheaf of poems.*)

(*Suddenly looking at him, faintly amused, faintly admiring*) Is this the picture of a man admitting his mistakes in public?

DENIS Courage sometimes overtakes what begins anonymously.

SWORD I admire you. (*Pause*) I should follow your example. (*Pause*) Mistakes abound. . . . Oh, yes, I assure you . . . by the drawerful.

(*Immediately* STELLA *leaves* MIRIAM'S *room, the latter gets up, gingerly, but determined. Feels her way into a dressing-gown of a misty grey colour, rather loose and long. Examines herself in the dressing-table mirror, trys to do something about her hair, make herself attractive.*)

(STELLA *goes downstairs. As she reaches the living-room,* ENTER MRS SIBLEY, R., *with loaded tray.*)

MRS SIBLEY (*glancing towards study*) All books . . . all talk. . . . (*Begins to unload tray*) Won't come and eat it even when it's here.

STELLA (*very carefully*) Mrs Sibley, may I boil an egg for Mrs Sword? I think she might try a light-boiled egg.

MRS SIBLEY She won't eat it.

STELLA It's worth trying.

MRS SIBLEY You think you know, but I know. I've been here long enough. But shan't be much longer. Not in a house like this. Everyone peculiar.

(EXIT STELLA, R., *to kitchen during the foregoing.*)

DENIS (*to* SWORD) Doesn't there come a time when you can resist trying again? At your age. . . .

SWORD (*bitterly*) At my age! The creative urge drives the uncreative as mercilessly as alcohol the alcoholic.

DENIS Some are cured, though.

SWORD (*holding his head on one side, as though listening*) Some are cured!

(MRS SIBLEY *approaches the study door.*)

MRS SIBLEY (*appealing*) Now, will you gentlemen chat it out at the breakfast table, please? There's ever such a nice dish of sowty kidneys ... if they haven't turned leathery.

(PROFESSOR SWORD ENTERS *the living-room, followed by* DENIS.)

SWORD (*suddenly turning on* MRS SIBLEY *an apologetic though potent kind of charm – he is very handsome besides*) Poor Mrs Sibley ... you must forgive us for treating you the way we do.

MRS SIBLEY (*overcome*) Well, I mean to say ... it's your own home, Professor Sword . . . and all that. All I want is that everything should be ... nice.

(MRS SIBLEY *turns tail.* EXIT, R. DENIS *and* SWORD *sit at dining-table.*)

(MIRIAM SWORD *has begun to feel neglected again. Has gone to her window. Stands looking out, in profile, hair straying in spite of her attempt to tidy it.*)

MIRIAM (*sighing*) Another day.... Already a glare.... I like it best when the mist creeps up from the valley ... softening the shapes ... the sound of goat-bells in the mist.... (*Brisker, almost angry*) That goatwoman is free! Wonder how she managed to buy her freedom....

SWORD (*dishing out kidneys*) Food! The greatest stimulus to thought.

DENIS (*accepting plate*) Thanks! I'll take the hint.

SWORD (*smiling*) I'm not rude, you know. Not really.

(MIRIAM *suddenly tears herself angrily away from the window.*)

MIRIAM Where is she? What's holding her up, I wonder?

(MIRIAM *comes out on the landing, to head of stairs. Looks over.*)
(*Calling*) Sister Summerhayes ... ?
(*Catches sight of* SWORD *and* DENIS.)
Oh....

DENIS (*to* MIRIAM) Stella ... (*correcting himself*) Sister Summerhayes went to get you your breakfast, Mrs Sword.

MIRIAM Oh.... She takes so long.

SWORD (*without looking up*) How are you feeling, Miriam?

MIRIAM Are you inquiring about my health?

SWORD What else?

MIRIAM No ... of course ... nothing else.... (*Rather shrill*) If you really want to know, I have a splitting head from lying awake half the night, and a touch of gout in my left foot, and....

SWORD (*calmly, interrupting*) I don't believe you.

(MIRIAM *returns abruptly to her room. At once comes back to head of stairs.*)

MIRIAM (*imperiously*) Hugo, will you tell that girl.... (*Her voice breaking*) Ask her to bring up something for herself ... so that we can have breakfast together. (*Almost a whimper*) I think I'm beginning to feel lonely....

(*She trails back disconsolately into her room, throws herself in the easy chair. At same time* ENTER STELLAR., *with* MIRIAM'S *breakfast tray.*)

SWORD (*to* STELLA) My wife is in need of sympathy, Sister. Will you take up something for yourself ... and eat it with her. That, it seems, is what she wishes.

(*He opens a book, props it up in front of him.*)

STELLA Couldn't be easier.

DENIS (*helping her*) I can recommend the controversial kidneys.

(MIRIAM *waits upstairs, tossing her ankle, arranging the skirt of her dressing-gown.*)

MIRIAM (*suddenly holding both hands to her face*) What a mess! It's a terrible thing how the people we meet late in life can't possibly know we weren't always....

(*She knots her hands in her laps, waits. During the foregoing* STELLA *has helped herself to a cup and some additional pieces of toast. Goes upstairs with the loaded tray.*)

(*Looking about, agitated*) That's why the *solution* is so admirable. After the first glass, one's thoughts flow so brilliantly, to meet the stranger. One may even become beautiful ... just for a moment ... before the ugliness sets in.

(STELLA *goes into bedroom with tray.*)

STELLA Thought I'd walked out?

MIRIAM (*fretful*) No. . . . Well, I did wonder . . . if something. . . .

STELLA It was Mrs Sibley. She turns the boiling of an egg into a major operation.

MIRIAM Operations are Mrs Sibley's profession.

STELLA Anyway, here's the egg.

MIRIAM (*shaking her head*) You must let me off the egg. I promise you I'll drink *lots* of *milky* coffee. But let me off the egg . . . just this morning.

(STELLA *sighs. Pours the coffee.*)

Eat it yourself. You're so healthy.

STELLA (*guiltily*) I love to eat!

(MIRIAM *accepts coffee. Drinks cautiously and carefully.*)

MIRIAM That young man down there . . . do you like him?

STELLA Well enough. That's to say . . . I don't think I know him yet.

MIRIAM You're usually so spontaneous.

(STELLA *sits on the edge of the bed, tucks into the kidneys while trying to appear less ravenous than she is.* MIRIAM *sits forward in her chair, sipping coffee meditatively, holding the cup in both hands.*)

I don't think my husband likes him. Hugo hates everyone . . . everybody but himself. He only asks Mr Craig so that he can tell somebody how he has suffered at my hands.

STELLA (*between mouthfuls*) Professor Sword has never discussed you with me . . . only the medical background.

(MIRIAM *throws back her head, and laughs.*)

(SWORD *has continued to read.*)

DENIS Excuse me, sir. Do you mind if I interrupt? I'm going to stretch past you and grab the jam.

(SWORD *lays aside his book.*)

SWORD (*passing jam*) Not at all. As a matter of fact I wasn't reading. I got into the habit of propping up a book at meals. . . .

MIRIAM (*reaching across, gently squeezing* STELLA'S *knee*) I'm glad I have you here. You won't leave me, will you?

STELLA (*putting aside the plate*) Not unless you want me to.

MIRIAM (*apprehensively*) But you haven't seen me yet . . . not like that.

STELLA I shan't.

MIRIAM Oh ... everybody does in time.

SWORD (*fiddling with the leaves of his book*) ... a book can act as a defence ... at least when the enemy is literate.

DENIS (*amazed*) But ... since when am I the enemy?

SWORD (*almost anguished*) No, no, no! (*Recalling*) It all began. ... Miriam, you see, is not all that literate. But she was overawed by learning in the beginning.

DENIS Mrs Sword strikes me as having rather intellectual interests.

SWORD (*correcting*) Aspirations.

MIRIAM In the end, everyone sees the worst.

STELLA I shan't. Not if we have faith in each other.

MIRIAM It's easy enough in the beginning.

SWORD (*half to himself, half to* DENIS) ... Never an intellectual. Miriam has her intuitions. That, I think, is what made it worse. Miriam might have been an artist of a kind. With Miriam's intuition and my mind I could have been an artist. Oh yes, a considerable one. ...

(DENIS *shows unwillingness to listen further. Gets up, sidles about.*)

SWORD ... if the two halves could have been fitted together ... do you see? ... but they didn't fit. ... (*Realizing*) I gather you're embarrassed.

DENIS (*evasively*) No ... oh, no. Stretching my legs.

(*He goes and sits on the upholstered seat near the glass doors. Takes refuge in the magazines.*)

MIRIAM (*sitting forward*) Listen! I can almost hear him down there, telling his guest about his wife.

STELLA You imagine things.

(*She goes and puts down the tray on the bedside table.*)

And here's your lovely little ring. You might lose it. (*Bringing the ring*) I've been admiring that ever since I first saw it. What's the stone?

MIRIAM (*slipping on the ring*) A moss-agate.

SWORD (*ostensibly to* DENIS, *though more to himself*) There came a time when she lost her wedding ring on purpose ... said it slipped off her finger. ...

MIRIAM (*to* STELLA) My fingers grew so thin, everything else slipped off. But the moss-agate stayed with me.

STELLA It's lovely. (*Begins to make* MIRIAM'S *bed*)

MIRIAM I'd love to give it to you....

STELLA (*horrified*) Oh, no ... I wouldn't have mentioned....

MIRIAM But it's the one thing I'm attached to. My only possession.

STELLA (*amazed*) What ... in this house ... full of beautiful things?

MIRIAM Those are his. (*Pause, looking at the ring*) But the ring is an heirloom ... something I have from my family. Some day I'll tell you about it....

SWORD (*half to* DENIS, *more to himself*) ... had delusions about her family.... She was a pawnbroker's daughter. I married her from Newtown. She was pretty then. Would you believe it?

DENIS (*looks up, stares at* SWORD *almost vindictively*) Yes?

SWORD (*turning round, surprised, annoyed, but restraining himself*) She was, too. But sensual. Those first years she led me a dance.

DENIS (*getting up in desperation*) Is no one to be allowed to enjoy the flesh?

SWORD (*drily, almost primly*) Within reason.

DENIS Who's going to decide where reason begins or ends?

SWORD Not Miriam.

MIRIAM (*sitting forward in her chair*) Listen to them down there! I can imagine the lies he's telling. Hugo was always an awful liar. Beware of handsome men, Sister Summerhayes. They lie worse than the plain horse-faced ones.

SWORD She took to the bottle. That is something I've never mentioned. But you know. Everybody knows....

DENIS (*taking him by the shoulders, affectionately, as a son*) Look here, haven't you *anything* to hang on to?
(*Pause.*)

SWORD (*extricates himself, goes a little apart*) Yes.... I have.... You'll be shocked.... I have a faith....

DENIS (*kindly*) I think I knew that too.

SWORD But sometimes I suspect God only helps the strong.
(*He goes off into his study.*)
(EXIT DENIS, BACK *through glass doors.*)

STELLA (*to* MIRIAM) Why don't you let me brush your hair?

MIRIAM Not a very nursey thing to do.

STELLA A nurse isn't an animal apart.

MIRIAM She ought to be.

(STELLA *brings hairbrushes, and starts to brush* MIRIAM'S *hair.*)

MIRIAM Doesn't do to become involved.

(STELLA *brushes rhythmically.*)

STELLA No-oh!

(*Silence.* MIRIAM *sits with eyes closed.*)

I remember . . . I remember a girl I trained with. We were friends . . . as much as there was time for friendship. Ann became involved with a private case . . . an old lady dying of cancer. . . .

MIRIAM (*from behind closed eyes*) Well?

STELLA Ann threw herself out of a window.

(SWORD *reading manuscripts in study.*)

SWORD (*looking through papers*) When we were young . . . when we wanted most to be poets . . . our tragedy was we had never lived a tragedy.

(*He throws a manuscript aside, starts on another.*)

MIRIAM (*half-listening to* STELLA) Sad. I almost killed myself once. Then I thought no one might appreciate it.

(STELLA *brushes harder, frowning.*)

STELLA Doesn't it help you if I brush your hair?

MIRIAM Pure bliss!

(*Silence.*)

May I call you Stella?

STELLA If that's what you want.

MIRIAM (*from behind closed eyes*) So reliable . . . always there . . . always recurring . . . Stella!

STELLA Oh, every one of us has her vices.

MIRIAM (*disbelieving*) What is yours?

STELLA Gluttony.

MIRIAM Restful, gluttonous Stella Summerhayes.

STELLA Sometimes my dad and I, when we're alone together . . . we have an orgy of raw kippers. There was one time we ate seventeen between us.

MIRIAM I don't think I could become attracted to a raw kipper.

STELLA You ought to try.

MIRIAM What's your father like?

STELLA I can't tell you . . . exactly. (*Pause*) Good. (*Pause, during which brushing continues*) Didn't you have any children, Mrs Sword?

MIRIAM A daughter.

(STELLA *does not dare inquire any farther.*)

(*At last*) She went away. I think her parents were too much for her.

STELLA And where is she?

MIRIAM In London. She's a fashion designer.

STELLA Is she brilliant?

MIRIAM Neither brilliant like her father, nor mad like her mother. She has what is necessary to remain the right side of sanity.

STELLA (*brushing*) Married?

MIRIAM No. And seems to be taking good care she won't be. She lives in Shepherd Market ... with a very bossy woman friend.

(SWORD *downstairs still plodding through the manuscript.*)

SWORD (*reading*) 'Mary, Mary, Mary. . . .' (*Angrily*) How we blaspheme in the name of purity!

MIRIAM (*to* STELLA) Her name is Mary. You must be of an age. Oh, Stella, how glad I am you're here!

STELLA (*turning her round by the shoulders to look at herself in the glass*) Now ... don't you look beautiful?

MIRIAM (*unconvinced*) My hair streaming ... ? Like a hundred hags in a high wind!

STELLA (*half laughing*) Mrs Sword, you must have a *little* courage!

(SWORD *throws aside his papers. Appears moved by an impulse. Gets up, comes into the living-room.*)

SWORD (*calling*) Mrs Sibley?

(*He approaches door* R., MRS SIBLEY REAPPEARS *through it. Carrying empty tray to start clearing table. She is depressed again by now.*)

(*Inhibited*) Mrs Sibley ... I have an idea.

(MRS SIBLEY *goes past him, starts to clear.*)

(*Trying it out*) I'm going to take them out ... for the day ... drive them round the mountain towns.

MRS SIBLEY All right for those who have the time.

SWORD A pity to waste the sun. (*Looking at the back of his hand*) Who would think we live in a country of the sun?

MRS SIBLEY Down at Kurrajong . . . that's at Elsie's place . . . they're always slipping off on a jaunt. Keeps the kiddies out of mischief. (*Suddenly suspicious*) Here . . . what about *Mrs* Sword? Is she goin' to ride around the towns?

SWORD (*caught*) No. My . . . wife always complains about my driving.

MRS SIBLEY That's all very well! Your drivin'! What'll you say if anythin' goes wrong with me sittin' at the wheel at home?

SWORD It hasn't before. She's grown quite fond . . . quite dependent on you, Mrs Sibley.

(*He turns away, as though it is decided. Stalks towards the stairs while listening for further protests.*)

MRS SIBLEY Not how it ever appeared to *me.* . . .

SWORD (*going upstairs, still pacifying*) Talk to her . . . humour her . . . allow her to tell you about herself.

MRS SIBLEY I've got the work.

SWORD . . . tell her about *your*-self.

MRS SIBLEY I'm not educated. I haven't got the time for anything to happen to *me*.

(SWORD *is about to go into his room. Then changes his mind, approaches his wife's door with repugnance. Knocks on invisible door.*)

SWORD May I come in, Miriam?

(MIRIAM *does not answer. Activity arrested in the room.* STELLA *moves to door as if to open, when* SWORD *stiffly enters.*)

(*Awkwardly*) I've come . . . to say . . . to tell you both, in fact. Miriam . . . I'm thinking of driving Sister Summerhayes and young Craig round the mountain towns.

MIRIAM Ugly little towns! (*Sharply*) And how do you know they'll want to go? (*Looks at* STELLA *hopefully*) Stella may not want to career over the mountains with an old man who's a shocking driver.

(*She continues looking at* STELLA, *as though the latter's loyalty is at stake.*)

STELLA (*to* MIRIAM) Perhaps that isn't altogether fair. I mean . . . he drove me very carefully the morning he brought me from the station. But I'm going to stay with you, Mrs Sword. I'm going to show you those snaps.

MIRIAM (*pleased, but pained*) Yes. (*Murmuring with a wistful childishness*) The photographs....

SWORD Then there's nothing more to discuss.

(*He turns as if to go out.* MIRIAM *hides her face in her hands.*)

MIRIAM (*wrenching it out masochistically*) No. Stella ... you must go, dear. Afterwards you shall tell me all about it. Mrs Sibley will be here ... to argue which tablets I must take. We've done it all before.

STELLA (*on the horns of a dilemma*) Mrs Sword ... I....

MIRIAM (*removing hands from her face, hard, matter of fact*) Yes. Yes. You must go. It will give Hugo so much pleasure to show off a young girl in those shocking little towns.

STELLA (*embarrassed*) If you think then ... I'll speak to Mrs Sibley before I go.

(STELLA *leaves the room without looking at* SWORD. *She is about to go down stairs, but turns into her room, begins quickly to make the bed, and tidy.*)

(MRS SIBLEY *coming and going in the living-room.*)

SWORD What a technique you've developed, Miriam, over the years, for humiliating yourself and others.

(*He moves back into the room. Prowls round his wife.*)

MIRIAM Yes! Isn't it awful?

(*She begins quietly to whimper. He stands behind her, touches her hair.*)

SWORD I even remember the first time. It was just after Mary was born. I stuck a bit of tinsel on a Christmas tree. You laughed, and accused me of being 'artistic'.

MIRIAM (*softly*) How we remember! Normal people don't remember all the painful things....

(*She suddenly seizes his hand, kisses, almost devours it. He submits for a moment, then withdraws it as though repelled.*)

(*Looking at him fiercely*) It was the first time you've let me touch you in I don't know how many years. How did I suddenly become less disgusting?

SWORD You are over-exciting yourself, Miriam. (*Goes towards door*) You are at your best when you are less excited. (*At the door*) Is there anything you need? (*He looks back.*)

MIRIAM (*desperately*) No.

(*He returns, stoops and kisses her on the forehead. Turns again and leaves the room, his expression strained.* MIRIAM *sits rigid and trembling, staring ahead.* SWORD *goes into his room.* STELLA, SWORD *and* MIRIAM *are now visible in their separate rooms.* STELLA *continues with bed-making and tidying.* SWORD *fiddles with this and that.*)

(ENTER DENIS CRAIG *through glass doors,* BACK.)

MRS SIBLEY (*about to depart with last of crockery, to* DENIS) You've got a nice day's drive arranged. . . .

DENIS Oh?

MRS SIBLEY With Professor Sword and Sister What's-'er-Name. (*Not without a touch of admiration*) He fancies himself, you know, driving along in that tweed cap. . . . But I'm to be the sucker, as they say . . . if anybody is. . . .

DENIS Mrs Sibley, you and I appear to be the minor characters of the piece. That alone ought to make us happy.

(EXIT DENIS L. *through the front door.*)

MRS SIBLEY Don't know what that signifies. . . . (*Looking after him*) They're all talk, talk, and nothing ever said. . . . (*Carries out tray,* R.)

(SWORD *looks at his face in the dressing-table glass. Suddenly and firmly goes and kneels beside his bed, his hands held in the traditional Gothic attitude of prayer.*)

SWORD (*praying*) O Lord, help us to overcome our revulsion. . . . Spare us the humiliation of humiliating others. . . . Teach us to translate knowledge into wisdom. . . . Make clean our hearts, so that we may . . . love . . . that we may love purely . . . without expectation . . . at last. . . .

(SWORD *suddenly, chin-on-breast, appears at a loss, clenching his hands.*)

(STELLA *stands* CENTRE *of her room, arms around herself, an expression of pure serenity.*)

STELLA All these days I haven't written. *He*'ll never write. We were always closest, though, when we were silentest . . . when I sat in the workshop, and listened to the sweep of his plane . . . the shavings falling. . . . Oh, it's good to know that what is good, true, exists. . . .

(STELLA *shakes off her mood. Quickly does one or two things to her hair.* SWORD *rises from his knees. Takes his tweed cap and a stick. Starts to go downstairs.*)

MIRIAM (*looking at herself in the glass*) They'll come back blinded ... faces ablaze ... voices bleached ... changed. ...

(STELLA *comes in quickly. Stands for a second.*)

STELLA Now, you know about the tablets . . . the big ones before lunch. . . .

MIRIAM I know *everything*!

STELLA (*half resolved*) Shan't I go with them?

MIRIAM Go! (*Wanly, martyred*) I shall stroll in the garden, amongst the ... plants. ...

STELLA (*smiling, softly*) Good-bye!

(*She takes up the tray from the bedside table.*)

SWORD (*calling from bottom of stairs*) Sister Summerhayes? Meet you at the car.

(*He goes out front door.* STELLA *runs downstairs, carrying tray.*)

(*Calling*, OFF) Denis? Where are ... ?

STELLA (*calling, running towards kitchen door*) Mrs Sibley!

(MRS SIBLEY *comes out. Takes tray.*)

The main thing is to talk to her once in a while. ...

MRS SIBLEY *She*'ll talk.

STELLA But tell her something. Tell her about your *grandchildren*. So that she won't think she's living on the moon.

MRS SIBLEY She thinks it's my grandchildren that's livin' on the moon.

(EXIT STELLA, L., *by front door.* MRS SIBLEY EXIT R.)

(MIRIAM *watches the departure from her window. Sound of car driving away. It becomes obvious at once that an idea is developing in* MIRIAM'S *mind. She comes downstairs, gliding, in her long gown, trailing sleeves. Goes and listens at door,* R. *Sound of* MRS SIBLEY *singing.* MIRIAM *goes into hall. Glances out of front door. Comes back as if to make sure of* MRS SIBLEY. *Returns to hall, and sits down at telephone in a state of nervous luxury.*)

MIRIAM (*telephoning, in an excited, peremptory voice*) Blackstone 268. . . . (*Irritated*) No! No! 268. . . . They're not ... ? (*Relieved*) Oh . . . *thank* you. . . . (*Pause*) Mr Cantwell? (*She relaxes a bit, a mixture of the languid and the intense*) Mrs Sword here. . . . Mrs Sword. . . . I wonder whether you could deliver a few bottles of whisky . . . ? (*Quickly*) Yes, yes, I know. . . . I know the Professor spoke. . . . I *know* none of the tradesmen are *supposed*. . . . (*Imploring*) But please listen to me, Mr Cantwell. (*Again languid*) I have an interesting proposition to make. . . . (*Looks at her ring*) You remember that curious ring you so much admired . . . the day we called at the store, and bought the broom? . . . My moss-agate ring? . . . You could have it, Mr Cantwell, on the understanding that you bring me *at once* . . . a dozen of Scotch. . . . Only Australian? . . . Oh. . . . A dozen Australian then. . . . Six? . . . Oh, but really. . . . (*Desperately calling*) Mr Cantwell? Mr Cant . . . ? (*Rattling the telephone frenziedly, then speaking to exchange*) You cut me off, or something. I was speaking to Blackstone 268. . . . (*Pause*) Mr Cantwell? (*Pause*) Six then . . . six Australian . . . provided you deliver at once. . . . Yes, you heard. My moss-agate ring. . . . I can assure you . . . the Professor won't be here. . . .

(*She replaces the receiver. Gets up. Undecided. Thinking. Finally goes and opens kitchen door.*)

(*Calling*) Mrs Sibley?

(ENTER MRS SIBLEY.)

Mr Craig mentioned seeing some beautiful lettuces down at Sanders'. You know . . . that roadworker's. . . .

(MRS SIBLEY *begins to make discouraging noises, wrapping her hands in her apron.*)

(*Raising her voice, brutally*) . . . that temporary camp. The pregnant wife . . . she's grown a few vegetables. Little lettuces with tight hearts. . . .

(MRS SIBLEY *moaning and sceptical.*)

(*Wheedling now*) I do wish you'd go down . . . say, in about an hour . . . finish the housework first, of course. I have such a craving for a fresh spring lettuce. Ask Mrs Sanders to give them on credit. The Professor will pay tomorrow.

MRS SIBLEY (*unenthusiastic*) Down to that gipsyfied camp? The stones roll from under your feet. . . .

MIRIAM But a fresh little lettuce. . . .

MRS SIBLEY And if anything happened to you? It wouldn't be worth it. Not for a lettuce.

MIRIAM (*turning away*) He hasn't left me anything to give you.

MRS SIBLEY (*offended*) Here! That's not nice, Mrs Sword!

(MIRIAM *starts to go upstairs.*)

MIRIAM God will help me!

MRS SIBLEY What ... to a lettuce?

(MIRIAM *continues to mount. Does not answer.*)

Didn't think *you'd* drag in God! Didn't think you *believed.*

MIRIAM (*ascending*) Oh, but I do! That's the point. It's just that ... nobody believes anyone believes. (*She reaches the landing*) But we're wasting our breath. I'm going in to get dressed now.

MRS SIBLEY Never knew *you* get dressed of a morning!

MIRIAM Perhaps not. But the unexpected sometimes happens. That is what makes life bearable ... (*she goes into her room*) ... even now.

ACT TWO

SAME AS ACT I, SCENE THREE. *Towards midday. Still sunny outside, though the bright blaze of early morning has died down somewhat.*
MIRIAM SWORD *upstairs in her room. She is dressed in a white blouse
and long dark skirt – very severe and unrelieved. Her hair is done, face
appears pared to the bone.*

Downstairs MRS SIBLEY ENTERS *at once and precipitately through
the glass doors,* BACK C. *Slams them viciously. Peers out in a direction
R., now that she is protected by the closed doors.*

MRS SIBLEY (*peering out*) Filthy beast!
   (MIRIAM *comes out of her room. On the landing she looks nervously
   at her watch. Starts to come downstairs. She is very jumpy, agitated
   in all her movements now. When she reaches the bottom of the stairs
   she and* MRS SIBLEY *grow conscious of each other's presence.*
   MIRIAM *is appalled, irritated,* MRS SIBLEY *anxious to blame somebody for something.*)
   Went out to fetch a bit of parsley . . . over there from under the
   tap. . . . There's a stinkin' billy-goat in amongst the roses!
   (MIRIAM *draws a deep breath. Goes quickly to the glass doors, and
   looks in direction indicated by* MRS SIBLEY.)
MIRIAM (*looking out*) That must be . . . it can *only* be Miss Quod-
   ling's. He'll eat the garden out. . . .
MRS SIBLEY If you could call it a garden. A few poor raggedy rose-
   bushes!
MIRIAM But goats do love roses.
MRS SIBLEY Down at Kurrajong, at Elsie's place. . . .
MIRIAM (*wildly*) Something will have to be done!
MRS SIBLEY What can a couple of women do?
MIRIAM (*with an expression of desperate cunning*) Someone I knew
   once kept goats . . . and the goats used to get in . . . into the
   house. (*Emphasizing*) The *buck* broke in. They found him lying

on one of the beds. The stench was *ghastly*! They had to fumigate the whole house.

MRS SIBLEY (*horrified*) On the beds?

MIRIAM On the bed!

MRS SIBLEY (*quickly*) Not if you keep the doors shut!

(*She goes to the open front door, and slams it shut.* MIRIAM *glances desperately at her watch.*)

MIRIAM But a buck, Mrs Sibley, is fantastically strong when roused. A buck can batter....

(MRS SIBLEY *has returned to living-room. She is frightened by now.*)

I've known ... I read how a buck once knocked down a strong man, and trampled and battered him to death.

MRS SIBLEY Next week I'm getting out! Elsie would never forgive herself if she knew her mother was exposed to a situation like this!

MIRIAM (*softly, wooing*) But a buck is quite gentle with his owners. They become terribly attached.

MRS SIBLEY Didn't ought to let them escape.

MIRIAM I expect Miss Quodling wouldn't have any difficulty in catching hers. (*Suddenly bursting into tears*) I do wish you'd go, Mrs Sibley.... It *is* frightening ... I can just imagine how glass doors....

MRS SIBLEY (*frightened, turning this way and that*) Oh, dear! Where does she live... this person with the goats?

MIRIAM (*stops crying – pointing in direction of front door*) You know that first loop in the road ...? You turn where you see the kerosene tin nailed to the stump.

MRS SIBLEY (*tremulous*) Ye... ehs....

(*She moves towards the front door.*)

MIRIAM (*quickly, realizing*) Oh ... not that way, Mrs Sibley. I forgot! Not when you can take the short cut.

MRS SIBLEY (*coming back, though doubtful*) I don't want none of those mountain tracks.

MIRIAM But this is so much shorter ... and far less steep.

(*Takes* MRS SIBLEY *by the arm, leads her to the glass doors, pointing through them in a direction,* L.)

U

Look! Go to the bottom of the orchard. You'll pick up the track just down there . . . behind that big blackwood standing on its own.

MRS SIBLEY (*looking through doors in opposite direction*) And what about the billy? What if 'e goes me?

MIRIAM (*pointing in opposite direction*) Not if you edge along there. See? The other side of the rosemary hedge.

(*She opens the doors, pushes* MRS SIBLEY *out.*)

MRS SIBLEY (*almost in tears*) Never bargained for this sort of thing. Runnin' messages out of doors. . . .

(MRS SIBLEY *disappears.* MIRIAM *returns* C., *holding her hands to her cheeks, very tense. Almost at once the sound of a car is heard approaching.* MIRIAM, *in a state of exhausted relief, touches her hair. Goes quickly and throws open the front door. Stands looking out. The sun lights up her strained smile. Sound of car door banging.*)

ENTER CANTWELL, *a middle-aged grocer. Shirt sleeves rolled half-way up his forearms. Long white apron. Hatless. The grocer's pencil behind one ear. He is breathing rather fast and resentfully. Probably a cautious man at the best of times. He is carrying an open carton in which necks of half-a-dozen whisky bottles are visible.*

MIRIAM (*genuinely moved*) I'm so grateful, Mr Cantwell. You don't know. . . .

(*She leads him into the living-room.*)

CANTWELL (*looking round*) It's *your* funeral, I suppose.

(*He continues to hold the carton.*)

MIRIAM You needn't be afraid. I'm quite on my own.

(CANTWELL *grunts.*)

MIRIAM Won't you put down that heavy box?

CANTWELL Where's the ring?

MIRIAM (*laughing coldly*) Surely you trust me?

CANTWELL Does the Professor trust his wife?

(*Silence. Then* MIRIAM *takes off the ring without looking at it. Holds it out towards* CANTWELL *at arm's length. He puts down carton, takes ring with signs of repressed excitement.*)

MIRIAM (*sighing*) Yes. There it is!

(CANTWELL *quickly puts ring in a waistcoat pocket.*)

CANTWELL Where'll I put the grog?

MIRIAM (*without hesitation*) In the sideboard ... over there.

CANTWELL Bit obvious, isn't it?

MIRIAM That's why. I know my husband. He's a subtle man.

(CANTWELL *carries carton of whisky over to sideboard against wall* L. *Stoops, and starts to stow it inside.*)

(*Unable to restrain herself*) You must excuse me if I.... (*She goes to sideboard, takes one of the bottles from the carton*) I've been so depending on it.... (*Takes glass out of sideboard*) I have these terrible migraines, you know ....

(CANTWELL *does not comment, continues to dispose of bottles in sideboard. She tears foil from bottle with trembling hands. Pours herself a good third of a tumbler.*)

(*Trembling*) ... at times ... quite ... agonizing....

(*She takes a deep, relieving draft.*)

(*Eyes closed, home at last*) You don't know ... how it helps.

(CANTWELL *straightens up.*)

CANTWELL (*eagerly*) What about this ring ... got a history?

MIRIAM (*taking whisky bottle by the neck, carrying it very practised, with one hand, glass in the other, to the table* C.) Oh yes. It has a history. (*Dreamy*) It was given to an ancestress ... on *my* side ... by one of the French kings....

(CANTWELL *has taken ring out of his pocket. Examines it. Fascinated.*)

CANTWELL That'd be some time ago, wouldn't it?

MIRIAM (*sighing*) Several hundred years. (*Dreamily, as she sits at the table with her bottle and glass*) She saved him from the attack of a wild boar ... while he was out hunting....

CANTWELL Waddayaknow! Been in the family all these years!

MIRIAM We were a great family then. As time went by, we became ... less important. (*Pause*) In fact, by my generation ... we had sunk pretty low. (*She sinks her mouth in the glass, then, after drawing breath*) My father was a pawnbroker, Mr Cantwell. He was a dear, good, hopeless man.

(CANTWELL *continues examining the ring.*)

(*Without real interest*) I expect you'll give it to your wife, won't you?

CANTWELL (*contemptuously, pocketing ring*) Nah! I'll keep it. For meself. Look at it once in a while.

(MIRIAM *eyes him with faint surprise.*)

MIRIAM You're a strange man . . . in that little shop.

CANTWELL It's a livin'.

MIRIAM But strange.

CANTWELL Why shouldn't *I* own one or two . . . (*terribly embarrassed, secretive*) . . . beautiful things? (*Pause*) Once when I was a boy I seen a coloured supplement of one of those French cathedrals. Charters, I think it was. (*Attempting to convey with his hands*) A rose window . . . all in colour! (*Pause*) I said I'm goin' there. (*Pause*) But I didn't.

MIRIAM (*sipping, dreamily*) So you keep one or two . . . beautiful things. You take them out and look at them . . . in that dark little room . . . behind the biscuits and the flour. . . .

CANTWELL Why not?

MIRIAM (*shaking her head, half ecstatic, half tragic*) No reason. Every man to his own visions.

(*She suddenly rouses herself, assuming a conventional social voice.*) Oh, I forgot. . . . How miserable of me! Get yourself a glass, Mr Cantwell, from out of the sideboard.

CANTWELL (*shaking his head*) Thanks! Never touch the stuff.

MIRIAM (*listless, raising her eyebrows, though really not interested*) Seventh Day . . . or something of that description?

CANTWELL (*proudly*) An Anglican all me life. Warden for the last six years.

MIRIAM (*shaking her head*) It amounts to the same thing. We're all worshipping the same God.

CANTWELL (*unable to restrain disapproval*) Doesn't seem to help you much.

MIRIAM (*guzzling her drink*) What . . . because I find Him at the bottom of the glass?

CANTWELL (*shocked*) Not what I was ever taught.

MIRIAM (*closing her eyes*) Different people . . . different approach. (*Suddenly opening her eyes*) You know, Mr Cantwell, you've done me the most glorious disservice anyone has ever done a person. I'm truly grateful. (*Sincerely*) I only hope your warden's conscience isn't going to suffer for it.

CANTWELL What about your own, eh?

MIRIAM Mine, poor thing! It's so frayed it hardly holds together any more. (*Pours herself another drink. Swallows a good draught*) Oh, dear God, yes! It brings Him close. Wonderfully close . . . (*shuddering, then closing her eyes*) . . . when it isn't terribly. . . .

CANTWELL (*looking round uneasily*) I ought to be makin' tracks. (*Picks up the empty carton.*)

MIRIAM Don't be afraid. He won't be here . . . not for some time yet. He's found an . . . occupation.

CANTWELL All the same, I gotta be on my way.

MIRIAM (*resigned*) Oh, I see! You're afraid of me! In the end you're all afraid. I'm the only one who isn't.

(CANTWELL *makes for the door without saying anything further.*) (*Raising her voice, though not turning her head*) Anyone who's been in hell is . . . not. I'm only afraid, Mr Cantwell, when He reaches down with His hand, and I can't touch . . . not even the tip of His cool finger. (*Turning round, to aim at* CANTWELL'S *departing back*) Hell shrieks in the end!

(EXIT CANTWELL *through front door, very slightly hunched.* MIRIAM *returns to her drink. Swallows. Pours another.*)

(*Laughing, tenderly*) Poor little man! A rose window . . . and a moss-agate. While the wife . . . she smelled of aniseed balls and armpits. Well. . . . My lovely moss-agate . . . (*slowly, in measured tones*) . . . all those hundreds of years filled with a mist that unravelled at *last* on . . . (*with bitter emphasis*) . . . *Bald Mountain*! (*Sounds of car driving away.*)

(*Disturbed*) Will he, I wonder . . . appreciate my moss-agate . . . or has its beauty *evaporated* . . . like the mists . . . and the love of men . . . ?

(MRS SIBLEY *is seen at the glass doors,* BACK. *She appears from the* L. *side, looking around cautiously, apparently for the buck.* MIRIAM *hears her arrival. Looks round. Hides her glass expertly in the bowl of flowers on the dining-table. Walks, very controlled, to the fireplace, hides the bottle behind the unlit logs.* MRS SIBLEY *outside suggests she has caught sight of the buck in the distance of the garden,* R. *She slips in through the glass doors.* MIRIAM *has continued leaning against the mantelpiece, her back turned, toying with her hair.*)

MRS SIBLEY If I'd known. . . . It was that steep . . . nearly broke me ankles. Then you would'uv looked funny!

MIRIAM (*very controlled, cold*) We're insured against all the minor disasters. It's only the major ones we weren't able to allow for.

MRS SIBLEY You upper class people . . . you don't only *talk* different, you *mean* different on top of that.

MIRIAM (*laughing, low and hoarse, but always controlled*) Didn't they tell you, Mrs Sibley, I'm the lowest class of all?

MRS SIBLEY I was taught not to listen to what anybody says. You've got to form yer own opinion.

MIRIAM (*remembering, again disturbed – she would like to turn, but doesn't dare*) But did you find her? Is she coming?

(MRS SIBLEY *assumes an attitude of haughtiness.*)

MRS SIBLEY Is she coming! She was hot on me heels. Smell. . . . That goat person leaves 'er own billy standing!

(MRS SIBLEY EXIT, L. MIRIAM *stoops, fishes out the bottle from behind the logs and has a swig from it. At the same time* MISS QUODLING *appears the other side of the glass doors. She is dressed much as before, except that she has sloughed a cardigan or two, and is wearing a pair of army boots instead of the gumboots. Carrying a coiled rope.*)

MISS QUODLING (*calling*) Sam! Just you wait! You independent man! We'll see who matters here!

(MISS QUODLING *descends* R. *the other side of glass doors in pursuit of her buck.*)

(RE-ENTER MRS SIBLEY. MIRIAM, *who has turned to observe* MISS QUODLING, *immediately turns her back again, hides the bottle once more behind the logs, assumes rather an unnatural position as she concentrates on the fireplace.*)

MRS SIBLEY What about your lunch, Mrs Sword? There's that bit of fillet the Professor brought from Blackstone a couple of days ago. Ought to be nice and tender. Shall I toss the fillet in the pan . . . with a little bit of salad to it?

MIRIAM (*harshly*) I'm not hungry. (*Hanging her head*) You're so kind! (*Clenches her hand against the mantelpiece.*)

MRS SIBLEY You've got to eat *something*!

MIRIAM Perhaps later . . . perhaps I'll eat a slice of cinnamon toast . . . and drink a cup of coffee. But even coffee tastes like mud.

MRS SIBLEY Got to keep your spirits up. You won't make any headway if you keep on givin' in.

MIRIAM (*looking into the fireplace*) I know my own capacities. They may be poor, but they are my own. (*Pause*) Better light the fire tonight, Mrs Sibley. (*Pause*) It's going to be cold. Already I can feel it!

MRS SIBLEY Yes, Mrs Sword. (*She is about to go out by the door,* R.) The goat person, Mrs Sword, decided on the way that she's goin' to come in and pay her respects.

MIRIAM I'll expect her then. Miss Quodling's always been an understanding soul.

MRS SIBLEY But high. . . . (*Remembering her encounter with* MISS QUODLING *she takes an inordinately deep breath*) Oh, dear! (*Shaking her head, shuddering*) High!

(EXIT MRS SIBLEY, R., *as* MIRIAM *comments.*)

MIRIAM (*smiling wryly*) Whatever is high hides the depths that have to be hidden. . . .

(MISS QUODLING *appears* BACK *at the glass doors. She is without her rope. Peers in, not yet seeing* MRS SWORD. *Knocks as loudly as possible.* MIRIAM *turns.*)

(*Her back supported by the mantelpiece, calling*) Come in, Miss Quodling. I couldn't be more pleased.

(MISS QUODLING ENTERS. *She, too, is pleased, though respectful.*)

MISS QUODLING Sorry to have given anybody trouble.

MIRIAM What have you done with him?

MISS QUODLING Roped 'im to the fence.

MIRIAM Good thing you've left us one.

MISS QUODLING (*cautious*) Eh?

MIRIAM All that firewood you carry off . . . before some of us are awake. . . .

MISS QUODLING (*stroking her nose*) Can't have chosen the darkest nights.

MIRIAM (*sombre*) No night is dark enough for those who lie awake. We develop the habit of seeing . . . hearing. . . . (*She moves away from mantelpiece towards table* C., *controlled, but not quite perfectly*)

We can pick our way between the logs. We know the touch of the
ferns....

(MISS QUODLING *has been observing shrewdly.*)

MISS QUODLING (*sympathetic*) You're not on it again, are yer?

(*Pause.* MIRIAM *turns to face her.*)

MIRIAM (*soberly*) Yes.

MISS QUODLING Well, I won't tell.

MIRIAM No need. (*Takes the empty tumbler out of the bowl of
flowers.*)

MISS QUODLING No need.

MIRIAM Truth has a certain smell.

MISS QUODLING I'll say!

MIRIAM (*formally*) Can I tempt you to a drop?

MISS QUODLING Seeing as you've fallen . . . I'd be prepared to
follow suit.

(MIRIAM *goes to sideboard. Rummages amongst the glasses, brings
one out, together with a fresh bottle.*)

MIRIAM I've often wondered, Miss Quodling, how you broke free?

(*She brings bottle and second glass to table,* C.)

MISS QUODLING Ha! It wasn't always free.

MIRIAM Or *is* it now?

(*She tears foil off the bottle, and drops it with a grand gesture where
she stands.*)

MISS QUODLING I was a prisoner as a girl all right. My life was
lived on the end of a duster....

(MIRIAM *pours a strong one in each glass.*)

MIRIAM At this point my husband would like to know . . . whether
the duster was . . . (*imitating* SWORD) . . . meta-*physical.*

MISS QUODLING Don't know about the meta-what's-this. I only
know my auntie was a terror for the dustin'....

MIRIAM (*softly, incidentally, raising her glass a moment before taking
another good slug*) Here's life, then....

(*Sighs. Sways slightly. Sits down at table with her glass.*)

MISS QUODLING (*crooking her finger*) Cheerio, Mrs Sword!

(MISS QUODLING *drinks and sits.*)

MIRIAM I was always a bit doubtful about the meta . . . metaphysical....

MISS QUODLING Dust! Dust! It was all tables. Little tables. And things. I've never seen so many things. . . .

MIRIAM The *physical*. . . . Now the physical. . . . But oh, no! Raise your mind to a higher plane . . .

MISS QUODLING I bust a shepherdess once. A bit of a china ornament! You wouldn't of known as anyone could create like Auntie did on that day. . . .

MIRIAM (*suddenly stretching her arms above her head in an attitude of languid sensuality*) . . . when the body is such a beautiful thing. . . . (*Lets her arms fall in hopelessness and disgust*) *Was* is perhaps the word.

MISS QUODLING . . . 'Pull the blinds,' she said. Mind you, there was no need . . . we practically lived behind holland. 'Pull the blinds,' however, she said . . . 'my head . . . couldn't be more broken than a little china shepherdess. . . .'

MIRIAM (*earnestly*) I understand. . . . (*Takes a good long pull at her glass*)

MISS QUODLING (*happy*) Don't it get yer down? (*She follows suit and drinks*)

MIRIAM I understood from the beginning. Oh, we made love . . . and so forth. We could have drunk each other up . . . and often did.

MISS QUODLING Sometimes the young fellers would come. They'd come on Sundays, and sit amongst the little tables. As I was sayun, Auntie's was full of little tables. I'd put on my good muslun . . .

MIRIAM (*bitterly unhappy, rocking*) Oh, God, the mornings. The exhausted mornings . . . when one comes alive again at dawn! You remember the light then? How it lies along the flanks . . . not quite flesh . . . not quite moonlight . . .

MISS QUODLING . . . my good muslun with the cherry sash. You wouldn't believe, eh? Settin' on the horsehair sofa Auntie said was gunna be mine. . . .

MIRIAM . . . that you never quite possessed. . . .

MISS QUODLING Who wanted to possess . . . whether a sofa . . . or a man?

MIRIAM Hugo was a god. . . .

313

MISS QUODLING Never knew a god . . . only men. The young fellers . . . (*sighing*) . . . some of them were right enough. . . .

MIRIAM Sometimes at dawn you would have said his head was carved in marble. . . .

MISS QUODLING You can enjoy lookun at a handsome man. But not to keep. . . .

MIRIAM . . . not even for a moment. Not for the most joyful . . . saddest moment of all. (*Pours herself another drink*)

MISS QUODLING I liked to *think* about the men, though. There was one feller . . . sat opposite me in the train . . . looked at each other, we did, all the way to Strathfield. I thought about 'um for twenty years. (*Pause*) Wondered what 'is voice would 'uv sounded like.

MIRIAM His voice was always cold, though. Perhaps it was only to be expected. A god with a marble voice. . . .

MISS QUODLING Rather leathery, he was. Scabs on the knuckles. Knocked 'em on the fenceposts perhaps. . . .

MIRIAM . . . The trouble with my god . . . he developed a Gothic soul. . . .

MISS QUODLING (*depressed*) Don't know about the Gothic. . . .

MIRIAM His hands learned to pray for salvation . . . from what . . . I can't for the moment remember. . . .

MISS QUODLING Don't know about salvation. All I know . . . it was all rooms, and little tables, and china shepherdesses that broke. When Auntie died, I cut and run. Bugger the young fellers, I said . . . and the horsehair sofa. . . .

MIRIAM Oh, yes . . . I remember, how I remember! Salvation from the devils of flesh! And I . . . (*laughing frantically*) . . . the worst . . . the worst devil!

(*She walks unsteadily to look at herself in the mirror over the sideboard.*)

MISS QUODLING Never let the horns grow so far . . . not when you know . . . burn them in the early stages with a little caustic stick.

MIRIAM (*turning, appealing*) Miss Quodling, am I your idea of the Devil?

MISS QUODLING (*looking*) You? You're sick!

MIRIAM (*returning to table, and pounding it with her fists*) And you . . . you found it! You escaped! You found your freedom . . .

MISS QUODLING Who found who or what . . . who can say? I've
got my goats. Had them too many years to remember. . . . There's
Dolores. She's certainly a horny one. I've got to admit that. Left
'em so long . . . the caustic stick wouldn't work. . . .

MIRIAM (*dazed*) . . . wouldn't work. . . .

MISS QUODLING (*smiling ecstatically*) My Dolores! You remember
Dolores?

(MIRIAM *shakes her head.*)

Well, I expect I'll never be free while there's that Dolores. Comes
in and lays down sometimes in front of the fire . . . as if it was the
lounge-room of a brick home, and her a Christian.

(MIRIAM *almost loses her balance, closes her eyes, and has to sit.*
MISS QUODLING *rises. Outside the day is becoming overcast.*)

'Ere! You *are* sick!

MIRIAM (*shakes her head*) Drunk!

MISS QUODLING Bit tipsy meself, if it comes. . . .

MIRIAM Drunk! Drunk! Ever since he kissed me on the mouth
in the Enmore Road!

MISS QUODLING Better be makun tracks . . . I s'pose.

MIRIAM Yes, there's always a time . . . to go . . . when you have
somewhere . . . to go *to*.

MISS QUODLING But you're *there*, it seems ter me.

MIRIAM Oh, yes . . . for ever . . . or somewhere else.

MISS QUODLING Well, Mrs Sword, I must thank you for a very
charming entertainment. If you come ter think, we've talked about
practically everythink. (*Goes towards the doors*, BACK) I'll hope
to repay the compliment, any time you'll do me the 'onour . . .
pardon me . . . *h*onour.

(MISS QUODLING EXIT BACK. *Disappears* R., *calling.*)

(*Calling*, OFF) Samson? Can't you learn you'll do no good pullun
on that rope? You're caught! Caught! Silly old devul! . . . Silly
old god! . . . (*Laughter*) . . . Ah, dear!

(MIRIAM *sits motionless in her chair.* ENTER MRS SIBLEY, R.
MIRIAM *makes no attempt to hide bottle and glasses, but* MRS
SIBLEY *is for the moment too interested in the departure of* MISS
QUODLING.)

MRS SIBLEY (*advancing into dining-room, but diverging into study, where she stands looking through the window while addressing* MIRIAM) That person seems to be actin' queer . . . if you ask me. . . . Of course I could see on the way up, she's a little bit off 'er rocker, but now . . . it looks . . . to *me* . . . as if she might of 'ad a couple. . . .

(MRS SIBLEY *whips round in horror. Comes running into the dining room.*)

(*Appalled*) Mrs Sword, you didn't. . . .

(MIRIAM *does not turn or answer. Continues sitting on her upright chair.*)

(*Catching sight of bottle and glasses*) What'uve you gone and done ter me . . . ? (*Bursts into tears*)

(MIRIAM *remains unmoved.*)

(*Wringing her hands, terrified, crying*) What am I goin' to say?

MIRIAM Let the situation speak for itself, Mrs Sibley.

MRS SIBLEY Situation! I'm goin' to send a telegram to Elsie. . . .

MIRIAM (*wearily*) Oh, yes . . . (*forcing herself up*) . . . when you've got it snug . . . somewhere . . . burrow in . . . burrow in. . . . (*She is rather staggery.*)

MRS SIBLEY That's all very well. In between, I've got to face the music. I'm the one. . . .

MIRIAM (*taking her bottle and glass*) I shall bear the brunt of it. (*Going towards stairs*) I know the score off by heart . . . (*mounting*) . . . from the opening roll of drums . . . down to the last crash of brass. (*Laughing softly, bitterly*) For *brass* . . . substitute . . . *glass*. Oh, yes . . . I've been through it. . . .

(*She has reached the landing.*)

(*Turning for a moment*) . . . and shall go through it. He won't spare me . . . any of his virtuosity. . . .

(*She continues along the landing, feeling her way into her room by the* [*non-existent*] *wall.*)

(MRS SIBLEY *appears petrified. Suddenly wrenches herself into action. Goes into the hall, to the telephone. Has a quick look at the book. Business of making call.*)

MRS SIBLEY (*panting*) Is that Blackstone P.O.? (*She pronounces the letters*) . . . Well, I want to send a telegram, please. . . . Eh? . . . Ordinary? I don't know that it's . . . yes, ordinary then. . . . To

Mrs Elsie Goodenough, View Farm, Kurrajong. . . . Eh? . . . (*Breathing hard*) What do I want to say? . . . Well, she's my daughter. See? And what I want to say is . . . (*it all comes pouring out*) . . . they've got to come up ter-morrer, and fetch me in their own car. I'll pack me port tonight. See? A person can only stand so much. I mean . . . it begins to get on yer nerves. . . .

(MIRIAM *has put down bottle and glass on bedside table. Stands for a moment contemplative at* CENTRE. *Hands joined as though for prayer, but carried low and listless, not in the suppliant attitude.*)

MIRIAM . . . sometimes you get to the bottom of the glass, and find it's . . . empty. Perhaps you imagined . . . it was ever anything else. . . .

MRS SIBLEY (*at telephone, offended*) Eh? . . . Sort it out. But I told you, didn't I?

MIRIAM (*rubbing her forearms*) . . . but cold. . . . (*Goes to window, looking out*) The sun is off. . . .

MRS SIBLEY (*at telephone*) Blackstone? (*Banging the bar of the set*) Blackstone! . . . Oh! (*Again tearful*) Some people are that rude. . . .

MIRIAM (*sad, dreamy*) But the mists will come . . . feel them already . . . the long, lovely mists . . . out of the valley. . . .

MRS SIBLEY (*blowing her nose*) A person's got to have education in a world like this.

(*Sounds of car approaching.* MRS SIBLEY *electrified. Quickly pockets her handkerchief.*)

MIRIAM (*still at her window*) . . . softer . . . kinder . . . than *cars*.

(MRS SIBLEY *rushes at front door to confirm.*)

MRS SIBLEY (*looking out*) Oh, dear . . . yes!

(*She scuttles across living-room, and* EXIT R., *to kitchen quarters.*)

MIRIAM (*leaving window*) I'm never exactly frightened . . . but am . . . *frightened.*

(*She falls on the bed in a position of grotesque helplessness, her face against the pillow. At first crying softly, then still.*)

(*Sound of car door,* OFF. *Then* ENTER STELLA *and* PROFESSOR SWORD. *Both rather flushed, dazed. In addition, the* PROFESSOR *could be feeling his age. He is glad of the support of his stick.* STELLA *carrying the tail of a lyre-bird.*)

(*Sound of car reversing, probably into a garage.*)

SWORD I feel guilty . . . making him drive home.

STELLA He loved it. Didn't you notice him taking the hairpin bend? (*Speaking without malice, however*) Once in a while, everybody needs the chance to show off.

SWORD (*irritably, self-engrossed*) Yes. But one likes to carry out what one had intended to do! I undertook to drive us there and back. (*Pause*) Two climbs in a day have made me feel my age.

STELLA (*stroking the lyre-bird's tail*) If we hadn't got out and walked, we wouldn't have found the lyre-bird's tail. (*Pause*) I wonder what killed it.

(SWORD *is too preoccupied to hear.*)

SWORD You don't think *I* was showing off, do you? . . . suggesting we plunge down into that gully?

STELLA Oh, no. It seemed the natural thing to want.

SWORD Well, it wasn't. It was most unnatural. But old men feel the need to prove themselves.

STELLA You did! And if you hadn't exhausted yourself, you wouldn't have let Denis drive home.

SWORD It gave *us* the chance to make a little conversation.

STELLA (*mystified*) We talked . . . yes. I never really believe people make conversation . . . except in books.

SWORD They like to think they do in life. Anyway, I enjoyed talking . . . with you. (*Drily, carefully*) Sister Summerhayes . . . to me this has been one of the happiest days.

STELLA (*pushing back her hair, radiant*) It was lovely. I'll write and tell my father.

SWORD You're very fond of your father.

STELLA He's what I've got.

SWORD He's very pervasive. But I haven't visualized him yet.

STELLA Professor Sword, I hope I'm not taking a liberty . . . but you remind me a little of my dad. . . .

SWORD (*could be disappointed*) Oh?

STELLA Of course he's a simple man. You'd find him boring. He's quieter. Dad doesn't *talk*, let alone make conversation. But we don't need to. We understand each other.

SWORD That is a luxury I've never enjoyed.

STELLA (*turning on him*) Oh, I shouldn't, I suppose . . . I'm not clever . . . and you're a university professor. . . .

SWORD (*laughing it off*) You can be devastating in your judgments.

STELLA No! Let me explain, please, if I can . . . in my own way. I think you try too hard. . .

SWORD (*drawing in his chin*) How?

STELLA . . . to know more than you know already. Knowing is not understanding. (*Pause*) Now, my father . . . doesn't know all that much . . . but understands. That's why I love him.

SWORD (*put out*) What does your father understand?

STELLA This may sound silly. . . . (*Pause*) Well. . . . Moments of silence. (*Pause*) Bread. (*Laughing*)

SWORD (*raising his eyebrows*) Bread?

STELLA I knew you'd boggle at that one! But it's true.

SWORD Your father is lucky.

STELLA But to know *as well as* understand . . . you could be luckier.

SWORD Your father is lucky to have a daughter.

STELLA You have one.

SWORD She gave us up.

STELLA So Mrs Sword told me.

SWORD (*thoughtfully, intent on* STELLA) The sun has brought out the best in you, Sister Summerhayes. You'll match him if you aren't careful. . . . You're glowing!

STELLA I do burn easily.

SWORD (*with thoughtful enthusiasm*) How it suits you!

(STELLA *lowers her eyes. Embarrassed.*)

STELLA I must go and see how my patient . . . (*she turns and starts to mount the stairs*) . . . show her my precious lyre-bird's tail.(*She runs up the rest of the way*)

SWORD (*watching her, speaking not quite with professional gallantry, engrossed rather in his own thoughts*) If the fox could have known his sacrifice would be accepted. . . .

(SWORD *goes rather wearily into his study.*)

(*Upstairs* STELLA *knocking on* MIRIAM'S *door.*)

STELLA Mrs Sword?

(*She listens.* MIRIAM *does not move, or reply.*)

SWORD (*making an even worse mess of the papers on the table in his study*) The same search for God and self. . . .

STELLA (*softly*) Mrs Sword. . . .

(*She goes into* MIRIAM'S *room. Takes it that the latter is sleeping. Goes quietly and sticks the lyre-bird's tail in an empty vase on the dressing-table.*)

(*At same time* SWORD *goes abruptly, unlocks a bottom drawer in his desk, takes out a bundle of papers. Sits down with them at the table, like a man about to indulge a private vice.*)

(STELLA *approaches* MIRIAM'S *bed to see whether she can make her more comfortable.*)

(*Suddenly realizing*) Mrs Sword!

(*Catches sight of bottle and glass on bedside table.* MIRIAM *stirs, awakes.*)

You're *sick*!

(MIRIAM *raises herself slightly on one elbow.*)

MIRIAM Not sick . . . just . . . sick. . . . (*She falls back on the bed*)

(*In the study* SWORD *continues to glance through the bundle of papers, triumphantly revolted.*)

SWORD She'd give that moss-agate to lay her hands on evidence like this. . . .

STELLA (*feeling and chafing* MIRIAM'S *hands and wrists*) But how did you . . . ?

MIRIAM My moss-agate ring.

STELLA (*desolate*) Your moss-*agate*! That's what you loved most.

MIRIAM Not enough . . . it seems.

STELLA (*very concerned, helping her into a more comfortable position*) If you have the will to *un*-do, then we must give you the will to *do*.

(STELLA *throws a rug over* MIRIAM, *wraps it round her.*)

MIRIAM (*moving her head from side to side*) Sometimes, in its absence, the will works. . . . Sometimes . . . when you are weakest . . . great strength will come without the asking. I have had such splendid moments, Stella, in my weakness. I could see *almost* . . . to the end of the tunnel.

(SWORD, *in the room below, flipping over the pages, more and more engrossed.*)

STELLA (*decided, to* MIRIAM) I'm going to give you something to help.

MIRIAM (*recoiling*) You're not going to dope me!

STELLA Not dope . . . calm. (*She goes towards the door*)

MIRIAM Some of the others used to dope me . . . so's they could take their corsets off, and try themselves out on Hugo. (*Laughing*) What a hope!

STELLA I'm not going to dope you.

(STELLA *leaves* MIRIAM'S *room, goes along landing to her own, where she unlocks a drawer, takes out a bottle of tablets.*)

(*As soon as she is left alone* MIRIAM *at once props herself up. Pours herself a shaky drink. Downs it rather sloppily.*)

(*Simultaneously* DENIS CRAIG ENTERS *house through front door. He is sunburnt from the afternoon drive. Moves slowly, contentedly. Looks around for a moment, then goes into* SWORD'S *study.*)

MIRIAM My darling little Stella, it's you I love almost the most. . . . (*On catching sight of* DENIS, SWORD'S *first impulse is to hide what he is reading, but this is obviously no longer possible.*)

SWORD Ah . . . there you are . . . Denis!

DENIS (*lazy for words*) Wondered what you'd done with yourself. Place's so quiet.

SWORD (*drily, returning to his occupation*) I'm having a read . . . as they say.

DENIS (*kindly*) Ruin your eyes if you're not careful. It's turned so bloody dark since the sun went in. (*Switches on light.*)

SWORD (*absent*) It's late. The mists are coming. . . .

(DENIS *flops down in armchair, legs apart.*)

(STELLA *has re-locked her drawer.* RE-ENTERS MIRIAM'S *room.* MIRIAM *has replaced her glass on hearing* STELLA *come.* STELLA *switches on light. Pours water from jug on small medicine table.*)

(*Making an effort, to* DENIS) Tired? (*He is not really interested, continues reading.*)

DENIS Bit done up. I'll have a shower. Take the ache out of my calves. (*Continues to sit.*)

(STELLA *brings the tablets and water to* MIRIAM.)

STELLA There. You don't really need them, though. You're already so much calmer. (*Coaxing a child*) Aren't you?

MIRIAM (*childlike*) Yes. (*Swallows pills, sips water almost contented*) Some of those other nurses used to give me injections. Some of them play darts on you . . . some of them grind it in as though they hope they'll never have to do it again.

(STELLA *receives back glass of water from* MIRIAM, *is about to return it to the table.*)

(*Indicating bottle at bedside*) Aren't you going to remove the cause?

STELLA Is it?

(MIRIAM *has a momentary fit of whimpering.* STELLA *disposes of glass of water.*)

(*Drawing up a chair*) No. I'm going to stay with you now . . . make amends. . . .

MIRIAM Don't become involved . . . darling Stella . . . with the patient. It could be too much for you. Remember the friend . . . who died of her involvement.

STELLA Fancy remembering that! (*Pause*) Ann, I think, didn't have faith.

(*She sits smoothing back* MIRIAM'S *hair.*)

MIRIAM Faith in what?

STELLA In life, I suppose.

MIRIAM I wonder what . . . you know. . . .

(STELLA *continues sitting, smoothing* MIRIAM'S *hair, holding her hand.*)

DENIS (*looking at* SWORD) Didn't know you approved of the literary effusions of others.

SWORD (*laughing*) Of others!

(*He gets up. He is a little feverish, jerky in his movements, as if about to be overwhelmed by the dangerous desire to confide. Suddenly thrusts the manuscript on Denis who browses during the following.*)

(*Walking up and down, filling and lighting a pipe, excitedly*) There are moments when the necessity is there . . . to express some . . . thing . . . when you are bursting with it . . . the inexpressible all . . . or nothing. (*Suddenly pulling himself together, finishing more rationally, a little ashamed*) Well, that's how it is!

(DENIS *continues to look through the manuscript.* SWORD *goes and sits down at desk, busy with something unnecessary, shoulders slightly hunched, waiting for a verdict.*)

MIRIAM (*stirring, drowsily, to* STELLA) Tell me something, Stella.

STELLA What sort of thing?

MIRIAM (*very drowsy*) About yourself . . . when you were Mary's age. . . .

STELLA (*humouring her*) Well . . . we'll have to think. (*Pause*) I used to dress up sometimes. . . .

MIRIAM Dress up?

STELLA Yes. Dress up in Mother's clothes. They were there still. I'd act around a bit. I could be quite comical at acting. There was one hat, with a feather in it. . . .

MIRIAM (*anxiously*) What colour?

STELLA Green, I think. Yes. An emerald feather!

MIRIAM Lovely. (*Pause*) Even Stella has worn disguises. . . .

STELLA I used to make my dad laugh . . . dancing . . . and acting. Then suddenly he said it mustn't happen any more. We packed up all the clothes, and he took them to the Salvation Army.

MIRIAM How *miserable* of him!

STELLA (*gravely*) They were my mother's clothes.

MIRIAM Oh, yes . . . sad. . . .

DENIS (*looking up from the manuscript*) You were young, too, Professor Sword!

SWORD (*agitated*) Young! You could follow the whole muddy stream *if* you were so disposed, right down to its last trickle . . . (*pausing, then savagely*) . . . the sludge of an uncreative . . . lascivious . . . *literate* mind. . . .

(DENIS *hands back the manuscript.*)

Disgusted?

DENIS No.

SWORD Because I am . . . when I'm not fascinated.

DENIS Not disgusted. It's just that, when it comes to the point, I'm not a good buyer for other people's secrets.

SWORD (*touching him lightly on shoulder*) Sentimental old Denis! I thought it would have been in your line.

DENIS It was.

SWORD Then what has converted you so suddenly?

(DENIS *doesn't answer at once.*)

323

DENIS The need to love, perhaps ... something true and permanent.

SWORD (*sitting down abruptly, horrified*) Oh, I loved my wife. I loved her. (*Pause*) So much so, I had to resist.

DENIS Why?

SWORD Love, as I understand it, is too difficult for men.

DENIS So you fetch out the tongs of self-mortification, and twist it into shapes it was never meant to take.

SWORD If one is guided ... then one must obey.

DENIS I was never yet illuminated!

(SWORD *gets up, goes out of the study in agitation, into the living-room.*)

SWORD You're right, Denis. I shouldn't have started all this. It never pays to undress in public. The most sympathetic audience is shocked by an old man's nakedness.

DENIS (*following, sincerely*) I hope not. . . . Talk, if it's going to do you any good.

(SWORD *has come down,* C.)

SWORD (*contemptuously*) Ever since we came to live in this house, we've been filling it with talk! (*Removed temporarily from his surroundings*) The mists have more to show for their activities. . . . Down in the gully the sassafras grows green, the ferns never want for moisture, the rotting leaves create ... silence.

(*Mist is visible in the waning light outside. Although there is artificial light in the study and* MIRIAM'S *bed-room, a natural dusk prevails in the living-room.*)

(SWORD *appears to have trodden on something near the dining table. He stoops and picks it up.*)

(*Upstairs* MIRIAM *stirs.*)

STELLA (*tenderly, leaning forward on her chair*) Are you feeling more rested?

MIRIAM (*thankfully, softly*) I was never more at peace. . . .

(SWORD *examines the foil* MIRIAM *has torn from the whisky bottle earlier on.*)

SWORD (*his voice trembling*) Turn the light on, will you, Denis. It's dark all of a sudden.

(DENIS *switches on light in living-room.* SWORD *confirms his suspicions. Gesture of anger and frustration. Looks around him help-*

*lessly. Catches sight of the empty glass left on the table. Takes hold
of it. Looks into it, smells it.*)

(*Accusingly, to* DENIS) Have you been *drinking?*

DENIS (*drily*) Not a drop since I arrived.

SWORD Nobody drinks who comes to this house . . . because there
isn't a drop to drink . . . or shouldn't be. (*Pause*) But somebody
. . . *somebody* has been drinking.

(ENTER MRS SIBLEY, R., *with cloth. She walks in a slow shuffle.
Appears to be defending herself with one shoulder, about to disown a
situation.*)

(*Holding out the glass, shouting*) Mrs Sibley?

MRS SIBLEY (*querulous*) Don't use your voice on me, Professor
Sword. I'm going tomorrow. So it doesn't apply.

(SWORD *is stung. Throws the glass on the floor, smashing it. Starts
a search, moving sculpture, ornaments on the mantelpiece. Suddenly
stoops, catching sight of the half-empty whisky bottle* MIRIAM *has
hidden behind the logs. Snatches it out, pours contents on logs, throws
the bottle into a corner of the room.*)

(MRS SIBLEY *has been ignoring, methodically laying and smoothing
the cloth.* DENIS *standing helplessly by.*)

DENIS (*as the bottle hurtles*) Here, hold *hard!* (*He tries to laugh it
off*) This won't help either of you!

(SWORD *pays no attention. Goes into study. Throws a couple of
cushions on the floor. Returns to living-room. Sweeps cushions off the
upholstered seat which forms an angle with the glass doors. Falls
abruptly on all fours to look beneath the frill. Gets up, goes to sideboard. Pushes aside a flower arrangement in a tall vase, so that it
topples over sideways.*)

(EXIT MRS SIBLEY, *dignified, still ignoring.*)

(SWORD *neglects to look in the sideboard as* MIRIAM *had expected.
All his movements are determined, automatic, dreadful. His breathing can be heard.*)

SWORD (*panting*) Somewhere. . . . She never did anything by half-
measures. . . .

(*Turns. Suddenly races up the stairs.*)

(*Shouting*) Sister Summerhayes!

(STELLA *gets up, startled. Comes out on to the landing.*)

Your patient's been on the loose!

STELLA (*calmly*) So I found. But she's sleeping now.

SWORD She's never slept. I doubt even in her own sleep. Certainly not in mine. (*Goes into* MIRIAM'S *room.*)

STELLA (*following him*) Don't blame *her*, Professor Sword. I'm the one to blame.

(MIRIAM *rises on an elbow. She and* SWORD *look at each other, she with apathy, he with disgust.* SWORD *catches sight of bottle and glass at bedside.*)

SWORD (*snatching them, to* STELLA) Looks as though you even encourage it!

(*Goes and throws bottle and glass out of window. Sounds of splintering glass.*)

STELLA I must be allowed to follow my own methods. (*Commanding*) Will you leave us now?

MIRIAM (*getting into sitting position on the edge of the bed*) That is something he can never do. He'll still be watching from other rooms.

(DENIS *has run up the stairs at the sound of breaking glass.*)

DENIS (*at door of* MIRIAM'S *room*) Stella . . . will you call me . . . if you need me?

STELLA (*taking* SWORD *firmly by the arm*) I need nobody . . . nothing . . . except my patient's confidence.

SWORD (*more relaxed, thoughtful, as he is forced towards the door*) How strong you are . . . for one so small. . . .

(*He comes out on the landing, and begins to descend stairs, followed by* DENIS.)

MIRIAM (*gratefully*) You will protect me, Stella. But I'm not in need of it. Not the part of me that matters.

(*She makes her way unsteadily to landing, followed by* STELLA, *who trys to draw her back.*)

(*Again over-excited*) . . . It has always made him so ashamed . . . that he can't reach the part which matters. . . .

(SWORD *has arrived at foot of stairs, followed by* DENIS.)

The things he can't accomplish! (*Shouting after him*) Better get on with your search, Hugo! There's still so much to find.

SWORD Search! Why haven't I let it kill you . . . long before this?

MIRIAM (*shouting from landing*) Perhaps you never thought about that before! But why not? Don't you realize it has given me a glorious, terrible life *you* will never know?

(SWORD *moves slowly, automatically, to sideboard. Twitches open the cupboard. Realizes what he has found.*)

There! You see? So simple! (*Laughing, then raising her voice, taunting*) Smash it, Hugo! Smash! Smash! Try to smash what is left of me! The verdict will only be *manslaughter*!

SWORD (*turning on her*) Even if it were murder....

(DENIS *has gone and leant against the upright,* R. *looking out through the glass doors.*)

DENIS It's almost dark on Bald Mountain. Tonight the rocks will cut the moonlight with razors....

(ENTER MRS SIBLEY, R. *Frightened, tentative.*)

STELLA (*from landing*) Professor Sword, you must control yourself... or I'll have to ring for the police!

MIRIAM He'd wriggle out! (*Looking down at him*) You ... *intellectual*!

(MIRIAM *spits at* SWORD. STELLA *leads her back into her room.*)

MRS SIBLEY (*trying* DENIS'S *arm*) Mr Craig, you're the only one I can expect anything of. Help me will you ... in the morning ... to send the telegram to my daughter?

DENIS (*turning, distracted*) Yes? The ... what?

MRS SIBLEY (*piteously*) The telegram!

(SWORD *turns away from the stairs. He is holding himself rigidly, his face pale and drawn.*)

SWORD We'll never get through ... never ... never ... however long we live ... however many messages we send....

ACT THREE

SCENE ONE · SAME AS ACT II

Later that night. The upper part of the house is in darkness. Down below PROFESSOR SWORD, STELLA SUMMERHAYES *and* DENIS CRAIG *are seated at the dinner-table, the two men at either end,* STELLA *in the middle, facing audience. The scene is unchanged, except that any signs of damage have been cleared away, and the fire is burning in the hearth,* R. *It is soon obvious that the meal has been more a ritual than a pleasure. Almost at once* STELLA *puts her knife and fork together beside a practically untouched helping. During the opening dialogue, which should be delivered in a dry, forced manner, the men eat by desultory mouthfuls. Finally put down knives and forks without finishing what is left on their plates.*

DENIS (*breaking a silence, to* SWORD) What about James?

SWORD Who? Oh! (*Laughing faintly*) Henry! (*Sighing*) Tried very hard, didn't he?

DENIS Did accomplish a certain amount.

SWORD Oh, yes. He did, I suppose . . . (*another sigh*) . . . in the end. (*Pause.*)

DENIS When I was twenty or so, I would have given years of my life to write a Henry James.

SWORD Might have become a fashionable success. (*Pause.*)

DENIS I wrote my MA thesis on him instead.

SWORD I was aware of it. (*Pause.*)

DENIS (*trying again*) *Trollope,* then?

SWORD (*vague*) *What* about Trollope?

DENIS (*irritated*) What *about* him?

SWORD (*clearing his throat*) I find him altogether . . . intolerably . . . flat.

(DENIS *sits back ruffling up his hair.*)

(*Sighing*) Of course there are one or two of the Barchester novels. (*Grudgingly*) Yes . . . one . . . or *two*.

DENIS (*in quiet desperation*) Is this the night the books got burnt? Or are we just being bloody Australian?

SWORD (*nettled*) Critical judgment has to be kept alive, you know. It dies when set in rigid moulds.

DENIS Or do we suspect enthusiasm . . . until *rigor mortis* sets in?

SWORD Oh, I'm the last to discourage *enthusiasm* . . . *unless* it declines into a 'crush'.

(*Pours himself a glass of water.*)

(*Remembering*) Water, anybody?

DENIS (*gloomy*) Yes . . . water!

(STELLA *rouses herself to pass the jug.*)

SWORD Do you agree, Sister Summerhayes? Or are we boring you?

STELLA I know my limitations.

SWORD Do you read perhaps . . . occasionally?

STELLA (*shaking her head*) Not very often.

DENIS She's busy making the wheels go round.

STELLA When I have a moment, I like to sit and look. I find it very satisfying.

SWORD (*thoughtfully*) Ye-ehs. (*Pause*) It can be rewarding. (*Pause*) On the other hand, it can be most distasteful.

STELLA There's always two sides to the coin.

(ENTER MRS SIBLEY, R., *with empty tray. Peers at the plates.*)

MRS SIBLEY Tt tt! None of yez eatin'? There are people who'd tell you my veal loaf's my best turn.

SWORD I thought *I*'d done more than justice to it, Mrs Sibley.

MRS SIBLEY (*mumbling and grumbling as she clears away*) None of yez eatin'. . . .

SWORD (*to* STELLA) And when you sit and stare . . . or, as you say, *look* . . . are you led to interesting conclusions by what you see?

STELLA Not exactly. It's the things themselves . . . (*out of her depth, but trying*) Oh . . . table . . . chair, for instance. Or that jug. Even the ugly things have a kind of truth, if you look at them long enough.

329

MRS SIBLEY (*turning at door,* R., *with her laden tray*) There's apple pie.

(SWORD, STELLA *and* DENIS *shake their heads.*)

(*Rather haughty*) Well, I won't waste me apple pie if nobody's eatin'. (EXIT R.)

SWORD (*thoughtfully*) Interesting. Provided you don't accept these ugly objects. Provided you can transform . . . or find some reason in their ugliness. (*Unhappy*) Though it's almost always impossible.

STELLA No. You can't transform the ugly truth.

(*Silence.*)

SWORD (*his voice a bit unnatural*) Returning to Henry James. . . .

(DENIS *shifts position in his chair, sits sideways, as if to avoid the subject mentioned.*)

. . . Miriam had quite a crush on him in the early years of our marriage. (*Pause*) I think she felt it was a kind of . . . *obeisance* to the intellect.

DENIS (*simply*) Perhaps she understood him.

SWORD (*unpleasantly taken aback*) She may have! (*Pause*) In any case, she went so far as to write a novelette.

DENIS Oh! What became of the . . . novelette?

SWORD I believe she thought better of it. I believe it was destroyed.

DENIS The more innocent are so often wiser.

SWORD I think . . . yes . . . it was the right move. It was all sentiments and style . . . though it had its moments . . . its stilted moments.

(STELLA *gets up. Goes to the sideboard,* L., *and takes up a torch which is standing on it.*)

DENIS (*turning to her*) Had enough?

STELLA (*smiling, ignoring the tone of his voice*) I have a letter to write. (*Going towards stairs rather wearily*) Tired, too. It's later than usual. I'll be ready to turn in.

SWORD Does this mean we ought to say goodnight?

(*He gets up, suddenly very punctilious.*)

STELLA (*pausing, facing them*) I expect so. There's still my patient. But I shan't be long after that. Goodnight, Professor Sword.

SWORD Goodnight, Sister Summerhayes . . . (*hesitating painfully*) . . . and thank you.

330

(*She does not answer, but mounts the stairs.* DENIS *watches her without speaking.*)

(*To* DENIS) A sober girl. (*Pause*) At her age Miriam was twirling half the night. She seemed to attract the more rackety type of physicist . . . and fourth year students who like to dance.

DENIS Sounds fine.

SWORD Oh, the dancing! I wonder they stood up to it.

(SWORD *goes into his study, switches on the light. He is followed by* DENIS.)

(STELLA *has turned on the light on the landing. Goes softly to* MIRIAM'S *room. Opens the invisible door. Shines her torch carefully into the darkness.* MIRIAM *is lying rigid in her bed. She opens her eyes.*)

STELLA (*approaching, softly*) Not asleep.

MIRIAM (*motionless*) No. Oh, I dozed . . . I think! For a moment I was in the thick of things. . . .

(*Pause.*)

STELLA I can give you another little dose, if you like . . . (*quickly*) . . . just to settle, not to dope.

MIRIAM (*petulantly*) No.

STELLA (*squeezing her wrist*) That's good, you know! That's good! (*She switches on the bedside lamp.*)

MIRIAM How?

STELLA It means that, between us, we'll discover the will. . . .

MIRIAM Oh, the will . . . I haven't the strength. . . .

STELLA I shall be the strength.

(*She starts doing things to the pillows, raising her patient on them slightly, straightening the sheets.*)

MIRIAM Did they empty the sideboard?

STELLA They emptied it.

(MIRIAM *draws a deep breath, closes her eyes again.*)

(SWORD *has taken his pipe and tobacco pouch from the study mantelpiece.*)

SWORD (*indicating fireplace in study corner,* R. BACK) Put a match to the fire, Denis. This little one. We'll need it tonight.

(DENIS *stoops and lights fire.*)

MIRIAM I wouldn't mind dying, Stella, if you were here to tuck me up in my last sheet.

STELLA Well, I shan't! See? Don't you know about the creaking gate?

MIRIAM What about it?

STELLA It lasts longest.

MIRIAM (*chuckling*) I like that! The creaking gate . . . !

(STELLA *continues to potter, tidying things on tables and dressing-table.*)

SWORD (*filling his pipe, reminiscing*) Only a few years ago . . . she was showing quite an improvement . . . we went to a ball . . . oh, some dreadful vice-regal thing. . . .

(DENIS *has sat down with a book, and started to look at it.*)

She bought a dress . . .

DENIS (*glancing through book*) Old bore in the end!

SWORD . . . simple enough in itself . . . but somehow extravagant for her. I must say I was tempted to refer to it as her *fancy* dress . . . and did.

DENIS (*nibbling a nail, looking through book*) I bet you did! Bloody old bore!

(STELLA *suddenly notices a white dress lying across the easy chair in* MIRIAM'S *room.*)

STELLA (*surprised*) What's this, Mrs Sword?

MIRIAM A dress.

STELLA Yes. I know . . . a *dress*. But what dress?

(*She holds it up. Even in its slack state, it must suggest a poetry of its own.*)

MIRIAM One I was fond of. I brought it out . . . I was looking at it just before I turned out the light.

SWORD (*restlessly*) Of course I didn't take my eyes off her all the evening, so we got through. She didn't have a chance to . . . bend her elbow.

DENIS (*turning pages of book*) *Persistent* old bore. Perhaps that's why one continues to put up . . .

STELLA (*admiring*) It's a lovely dress.

MIRIAM (*stirring*) Oh, and a success! Let me tell you! (*With an odd astringence*) Men used to look at me, Stella . . . right to the end . . . and I wasn't always . . . *drunk*.

STELLA I've often found men are at their worst when I'm stone cold sober.

MIRIAM (*delighted*) What a trick you are at times!

STELLA Shall I put it away?

MIRIAM (*resentful*) No. You can leave it. Perhaps I'll turn on the light in the night. It'll be something to look at.

(STELLA *lays the dress where it was.*)

SWORD I followed her *everywhere!* Into the supper room . . . amongst the cinerarias and palms. (*Drily*) They began to think I was jealous of her . . .

DENIS (*looking at* SWORD, *almost savagely*) Aren't you?

(SWORD *half-averts his face with a queer nervous jerk.*)

SWORD . . . whereas it's she who's always been jealous of me.

STELLA Is there anything more I can do for you, Mrs Sword?

MIRIAM Pray for me, Stella.

STELLA (*embarrassed*) I was never taught to pray. But I'll be here, close by, as long as you need me. I'll will you to strength and happiness.

MIRIAM (*disconsolate*) This *will* thing of yours . . . I never had much faith in that.

STELLA You will!

(*It is time for 'lights out' and* MIRIAM'S *masochistic tendency takes over.*)

MIRIAM (*feverishly*) You're distressingly *bright*, my dear, at times.

STELLA You won't hurt me, you know, only yourself.

MIRIAM (*ignoring, looking at* STELLA *piercingly*) Is your . . . little . . . too pretty . . . face, one of those I must learn to hate?

STELLA You'll have to decide whether that's what you want to think. (*Pause*) Goodnight, Mrs Sword. (*She goes to switch out the light*)

MIRIAM (*scarcely audible, wounded by her own nature*) Stella!

(STELLA *switches out the light. Goes out to landing by light from her torch, and into her own room, where she turns on light, deals her hair one or two brisk strokes with the brush, and takes up a pad and Biro from the dressing-table. She settles down at table, C.*)

DENIS (*rising, to* SWORD) I'll be hitting it, I think.

(SWORD *grunts. He has taken the wastepaper basket, and is seated at table* C., *sorting and destroying papers.*)

(*Observing*) What are you up to?

SWORD Destroying a lot of rubbish.

DENIS I thought we'd decided that was the author's prerogative.

SWORD A man needn't stick to his principles, need he? Wouldn't be human if he did.

DENIS That's what I've been trying to preach.

(SWORD *grunts.*)

DENIS Well.... (*Continuing with the formalities*) Goodnight, sir.

SWORD (*without looking up, absorbed, also perhaps a bit sulky*) Goodnight.

(DENIS *goes into living-room. Switches off the light. Through the glass doors a lopsided moon has risen. It can be seen through strands of cloud or mist.*)

STELLA (*writing, quickly, spontaneously*) . . . am missing you so much in this place . . . it is all right . . . no, it is heaven . . . a forest of dark sassafras and scrub, rising to bare rocks and sunlight. . . . All day I've been driving at a hundred over the mountains. . . . I'm tingling now . . . but tomorrow shall look a sad *prawn*. . . . Well, Dad, the case is an interesting, a pathetic one. Mrs Sword....

(*As* DENIS *walks slowly towards the door,* BACK C., ENTER MRS SIBLEY, R. *She moves carefully. Passes the study door, from which the light falls on her. She glances in, anxiously, and moves on with greater care.*)

DENIS (*to himself, looking out through the glass doors*) The moon never fails to do her stuff. She's most poignant when she's most lopsided....

MRS SIBLEY (*in a loud whisper*) I'm sorry I didn't draw the curtains. I was too upset . . . and occupied.

DENIS You did me a service, Mrs Sibley. Otherwise I might have missed the moon.

(MRS SIBLEY *glances that way, surprised.*)

MRS SIBLEY Oh, the moon. . . . It comes and goes, doesn't it? (*Pause*) Mr Craig, you won't forget the promise you made?

DENIS What promise, Mrs Sibley?

MRS SIBLEY The telegram!

DENIS Telegram?

MRS SIBLEY The telegram to my daughter . . . that I spoke of . . . that you was going to help me send in the morning.

DENIS (*laying a hand on her arm*) Oh yes, the telegram! We'll see about it tomorrow.

MRS SIBLEY Because when people cheek me on the phone . . . it gets me flustered. (*Her breath tears, and she almost can't go on*) And I've got to get out of here. Down there it isn't all this mist. The sun shines at Kurrajong. Elsie's been lucky. She's struck it good. Of course there's still the mortgage to pay off. Of course there's the wax on the oranges . . . the soot. . . . But Bob's good. He knows what to do. . . .

DENIS (*weary*) Yes, yes, Mrs Sibley. In the morning.

MRS SIBLEY (*tearful*) I love those blessed oranges. I love to watch the children . . . playing in and out the trees. That's what I know . . . what I understand.

DENIS (*moving towards stairs*) Yes, yes, there's nothing like your own.

MRS SIBLEY Perhaps when they take me down there, they'll let me stay. I'll bake them a dinner once in a while . . . and do little things for the kiddies. They're bold at times . . . but I think . . . I think they like their nan. And they're what I know . . . what I need.

DENIS Yes, yes, continuity is reassuring.

MRS SIBLEY Eh?

DENIS I mean . . . of all of us . . . you stand the best chance.

MRS SIBLEY (*puzzled*) Oh? (*Sighing, hopefully*) You won't forget, then?

(*She shuffles* OFF, R., *slightly reassured.*)

(DENIS *mounts the stairs.*)

STELLA (*writing*) As for Professor Sword . . . (*suddenly pauses, looks up, sits staring straight ahead, murmuring*) Professor Sword. . .

(*On reaching top of stairs,* DENIS *turns along landing towards door at end,* R., *beyond which his room probably lies.*)

(*In a renewed burst of writing*) . . . he is passionate, arrogant, violent at times, but I canot dismiss him altogether . . . because I, pity him . . . (*pause*) . . . and because . . . I suppose . . . he reminds me . . . a little . . . of you. . . . (*Laughing, writing*) Oh no, not really!

(*Before reaching end of passage* DENIS *is compelled to turn back. He approaches* STELLA'S *room. Knocks.* STELLA *comes to the door.*)

DENIS (*quietly, apologetic*) I saw your light.

STELLA (*surprised, a little put out by interruption*) Yes?

DENIS I've been thinking about you.

    (STELLA *stiffens almost imperceptibly, does not answer.* DENIS *moves into the room, takes her in his arms.*)

    (*With genuine tenderness, laying his cheek against hers*) Oh, Stella! You are the great good, the true simplicity most of us aspire to!

STELLA (*gently extricating herself*) Denis, it's late.... (*Quickly*) Oh, you've begun to show me I can trust you.... (*Touching his cheek*) I *know* I can! (*Leaning against him, frowning*) It's myself. I mightn't be able to return ... in every way....

DENIS You? Always so confident in giving?

STELLA That's different. When it comes to oneself ... that's the last stronghold of doubt. (*She moves away.*)

DENIS I'm learning to wait, Stella, now that it's worth while.

STELLA Yes. You must give me time ... to understand ... what I have to do.

DENIS Goodnight.

STELLA (*she kisses him gently*) Goodnight.

    (DENIS *goes along the passage, and* EXIT R.)

SWORD (*still examining papers at study table, now destroying in more desultory fashion*) That girl.... An uneducated girl ... can show one things ... one hadn't seen....

    (STELLA *has seated herself again and taken up her pen.*)

STELLA (*absorbed, writing*) ... his mouth is cruel. Yours is kind, kind, even when it warns, or judges. That, I think, is why I love my father ... and yet this Professor Sword is a man I would also like to ... (*pause*) ... respect....

SWORD (*staring at paper before him*) She has a kind of purity that will bear looking at ... again.

STELLA (*writing*) Goodnight now. We are neither of us much on paper, we know. (*Pause*) How are you making out for laundry? Do you air your pyjamas before you put them on fresh on Sunday?

    (STELLA *dashes off end of letter.*)

SWORD (*staring ahead of him*) If one could give expression to the moments that have moved one most. ... That girl stroking the

lyre-bird's feathers. . . . (*Suddenly tearing up the paper, savagely*)
Any woman, after all, is one of the messier varieties of fruit. . . .
(*During* SWORD'S *speech* STELLA *seals and addresses letter. Gets
up, yawns. Starts to undress.*)
(LIGHTS ARE LOWERED *for a few moments to denote passage of
time.*)

When the action continues MIRIAM'S *room is in full light. She is
wearing the white dress, and is sitting upright, tense and nervous, in
the easy chair. Her hands are knotted. She has attempted to do something about her hair, and looks beautiful in a strange, poetic way, like
someone returned momentarily from the dead.*
STELLA'S *room in darkness.*
The light is still on in SWORD'S *study. He has unknotted his tie and
unbuttoned his collar. The table,* C., *is now tidied. A few papers
arranged in neat piles. As part of the tidying process* SWORD *is seen
standing a block of four or five books in a bookcase. Waste paper
basket beside table is full. Surplus of crumpled paper on floor.*

SWORD Futile . . . this tidying business. . . . If you could tidy an
untidy mind . . . something might be accomplished. . . .
(*He rakes fire together. Switches off light. Comes out into living-
room, which is lit only by moonlight through glass doors.*)
. . . On the other hand, it might be intolerable too . . . like living
in a hospital.
(*He starts to mount the stairs.*)
(MIRIAM *gets up, agitated, touching her cold arms, wringing her
hands.*)
MIRIAM (*caged by her room*) O Lord, if I only had it now! (*Parting
the curtains*) The moon never looked more lopsided. Oh, Lord, I
never felt emptier. . . .
(*She lets curtains fall back into place, puts the back of her hand
against her mouth in passing desperation.*)
(SWORD *reaches landing. Switches light on. As he is about to turn
into his own room, he apparently notices light under* MIRIAM'S
[*invisible*] *door. Slowly opens door.*)
SWORD (*tentatively*) Miriam?

(*She is standing* C., *her dress streaming with a white light.*)

(*Entering, angrily*) Good God, what's come over you?

MIRIAM What does *come over* us half the time? Regret . . . I suppose . . . or hope. Or both together.

(*She is terribly nervous, uncertain now that she has done right.*)

SWORD Isn't it a little ridiculous to dress up in the middle of the night?

MIRIAM Night or day . . . aren't they different faces of the same?

SWORD But that dress . . . I was thinking about it earlier. . . .

MIRIAM (*defiantly*) It was my last throw.

(SWORD *goes to her. Puts his arms around her, kisses her, but coldly.*)

SWORD We should have *learnt* to love each other.

MIRIAM (*bitterly*) Perhaps we weren't made for it.

SWORD Even scorpions love each other after their fashion.

MIRIAM (*moving her arms*) Will you let me go, Hugo? I'd like to . . . keep my . . . dress.

(SWORD *releases her, moves away.*)

SWORD And that book you wrote . . . that novel. . . . I was remembering that too, tonight. I never gave you an opinion. (*Slowly, unwillingly*) I think it may have had . . . some slight . . . literary merit.

MIRIAM I destroyed it.

SWORD Few of us haven't destroyed our works . . . rashly or wisely.

MIRIAM I destroyed it. (*Turning on him, fiercely*) Hugo, it may have been the first murder you committed!

SWORD (*wincing, more for her absence of taste*) Oh, come!

(MIRIAM *throws herself on the bed.*)

MIRIAM Leave me, will you. . . .

(SWORD *goes to her, touches her now with genuine regret.*)

SWORD Miriam . . . I never say the things I mean to say! They seem to . . . turn on me. . . .

MIRIAM Oh, leave me! Leave me!

SWORD You'll ruin that dress . . . and you're fond of it.

MIRIAM (*against the sheets, racked*) My *dress*!

(SWORD *switches off the light. Goes into his own room. Light on.*

Takes a quick turn round the room, stiff, hunched, contemplating some move. Then sinks slowly to his knees beside the bed.)

SWORD (*muttering, wincing*) Stiff....

(*He raises his hands in the conventional Gothic attitude of prayer. Closes his eyes tightly. Pauses a moment, searching for the right words.*)

(*Praying*) O Lord, counsel us ... (*coughs drily*) ... advise us....

(*Frowning for something ill-chosen, then opening his eyes wide, staring at the wall ahead in desperation*) Prevent us, Lord, from drying up too soon. (*Moistens his lips. His posture slackens*) Allow us to enjoy the sun even when it is burning us up ... the smell of summer ... all smoothness, ripeness. Is it sin to love the purity of innocence ... to love honesty ... to bow to Goodness without knowing the touch of her hand? Until now, O Lord, I have lived off abstractions ... when love perhaps ... is not the sensual demon ... I thought it to be.

(*Suddenly tears his hands apart. Gets to his feet. Stands grotesquely undecided.*)

(*Head hanging as he wrestles*) May the spirit never accept the flesh?

(*As* SWORD *finishes his prayer* MIRIAM *switches on the light in her room. She is obviously in a highly emotional state. She throws open the door of her room almost at once, comes out on the landing, listens for a moment in great anguish. Descends the stairs, her white dress trailing. Lets herself* OUT *through front door which remains ajar.*)

(SWORD *begins to walk slowly, automatically, out of his room, along the landing. Comes to a standstill at* STELLA'S *door. Pauses. Knocks.* STELLA'S *room remains in darkness.* SWORD *knocks again.*)

STELLA (*waking, alarmed, calling from darkness*) Yes ...? What is it? I'm coming, Mrs Sword!

(*Bedside lamp is switched on.* STELLA *waking. Her hair is undone. Her face wears an expression of anxiety. Gets out of bed as quickly as possible. She is wearing a nightgown. Feels for her slippers from edge of the bed.*)

(SWORD *makes no move outside the door.* STELLA *throws open the invisible door.*)

Y*

(*Amazed*) Professor. . . . Is it Mrs Sword?

SWORD (*drily*) Not as far as I know.

(STELLA *is relieved, but upset.*)

STELLA (*gasping*) Oh, dear! I'm glad! . . . I was dreaming of your wife. . . . In some way she needed . . . I know! We were lost together in the bush . . . but just so far apart. . . . We couldn't *help* each other!

SWORD May I come in?

STELLA (*slowly*) If you feel you must.

SWORD I would like to talk to you, Sister Summerhayes. It's I who need your help. . . .

(SWORD *comes in.* STELLA *does not quite retreat inside her room, but is obviously nervous.*)

STELLA If I can be of any. . . .

SWORD (*looking at her, thoughtfully*) Sleep has made you look younger. . . .

STELLA (*holding her hand to her eyes*) You can't expect to wake a person up, and not catch them unawares!

(SWORD *looks at himself a moment in the dressing-table mirror.*)

SWORD Younger. . . .

STELLA (*worried*) I'm going to Mrs Sword, Professor . . . if you'll let me.

SWORD I've just left her. She's well enough.

STELLA Then don't you think you'd better get some sleep yourself?

SWORD Yes. . . . I should. . . . (*Looking at her*) Stella Summerhayes, Miriam has sometimes tried to suggest that I'm the one who is sick. I think . . . perhaps . . . she is right.

(STELLA *sits on the edge of the bed, unhappy at the turn affairs have taken.*)

STELLA Then what do you expect of me, Professor Sword? You must consult somebody who's qualified. . . .

SWORD But no real sickness is ever specific. . . . Can't you understand? . . . It's a corrosion of one's better self.

(STELLA *does not answer. She smoothes the folds of her nightgown.*)

Just to be with you, Stella, *heals* . . . gives . . . hope of recovery. *Stella!*

(*He slips down on his knees beside her, then sitting so that he faces* FORWARD, *head against her thigh.*)

So cool . . . so warm. . . . Your silences soothe more than other people's words of advice.

STELLA (*in some distress*) You're asking for something I'm not in a position to give . . . even if I wasn't ignorant.

SWORD Your heart knows. I've seen already.

(*Silence. For a moment she touches his hair, but her expression is remote, her face lost in thought.*)

Why did you touch my hair?

STELLA Because I'm sorry for you.

SWORD You see?

STELLA And would be sorry . . . for anybody. (*Change of tone*) Oh, do get up, Professor Sword! I don't like to see a man like you sitting on the floor!

SWORD (*laughing*) A man like me? If you could see me! You know how one appears to oneself?

STELLA (*agitated*) Yes! *My*self to *my*self! Yes! But you . . . please . . . a man of importance.

(SWORD *gets up. Sits beside her on the bed.*)

SWORD Don't humiliate me, Stella. A man *knows* what his own importance amounts to, even when he won't always admit it.

(*They sit looking at each other.*)

STELLA I was writing to my father tonight. . . .

SWORD (*frowning*) Your father?

STELLA I wanted to describe you. . . . (*Pauses*)

SWORD Well?

STELLA But couldn't. (*Pause*) You're too fine . . . too cruel . . . at the same time. (*Pause*) There are times when I hate to look at your mouth. It is so . . . so. . . .

(*She stares, giving way to her thoughts, and a natural fascination. For a moment their mouths come together.* STELLA *immediately jumps up, disturbed.*)

You see . . . there are moments when you remind me of him . . . but you're not like . . . because he is so honest . . . kind.

SWORD (*getting up from the bed*) I'm condemned then.

STELLA (*distraught*) Hugo! Hugo!

SWORD (*ironic*) Hugo!

STELLA That is how she called ... as we tried to find each other in the dream.

(*She has moved away across the room.* SWORD *has followed. Attempts to fondle. She avoids him.*)

Then he came....

SWORD Who?

STELLA He did. (*Warding off* SWORD'S *advances*) No!

SWORD You see?

STELLA (*protesting*) No! ... I don't see anything ... any longer.... You won't allow....

SWORD Was it your father? (*He takes her*)

STELLA No.... I don't know ... who it was. It was a dream.

(*She retreats round the room.*)

SWORD (*following*) Perhaps it wasn't your father ... or was.

STELLA (*retreating*) Go, now! You'll have disgusted yourself more than enough already.

SWORD Stella!

STELLA You'll remember.

SWORD Could remember together....

STELLA (*restraining herself*) Go! Go! Don't you see ... how you'll destroy ... everything you respect most....

(*They struggle together over the bed. Panting. Then* STELLA *seems to get the upper hand.*)

(*Between her teeth*) Do, please!

(SWORD *moves away. Again he is holding himself stiffly, correctness assuming control.*)

SWORD (*stiffly*) You won't admit it, then?

STELLA How?

SWORD You touched my hair. You called me by my name. In other circumstances ...

(*Silence.*)

... we could love each other ...

(*Silence.*)

... if your father ...

STELLA (*harshly*) My father? I wasn't thinking of my father....

SWORD ... but talk ... almost incessantly....

STELLA (*sobbing*) He's my father!

SWORD And I ... could be ... your father.

(STELLA *turns to face him.*)

STELLA Oh, don't ... don't! Because I respected ... loved if you like....

SWORD Because I was your father ... almost....

STELLA (*turning away, holding her hands to her temples, crying in horror*) My father! My dearest father!

SWORD I'm sorry, Stella.

STELLA (*from the depths*) Oh! Oh!

(*He goes to her. Kisses her very gently.*)

SWORD I would prefer not to be myself. (*Pause*) If we had been able to escape together, we might have spoken simply ... about the simple things ... or whatever mattered ... to us.

(*He goes out of the room.* STELLA *falls in the easy chair.* SWORD *walks along the landing. He is about to turn into his own room, but notices the light from* MIRIAM'S.)

(*Approaching*) Miriam?

(*When he receives no answer he goes in. Quick turn round the deserted room. Runs out on to the landing. Down the stairs. Switches on the light. Quick search round the downstairs rooms. Then* EXIT *by front door.*)

(*Calling,* OFF) Miriam? ... Miriam!

(*His voice dies away.* STELLA *gets up. Goes to wardrobe, takes out her cloak, puts it on over her nightgown. Leaves her room, walks downstairs, so slack she could miss a step by accident, but does not care.*)

STELLA (*on the stairs*) This house....

(*Arrived at the foot of the stairs, she walks directionless at first through the living-room.*)

Could he really mean ...? (*Tortured*) Dirt! Dirt!

(*Claps her hands to her mouth. Then removes them.*)

My own *father* ... !

(*She leaves the house through the glass doors,* BACK. *Walks away slowly through the moonlight.*)

SCENE TWO · SAME AS ACT ONE, SCENE TWO

ENTER MISS QUODLING R. *She is wearing a Digger's old buttonless coat over the many cardigans. Man's hat. Army boots. Carrying a hurricane lamp, with which she has been searching this way and that.*

MISS QUODLING (*tossing the light in different directions, calling*) Jessica? . . . Jess? Jess? Jess? . . . You godforsaken Jessica! (*Pause. Heavy sigh*) It's not for pleasure a person goes roamun round the bush at night . . . or perhaps it's mornun. You forget which. (*Pause, voice trailing*) Lookun for a goat that's slipped 'er bell. . . . (ENTER TWO HIKERS *down the incline,* R. *They are youngish men, of the same age, well-built, though of a city type. Windjackets and shorts. Rucksacks on their backs.* SECOND HIKER *is carrying an axe suspended by a loop of cord from his rucksack, the axe-head leather-covered.*)

FIRST HIKER (*to* MISS QUODLING) 'Day!

MISS QUODLING (*holding up her lantern*) That what it is? . . . Who are you, anyway, burstun through the scrub like a mob of steers?

FIRST HIKER We're a couple of characters taking a walk.

MISS QUODLING Characters! I'll say!

SECOND HIKER Thought we'd get an early start. We don't have all that long before we'll be shut up again.

MISS QUODLING (*slightly contemptuous*) Ah! City!

FIRST HIKER (*indicating his companion*) I wanted this young cove to see the sunrise from Bald Mountain.

(*Noises of good-natured protest from* SECOND HIKER.)

We reckoned on following the track down Hermit Valley . . . then out through Blackstone . . . (*confessing*) . . . but got a bit bushed already.

MISS QUODLING I'm not surprised. There's many gets bushed around Bald Mountain by day. Never knew why they called it *Bald* . . . unless it growed away from its name.

SECOND HIKER (*to* MISS QUODLING) Cigarette?

MISS QUODLING I wouldn't insult my lungs!

FIRST HIKER Bit lost yourself, aren't you?

MISS QUODLING Don't tell *me* I'm lost! I know this 'ere mountain like my hand. Why, there's people will tell you . . . people that *know* . . . that I *am* the mountain!

FIRST HIKER Go on!

MISS QUODLING Yairs. (*Pause*) No. I was out lookun for a doe that must have kidded yesterday afternoon, an' hid 'er kids the way they do. It's my Jessica.

SECOND HIKER (*flippant*) Jessica sure knows how to be a nuisance.

MISS QUODLING (*sternly*) It's never a nuisance where a goat's involved.

SECOND HIKER (*not interested*) Well . . . you know what you like, I suppose.

MISS QUODLING Nobody knows better.

(*Pause.*)

FIRST HIKER What about directing us a bit . . . telling us the way to the lookout.

MISS QUODLING This isn't a tourist resort. There isn't any lookout.

FIRST HIKER Whatever it is then.

MISS QUODLING If it's direction you want, you couldn't have struck luckier. Follow this 'ere track down. . . . (*She points* OFF, L., *explaining as she must have many times before*) When you get to the bottom, there's a turn to the right. Don't take that. Follow along the edge of the gully until you reach a timber home. The home is mine. See? Just a little further on you'll find the lookout. . . .

SECOND HIKER Yeah?

MISS QUODLING (*sternly*) Only it isn't a lookout. See?

FIRST HIKER Okay. Hope you find the goat.

MISS QUODLING (*proud*) Oh, I shan't *find* the goat. A goat makes sure yer don't . . . even when you've been lookun all yer life.

(HIKERS *begin to move*, L.)

FIRST HIKER Thanks for the info, Mrs . . . er. . . .

MISS QUODLING *Quodling*'s the name. *Miss.* (*To* SECOND HIKER) Got a good lump of an axe hangin' off of yer. Goin' ter murder a tree or two?

SECOND HIKER (*sheepish*) Thought I might try my hand on a couple.

MISS QUODLING (*gesticulating angrily, so that the light jumps*) Well, these are all my trees. See? As fur as you can look. And further still.

(ENTER MIRIAM, R. *She stands watching, motionless, at top of the incline.*)

SECOND HIKER (*to* MISS QUODLING) What about the Crown?

MISS QUODLING The Crown? I'm the Crown!

FIRST HIKER Wouldn't be surprised.

(HIKERS *laugh.*)

MISS QUODLING Eh?

(*She joins them in their laughter.*)

(*Laughing*) I'm tellun *you!*

(HIKERS *move off.*)

FIRST HIKER See yer later then!

SECOND HIKER See yer some more!

(TWO HIKERS EXIT L.)

MISS QUODLING (*calling after them*) Don't forget what I told yer, boys! After yer reach the private home, you're as good as there. (*Shouting at the top of her voice*) A false step won't bring yez closer ter Sunday, though.

(*Silence.* MISS QUODLING *could be a little depressed.*)

(*Sighing*) Ah, dear! Goats! (*Pause*) Cold's got inter me shoulder again.... (*Shrieking*) Jessica? You cross-eyed-lookun Jessica!

(MISS QUODLING *turns this way and that, making the lamplight dance.*)

One day I'll let yez all go to hell.... (*Turning* R., *in the direction in which* MIRIAM *is standing*) Did I see the white end ... (*peering*) ... of a bloody ... otherwise ... pretty little ... goat?

(*Light reveals* MIRIAM *standing at top of the incline. Her hair is astray. Her face is pale. Her white dress, though torn in places, still suggests a poetry of its own. She does not look up immediately.*)

(*Amazed*) Strike a light! What's this? Mrs Sword ... and all dressed up!

(MIRIAM *does not answer.* MISS QUODLING *attempts to jolly her.*) Goin' to a ball, eh?

MIRIAM (*bitterly*) No. I came from it.

(*She staggers down the incline towards* MISS QUODLING.*)

(*Her emotions threatening her at last*) Miss Quodling . . . I . . . I had to find . . . somebody.

MISS QUODLING Steady on! You're right now. . . . (*Puts out her hand to steady* MIRIAM, *takes her by her bare arm*) Golly, but you're cold! Eh, dear? And no wonder. All dressed up for Government House!

MIRIAM If I could feel . . . I might feel cold.

MISS QUODLING Bit shivery, though. Here!
(*She takes off her Digger's coat. Puts it round* MIRIAM'S *shoulders.*)
May be a bit dirty . . . but it's honest. (*Pause*) And it don't smell. You must know by now that a goat never *smells*.

MIRIAM (*hanging her head*) Thank you. I'm terribly . . . grateful.

MISS QUODLING Jessica or no Jessica, we'll go along home to my place. . . .

MIRIAM If I could only sit awhile. . . .

MISS QUODLING You'll sit . . and if yer don't want ter tell . . . well, I'm not askun. (*They begin to move* L.) I was never one to ask. (*Pause*) Of course if I *find out* . . . that's because I'm not stupid.

MIRIAM (*gratefully*) I shan't interrupt you in any way.

MISS QUODLING Nothing can interrupt the sunrise or the goats.

MIRIAM Or if I could help. . . .

MISS QUODLING Help! You're gunna sit by the fire. It's got to the lazy stage by now, but a kick works wonders with a lazy fire.

MIRIAM (*almost in tears of joy*) I can't think . . . if I hadn't found you. . . .

MISS QUODLING Well, you found!
(MISS QUODLING *puts her arm round her as they* EXIT L.)
(*Calling*) All I can say is, damn you, Jessica . . . wherever you are. (*Fainter, grumbling*) Won't recognize yer voice . . . when they make up their minds not to. . . .

SCENE THREE · SAME AS ACT ONE, SCENE ONE

Again the first light of morning. Cold and colourless. Intermittent bells and bleating from the yardful of does, stamping and grunting from the buck's pen. The light will continue to increase, and the sun rise eventually. Very faint smoke at first from MISS QUODLING'S *chimney.*

ENTER MISS QUODLING *and* MIRIAM L. MISS QUODLING *supporting* MIRIAM, *who is already calmer, and soothed.*

MISS QUODLING (*speaking very gently, both to soothe her companion and because she is expressing her private thoughts*) When I came 'ere in the beginnin', I was afraid. Wouldn't of admitted it, of course ... not to anyone on earth ...

(*Dreamlike picture as the two women drift slowly across the scene.*)
... but I was. I'd run away from ... life, I s'pose. And here I stood. (*They halt*) On this very spot. It was just as if I was the first person born in an empty world. It was huge, and lonely, and I had to get used to it....

(MIRIAM *nods. Sad, dreamy.*)
Then it seemed ter get used ter *me*. I *was* born. Look! (*Makes a gesture with her arm*) You can *feel* the light when it first begins. Can't you feel its touch? Eh? Soft....

(*They move across to the gap between shack and goatyards.*)
(*Pointing* OFF, *direction* R.) Look!

(MIRIAM *leans against* MISS QUODLING. *It is almost as though they are a pair of lovers.*)

MIRIAM (*sadly, sighing, recovering her vision*) Beautiful! They haven't all gone out yet.

MISS QUODLING Bit cheap, perhaps. I call them the rhinestones of Sydney. Too much glitter. (*Reverie*) When I was a young girl at Auntie's, there was a flash young feller used ter come around. Thought 'e could catch me with a rhinestone necklace. Well, I wasn't taken in. (*Drily*) I kept the necklace, though. It was pretty enough ... till the stones fell out. The whole thing fell apart. (*She leads* MIRIAM C.) This won't fall apart. Not Bald Mountain. Not.... (*Suddenly fierce, quite hysterical*) You can't believe what they tell yer in the papers. Now can yer? Anyway, I don't read the papers any more.

(*They pause,* C. *Then* MISS QUODLING *takes* MIRIAM *tenderly by the hands.*)

(*As though to a child*) I'm gunna take you in now to sit by that bit of a fire.

MIRIAM (*weary, but happy*) Yes ... the fire. ...

(*They move towards the shack.*)

MISS QUODLING Then you won't be cold any more.

MIRIAM I'm not cold ... only dead.

MISS QUODLING Wait till we rake the ashes. Then you'll see. ...

(MISS QUODLING *and* MIRIAM EXIT *into shack. Interior suddenly illuminated by the hurricane lamp.*)

(OFF) There ... as it burns, push this fencepost further in. One of yer own posts, too. You'll soon have quite a nice little ... blaze. ... P'raps you might like ter fan it yerself ... for company like. ...

(MISS QUODLING *is seen to move across the visible window.*)

(OFF) Forgot this back door when I went out. (*Sound of invisible door closing*) It can blow cold on this side ... out of the valley. 'Ere ... you sit down by the fire. ... No more black thoughts. I'll shut the window, too. Yer don't want ter look out. ... (*Sound of window shutting on other side of shack*) It's sad sometimes at this hour. (*Pause*) There, you're real snug now.

(*Smoke increases from the chimney. From the increase in light it would appear the sun has begun to rise* OFF R. MISS QUODLING *appears at door, wearing her gumboots now, singing tunelessly. She is carrying the little iron milk-can and the billy. Twitches the rag off the veranda line. Slings the rag across her shoulder. Moves across to the does' yard. As she goes into the yard a chorus of bleating, accompanied by agitated bells. Sounds die.*)

(*In yard*) Well, youse! Thought I'd forgot. ... Now, *Fairy*! Fair*ee*! ... And my galopshous Dolores! How're you feelun, Dolores? Good?

(*Sounds of metal on metal. Buck grunts and shakes his fence.*)

(*Shouting*) You, Samson! You'd drive a woman to the edge! Fat lot you bucks care about a person. It's just a matter of supply.

(ENTER STELLA, L. *She is still wearing the long cloak over her nightgown. Could have been sleep-walking.*)

(*To herself, in yard*) It'd break yer heart . . . I wouldn't let my heart break . . . not even for a goat. . . . Or would I?

(STELLA *moves slowly across the scene.*)

STELLA The mornings wash so clean . . . but not clean . . . enough.

(*She approaches the apple tree. First sunlight strikes her.*)

She said the trees on Bald Mountain . . . bear *little* . . . runty . . . played-out fruit. . . .

(*She completes a circle in silence, then looking around her.*)

You can almost believe in what you see. Such peace! If it wasn't . . .

(*She turns, making for the gap between yard and shack.*)

(*Crying, softly, brokenly*) My own father!

(EXIT R., *behind the shack, towards the sun.*)

MISS QUODLING (*furious*) Look, Dolores, if you do that again I'll fetch you such a crack. . . . (*Almost crying*) All I ask is that everybody acts *reasonable*!

(*Sound of* SWORD *calling* OFF R., *foreground.*)

SWORD (OFF, *calling*) Miriam? . . . (*Closer*) Miriam!

MISS QUODLING Wish I was a goat meself. Then there wouldn't be any difference. No difference at all.

(ENTER SWORD R. FORWARD *of shack. He is dishevelled, rather wild. Shirt open at the neck, tie gone, shoes muddy.*)

SWORD (*calling outside shack*) Anyone there? (*Walking about, looking*) Miss Quodling?

MISS QUODLING (*looking over the fence*) Who the devul's that? (*Angry*) As if I hadn't had interruption enough! (*Noticing* SWORD, *with some distaste*) Oh, it's you, is it?

SWORD I'm looking for my wife.

MISS QUODLING Well, I've got me milkun.

(MISS QUODLING *continues with her work in the yard.*)

SWORD But my wife, Miss Quodling. . . .

MISS QUODLING Yer wife! Should'uv thought about 'er sooner. Wives don't keep, you know. They'll go a bit off.

SWORD (*mechanically*) I'm looking for my wife.

(*He flops down exhausted on a log outside yard gate. Sits with his*

*legs apart, hands clasped between them, head bent. Silence, except for
bells and occasional bleating.*)

Have you seen her? (*Beseeching*) Miss Quodling?

MISS QUODLING (OFF) I've seen ghosts in my day . . . on Bald
Mountain.

(*Pause.*)

(*Furious*) Fairy, will you take your foot . . .

(*Pause.*)

(*Looking over the fence, raising her voice again for* SWORD) I've
seen ghosts . . . and a fireball . . . and bushfires so close they
burnt the bark off this blinkun fence. . . .

SWORD Won't you have pity, then, Miss Quodling?

MISS QUODLING Pity!

(*A burst of sly laughter.*)

That's a word we all of us use when we're stuck for a way out!

(*Sound of* MEN'S VOICES *shouting in the distance,* OFF R., MISS
QUODLING *emerges from the yard.*)

What's that? Did you hear, Professor Sword?

SWORD (*not interested*) Somebody calling.

MISS QUODLING Calling for what?

(*She goes* BACK *towards the gap, looking in the direction* R.)

(*Shading her eyes against the glare of the rising sun*) It's those two
boys I seen this mornun. One of 'em, anyway. (*Without much
concern*) Hope nothun's wrong. They've lit a fire down there, just
below the . . . (*grudgingly*) . . . lookout. Must've stopped for a bite
of breakfast. (*Turning away, reassured*) Yairs.

SWORD Miss Quodling, I'm asking you to help me.

MISS QUODLING Who am *I*?

SWORD (*ignoring it*) For certain reasons . . . my wife left the house
this morning . . . (*waving his hand, distracted*) . . . or night.

MISS QUODLING Oh, I don't ask you to give me reasons. Everythink explains itself in time.

SWORD (*incoherently*) I've tried, Miss Quodling . . . I've tried. . . .
But in the end . . . one is *weak*. (*Abruptly*) That's all . . . if you
despise me for it.

MISS QUODLING Well, now! Well!

(*She struts about rather arrogantly.*)

351

SWORD I was the lost one, you see . . . long before Miriam got lost . . . long before she drank her mind, her beauty, away . . . into a state of sluttishness. Perhaps I mightn't admit it even now . . . except that you and I are here on the edge of the world . . . and might so easily slip over, into this merciless morning light . . . or have slipped already . . . along with the illusions of importance and grandeur we had until very recently.

MISS QUODLING (*without mercy*) Speak for yerself, Professor Sword. You'll climb back, anyway. You're an expert at it.

SWORD (*suddenly naïve*) Your opinion of me isn't very high.

MISS QUODLING Perhaps if I understood all those letters after yer name. . . . But I don't! (*Laughing, turning her head, trying to disguise the truth*) Ah, dear! You're such a *boy!*

(SWORD *wears an expression of undisguised bitterness.*)

(*Severely*) What you should'uv married was something between yer own mother and the Virgin Mary.

(SWORD *makes an attempt to interrupt.*)

But that wouldn't of solved the problem. You would'uv been lookun for *reasons* even then. As if reasons wait to be found. They choose!

(*Sound of buck grunting and shaking his gate.*)

Listen to that buck tryun to get out! He would, too, if he could!

SWORD (*shocked*) But we're not . . . just . . . animals!

MISS QUODLING (*sad*) Ah, no! We're not! (*Almost whispering*) We're not, we're not, we're not! And kill ourselves because of it.

(ENTER FIRST HIKER, R., *from behind shack. He is breathless from climbing and running.*)

(*Turning*) Look who's here! It's one of me two hikers. What's got inter you so early?

HIKER (*panting*) It's . . . Miss Quodling. . . . There's a woman . . . gone over . . . (*gasping for breath, pointing in direction from which he has come*) . . . back . . . just along there.

MISS QUODLING Fell?

HIKER Who's to say?

(*Pause.*)

SWORD (*agitated*) But what woman?

HIKER How do I know?

SWORD No! No!

HIKER There she stood . . . against the light. . . . From down below . . . there was a rare glare around her. (*Fighting for his breath*) She was white . . . you would have said it was a statue . . . so stiff and white. . . .

MISS QUODLING She didn't fall.

HIKER I didn't say it. (*Pause*) She seemed to topple out of the sun. (*Pause, very moved*) Now she's lying at the foot of the cliff . . . broken.

SWORD (*rounding on* MISS QUODLING) And now Miss Quodling . . . will you tell me?

MISS QUODLING (*shocked and frightened*) She was there a moment ago. Sitting by the fire. She was *there* . . . (*very shaken*) . . . but there's never any knowun what gets inter people's heads. (*She begins slowly to approach the shack*) I'll go an' see . . . Professor Sword.

HIKER Well. . . . I'll make for Blackstone . . . fetch the police, and ambulance.

(*He is about to move* L. *when* ENTER DENIS CRAIG *in haste. He is wearing sweater and slacks. Pulls up on catching sight of the group outside* MISS QUODLING'S.)

DENIS Have you found her, then?

SWORD Perhaps. . . .

DENIS I was afraid. . . .

SWORD We may have cause to be.

DENIS What . . . cause?

SWORD She threw herself over the cliff.

MISS QUODLING Oh, we don't know for. . . .

DENIS (*slowly*) If Stella Summerhayes is dead . . . how shall we believe . . . in life?

SWORD Stella?

DENIS Left the house. (*Clearing his throat*) I went to her room. I felt uneasy . . . felt she needed. . . .

SWORD (*torn between possibilities*) But Stella! When I thought Miriam. . . .

MISS QUODLING (*to* DENIS) We don't know, Mr Craig.

SWORD Stella or Miriam ... the cause is much the same.

DENIS (*nerving himself*) I'll go on down ... see what I can do.

HIKER (*taking* DENIS *by elbow*) My mate's down there ... staying with her. (EXIT HIKER L.)

(ENTER MIRIAM *from shack. She has abandoned* MISS QUODLING'S *coat, so that her torn ball dress looks doubly incongrous and shocking in the early light.*)

DENIS (*catching sight of* MIRIAM) I'll go on down ... to Stella.

(EXIT DENIS *quickly* R., *behind the shack, in direction of the lookout, hiding his emotion.*)

MIRIAM (*quickly, bewildered, as if waking*) Stella? Where is Stella? It's Stella I've been looking for.

MISS QUODLING You won't find her, my dear. She's gone.

MIRIAM (*incredulous*) Gone?

(SWORD *has gone aside, and is standing alone.*)

MISS QUODLING Threw herself over.

MIRIAM (*confused*) But Stella! She was my only ... remaining ... hope! (*Distraught*) My little Stella! Mary! My darling, darling Stella!

SWORD Miriam, I killed Stella Summerhayes.

MIRIAM (*holding her head, hopeless*) Oh, Hugo, Hugo! We both did. We are the destroyers! Destroying to keep our pride intact.

(*She feels her way down from the veranda.*)

MISS QUODLING (*coaxing*) Take your wife home, Professor Sword. She needs looking after.

SWORD (*helpless, stricken*) Yes. ... Yes. ... We must try again.

MIRIAM (*dull from crying*) If we're able to.

SWORD We must try again.

MIRIAM Yes. Even when we fail.

SWORD Failure is sometimes the beginnings of success.

MIRIAM Yes. We must try.

SWORD (*looking at her, helplessly*) It's time we went back to the house then.

MIRIAM (*looking back at him with an expression of desperation*) The house?

SWORD (*dully*) That is where we live. . . .

    (MIRIAM *turns. As they* EXIT *she precedes* SWORD *by several feet. They walk like automata towards the next round.*)

    (MISS QUODLING *moves back.*)

MISS QUODLING You left us too soon, Stella. (*Breaks a branch off apple tree*) Too soon . . . too good. I warned you, didn't I? . . . they'd get you. (*Shouting, throwing the apple blossom into space*) I warned you, though. (*Quieter*) Well, it's the way of human beings. Now the others'll go away. They do . . . always in the end. There'll be nothing on Bald Mountain . . . but goats. . . .

(*She goes and throws open the gate at* BACK R. *corner of yard. Stands watching as the goats scramble down the mountainside.*)

There'll be the Bald Mountain I remember as long as I care to remember. . . .

(*A spare, prickly musical accompaniment.*)

. . . the bare patches, with the sour grass, the brackish water seeping through. . . . Swords amongst the rocks. . . . In the spindly scrub, the prickly flowers . . . no scent much . . . but the smell of sun. . . . Whole mornings I'll lie and watch a beetle or ants struggling with rocks of sand . . . listen to the sound of pellets scattering, as my goats browse off leaves . . . and sun. Their yeller eyes know as much as they're allowed ter know. Only I know everything. Only I can say: Run, goats! Jump! Skip! This is the world of goats. *My* world! My. . . .

(*Pauses, horrified.*)

(*Calling*) Not you, Dolores. Hey Face-ache Dolores! Not at your age. You can't . . . (*screaming*) . . . LEAP. Dolores! (*Aghast*) Dol-or-es! (*Sobbing*) My old Dolores!

(*She turns back*, C., *broken, sobbing.*)

Then there *is* something that knows more . . . something that gets us all in the end . . . through the heart.

(*She stands* C., *wooden, staggering, holding out her arms, reaching as far as she can with her stiff fingers, in a tirade. Music rises in accompaniment.*)

(*Shouting*) But when there is nothing left . . . not even Bald Mountain . . . after they've ground it into dust . . and all livin' things with it . . . like they tell yer . . . if you can believe. . . . (*Beside herself*) But you can't! Can yer? You can't! There is no such thing as *nothun*! (*Softer*) The silence will breed again . . . in peace . . . a world of goats . . . perhaps even men!

CURTAIN

BIBLIOGRAPHICAL NOTE

MAY-BRIT AKERHOLT

This bibliographical guide is a representative selection of critical material on the four plays in this volume.

The press reviews indicate the wide range of critical attitudes towards productions. It is interesting to compare the largely adverse criticism of *A Cheery Soul's* first production, in the press as well as in literary journals, with the critical acclaim of Sharman's production of this play in 1979, particularly in light of an article by Carroll in 1976. He maintains that one day soon 'the Australian theatre will have the resources and the experience to do [White's plays] full justice'.

Tasker comments on the originality of style and mode in White's plays generally in an article about the stage history of *The Ham Funeral*, with notes from the rehearsals of its first production. Several articles refer to specific productions, for instance Bray's, which takes its basis in Tasker's *The Ham Funeral*. Bray is one of many who claim that White anticipates playwrights like Beckett, Ionesco and Pinter in his use of forms later exploited by these writers. Phillips is concerned with theatrical styles and methods and their relationship to themes and characterisation in a review article on *The Season at Sarsaparilla*; he also has some interesting ideas on the play's language. A particularly good article on the varied uses of language in White's drama is that of Brissenden; see also Herring's discussion on dramatic dialogue.

White's extensive use of irony is dealt with by most critics; for some interesting and quite diverse comments, see Bradley and Brissenden.

There is no escaping the labels 'Freudian' and 'Jungian' as far as literary criticism of White's works is concerned. The Indian critic Ahuja finds, apart from a blend of existential thought and expressionist mode in all the plays, that the Freudian Oedipus complex is the central theme of *The Ham Funeral* and the Electra complex of *Night on Bald Mountain*. In a truly academic exercise in modernism he views White's work as a 'process of assimilation and synthesis' of the themes, forms and visions of writers from Swift through to Shaw and Toller, including Freud, Nietzsche, Voltaire, Strindberg and Chekhov. Douglas also isolates elements of Freudian psycho-analysis and Jungian analytic psychology (*The Ham Funeral*) in his article on early symbolist and expressionist dramatic conventions in White's first two plays, with particular reference to Strindberg. Expressionism is also the main theme of the American critic Whitman who discusses the indebtedness of White to Strindberg. Dyce's book on the four plays refers to the uses of expressionist forms, and she has a lengthy discussion of Jungian influences in her chapter on *The Ham Funeral*.

Archetypal motifs and patterns are identified by most writers. A feature is the unity of opinion that *The Ham Funeral* is a 'morality play'. Hanger claims it has the universal character of a modern morality and allegory as opposed to the specific details of time and place in *The Season at Sarsaparilla*. And in a discussion which generally rejects *A Cheery Soul* for its lack of dramatic unity and *The Season at Sarsaparilla* for its failure to blend naturalistic approaches to characterisation with 'more schematic, more fable-like' ones, Taylor argues that *The Ham Funeral* succeeds because it is a psychological morality play 'firmly located within the realm of the fable'. Taylor's rejection of *A Cheery Soul* concludes that the play fails to give theatrical life to 'what should have been left a short story'. Akerholt, however, finds the dramatisation of the story generally successful. See also Kiernan on the translation of story to stage play.

Several critics deal with the relationship between prose fiction and drama. In a detailed argument on *The Ham Funeral* Loder points to the play's relevance to White's novels, placing it in the context of the whole cannon. Burrows, in a careful analysis of the four plays, claims that *Night on Bald Mountain* signals that 'White the dramatist has slowly approached the achievement of the novelist'. This view of White's fourth play is in contrast to that of the majority of critics, who seem to agree that it falls between the two stools of tragedy and melodrama. Kruse, however, questions this opinion in an entertaining article in which he maintains that 'one obvious message is that critics can be seen as a den of witches on top of a mountain' and that the characters themselves are literary allusions in a play of puns which 'challenges assumptions about realism through its language'. In elaborating on the 'word-puzzles' of the play, he writes a Nabokovian argument in which the critic himself plays word-games with the text – and the reader? 'It takes all kinds to make a tasty dustbin'.

PERFORMANCE PRESS REVIEWS

The Ham Funeral
At the Union Theatre, Adelaide, November 1961 and on tour:
  E. Riddell, *Sunday Mirror*, Sydney 24 June 1962; *Sydney Morning Herald* 11 July; K. Kemp, *Bulletin* 12 July; D. Rowbotham *Courier Mail*, Brisbane, 24 October 1962.

The Season at Sarsaparilla
At the Union Theatre, Adelaide, September 1962 and on tour:
  The Times, London, 22 September; G. Hutton, *Age*, Melbourne, 13 October; H.A. Standish, *Herald*, Melbourne, 17 October; K. Kemp, *Bulletin* 1 June 1963.
Revival by Old Tote Theatre Company, November 1976:
  G. Pascall, *Australian*, 8 November 1976; D. Marr, *Bulletin*, 13 November 1976.

A Cheery Soul
At the Union Theatre, Adelaide, November 1963:
  H.A. Standish, *Herald*, Melbourne; and G. Hutton, *Age*, Melbourne, both 29 November 1963.
Revival by the Sydney Theatre Company, January 1979:
  H.G. Kippax, *Sydney Morning Herald*, 18 January; V. Emeljanow, *National Times* 29 January to 3 February; P. Corris, *National Times* 4–10 February; K. Brisbane, *Theatre Australia* March 1979.

Night on Bald Mountain
At the Union Theatre, Adelaide, March 1964:
  Brek (H.G. Kippax) *Nation* 21, March 1964, M. Rodger, *On Dit* 32, 26 March 1964.

CRITICAL STUDIES, 1962–67

D. Bradley, '*The Season at Sarsaparilla*:
  Patrick White's "Charade of Suburbia"', *Meanjin* 21, 4, December 1962 pp 492–94.
J.J. Bray, '*The Ham Funeral*' *Meanjin* 21, 1, March 1962, pp 32–34.
R.F. Brissenden, 'The Plays of Patrick White', *Meanjin* 3, 1964; reprinted in *Contemporary Australian Drama*, ed P. Holloway, Sydney, Currency Press 1981.
J.F. Burrows, 'Patrick White's Four Plays', *Australian Literary Studies* 2, 3, June 1966, pp 155–70.
E. Hanger, 'The Setting in Patrick White's Two Plays:
  Unlocalized in *The Ham Funeral*, Australian in *Season at Sarsaparilla*', *Proceedings*, IVth Congress of International Comparative Literature Association, Fribourge 1964, ed. Francois Jost, The

Hague and Paris: Mouton 1966, pp 644—53.

T. Herring, 'Maenads and Goat-Song: The Plays of Patrick White', in *Ten Essays on Patrick White*, ed. G.A. Wilkes (selected from *Southerly*, 1964—67). Sydney, Angus and Robertson 1970, pp 147—62.

H.G. Kippax, 'Australian Drama Since *Summer of the Seventeenth Doll*', *Meanjin* 23, 2, September 1967, pp 229—42.

H.G. Kippax, Introduction to *Four Plays by Patrick White*, Melbourne, Sun Books 1967, pp 2—10.

E. Loder, '*The Ham Funeral*: Its Place in the Development of Patrick White', *Southerly* 23, 1963, pp 78—91.

A.A. Phillips, 'The Dogs Have Their Day', *Overland* 25, December 1962—63, pp 33—34.

RETROSPECTIVE CRITICISM, 1973—85

C. Ahuya, 'Modernism in Patrick White's Plays: An Exercise in Synthesis', *Literary Criterion* 4, Summer 1975, pp 53—63.

M-B. Akerholt, Female Characters in the Plays of Patrick White and Dorothy Hewett', *Westerly* 1, 1984.

M-B. Akerholt, 'Story into Play: The Two Versions of Patrick White's *A Cheery Soul*', *Southerly* 4, December 1980, pp 460—72.

D. Carroll, 'Stage Conventions in the Plays of Patrick White', *Modern Drama* 19, Tulane, March 1976 pp 11—23; reprinted in *Contemporary Australian Drama*, op cit pp 194—207.

D. Douglas, 'Influence and Individuality: the Indebtedness of Patrick White's *The Ham Funeral* and *The Season at Sarsaparilla* to Strindberg and the German Expressionist Movement', in *Bards, Bohemians and Bookmen: Essays in Australian Literature*, ed. Leon Cantrell, St Lucia, University of Queensland Press, 1976, pp 266—80.

J.R. Dyce, *Patrick White as Playwright*, St Lucia, University of Queensland Press, 1974.

P. Fitzpatrick, 'Patrick White' in *After 'The Doll': Australian Drama Since 1955*, Melbourne, Edward Arnold, 1979, pp 49—68.

B. Kiernan, *Patrick White*, Macmillan Commonwealth Writers Series, London 1980.

D. Malouf, 'The Void', *Quadrant*, September 1977, pp 26—27.

L. Rees, 'The Plays of Patrick White' in *A History of Australian Drama, Vol 1: the Making of Australian Drama from 1830s the the Late 1960s*. Sydney, Angus and Robertson 1973, pp 333—52.

A. Taylor, 'Patrick White's *The Ham Funeral*', Meanjin 32, 3, September 1973, pp 270—78.

R.F. Whitman, 'The Dream Plays of Patrick White', *Texas Studies in Literature and Language* 21, 2, Summer 1979, pp 240—59.

HISTORICAL DOCUMENTS

A. Barclay, 'Jim Sharman Directs Patrick White's Most Challenging Play', *Theatre Australia* 3, 8 March 1979, pp 15–17, 34.

R.F. Brissenden, 'Rejection by Adelaide: The Mark of a Great Play', *Australian* 6 January 1968.

W. Latimer, 'The Painting that Inspired an Australian Play', *Pix*, 14 July 1962, pp 57–60.

J. Tasker, 'Notes on *The Ham Funeral*', *Meanjin* 23, 3, September 1964, pp 299–302.

BIOGRAPHICAL REFERENCES

R.F. Brissenden, *Patrick White*, Writers and Their Work, London, Longmans, Green and Co, revised edition 1969.

G. Dutton, *Patrick White*, Australian Writers and Their Work, Melbourne, Lansdowne Press, revised edition 1962.

R. Glover, 'There's Still a Lot of Black in White', *Sydney Morning Herald Good Weekend*, 18 May 1985.

D. Leitch, 'Patrick White: A Revealing Profile', *National Times*, 27 March – 1 April 1978.

P. White, *Flaws in the Glass*, a self portrait, London, Jonathan Cape, 1982.